Praise for
THE WOMAN THEY COULD NOT SILENCE

'This book will fill you with rage, despair, and determination. Moore has written a masterpiece of nonfiction, giving voice to the life of Elizabeth Packard, a crusader of humanity, who countless men tried to subdue. With elegant prose, and an epilogue that will leave you reeling, *The Woman They Could Not Silence* will linger long after the last page is read.'

Nathalia Holt, *New York Times* bestselling
author of *Rise of the Rocket Girls*

'What a story — and what a telling! Kate Moore has hit another one out of the park. In the best tradition of *The Radium Girls*, Moore recounts the stunning true account of a woman who fought back against a tyrannical husband, a complicit doctor, and 19th-century laws that gave men shocking power to silence and confine their wives. By challenging these norms, Elizabeth Packard became a heroine on the scale of the suffragists. In Moore's expert hands, this beautifully written tale unspools with drama and power and puts Elizabeth Packard on the map at the most relevant moment imaginable. You will be riveted — and inspired. Bravo!'

Liza Mundy, *New York Times* bestselling author of *Code Girls*

'*The Woman They Could Not Silence* tells the captivating story of Elizabeth Packard, a forgotten heroine whose harrowing ordeal in an insane asylum seems straight from the mind of Stephen King — except every word is true. Blending impeccable research with novelistic flair, Kate Moore brings the indomitable Packard to brilliant life and proves she belongs among our most celebrated women leaders.'

Karen Abbott, *New York Times* bestselling
ts of Eden Park

'What an incredible narrative about a singular historical woman. In *The Woman They Could Not Silence*, Kate Moore once again utilises her astonishing talent in discovering the important, forgotten women of history. In bringing to life the account of Elizabeth Packard, wife and mother of six, Moore shares the stories of many sane women committed to insane asylums simply because they did not abide by the societal expectations about women, and the one woman who successfully challenged these practices. Through these pages, Moore enthralls as she ensures that such women will be silent no more.'

Marie Benedict, *New York Times* bestselling author

'With path-breaking research and electric prose, Kate Moore reveals just how crazy marriage laws once were — and one unbeaten heroine helped make them sane.'

Elizabeth Cobbs, *New York Times* bestselling author
of *The Hello Girls: America's first women soldiers*

'Heartbreaking and devastatingly important — Kate Moore has a rare gift for combining impeccable research and brilliantly mesmerising storytelling. *The Woman They Could Not Silence* yanks back the curtain on the tragic and once-hidden injustices that ruined women's lives — and gives even more power to the one brave and undaunted voice that refused to be silent. You will cry, and then you will cheer, and then your life will be changed forever.'

Hank Phillippi Ryan, *USA Today* bestselling author
of *The First to Lie* and *Her Perfect Life*

'Told with the urgency and passion of a novel, Kate Moore's deeply researched and thrilling study of Elizabeth Packard's fight against the power of psychiatric patriarchy in 19th-century America will keep you up at night and illuminate women's ongoing battles for authority and respect.'

Elaine Showalter, literary critic, professor emerita at
Princeton University, and author of *The Female Malady*

Praise for
THE RADIUM GIRLS

'Moore's well-researched narrative is written with clarity and a sympathetic voice that brings these figures and their struggles to life ... a mustread for anyone interested in American and women's history, as well as topics of law, health, and industrial safety.'

Library Journal, starred review

'[This] fascinating social history — one that significantly reflects on the class and gender of those involved — [is] Catherine Cookson meets *Mad Men* ... The importance of the brave and blighted dial painters cannot be overstated.'

Sunday Times

'Kate Moore's gripping narrative about the betrayal of the radium girls — gracefully told and exhaustively researched — makes this a nonfiction classic. I particularly admire Moore's compassion for her subjects and her storytelling prowess, which brings alive a shameful era in America's industrial history.'

Rinker Buck, author of *The Oregon Trail: a new American journey* and *Flight of Passage: a true story*

'This timely book celebrates the strength of a group of women, whose determination to fight improved both labor laws and scientific knowledge of radium poisoning. Written in a highly readable, narrative style, Moore's chronicle of these inspirational women's lives is sure to provoke discussion — and outrage — in book groups.'

—*Booklist*, starred review

'*Radium Girls* spares us nothing of their suffering ... Moore is intent on making the reader viscerally understand the pain in which these young women were living and through which they had to fight in order to get their problems recognised ... The story of real women at the mercy of businesses who see them only as a potential risk to the bottom line is haunting precisely because of how little has changed; the glowing ghosts of the radium girls haunt us still.'

NPR Books

'*The Radium Girls* by Kate Moore is powerful, disturbing, important history.'

Karen Abbott, *New York Times* bestselling author

'Kate Moore has dug deep to expose a wrong that still resonates — as it should — in this country. Exceptional!'

San Francisco Book Review

'Kate Moore ... writes with a sense of drama that carries one through the serpentine twists and turns of this tragic but ultimately uplifting story. She sees the trees for the wood: always at the center of her narrative are the individual dial painters, and the list of their names at the start of the book becomes a register of familiar, endearing ghosts.'

Spectator

'In this thrilling and carefully crafted book, Kate Moore tells the shocking story of how early-20th-century corporate and legal America set about silencing dozens of working-class women who had been systematically poisoned by radiation ... Moore [writes] so lyrically ... FIVE STARS.'

Mail on Sunday

'Heartbreaking ... What this book illustrates brilliantly is that battling for justice against big corporations isn't easy ... [The radium girls' story is] a terrible example of appalling injustice.'

BBC Radio 4 Woman's Hour

'Like Dava Sobel's *The Glass Universe* and Margot Lee Shetterly's *Hidden Figures*, Kate Moore's *The Radium Girls* tells the story of a cohort of women who made history by entering the workforce at the dawn of a new scientific era ... Moore sheds new light on a dark chapter in American labour history; the 'Radium Girls', martyrs to an unholy alliance of commerce and science, live again in her telling.'

Megan Marshall, Pulitzer Prize–winning author
of *Margaret Fuller: a new American life* and
Elizabeth Bishop: a miracle for breakfast

'Carefully researched, the work will stun readers with its descriptions of the glittering artisans who, oblivious to health dangers, twirled camel-hair brushes to fine points using their mouths, a technique called lip-pointing ... Moore details what was a "ground-breaking, law-changing, and life-saving accomplishment" for workers' rights'.

Publishers Weekly

'Compelling chronicle of women whose work maimed and killed them, while their employers, their doctors, and their government turned a blind eye to their suffering.'

Seattle Times

The Woman They Could Not Silence

Kate Moore is a multiple *Sunday Times* bestselling author who has written more than 15 books across various genres, including history, biography, and gift. Her last book was the award-winning international bestseller *The Radium Girls*, which was selected for Emma Watson's Our Shared Shelf book club. She is based in London.

THE
WOMAN
THEY
COULD NOT
SILENCE

one woman, her incredible fight
for freedom, and the men who
tried to make her disappear

KATE MOORE

SCRIBE
Melbourne • London

Scribe Publications
2 John St, Clerkenwell, London, WC1N 2ES, United Kingdom
18–20 Edward St, Brunswick, Victoria 3056, Australia

Published by Scribe 2021

This edition published by arrangement with Sourcebooks

Printed and bound in the UK by CPI Group (UK) Ltd, Croydon
CR0 4YY

Scribe is committed to the sustainable use of natural resources and
the use of paper products made responsibly from those resources.

978 1 914484 00 1 (UK edition)
978 1 922585 08 0 (Australian edition)
978 1 922586 19 3 (ebook)

Catalogue records for this book are available from the National
Library of Australia and the British Library.

scribepublications.co.uk
scribepublications.com.au

For my Elizabeth,
and for John,
the best parents a woman could wish for.

CONTENTS

Author's Note   xvii

Prologue   1
Part One: Brave New World   3
Part Two: Dark before the Dawn   119
Part Three: My Pen Shall Rage   161
Part Four: Deal with the Devil?   231
Part Five: Turning Points   267
Part Six: She Will Rise   361
Epilogue   437
Postscript   451

Reading Group Guide   456
A Conversation with the Author   459
Selected Bibliography   465
Picture Acknowledgments   474
Abbreviations   476
Notes   478
Index   526
Acknowledgments   537

AUTHOR'S NOTE

This is not a book about mental health, but about how it can be used as a weapon.

It's a historical book. And as the people about whom I've written used their own contemporaneous terms to describe "madness"—such as *the insane* and *lunatics* and *maniacs*—I have used them too, though they're clearly not acceptable or appropriate in the modern age. As I hope this book will make clear, they were always blanket terms anyway, too broad and all-encompassing ever to be useful or sensitive to truth.

It's a nonfiction book. Everything in it is based on careful historical research. Every line of dialogue comes from a memoir, letter, trial transcript, or some other record made by someone who was present at the time.

It's a book that is set over 160 years ago. A lot has changed. A lot hasn't. We are only just beginning to appreciate exactly how a person's powerlessness may lead to struggles with their mental health. With that understanding, statistics showing higher rates of mental illness in women, people of color, and other disenfranchised groups become translated into truth: *not* a biological deficiency, as doctors first thought, but a cultural creation that, if we wanted to, we could do something about.

So in the end, this is a book about power. Who wields it. Who owns it. And the methods they use.

And above all, it's about fighting back.

There's no more powerful way to silence someone than to call them crazy.

—*Holly Bourne, 2018*

Confusion has seized us, and all things go wrong,
The women have leaped from "their spheres,"
And, instead of fixed stars, shoot as comets along,
And are setting the world by the ears!...
They've taken a notion to speak for themselves,
And are wielding the tongue and the pen...
Now, misses may reason, and think, and debate,
Till unquestioned submission is quite out of date...
Like the devils of Milton, they rise from each blow,
With spirit unbroken, insulting the foe.

—*Maria Weston Chapman, 1840*

PROLOGUE

If she screamed, she sealed her fate. She had to keep her rage locked up inside her, her feelings as tightly buttoned as her blouse.

Nevertheless, they came for her. Two men pressed around her, lifting her in their arms, her wide skirts crushed by their clumsy movements—much like her heart inside her chest. Still, she did not fight back, did not lash out wildly, did not slap or hit. The only protest she could permit herself was this: a paralysis of her limbs. She held her body stiff and unyielding and refused to walk to her destiny, no matter how he begged.

Amid the vast crowd that had gathered to bear witness, just one person spoke. The voice was high-pitched and pleading: female, a friend. "Is there no man in this crowd to protect this woman?" she cried aloud. "Is there no man among you? If I were a man, I would seize hold upon her!"

But no man stepped forward. No one helped. Instead, a "silent and almost speechless gaze" met her frightened eyes, their inaction as impotent as her own subjected self.

She didn't know the truth yet. In time, she would.

The only person who could save her was herself.

PART ONE

BRAVE NEW WORLD

A wife once kissed her husband, and said she, "My own dear Will, how dearly I love thee!"

Who ever knew a lady, good or ill, that did not love her own sweet will?

—Chicago Jokes and Anecdotes for Railroad
Travelers and Fun Lovers, 1866

Unruly women are always witches, no matter what century we're in.

—Roxane Gay, 2015

CHAPTER 1

––––

It was the last day, but she didn't know it.

In truth, we never do.

Not until it is too late.

She woke in a handsome maple bed, body covered by a snow-white counterpane. As her senses resurfaced after a restless night's sleep, Elizabeth Packard's brown eyes blearily mapped the landmarks of her room: embroidered ottoman, mahogany bureau, and smart green shutters that—for some reason—were failing to let in any light.

Ordinarily, her husband of twenty-one years—Theophilus, a preacher—would have been snoring next to her, his gravity-defying, curly red hair an impromptu pillow beneath his head. But a few long weeks before, he'd abandoned their marital bed.

He thought it best, or so he'd said, to sleep alone these days.

Instead, her senses were filled by the precious proximity of her slumbering six-year-old son. Unconsciously, Elizabeth reached out for ten-year-old Libby and baby Arthur too—the other two of her six children who'd taken to sleeping beside her—before remembering. Only George was there. The others were both away from home, in what she hoped was coincidence.

Elizabeth drank in the sight of her sleeping child. She could not help but smile at her "mother-boy"; George was at that adorable age where he had "an all-absorbing love for his mother." He was a restless child, for whom the hardest work in the world was sitting still, so it made a change to see him so at peace. His dark hair lay wild against his pillow, pink lips pursing with a child's innocent dreams.

He and her five other children—Arthur, Libby, Samuel, Isaac, and Theophilus III, who ranged in age from eighteen months to eighteen years—were truly "the sun, moon and stars" to Elizabeth: priceless "jewels," her "train of stars." She spent her days making their world as wondrous as she could, whether enjoying bath times in the bake-pan or gathering her children about her to tell them tales of her Massachusetts childhood. To see their "happy faces and laughing eyes" offered such blessed light. It was particularly welcome in a world that was becoming, by the day, increasingly black.

Such melancholy thoughts were uncharacteristic for Elizabeth. In normal times, the forty-three-year-old was "always rejoicing." But the splits that were even now threatening her country—with some forecasting an all-out civil war—were mirrored in her small domestic sphere, within her neat two-story home. Over the past four months, she and her husband had retreated behind those enemy lines, prompting much "anxious foreboding" from Elizabeth.

Last night, that ominous sense of foreboding had plagued her until she could not sleep. Around midnight, she'd given up and crept out of bed. She wanted to know what Theophilus was planning.

She decided to find out.

Quietly, she moved about the house, a ghostly figure in her night-dress, footsteps as muffled as a woman's gagged voice. To her surprise, her husband was not in his bed. Instead, she spied him "noiselessly searching through all my trunks."

Elizabeth's heart quickened, wondering what he was up to. He'd long been in the habit of trying to control her. "When I was a young lady, I didn't mind it so much," Elizabeth confided, "for then I supposed my husband...knew more than I did, and his will was a better guide for me than my own." She'd grown up in an era when the superiority of men was almost unquestioned, so at first, she'd swallowed that sentiment, believing "woman's chief office is to bear children" and that it was "natural for the moon [woman] to shine with light reflected from the sun."

But over the years, as Theophilus had at various times confiscated her mail, refused her access to her own money, and even removed her from what he deemed the bad influence of her friends, doubts had surfaced. The net he cast about her felt more like a cage than the protection marriage had promised. Once, he'd even threatened to sue a male acquaintance for writing to her without his permission, demanding $3,000 (about $94,000 today) for the affront.

In all their years together, however, he had never before rifled through her things at night. Fortunately, he was so engrossed in his task he did not see her. Elizabeth slipped back to bed, her sharp mind whirring, reviewing the events that had led them to this point.

The Packards had married in 1839 when Elizabeth was a "green" twenty-two and Theophilus a "dusty" thirty-seven. Theirs had been a clumsy, awkward courtship, throughout which Elizabeth feared her curt fiancé, fifteen years her senior, "did not seem to love me much." But as Theophilus was a long-time colleague of her father and Elizabeth an obedient daughter, she'd married "to please my pa," committing herself

Elizabeth and Theophilus Packard

to her new husband "with all the trusting confidence of woman."

At first, all had seemed well. Elizabeth had been raised "to be a silent listener" and her preacher husband contentedly became the sole mouthpiece in their marriage. "To make him happy was the height of my ambition," Elizabeth wrote. "That's all I wanted—to make my husband shine inside and out."

The problem in their marriage had been he didn't make her shine in return. Their characters were as opposite as it was possible to get. Where Elizabeth was vibrant, sociable, and curious, Theophilus was gloomy, timorous, and—in his own words—"dull." A typical diary entry of his read: "This Sabbath is the commencement of spring. Rapidly do the seasons revolve. The spring-time of life is fast spending. Soon the period of death will arrive." No wonder Elizabeth described their marriage as "cheerless." She wrote with feeling: "The polar regions are a terrible cold place for me to live in, without any fire outside of me." Her husband seemed "totally indifferent" to her. Sadly, she concluded that he did "not know how to treat a woman."

Nevertheless, she said nothing to him directly, enduring this "blighting, love strangling process silently, and for the most part uncomplainingly."

That is...until everything changed. In 1848, the first Woman's Rights Convention was held in Seneca Falls, New York, unleashing a national conversation about the rights of women. It was one in which Elizabeth and, less willingly, Theophilus took part. "Wives are not mere things—they are a part of society," Elizabeth began to argue, but Theophilus's belief, according to his wife, was that "a woman has no rights that a man is bound to respect."

Countless times, the couple had "warm discussion[s]" on the subject. It was Elizabeth, naturally blessed with "a most rare command of language," who triumphed in these fights. Yet her victories came at a cost. She felt the demonstration of her intellect prompted "jealousy...lest I outshine him." Theophilus was "stung to the quick," and his grievances slowly grew. He was the kind of man who counted them like pennies, recording slights in his diary with the miserly accuracy of a rich man unwilling to share his wealth. He grumbled crossly, "My wife was unfavorably affected by the tone of society, and zealously espoused almost all new notions and wild vagaries that came along."

Perhaps the notion that caused him most consternation: in Elizabeth's words, "I, though a woman, have just as good a right to my opinion, as my husband has to his."

The concept was dazzling. "I have got a mind of my own," she realized, "and a will, too, and I will think and act as I please."

Elizabeth's newfound autonomy was anathema to Theophilus. "Wives, obey your husbands" became a scriptural passage oft quoted in their home. But Elizabeth was no longer silently listening. She felt that Theophilus might, "with equal justice, require me to subject my ability to breathe, to sneeze, or to cough, to his dictation, as to require the subjugation of my...rights to think and act as my own conscience dictates." Defiantly, she kept on articulating her own thoughts, asserting her own self, inspired by the women's rights movement that it was her right to do so.

Theophilus's response was telling. He did not allow his wife agency. He did not encourage her independence. Instead, he wrote that he had "sad reason to fear his wife's mind was getting out of order; she was becoming insane on the subject of woman's rights."

On the morning of June 18, 1860, Elizabeth shifted uncomfortably in bed, her disquiet slowly intensifying. Beyond her bedroom window, the noise of the nearby prairie filtered through the closed green shutters. Elizabeth loved living in the Midwest. "Action is the vital element out here," she wrote approvingly. "The prairie winds are always moving—no such thing as a dead calm day here."

By this point, that lack of calmness applied to the Packards' marriage too, because their differences had only increased after the family moved west five years earlier. The change of scene had reflected Elizabeth's literally widening horizons. Shelburne, Massachusetts, where the Packards had lived for most of their marriage, was a place dominated by mountains and trees: a landscape that spoke deafeningly of what had always been and always would be. In contrast, the open prairies and wide skies of the Midwest seemed to herald endless possibilities—what *could* be, not what had been. Elizabeth felt strongly that "woman's mind ain't a barren soil," and once she was living in the fertile Midwest, she'd gotten busy planting seeds. "No man shall ever rule me," she declared, "for I ain't a brute, made without reason... I'm a human being, made with reason...to rule myself with."

She put that reason into practice. Soon, it wasn't just her appetite for women's rights that disturbed Theophilus. Elizabeth had a fiercely inquiring mind, and once she began to pull at the threads of their misogynistic society, the whole tapestry of their lives started to unravel. Both Packards were extremely devout, yet Elizabeth became wary of mindlessly swallowing what other people preached, including the sermons of her husband. Instead, she read widely about other faiths and philosophies until eventually her independent thinking led her to question her husband's creed.

In fact, almost by nature, Elizabeth and Theophilus worshipped different gods. To Elizabeth, God was love. But to Theophilus, He was a distant tyrant who dispensed His mercy so sparingly and secretly that one never quite knew if one had done enough to be saved. Where Elizabeth saw good in all, Theophilus believed everyone was damned unless they found *his* God—and that included himself. The pastor, fearful God would find out the least sin in his naturally dark heart, "used to tell God what an awful bad man he was, in his family prayers." Elizabeth commented wryly, "I was almost ashamed to think I had married such a devil, when I had so fondly hoped I had married a man."

Theophilus's beliefs extended to his children, too. He felt their hearts were "wrong by nature, and *must* be changed by grace." For their own good, he told them so, bluntly describing the hellish fate that awaited them until the children cried. Her heart hurting, Elizabeth would comfort them. She'd counsel, in opposition to Theophilus's teachings, "Be your own judge of your own nature…don't be deluded into the lie that you are bad."

Her "irreligious influence" caused Theophilus "unspeakable grief." He professed himself worried for his children's souls. When, each Sabbath, Elizabeth and the children would gather in her kitchen for "good talking times" after church, Theophilus could not contain his disapproval. He'd grumble as he retired alone to his study that they were "Laughing! On the brink of hell!"

Elizabeth was not laughing now.

She wondered anxiously what her husband's actions the night before meant. As she mulled over what she'd witnessed, her suspicions "assumed a tangible form."

"I was sure," she wrote, "arrangements were being made to carry me off somewhere."

Over the past four months, Theophilus had made it plain he wanted her gone. He could not cope with his newly outspoken wife, with her independent mind and her independent spirit—not least because Elizabeth did not keep her new character confined to their home. She asserted herself in public too, such as in a Bible class run by his church. Although at first she had been reticent—"[I] felt so small somehow," she confessed, "I didn't feel that anything I said was hardly worth saying or hearing"—as the weeks had passed she'd grown more confident until she frequently contributed, voluntarily reading her essays aloud.

But her opinions deviated from her husband's prescribed position. The classes were staged in part because Theophilus's Presbyterian church had recently switched from following New School to Old School doctrines—the latter a more conservative creed—and Theophilus needed to persuade his congregation to adopt the change. But to his horror, Elizabeth challenged him theologically and encouraged her classmates to think critically too. Though she'd write in her essays, "I ask you to give my opinions no more credence, than you think truth entitles them to," she was such a naturally persuasive person that, woman or no, her husband feared her influence. Elizabeth possessed "an irresistible magnetism." The pastor, in contrast, felt "unusual timidity" when it came to public speaking. Even without trying, she easily eclipsed him.

He asked her to stop attending the class.

"I am willing to say to the class," Elizabeth offered, "that as...Mr.

Packard [has] expressed a wish that I withdraw my discussions…I do so, at [his] request."

But that wouldn't do. That would only draw attention to her divergent views.

"No," Theophilus responded crossly. "You must tell them it is your choice to give them up."

Elizabeth exclaimed truthfully, "But, dear, it is not my choice!"

Her recalcitrance was new. Previously, Elizabeth had always been a peace-maker—"I had rather yield than quarrel any time"—but now that she'd begun to find her voice, she refused to be silenced. For decades, Theophilus's had been the only voice in the room. Was it too much to ask to share that space, now she'd ventured to speak the odd sentence? And did it really matter so very much that she did not think as he did?

But it *did* matter. As a preacher, Theophilus was supposed to lead his community, but now his own wife wouldn't follow him.

Yet Elizabeth refused "to act the hypocrite, by professing to believe what I could not believe." (An example: the new creed was ambivalent about abolition, but Elizabeth was *for* the freedom of the slaves.) She could not understand why Theophilus could not accept her independence. "I do not say it is wrong for others to do this," she pointed out, "I only say, it is wrong for *me* to do it." Yet in the face of her impassioned eloquence, Theophilus felt powerless and furiously impotent.

He conceived a plan. He kept it simple. Just seven words intended to silence her once and for all.

When the Packards next argued, he warned Elizabeth, if she did not conform, "I shall put you into the asylum!"

———

It wasn't quite as crazy an idea as it might at first have seemed. On the national stage, the women's rights campaigners were openly derided as "fugitive lunatics." Theophilus had simply adopted those same terms to describe his quick-witted wife.

Elizabeth had laughed, at first, at his outlandish threat. "Can [a woman] not even think her own thoughts, and speak her own words, unless her thoughts and expressions harmonize with those of her husband?" she asked archly. And did she not live in free America? It was written in the Constitution that freedom of religion was sacrosanct. Elizabeth saw no reason she should be any less entitled to that right—even if she was a woman.

But by the morning of June 18, there was no more humor. The more she'd spoken up for herself, the more her husband had undermined her. In the Bible class, he dismissed her ideas as "the result of a diseased brain." He told their neighbors she was sadly suffering from an "attack of derangement." His evidence was that she now acted "so different from her former conduct," his obedient wife having been transfigured into this harridan. Her unwillingness to adopt his viewpoint and insistence on her own made for "strange and unreasonable doings, in her verbal and written sayings." And then there was the killer proof: "her lack of interest in her husband." What could be madder than a woman who wanted to be more than just a wife?

Elizabeth had confronted him. "Why do you try to injure and destroy my character rather than my opinions?" She thought it nothing short of cowardly, the way he avoided debating her directly.

But he'd had to take action because Elizabeth had not been cowed by his threat. In fact, in May 1860, she'd only grown bolder. She took the courageous decision formally to leave his church. "To…be false to my honest convictions," she said, "I could not be made to do."

But the pastor feared others might follow in her footsteps. He had to ensure that no one else, whether wives or worshippers, replicated her revolutionary stance.

That morning of June 18, Elizabeth's eyes were drawn again to the green shutters in her bedroom. There was a reason they no longer let in light.

Theophilus had boarded them shut.

He also locked her in her room, supposedly for her health. He felt it best she be "withdrawn from conversation and excitement." Though Elizabeth knew the truth—that she was being "kept from observers... [because] my sane conduct might betray his falsehoods"—she'd been powerless to stop him.

But she was not entirely powerless now; she still had her powerful brain.

She used it.

After Theophilus's behavior the night before, Elizabeth's former forebodings shifted, sliding from suspicion into certainty. Thanks to her husband's warning, she could even color in the future he had sketched. A hulking, gray insane asylum loomed on her horizon.

Elizabeth knew the plan. She knew the perpetrator. The only question left was: when would he make his move?

At that moment, footsteps suddenly sounded outside her door.

CHAPTER 2

Was it a friend or foe…?

There was every likelihood it was the latter. To Elizabeth's consternation, when Theophilus had declared that she was mad, his parishioners had taken him at his word. They'd begun to weigh her behavior, looking for evidence to support his claim. Her "every motion; every look; every tone of the voice [became] an object of the severest espionage."

"As soon as [the allegation of insanity] has been whispered abroad, its subject finds himself…viewed with distrust," explained a leading nineteenth-century psychiatrist. "There still lingers something of the same mysterious dread which, in early times, gave him the attributes of the supernatural."

It was not so many years since the whisper would not have been "insane" but "witch"…

Elizabeth found the "crushing scrutiny" oppressive. "Whatever I say or do," she wrote in dismay, "[they] weave into capital to carry on [the] persecution." Though Elizabeth felt "an instinctive aversion" to being called insane, she could not narrow her eyes and speak sharply to those who whispered it of her or her unfeminine annoyance would be perceived as mad. If someone observed her snapping at her husband, perhaps because he had not cleaned the yard, the mere fact Elizabeth was "angry…and showed ill-will" became evidence of her unbalanced brain. There were those who thought her "dislike to her husband" was proof of her "derangement of mind."

Because in the nineteenth century—and beyond—women were supposed to be calm, compliant angels. They were even encouraged, for their health, to endeavor "to feel indifferent to every sensation." Those women, like Elizabeth, who displayed "ungovernable" personalities or "more than usual force and decision of character," or who had "strong resolution…plenty of what is termed *nerve*," were literally textbook examples of mental instability.

For some parishioners, however, her emotions were irrelevant. Simply her vocal presence in the Bible class, independence from her husband, and divergent religious views were signs enough of sickness.

They therefore supported their pastor in his plan. On May 22, 1860, the parishioners had signed a petition to have Elizabeth "placed in an Insane Asylum, as speedily as it can be conveniently done." Thirty-nine people signed the statement. "Just think!" Elizabeth later exclaimed. "Forty men and women clubbed together to get me imprisoned just because I chose to think my own thoughts, and speak my own words!"

Was it one of the thirty-nine lurking outside her door?

Elizabeth knew her home offered no sanctuary. Two days prior, on June 16, she'd watched as one parishioner after another had filed into her parlor, summoned by her husband to attend a mock trial of Elizabeth's sanity. Deacon Spring, of her husband's church, was the biased moderator.

"Such a pack of wolves around our house as we had," Elizabeth remarked darkly, "and no gun to shoot them with either."

She felt she was "suffocating and choking…in…a meddlesome and gossiping world." Lately, the wolves' hot breath had come even closer; Theophilus had usurped Elizabeth's domestic authority and brought another woman into their home. Twenty-three-year-old Sarah Rumsey, one of his most devout parishioners, had moved in, supposedly to help with the household chores. But Sarah was a teacher by trade and came from a wealthy family; Elizabeth knew she was no servant but a spy.

Frequently, Elizabeth had caught Sarah, her husband, and Theophilus's middle-aged sister, Sybil Dole, in "earnest conversation, which was always carried on in a whisper whenever I was within hearing distance." They would start, guilty, if she came across them suddenly. And Sarah would absent herself after any altercation, as though rushing off to make a record.

Was it perhaps Sarah's step she heard beyond her bedroom door?

The spy certainly had a lot to witness. Rows between the Packards had become increasingly frequent. Because just as Elizabeth did not stop asserting herself when she stepped outside the home, Theophilus did not stop his campaign against her when he returned to their house. In front of the family, across the dinner table, he told her bluntly she was insane and that she should stop talking.

But when Theophilus tried to silence her, Elizabeth felt her spirits rise. *So this was how it felt to dine with the devil.* This was not a Bible class; this was not his church. This was her home. These were her children. If she could not be herself here, then where in the world was there left her? Angry, she shouted at him: "[I will] talk what and when [I have] a mind to!"

The children, at least, had not abandoned her. They said of Theophilus's publicly known plan to take their mother to an asylum: "They will have to break my arms to get them loose from their grasp upon you, Mother, if they try to steal our dear mamma from us!" Elizabeth's only hope, that morning of June 18, was that one of the children might have risen and come to wish her good morning.

Perhaps her most staunch defender among them was her second-born son, Isaac, who was just six days shy of his sixteenth birthday. A "tender-hearted and devoted son" with "a mild and amiable temper," he'd strongly taken his mother's side in the Packards' civil war. He'd been greatly disturbed by what he termed the "wholly unfounded" rumors about her sanity and stepped up to defend her. He not only sounded the alarm to his big brother—eighteen-year-old Theophilus, nicknamed Toffy, who lived in Mount Pleasant, Iowa and was therefore not witness to the circling wolves—but also secured pledges of help from those Manteno townspeople who were *not* of his father's church. They said they'd step in if ever Theophilus tried to send Elizabeth to an asylum. Isaac worked in the local store, run by Mr. Comstock, and it had proved the perfect place from which to enlist support from the community.

Before she'd been locked in her ground-floor nursery, Elizabeth had tried to do the same. The world, after all, was wider than Theophilus's narrow realm. "She went from house to house everywhere complaining of her husband," Deacon Spring observed disapprovingly, while Theophilus grumbled that she'd "aroused a rabid excitement against me, *outside* of my own church and congregation."

Elizabeth's second son, Isaac Packard, as a young man

That was true. Sociable Elizabeth had many friends in the small farming village, which had a population of just 861. Her closest were the Blessings, who ran the local hotel, and the Hasletts, who ran Manteno; William Haslett was the town supervisor. They'd all been outraged by Theophilus's scheme. "That woman endured enough every day of her life for weeks," commented Mr. Blessing.

Theophilus was angry at the army she had raised. He invited a handful of her soldiers to his "trial" on June 16, hoping to convince them. But when a doctor among them refused to cast his vote—his reasonable justification being that he'd made no professional examination of Elizabeth and could hardly diagnose her based on hearsay—Theophilus, bitter, dismissed him as a "quack."

Isaac Packard had attended the trial. Inevitable though it had been, he'd been devastated by the verdict of insanity. It made him even more determined to assist his mother.

Determination that saw him standing ready on the morning on June 18—and standing outside his mother's door.

It was *his* tread Elizabeth had heard. She summoned her dark-haired son to her bedside, feeling the wolves' hot breath, desperate now to concoct some plan that might prevent her husband's perfidy.

She told Isaac to fetch his sister home at once. Libby was sleeping overnight at the Rumseys and Elizabeth felt suspicious of her absence, coinciding as it did with baby Arthur having gone to stay with Sybil Dole. Was it all part of Theophilus's plot?

Isaac promised he would fetch his sister. But he explained with a young man's grown-up pride that he had another, more pressing responsibility to attend to first. He'd been given special instructions by his boss that morning: "I must first go of an errand on to the prairie for Mr. Comstock." He vowed that as soon as he was done, they would go together to collect Libby and Arthur.

The plan confirmed, Elizabeth relaxed. She knew Mr. Comstock was "too noble to cheat you out of a single farthing." In fact, when her husband had first threatened the asylum, it had been Comstock she'd consulted for advice, for in addition to running the local store, the twenty-eight-year-old was a lawyer. Elizabeth had called on him with a sad heart, regretting such a visit should be necessary. Yet Comstock's "gentle respectful attentions" soon put her at her ease until she felt she "could look up and speak without my voice trembling." She'd wanted to know: Was it legally possible for her husband to commit her, given she was not mad?

Most states then had no limits on relatives' "right of disposal" to commit their loved ones. As one commentator wrote of the lack of legal protections for patients: "The insane were confined for their own good. It followed that there could be no motive for misdiagnosis, mistreatment, or unjust detention…there was no need to protect him from his protectors." But Comstock had good news. In Illinois, an insanity trial before a six-man jury was required before admittance to the state hospital. Theophilus's plan was impossible; Elizabeth had nothing to fear.

The information had, for a time, given her a feeling of comparative security. Mentally, she'd begun preparations for a trial. She'd felt her Bible class essays were her "only available means of self-defence," because she believed they provided evidence her views were sane. Once the church members' feelings about her had become clear, she'd made a point of putting "into written form *all* I have to say, in the class, to prevent misrepresentation." Words had become her defense, her armor, and the Bible class a chrysalis through which Elizabeth found her voice.

It had been a long time coming. After she'd married, Elizabeth had had to leave behind the "thorough, scientific education" she'd received as a girl and the teaching career that had followed. Over the years, she had longed—in vain—for a tithe of the time her husband had for study. He'd spent their decades together sketching out sermons, but her thoughts had always evaporated into nothing, like the steam above the saucepans on her stove.

The Bible class had changed all that. Her attendance had coincided almost exactly with her weaning baby Arthur from the breast; it was a chance to use her brain over body after decades of childrearing. Simply to leave her domestic realm had been enervating; her mind had opened like the door through which she walked. But the opportunity to write essays was even more transformative. Line by line, Elizabeth had begun to see *herself* take shape on the page.

With the essays so significant, in so many ways, she'd already taken care to conceal them in her room. Now, with the noose drawing tighter about her neck, she felt it safest to keep them on her person. She had therefore started sewing a pocket in her underskirt, knowing the ample girth of a cage crinoline would create the perfect hiding place.

But it was not finished yet. As she and Isaac discussed their plans that morning, she made a mental note to complete that pocket as soon as she possibly could.

———

Her musings were suddenly interrupted. While she'd been chatting to Isaac, her son George had woken and slipped quietly out of bed, dancing off into the dewy grass of their garden. He now returned and announced with a flourish, "I have picked some strawberries for your breakfast, Mother."

Elizabeth had barely begun to thank him when a deep voice cut into their conversation.

"Come, George," said Theophilus Packard, standing at the nursery door. "Won't you go with Father to the store and get some sugar-plums?"

With cool eyes, Elizabeth assessed her husband. She'd known his face since she was ten years old—this face of the man intent on her destruction. She could have sketched his features from memory: the "winter of perpetual frown" that furrowed his high forehead, his thin pink lips, and his reddish, mustache-less beard, which hugged the contours of his rounded chin.

Elizabeth knew his face so well—and her husband knew their son. If there was one thing in the world Georgie loved, it was sugarplums.

With a cry of excitement, he dashed off with his dad; Isaac went too, for the sugarplums could be found at Comstock's. Now every child was absent. Still smiling at her son's exhilaration, as soon as they'd gone, Elizabeth threw back the bedcovers, typically eager to start her day. She stripped off her nightgown, planning—as was her daily routine—to give herself a cold sponge bath.

As she moved about the room, her reflection was captured in its gilt-framed mirror. Petite at only five foot one, Elizabeth was a handsome woman. She had a nose as strong and straight as her principles, slim lips, and almond-shaped brown eyes—her intelligence was said to "gleam" in them. At that time of the morning, her long brown hair lay loose upon her shoulders. It was secretly starting to be silvered gray, but Elizabeth pasted it with sugar and water, a primitive gel that made her hair look black.

She was only halfway through her ablutions when a two-horse lumber wagon pulled up outside. Intrigued, she wandered to her boarded window and peered out through the cracks. To her surprise, she could see Theophilus; he must have entrusted George to Isaac. With him were four other men. Three she recognized as members of his church—Deacon Dole, who was Sybil's husband, plus Drs. Newkirk and Merrick—but the fourth was a "stranger gentleman" whom Elizabeth did not know.

As the men moved briskly toward the house, Elizabeth instinctively sensed danger. Moving swiftly, she crossed to her nursery door and locked it—of her own volition this time. Then she began to dress, as quickly as she could. The thought of her essays, hidden in her wardrobe, flickered through her mind, and she worked with yet more speed.

But the many layers of a nineteenth-century woman's wardrobe hampered her intent. She'd barely begun to pull on her drawers and her cotton chemise before the men were at the door. She heard their footsteps coming closer before the handle rattled. To her relief, the turned key kept them out. She turned back to her garments, rushing now, not wanting them to burst into the room with her underdressed and disarrayed.

When she heard the noise at the window, she was startled.

When she saw the gleam of the ax, she was scared.

She ran back to bed and threw the counterpane across herself. She needed it for modesty, body bare beneath her underclothes. She lay there trembling, tense and terrified, while the men outside rained blows upon the boards.

The wood splintered easily. With each blow, she felt it striking at herself, cutting cleanly through her confidence.

The ax made short work. All too soon, the men clambered through the window. They swarmed into the room, male bodies incongruously big and bold within her nursery.

The wolves were on the inside now.

CHAPTER 3

The two doctors came straight to her side. They seized her arm from beneath the bedclothes and professionally took her pulse. It raced, rampant; she was shocked and scared. Despite its rapid pace, Newkirk nodded at her husband. Whatever he was looking for, it seemed it had been found.

Theophilus stepped forward and said, "The 'forms of law' [are] now all complied with." He told Elizabeth to dress at once for a journey to the Jacksonville Insane Asylum. The train would be leaving at ten.

Elizabeth protested; she would *not* be committed without a *proper* trial. Thanks to Comstock, she knew the law. She knew her rights.

But Theophilus informed her, "I am doing as the laws of Illinois allow."

Although Elizabeth could not credit it, *he was absolutely right*.

Comstock, too, was a member of his church. Unbeknownst to Elizabeth, he'd also signed the parishioners' petition that Elizabeth was "so far deranged" she should be swiftly dispatched to an asylum. Yet he'd still not *exactly* lied to her. A six-man jury trial *was* required before commitment. But whether by design or not, Comstock had failed to mention one critical caveat.

The law did not apply to married women. They could be received at an asylum simply "by the request of the husband."

Because married women at that time in the eyes of the law were "civilly dead." They were not citizens, they were shadows: subsumed within the legal identities of their husbands from the moment they took their marital vows. "The husband and wife are one," said the law, "and that one is the husband." He spoke for her, thought for her, and could do what he wanted with her. The law gave him power "to deprive her of her liberty, and to administer chastisement."

In sending Elizabeth to an asylum, Theophilus Packard planned to do both.

The Illinois law in fact explicitly stated that married women could be admitted "without the evidence of insanity...required in other cases." The only safety net was that admittance only occurred "if the Medical Superintendent shall be satisfied that they are insane."

But Theophilus had already dealt with that. Though the state hospital was overcrowded, rejecting 75 percent of all applicants, Elizabeth had been selected as a patient on the strength of her husband's application.

Theophilus just needed to get her there.

Elizabeth's mind spun from what he told her. Under the laws of the United States at that time, a man's wife was his property: Theophilus could do as he wished. She later wrote in bleak despair, "I...have married away all the freedom I ever had in America."

Although the crisis had been coming for months, at this, its climax, she still felt betrayed. She and Theophilus had been married for twenty-one years. She had borne him six children. She had lived with him, laughed with him, sometimes even longed for him. She'd railed at him, rued for him, rubbed along with him for decades. She'd poured every ounce of energy she had into building their home and making their meals—into making a *life* together. Now, he was tearing her from it.

"If it had been an open enemy who had done it," she later wrote, "I could have borne it with comparative ease, but it is him, mine acquaintance, my equal, and one whom the world considered my best friend." She felt herself reeling from the revelation: "[The] man to whom I trusted...myself has proved a traitor."

She kept calm. Very quickly, she recognized that wailing and railing at the injustice would only add weight to her husband's claim that she was mad. Ironically, the harder she fought for her freedom, the more likely it was to be lost. How convenient for him if she acted in such a way to support his plan of banishment!

So she did not cry. She did not let herself think about her children. She channeled all her energy into self-possession, body and face becoming a blank canvas on which she let nothing show.

But inside, Elizabeth's mind was racing. She still hoped for some legal remedy, at least for some chance of self-defense. Securing her essays was therefore essential. Thinking quickly, she asked all present to leave her room so she could bathe and dress in private, intending to secrete her Bible class essays beneath her cage crinoline.

But Theophilus narrowed his eyes at her request. He insisted that Sarah Rumsey stay. Elizabeth protested—just think of the impropriety of bathing before this girl!—but he was resolute.

Under Sarah's watchful eyes, she dared not take the papers. Awkwardly, Elizabeth finished her ablutions and began to dress. She donned her wardrobe like armor, each garment a godsend that gave a touch more time at home. She heaved on her corset and her petticoats, spread out her heavy skirts across her cage crinoline.

Too soon, she ran out of items. With a sense of frustrating finality, she slung her traveling shawl across her shoulders and tied her bonnet ribbons beneath her chin. As she picked up her smart gold pocket watch, Elizabeth tried not to note the time, not to see how little freedom she had left. Already, the watch's message was meaningless.

All that mattered was that time was running out.

CHAPTER 4

She refused to walk to the station. It was one of the few protests she had left. Of course, it didn't make a difference. The two doctors simply swept her up in their arms and carried her to the waiting wagon.

All the way there, Elizabeth protested calmly, asking for a legal trial and vowing she would never leave her children voluntarily. She begged of Theophilus the chance to see them one last time before they left Manteno, but he bluntly told her no. It was not an accident that none were present. He was not about to bring them back to see her stolen from them.

As she tried to reason with him, Theophilus claimed, "It is for your good I am doing this. I want to save your soul...I want to make you right."

"Husband," Elizabeth sighed, "have not I a right to my opinion?"

"Yes," he responded, to her surprise. But he added, "You have a right to your opinions if you think right."

Elizabeth offered no physical resistance as she was lifted into the wagon, the men swinging themselves in beside her. Inside, she was screaming. With a crack of the reins, the horses began to move, bearing her swiftly away to the station. She barely had time to look back to drink in one last sight of her beloved home: to catch a fading glimpse of green shutters, floral beds in her well-tended garden, a painted porch she'd made beautiful herself.

Elizabeth's beloved home in Manteno

The passenger depot was located at the northwest corner of Division and Oak: a low-roofed, cream-clapboard building that was rooted right next to the railroad tracks. As they approached, Elizabeth's eyes rounded with astonishment. The place was absolutely packed, spilling over with citizens: the army Isaac had rallied to her defense.

Theophilus glanced nervously at the gathered crowd. "Wife," he said hesitantly, "you will get out of the wagon yourself, won't you? You won't compel us to lift you out before such a large crowd?"

Elizabeth smiled sweetly. "No, Mr. Packard," she replied at once. "I shall not help myself into an Asylum. It is *you* who are putting me there. I do not go willingly... I shall let you show yourself to this crowd, just as you are."

So in front of the mass of witnesses, Elizabeth was awkwardly lifted down and carried to the ladies' waiting room. There, she rushed to the window, eyes combing the crowd with relief. The countenances of all were etched with "deep emotion." Elizabeth felt that same deep well within her, her gratitude to Isaac rising like a wall of water. It washed her stricken soul clean. She had not been forsaken. All would be well.

She felt much more confident as Theophilus joined her in the waiting room. Outside, Deacon Dole was addressing the harried crowd; she could not hear his words. Calmly, she took a seat, skirts settling around her in a symphony of sighs.

Theophilus sat down next to her, bending his head to whisper in her ear. In tones "most bland and gentle"—as though she were a horse that might bolt with the least provocation—he urged her again to walk with him when the train arrived.

"Mr. Packard, I shall not," Elizabeth said firmly. "It is your own chosen work you are doing. I shall not help you do it."

Her steadfastness was unshakable. As she and her husband had battled these past few months, she'd become "more and more determined he should have no reason, in truth, for finding fault with me." Indeed, she'd recently begun to conceive of her stand for selfhood as "business that God has sent me to do." Her conscience told her she must fight for her rights, "to be...an example [to] women to raise them from being in bondage to man." She did so at this point more emboldened than ever, "holding on to God's cause with both hands."

She would *not* submit to him. As she put it, "A peace based on injustice...is a treacherous sleep whose waking is death. Your honor lies in waking out of it."

Elizabeth was wide awake now.

All too soon, the unmistakable sound of the train was heard. The iron horse rode into Manteno in a belch of steam and sparks. Elizabeth sat patiently on her seat, her passive resistance the only power she had.

Deacon Dole came to collect her. Having dealt efficiently with her traveling basket, he gazed helplessly at her body, not knowing how to seize her and maintain their modesties.

Eventually, with an impatient sigh, Elizabeth instructed him and another man to make a "saddle-seat" with their joined hands that she could sit upon. By now, she had been introduced to the "stranger gentleman" in her husband's gang—Sheriff Burgess from nearby Kankakee—and she asked him to tend to her skirts once she was settled. She knew instinctively that she could not appear in public with the least thread out of place; she was right to be concerned. The nineteenth-century medical notes of supposed madwomen place particular emphasis on their appearance. An unbuttoned blouse, an undone bun, or even simple carelessness of dress was considered damning evidence a woman's mind roamed free from its moorings.

The train's whistle sounded outside. Deacon Dole and his partner quickened their pace. Elizabeth was carried out of the waiting room and onto the teeming platform. From her elevated position, she had a clear view of all the citizens who'd come to save her. Without saying a word, she "imploringly and silently" looked to them for the protection they had promised. Any moment now, she told herself, they would step forward en masse and demand her husband stop his scandalous behavior.

But she looked to them in vain. No man defended her. A "silent and almost speechless gaze" met her eyes instead.

Elizabeth blinked, unsettled. The cavalry was there, all present and correct, but they were stiffly playing silent statues: an unmoving army that had surrendered all its arms.

Unknown to Elizabeth, Deacon Dole had told the crowd that the sheriff had a formal warrant for her committal and that anyone who interfered with this legal course of action was liable to be arrested.

And no man wants to lose his liberty.

Elizabeth's grip on her own was fading fast. She looked desperately from man to man, but

Against her will, Elizabeth Packard is carried to the train at Manteno station

their silent sympathy, "like dead faith," was of no account to her. "All the oppressor asked or needed was neutrals [who would] not...interfere," she later wrote. "The hungry wolf can carry his prey through the street in his clenched teeth... He can pace the platform of a crowded depot, and still thrust his fangs into her...and no dumb dog dares to bark to oppose him."

The dogs merely watched, mute, as the wolves took her: wordless witnesses as she was carried closer to the cars. Elizabeth felt her hope start to slide, the knowledge that her friends' words were weightless summoning it south. At times, she caught whispered sighs of encouragement. "You will not be there long," said the Methodist minister, whose church she'd joined after leaving her husband's. Another promise filtered through that they would get her out "in a few days." Mention was made of "speedy liberation under the habeas corpus act."

But no one dared to fight for her. No one dared to stand up for her or to intervene. Even Mr. Blessing later said, "I did not like to interfere between man and wife."

No, they were "double-minded" men, "unstable as water," part of a rising current that Elizabeth felt surrounding her—a current too powerful to resist. She felt her head slip under it, felt the pull of the undertow grabbing at her limbs. She wanted to scream—but if she screamed, she sealed her fate. She had to keep her rage locked up inside her, her feelings as tightly buttoned as her blouse.

Amid the vast crowd that had gathered to bear witness, just one person spoke aloud. The voice was high-pitched and pleading: female, a friend. "Is there no man in this crowd to protect this woman?" Rebecca Blessing shouted, pacing the platform. "Is there no man among you? If I were a man, I would seize hold upon her!"

But Rebecca was not a man. She had no power.

In a heartbeat, anyway, it was too late. Deacon Dole deposited Elizabeth at the doorway to the cars, and she was pulled inside, the door quickly latched behind her "to guard against any possible reaction of the public." With Theophilus, Dole, and Burgess as her bodyguards, she was ushered swiftly to a seat, the train already beginning to pull away, to build up speed, to bear her away from her home.

But it was not just her home Elizabeth was leaving. Her liberty lay scattered on the railroad track, her reputation for sanity dead beside it. But worst of all, her children...*her children*. Her Isaac, her Libby, her Samuel, her George. Her Arthur. Her Toffy. All gone. All left to this pack of wolves that had ravaged her.

"O!" she suddenly exclaimed as the world outside her window changed from familiar to strange. The word itself was a gulp of grief.

All morning, she had not cried a single tear. She had kept herself together; she had fought with dignity and drive. But a "deep gush of emotion" now overwhelmed her, her love for her children bursting the confines within which she had kept it caught. It rushed through her, unstoppable as a river headed to the sea, and she gave herself up to it, her head pressed to the seat in front, her body bent in pain.

Her sun, moon, and stars. Her sun, moon, and stars.

But the sky was black and empty.

As empty as her eyes that could not see her children now. She was blind as knowledge cruelly caught them in its net, as Isaac returned from his pointless errand to find that she was gone. For the first time in his young life, he tasted bitter truth: that promises are paper tracts too quickly torn. Libby, meanwhile, wept "almost unceasingly," her tears tinged by female fate. She was the only woman in the household now; her future was fast-fixed.

Though Arthur was too young to know, George was far too old. He tore himself from his keepers when the truth found him: he ran free, ran fast, ran after his mamma as quick as his legs could go. His mother had gone on the train, they'd said, so he determined to follow. But although he ran and ran and ran along the railway track, till his little legs could run no more, she never came any closer. He never caught sight of the train.

He could not find her. He could not reach her.

Elizabeth was lost to all her children now.

CHAPTER 5

It was a day's journey to Jacksonville, some two hundred miles to traverse. With the townspeople no threat, Burgess disembarked at Kankakee; Deacon Dole took his leave of them too. Only the Packards went all the way to the asylum.

By the time the train pulled in, it was well past 8:00 p.m. The sun had already dipped below the horizon, leaving a murky gray twilight in its place.

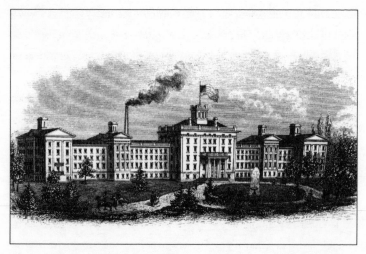

The Illinois State Hospital at Jacksonville, Illinois, in the early 1860s

The hospital was situated a mile from the town center—this repository of human souls kept distant from society. Elizabeth surveyed its shadowy walls with suspicion, her eyes having to squint to see in the indistinct dark. Five and a half stories high, it was three hundred feet wide: a central building and two generous wings, plus a lopsided extension that ran only to the west. As Elizabeth gazed at it, its endless rows of barred windows seemed to stare sightlessly back. It was the kind of place that inspired "awe both deep and lasting" as well as a "chilling sense" of the life within.

Elizabeth was quiet now, after all her words before. This was no time for essays or speeches or even prayer. As the Packards walked wearily along the brick pavement that led to the entrance, the steps of her buttoned boots spoke for her, each click of her heels saying *no no no*.

But there was no one left to listen.

Husband and wife reached the end of the path. The asylum loomed above them like Theophilus's God: tyrannical, secretive, its mercy out of reach. It had a grand, four-columned portico—the fluted pillars more in keeping with a stately home than a hospital—but the impression was still not welcoming. It spoke more of power, of a place that one entered unwillingly and always under force.

Elizabeth could see the front door clearly, wrapped within its white arched frame. She could see the glow of gaslights. And whether from night blindness or fear or even a fluttering breath of last-ditch hope, she chose to take her husband's arm. Gently, he guided her up the wide bank of stone steps that led them to the door.

Elizabeth tried to let her thoughts fall silent, but their voices were too loud for her simply to ignore. And among all the thoughts racing through her mind that night, there was perhaps one that rose a little higher than the others.

It slipped up like a secret, driftwood twisting on a tide of memory.

Not again. Not again.

How can this be happening to me again?

Because this was not Elizabeth's first time in an asylum.

History favors reruns.

———

She'd been nineteen the last time she was committed. On February 6, 1836, Elizabeth had entered the State Lunatic Hospital in Worcester, Massachusetts, on the legal orders of her father, Samuel Ware. She'd been right in the midst of her high-flying teaching career. At the time, Elizabeth was the principal of Randolph College in Massachusetts, a first-class school that employed "only the best classical educators." The cause of her insanity was reportedly "mental labor."

She was far from the first woman brought down by her use of her mind. In fact, people expected such outcomes. A visitor to an all-female school in 1858 remarked that its teachers were "training your girls for the lunatic asylum." While women had proven that they *could* study on an intellectual level, doctors lamented that the choice made them highly susceptible to "derangements of the nervous system." The problem was that when "minds of limited capacity to comprehend subjects" tried to do so, it ultimately led to mental breakdown. That was what had supposedly happened to Elizabeth.

In reality, doctors were policing women who stepped outside society's strictly defined gender spheres—work and intellect for men, home and children for women—in what could be described as a "medicalization of female behavior."

For similar reasons, one common cause of committal to an asylum in Elizabeth's time was "novel reading." Doctors believed that those who indulged in this "pernicious habit" lived "a dreamy kind of existence, so nearly allied to insanity that the slightest exciting cause is sufficient to derange." No wonder Theophilus and his co-pastor had tried to shut down the first public library that opened in Shelburne, Massachusetts. It was introducing "improper literature," and the preachers did not believe that churchgoers should risk their souls—or indeed their minds.

TABLE IV.

Supposed exciting causes of Insanity in cases admitted since December 1, 1864.

Domestic trouble	33	Sun stroke	
Religious excitement	32	Intemperance	2
Business anxieties	16	Novel reading	3
Death of friends	13	Fear	3
Puerperal	22	Brain fever	7
Disappointed love	15	Epilepsy	2
Over exertion	13	Paralysis	12
Vicious indulgences	25	Hereditary	6
Spiritualism	8	Unknown	19
Hard study	8		195
Physical injury	7	Total	446
Change of life	3		

Chart showing the supposed causes of insanity in those admitted to the Jacksonville asylum—including three patients admitted for "novel reading"

The psychiatrists at Worcester had not only been concerned with Elizabeth's overuse of her brain, however, but also her irregular menstrual cycle, as noted on her admittance form.

In the nineteenth century, doctors were certain that women's menstrual cycles made them liable, indeed likely, to go mad, despite no confirmatory scientific evidence. Whether they were menstruating too much or too little, were pregnant, breastfeeding, infertile, or menopausal, every single life stage relating to women's sexual organs was deemed saturated with risk. Mothers were encouraged to delay their daughters' periods—by making them take cold baths and avoid meat, feather beds, and those ever-pernicious novels—as the moment menstruation began, a woman was subject to its uncontrollable forces, which exerted a disastrous effect upon her mind.

It was a theory that dated back to ancient times. Documents from circa 1900 BC described how a woman's insanity sprang from the position of her uterus; in those days, it was believed to roam about her body, so treatments focused on sending it back to its proper place, mostly via malodorous or sweet-smelling substances, which were placed at either her vagina or her nostrils depending on which way the doctor wanted the womb to wend. The smelling salts that Elizabeth's peers frequently carried with them were a direct descendant of this centuries-old theory: when a hysterical Victorian woman swooned, a quick sniff of the salts would swiftly restore her sanity. It was no coincidence that the word *hysteria*, in fact, derives from the ancient Greek for *uterus*.

Elizabeth herself gave neither theory credence: her teenage committal was not caused by her period or her mental labor. To the end of her days, she maintained that her father had "very needlessly and unkindly" placed her in the asylum after she'd become *physically* sick with brain fever—what modern-day doctors believe to be meningitis or encephalitis. Elizabeth reported that the moment she'd recovered from her physical illness (and its then-standard treatment of venesection; she'd been bled excessively in her view), her mind had recovered as well.

Her medical record in many ways supports her account. Though most patients at the asylum stayed for months or even years, Elizabeth had been released in just six weeks.

As she walked into the Illinois State Hospital in June 1860, she could only hope this new incarceration would prove as short-lived as her first.

———

They were expecting her. As the Packards entered the ten-foot-wide hall, a young man in his midtwenties greeted her. By the light of the gas lamps, she could see he had soft blue eyes and a full black beard. Politely, he introduced himself as Dr. Tenny, the asylum's assistant physician. He was second-in-command at the asylum; the superintendent was away on business.

Tenny's manner, Elizabeth was relieved to find, was like that of "a tender brother," an impression heightened when no formal paperwork was completed that night. The doors to the offices that lined the hall stayed shut. Instead, Elizabeth was escorted directly to a women's ward in the original west wing. Theophilus did not join them. He would be provided accommodations within the stately guest apartments.

After twenty-one years, husband and wife went their separate ways.

It was the smell that hit Elizabeth first. As soon as she left the public realm of the reception hall, a "horrid and sickening stench" accosted her, what one doctor described as "the peculiar taint which apartments long occupied by the insane are apt to contract." She noticed, too, that the attractive furnishings that had graced the entrance hall were gone; cheap, uncomfortable items stood in their stead. Together, she and Tenny walked along a wide corridor, pausing only when they reached a certain door: the entrance to Seventh Ward. With a clatter of his keys, Tenny unlocked it.

An attendant came to meet them: thirty-six-year-old Mrs. De La Hay, who hailed from Tennessee. Yet she could show Elizabeth to no comfortable apartment. Due to overcrowding, every bed in Seventh Ward was taken. Elizabeth was ushered into a tiny room with a narrow settee bed instead.

It was, at least, private. With a heavy sigh, Elizabeth sat down on the bed's hard surface. She was served plain biscuits for supper. It was a world away from the meals she had once cooked for her family and herself. Given only a domestic sphere to conquer, Elizabeth had set about doing so in style; it was against her principles to half do anything. In Manteno, she'd grown her own fruits and vegetables—asparagus, currants, thimbleberries, and more—and spent her days roasting beef and baking "notion and custard-pies." Even Theophilus had admitted he couldn't find her equal as a cook.

As she forced down each dry mouthful, she wondered what her husband was eating that night as he dined at the doctors' table. It was renowned statewide for its magnificent meals, at which were served "all the viands, dainties and luxuries of the season."

Not long after she'd been shown to her room, a bell began to toll. Elizabeth listened to its mournful song. It came as a full peal at first, incongruently joyful, before morphing into a steady, somber sound that kept pace with her breaking heart.

By the time it reached its very last stroke, all the lights in the asylum were out.

Curfew had been called.

Elizabeth pushed her food aside. She swung her legs up onto the uncomfortable settee. There was no pillow. She bent her weary head to her folded hands instead and lay as though in prayer.

It was dark in the small room, light filtering fitfully through the barred window. In the sudden stillness after the silenced bell, she had thought, at first, there was quiet.

But there is no such thing in an asylum.

Gradually, "unearthly sounds" reached her ears. Cries and calls, screams and songs, uncanny laughter and a torrent of tears. The unsettled soundtrack of the troubled souls who lived within these walls.

Despite that chorus lifting all around her, rising from the floors below, Elizabeth had never felt so lonely. In this private room, she heard only her own breaths. She wasn't used to sleeping alone. Even after her husband had left her bed, her children had taken his place. A fever had recently afflicted the three youngest, so they'd all needed nursing through the night. Where were her children's bodies now, their sweet, snuffling sighs? Where was her darling Georgie boy, his tiny torso curved against hers, safe and sound and snug?

After eighteen years of mothering, Elizabeth was suddenly on her own again, but it wasn't like before. It felt as though something was missing, those "dear fragments" of herself now as much a part of her as toes or fingers. She didn't know who she was without her children. So her mind was filled with them, even as her bed was empty. Who was putting them to bed tonight? Who would comfort them when they cried?

She tossed and turned, question curling after question, but no answers came to ease the ache. She felt their absence almost as a phantom presence, yet soon even the imprint of their ghosts was gone, chased away by chattering cries.

Then, she was haunted only by madwomen, their voices rising through barred windows, carried to her on the hot night air.

CHAPTER 6

She stirred from sleep at the tolling of the bell. Despite all her worries, in the end, Elizabeth had slept. As the morning bell reached a crescendo, she reached for her watch: 4:05 a.m. Time to rise into this new world.

The night before, she'd begged of Mrs. De La Hay a bowl of cold water and a towel so she could at least take her sponge bath as usual. The familiar routine was reassuring. Carefully, she combed through her dark hair with the accoutrements she'd brought from home, angling her small mirror to see herself.

Her dark-brown eyes looked levelly back at her. Elizabeth Packard had not given up yet. She truly believed "submission is no virtue." Another day, another chance to show that she *was* sane. Because she knew this whole enterprise was simply her husband's attempt "to secure her subjection." With typically shrewd insight, she wrote, "That class of men who wish to rule woman, seem intent on destroying her reason."

But Elizabeth's reason was not destroyed yet. Though she didn't quite know how she would do it, she intended to accompany Theophilus back to Manteno, to return to her children as soon as she could.

At 5:30 a.m., a two-minute peal of the ever-present bell brought an attendant to her door.

Breakfast was served.

Elizabeth ventured out into the hundred-foot-long corridor that ran through the center of the ward. It was almost fourteen feet wide, its walls hung with a smattering of attractive engravings. Several doors branched off it to dormitories and private sleeping rooms. Although the hospital's original design had included parlors for the patients' relaxation, over-crowding meant these had long ago been converted into sleeping quarters too. Approximately twenty-eight patients were allocated to each of the asylum's eight wards. Elizabeth could hear the low, murmuring voices of the women of Seventh Ward as she walked toward the dining hall.

A ladies' ward at the Illinois State Hospital

At each step, a noxious smell infiltrated her every breath; the ward's water closets were separated from the other apartments by only a single door, and the pungent odor of the waste of so many patients was omni-present. Though Elizabeth did not know it, the smell was particularly toxic at that time. A devastatingly bad summer drought meant there was insufficient water to flush away the sewage. The resulting stink made the ward "almost uninhabitable from this source of offense." But Elizabeth just had to endure it and try to breathe through her mouth instead.

She paused on the threshold of the dining room. Perhaps to her surprise, she saw neatly dressed women sat around a long, oilcloth-covered table, set with glass and china. Seventh Ward was in fact "the most pleasant and highly privileged of all the wards" and its inmates considered the most sane. Therefore, as Elizabeth asked her attendant to introduce her, most of the women greeted her with "lady-like civility." Elizabeth, naturally gregarious, found herself almost among friends as she joined them at the table.

As they talked, she discovered that most of the women were well educated, middle-class, middle-aged, and married—just like herself. Nineteenth-century doctors believed patients "ought not to have [their sensibilities] wounded by being herded together in the same apartment with persons whose language, whose habits, and whose manners, offend and shock them," as they feared such unpleasant associations "may retard, and perhaps prevent, [their] cure."

Therefore, patients were segregated. Poor immigrant women were nowhere to be seen: they were assigned to the less luxurious wards, so that such "noisy, destructive" women, who were considered by doctors "vulgar and obscene" and of "low grade of intellect," would not affect the cure of these higher-class patients.

Nor were any of Elizabeth's new associates women of color. Very few were even admitted; in the preceding nine years, Jacksonville had treated fewer than ten *people* of color. This was perhaps partly due to discrimination—the asylum had a waiting list of 240, and places were prioritized for whites—but there was also a cultural bias, as certain types of insanity were considered to affect only the "highly civilized," which at that time meant white people. As one doctor explained, "We seldom meet with insanity among the savage tribes of men."

Moreover, when U.S. census records revealed that insanity was notably more common among free African Americans than slaves, psychiatrists mistakenly deduced that slavery must be advantageous to mental health. Those few people of color admitted to asylums therefore found the cause of their derangement often listed as just one word: "freedom." One physician even theorized that to run away from slavery was itself madness. To cure slaves of what he called "drapetomania," he prescribed "whipping the devil out of them" as well as the amputation of both big toes.

As she ate, crammed in among the other women, Elizabeth could not help but think back to yesterday's breakfast: sweet Georgie's platter of fresh strawberries, plucked from her fruitful garden. Here, the fare was "very plain and coarse, consisting almost entirely of bolted bread and meat." Luckily, the meal was over quickly, the attendants chivying the group to "hurry up!" even though many had not yet eaten their fill. Elizabeth left their squabbling voices behind, returning alone to her room. She wanted to plot her next move. Fortuitously, as it was "the use of my reason, rather than the loss of it" that had led to her committal, she had by then worked out exactly what she must do.

Her only chance of liberty was to persuade the asylum's superintendent to free her.

After all, he'd based her admittance solely on her husband's application, but he hadn't yet *met* her. She was determined to show she'd been committed merely "for THINKING." Once he realized the truth, she thought, he'd have to let her go.

She did not have long to wait to put her plan into action. As she sat there, deep in thought, a firm knock sounded upon her door, and into her room strode the only man who could save her now.

Dr. Andrew McFarland.

———

He was, Elizabeth could not help but notice, "a fine-looking gentleman." McFarland had a neatly trimmed goatee beard and a polished bald pate, with salt-and-pepper hair still scratching out his sideburns. Tall, he towered over her petite frame, dark eyes probing into hers. Instantly, she thought him a "true man, made in God's image." He was six months younger than her.

The superintendent shook her hand. Elizabeth believed "you can feel some people's hearts in their fingers," and the doctor's firm grip only increased her fulsome first impression.

There was much in his history to commend him too. McFarland

Dr. Andrew McFarland

hailed from Concord, New Hampshire, where he'd run the state asylum for seven successful years. Though professionally trained as a medic, he was "of the classic type of intellectuals" who pursued a breadth of study. He would quote Shakespeare in his psychiatry essays, found the poetry of Burns "an unfailing fund of amusement," and wrote his own artistic works, hailed by the local paper as "bearing marks of superior poetic genius." His intellect, Elizabeth would later claim, could "hardly be eclipsed."

Though there was no formal training in psychiatry at the time, he'd become an "enthusiast" in the field and, like all other alienists, learned on the job. With breathtaking arrogance, McFarland considered asylum superintendents—himself included—"the best men that society can produce." Yet his board of trustees echoed his self-assessment, finding his "executive ability...unsurpassed."

"There is no man in Jacksonville more universally respected than he," sighed one newspaper of the doctor, with all the longing of a love-struck teen.

Elizabeth almost seemed to share some of those sentiments as she took in McFarland's "kindly, dignified and professional presence." Only belatedly did she even notice that Theophilus was also in the room, creeping in the superintendent's shadow: a courtier to a king.

They'd come to bid her join them for an interview in the reception room. Elizabeth gladly accepted, happy "to be restored to the civilities of civilization."

She hoped this meeting would see her restored to them forever.

She walked with McFarland back to the main building, retracing her steps from the night before. Already, it was a happier journey, the June sunshine casting cross-stitch shadows on the wooden floor as it poured through the grated windows. McFarland strolled confidently by her side with a familiarity borne from six years on the job...and the fact that the asylum was also his home. He, his wife, and their four children lived in an expansive, eight-room apartment within the central building.

Yet his poise was also proof of his affirmed position within his profession. McFarland was at the top of his game: president of the Association of Medical Superintendents of American Institutions for the Insane (AMSAII) and a leader among his peers. Moreover, since he'd assumed the superintendency of the Illinois State Hospital in 1854, he'd licked the asylum into such shape that he'd written languidly in his last biennial report that there was such "harmony" within that "long periods of time elapse, leaving nothing to record of especial interest."

Little did he know that was all about to change.

CHAPTER 7

The doctor took a seat opposite the Packards in a big rocking chair while Elizabeth and Theophilus shared the sofa. It was McFarland who took the lead—Elizabeth's husband remaining speechless throughout—as the superintendent guided the interview through small talk to "the progressive ideas of the age, even to religion and politics."

With confidence, Elizabeth matched him conversational step for step. She was delighted never to be at a loss for what to say, despite the doctor's evident intelligence. Indeed, after so many years of being silenced by Theophilus, "dying by inches" as he'd crushed her self-esteem, the conversation felt to her like "a feast of reason and a flow of soul."

Hungry for the intellectual stimulation, she rather gorged herself. Her husband became a forgotten ghost, so insignificant that she did not talk about him and "particularly avoided any disparaging...remarks respecting Mr. Packard." Though her husband's presence might have made her feel unable to speak freely, Elizabeth never said so. Rather, she suggested Theophilus became a mere afterthought. Why bother with him when she could climb mind mountains with McFarland?

The doctor rocked gently in his chair and let her speak. Elizabeth took this to be a gallant deferential doffing of his hat, allowing her to take the floor. She wrote that unless her "womanly instincts very much deceived me," McFarland enjoyed their conversation just as much as she. He certainly seemed impressed. Though he wrote that he admired her "good looks," he was even more taken with her "extraordinary powers of mind."

How strange it must have been for McFarland to meet the subject of her husband's application. Did the two measure up? Elizabeth anticipated confidently they did not. Her husband had of course gladly shared with McFarland her medical history; Theophilus lamented that he hadn't been aware of "the sad risk incurred in marrying any person who has once been insane." Notwithstanding the fact that Elizabeth had performed her wifely duties impeccably for the past twenty-one years—so much so that even her enemies recognized that when it came to domestic accomplishments, she was "a model wife and mother"— Theophilus claimed she had only "*appeared* to human view to recover" from her teenage commitment. The truth, in his account, was to the contrary: the insanity had *always* been there—an invisible devil that had danced on her back for all this time and dared only now show its face.

But there was no sign of the devil in that morning meeting. In fact, Elizabeth judged it unnecessary for her to make an overt "plea of defence in favor of my sanity." What would be the point, when her own conduct made it clear? At the close of the interview, she returned contentedly to her ward, the dinner bell ringing in her ears for what she expected would be the first and last time. "I do believe," she wrote of the doctor, "that he became fully convinced in his heart that I was not insane, before our interview terminated."

She was so confident that later that afternoon, when she learned Theophilus had gone sightseeing without her, she grumbled about his selfishness, this now being the biggest slight in her mind. Jacksonville was known as "the Athens of the West," and Elizabeth had wanted to see its famous elm-lined roads and magnificent state institutions. She was cross she would not get to enjoy them before she and Theophilus returned home tomorrow.

She was offered a compromise: an attendant invited her to take a stroll within the asylum grounds. Elizabeth leapt at the chance. Asylum tourism was in fact a common pastime of the era: one New York hospital attracted up to ten thousand visitors a year, while Jacksonville itself received large numbers of visitors who came to enjoy not only the grand building and expansive grounds but also the human zoo of the asylum's inmates. It was an entertainment centuries old, once costing a shilling to see "the beasts" rave at Bedlam.

Another patient accompanied her. Their party of three paused briefly at the ward door while the attendant unlocked it before proceeding outside.

After the stink of the ward, fragranced by the many bodies of her fellow patients and the unflushed water closets, Elizabeth found "the pure air alone exerted an exhilarating influence." Yet there was also much to inspire her in the grounds themselves. The hospital sat within 160 acres of well-tended farmland. Fields of luxuriant wheat and corn stretched across the horizon, home to over one hundred swine and a dairy herd of thirty. Nor were these the only animals. Horses frisked across the fields, wild rabbits scampered, and the skies were alive with all manner of birds: eave swallows, purple martins, and "a cloud of swifts." Elizabeth noted with a gardener's interest the heaving vegetable patch, a misnomer for a vast output that included carrots, parsnips, pumpkins, and more. Closer to the building, an "ample expanse of flowers...exhaled their rich fragrance in clouds of balmy perfume" while an orchard of fruit trees, elms, and sycamores provided "shade as well as ornament." The scenery was "all but Paradisiacal."

But there was a snake in the grass. Elizabeth could not explore at will. At every step, she was shadowed by her attendant, who kept vigilant watch lest she try to run off. She was not allowed to be alone nor to wend her own way through the beautiful grounds. She was kept on a leash, a word or look yanking her back sharply should she try to pull away. "Is there no more freedom outside of our bolts and bars, than within?" Elizabeth sighed. On her return to the ward, the turn of the key at least felt honest: liberty audibly lost.

That night, Elizabeth was provided with a proper bed in a private room. She thought she could have borne one more night on the settee, given her stay would be so short, but as she settled down onto the comfortable, if narrow, mattress, she was appreciative. She had a long journey ahead of her tomorrow. She wanted to be well rested when she saw the children again.

———

It was the following afternoon before she heard anything more. McFarland had popped into her room briefly that morning, but as the meeting was "very pleasant and satisfactory," Elizabeth felt assured all was well. She likely made ready her traveling basket for the return journey, knowing she and Theophilus would be leaving that day.

At 3:00 p.m., as though on schedule, her husband appeared at her door and invited her to go with him. She was magnanimous in his defeat. She took his arm, without its being offered, and together they strolled to the reception room. Once there, husband and wife took a seat on the sofa, sitting side by side as they had so many times before.

"I am going to leave for Manteno in about one hour," he told her. Elizabeth may have nodded. Yes, they would make good time, would likely have to stay the night en route given the hour, but what a wonderful surprise for the children the next morning when she came sweeping back home. "I did not know," Theophilus added, "but that you would like to have a talk with me before I left."

Elizabeth paused in her imaginings. She could not fail to notice he had used *I* and not *we*. She drew away from him.

"Then you are determined to leave your wife in an Insane Asylum," she stated flatly. Despite everything, she could not believe it had come to this. A rush of anger seized her. "O, husband! How can you do so?" Her rage came out in hot tears.

Theophilus was unmoved. "I hoped we should have a pleasant interview before we parted," he griped, annoyed. According to what he professed, he was doing this for her own good and that of the children—to save their souls. Why couldn't she see it?

She begged and pleaded, told him to think of "those dear little motherless children."

He was adamant. "I shall see that they are well taken care of."

"But you cannot give them a mother's care," she cried. "O, how can my children live without their mother; and how can I live without my children?"

At the thought, she could not bear it. She rose from her seat, passion forcing her legs to pace, her feelings so intense she had to hold a handkerchief to her face to cover it. Still, her tongue tried to save her. Weaving words, she conjured

Elizabeth is overcome at the thought of living without her children

plaintive arguments, expressive pleas, entreating him to reconsider. She could not look at him as she cast her magic, perhaps too scared to see what was in his face. She paced the room instead, each length a last-ditch attempt to persuade him. She channeled all her emotion into walk and turn, walk and turn, to keep from breaking down.

Yet eventually, when he'd said nothing for some time, she dared risk a glance at him…

He was fast asleep on the sofa.

Elizabeth's pacing ground to an unhappy halt. The fight went out of her too. "I see it is of no use to say anything more," she said.

But there *was* still the doctor… Upon waking, that was where Theophilus went next: to see McFarland, leaving his wife in the reception room. Elizabeth felt she still had "a little ray of hope to cling to, as Mr. Packard had not yet left." Perhaps McFarland would step up and insist that Theophilus *had* to take her home.

She was not privy to their conversation in the doctor's office. She could not see the asylum's register. She did not know that the previous day, McFarland had made a new entry. On June 19, 1860, Elizabeth Packard—without her knowledge—had been formally admitted to the asylum.

In truth, her admittance was a foregone conclusion. Her husband's application had not only included his own account of her supposed madness; it contained two medical certificates from two different doctors also attesting she was insane. Both recounted her "derangement of mind," namely upon "religious matters," yet more telling were the doctors' more detailed assessments. One of the certificates was supplied by Dr. Newkirk, the member of her husband's church; he'd issued his certificate eight days *after* he'd signed the parishioners' petition, which ended any pretext of impartiality. He cited her "incessant talking" as evidence of madness.

The second was signed by a doctor from Kankakee, Christopher Knott, who'd been briefed beforehand by Theophilus that he "designed to convey" Elizabeth to the asylum. Such briefings were commonplace; as psychiatrists conceded there was a "deficiency of science" regarding insanity, they were reliant on families' accounts, at least in the first instance, to make their diagnoses. Really, certificate-issuing physicians simply rubber-stamped whatever a family said. So it had been with Dr. Knott. Without revealing his purpose to his so-called patient, he'd called at the Packards' home and deliberately engaged Elizabeth in conversation about religion "for the purpose of drawing her out." Yet to Knott, her religious beliefs were not her only symptoms; he also noted her "unusual zealousness" and prominent "strong will."

"Incessant talking." "Unusual zealousness." "Strong will." These were, in fact, textbook examples of female insanity in the nineteenth century. Doctors frequently saw pathology in female personality.

And so, with these certificates formally filed, Elizabeth's fate had been sealed. McFarland's cursive script in the asylum log recorded that Elizabeth was "slightly insane," with the "present attack more decided the past four months." This dated exactly to the time she'd joined the Bible class and begun forthrightly to express her opinions—in opposition to both her husband's wishes and his own beliefs.

Curiously, although the certifying doctors cited her religion as the main reason for her madness, she was *not* admitted as a case of religious insanity. This makes plain the importance of the doctors' other observations. Instead, in an echo of her time at the Worcester asylum, Elizabeth was admitted to Jacksonville because of her "excessive application of body & mind."

Or, as she herself expressed it, she'd been "placed there by her husband for THINKING."

Left alone in the reception room, Elizabeth waited anxiously by the window. Her little candle of hope was still burning, a tiny, precious flame. After a time, she saw Theophilus emerge onto the porch outside. At the bottom of the steps, a carriage waited.

He paused when he saw her standing there, trapped inside by a plan of his own making.

Would he beckon to her? Was she to join him after all?

On the contrary. He took time only to give her "one look of satisfied delight."

"Never," Elizabeth wrote with tight hurt, "had I seen his face more radiant with joy."

He threw her "kisses from the ends of his fingers," bowing his "happy adieu." No mention had been made by him of her recovery. He'd never said he hoped she should get better, that he hoped to see her soon.

As far as Elizabeth knew, he was leaving her there forever.

Theophilus bounded down the stone stairs with a much lighter step than his fifty-eight years might suggest was possible. Without giving her a backward glance, he disappeared inside the waiting carriage.

And Elizabeth's "dying hope" went out in utter darkness.

CHAPTER 8

After her husband's departure, Elizabeth had no choice but to return to Seventh Ward. The heavy door clanged shut behind her with horrible finality. To her surprise, however, the next sounds in her ears were sweet indeed: she found an outpouring of sympathy "from sister spirits who share my fate." Her fellow patients rallied around her, knowing exactly how her powerless position would be making her feel.

They shared their own stories too, and she discovered many had also been committed by domineering husbands. Some, like Elizabeth, had "no bruises, or wounds, or marks of violence...to show as a ground of her complaint" but nevertheless writhed "in agony from spirit wrongs." They knew, as Elizabeth did, that sometimes those controlling, invisible bruises were the most painful kind of all.

Other women had been physically abused before being dispatched to the asylum. One woman, committed by her "drunkard husband," was brought to the hospital with "half of the hair pulled out of her head," but she'd still been admitted.

"Of course the husband's testimony must be credited," Elizabeth observed sardonically, "for who could desire more to protect a woman than he?"

One psychiatrist openly defended this common practice of accepting a husband's word over his wife's, saying, "The manifestations of [insanity] are often very difficult to apprehend... It is necessary to have heard the private history of these women from their husbands to form an adequate idea of...the absurd ideas which have sprung up in their minds, the monstrous nature of their feelings, and the horrible acts they can commit." After all, in public, a woman might "preserve the appearance of sanity, and seem so reserved, mild, and well-disposed as completely to deceive the most skilful observers." But if a *husband* said she was mad *behind closed doors* then, quite simply, she must be.

Elizabeth railed, "It isn't fair for you to credit [men's] lies—and discredit [women's] truths!" But that injustice was set in stone in society, as evidenced by the experiences of the women she now got to know on Seventh Ward.

Sarah Minard became a particularly close compatriot. At forty-eight, Sarah was extremely elegant, the wearer of smart gold spectacles. She filled her private room with house plants—something to tend to, given she couldn't now mother her three children. No wonder she had "premature marks of age upon her head, which grief, not years had caused."

Sarah's husband, Ira, was a wealthy real-estate mogul who'd committed her for her interest in spiritualism—a religion then taking America by storm, with an estimated ten million followers. It was described by women's rights campaigner Elizabeth Cady Stanton as "the only religious sect in the world...that has recognized the equality of woman." Sarah herself protested, "It is not insanity, it is spiritual religion," but of course her defense did not matter. She'd been in the asylum for at least two years by the time Elizabeth met her.

Elizabeth made friends, too, with Maria Chapman, whose "busy fingers were always engaged with book, needle or pen" or with lifting her ear trumpet to her head, the better to hear her friends' chatter. Highly intelligent, Maria commanded "universal respect" on the ward. She'd been sent away for believing the teachings of Emanuel Swedenborg, a Swedish philosopher, because her friends did not. As Elizabeth later put it, "In many instances [it] is not Insanity, but *individuality*" that caused women to be committed.

Elizabeth was astounded to find such characters in the asylum. "It was a matter of great surprise to me," she wrote, "to find so many in the Seventh ward, who, like myself, had never shown any insanity while there, and these were almost uniformly married women, who were put there either by strategy or by force."

Women were sent to asylums for causing "the greatest annoyances to the family" or defying "all domestic control." The asylum was, in short, a "storage unit for unsatisfactory wives." They'd been, Elizabeth observed archly, "put here, like me, to get rid of them."

And that statement was truer in her own case than even Elizabeth knew. Because Theophilus had more motivation to get rid of her than she ever suspected.

Whatever the pastor later said, he *wasn't* just trying to save his children's souls.

He was trying to save himself.

There was a reason his church had recently flipped from New School to Old School doctrines. Openly, the switch had coincided with the church securing funding for its first permanent home. Even as Elizabeth was sent to the asylum, that money was paying for the upright boards and square tower that formed the new church building where her husband would now preach. The money had come with strings attached: the church had to switch its creed.

The suggestion had come from Cyrus H. McCormick, one of America's richest men, who'd donated $800 (about $25,000 today)—nearly half the total cost. McCormick was not only an extraordinarily wealthy individual but powerful in all the ways a man can be. At six feet tall and weighing two hundred pounds, he was a "massive Thor of industry" whom "men of lesser calibre regarded…with fear." Such was his intimidating aura that "smaller men could never quite subdue a feeling of alarm…in his presence." When he said "jump," one didn't ask, "How high?" One's feet were already in the air.

Although McCormick was himself devout, faith was not his motivating factor when it came to this more-than-generous donation. At the time, America was being torn apart by slavery, with many fearing these divisions might lead to the secession of the Southern states from the Union—even civil war. There were those in power determined to stop such splits by suppressing all talk of abolition, and McCormick was one. And the Old School's position on slavery was that it had "no authority" to pronounce on the matter; it stayed firmly on the fence. Therefore, McCormick pushed the Old School doctrines wherever he could. With his immense wealth, he was easily able to manipulate financial matters so that existing pro-abolition pastors lost their places and pro-slavery ones were hired instead. He didn't even try to conceal his plan; he was openly accused of "subsidizing the preaching of pro-slavery principles in the free Northwest."

McCormick was a personal friend of Deacon Spring of Manteno, so it had been easy for him to add Theophilus's church to his political plot. Despite the fact that the church had previously followed the pro-abolition New School creed, the church had taken the money—and turned its back on abolition as it did.

Elizabeth was unaware of these machinations. She knew only that her husband, who'd previously supported abolition, had suddenly stopped. They'd argued about it. "The oppressed ought always to find in us a fearless friend," she'd boldly told her husband. She thought it his duty to enlighten Deacon Spring—who, like McCormick, was not pro-abolition—on the merits of the cause. "I think he would respect you all the more, to see you true to your principles."

But Theophilus knew that was *not* the case. Spring and McCormick would likely fire him if he dared do that.

And Theophilus had a secret he'd been keeping from his wife—a secret that made that outcome an absolute impossibility.

He was deeply in debt—to the tune of $3,800 (about $118,000 today).

It meant the threat of losing his job hung over him like a guillotine's blade. No matter Theophilus's true beliefs, he had to toe the line—as meekly obedient as his wife was not. As he himself observed, "Self-interest is a powerful principle of action."

And this self-interest, with its related need to put the church first, was at least partly behind his emphatic insistence that his wife had to keep her mouth shut—and his following through on his threat to dispatch her to the asylum when she didn't. It was no coincidence that the very first time he'd made his threat had been after Elizabeth had voiced her pro-abolition perspective in front of Deacon Spring. Theophilus had told her himself he was attacking her sanity so that her opinions "may not be believed!" The pastor was acutely aware that if he could not control his wife—and her potential influence on his parishioners—he had no hope of controlling his congregation. And it was essential to McCormick and his political plan that Theophilus did just that.

Elizabeth knew none of this—that in standing up to her husband, she was also thwarting the interests of some very powerful men. The church leaders had been aghast when she'd left their church on principle, because who was to say this woman's independent exit might not inspire others to follow suit? Tellingly, although the deacons signed the petition to commit her on May 22, two days later, they tried another tack, when they and twelve others wrote to Elizabeth to beg her to rejoin their church. In the letter, they appealed to her reason—which suggested they thought she was sane.

Yet they hadn't been able to resist including a rebuke in the letter for the way she'd "so entirely disregarded the counsels of your husband." Her political views were not the only problem for them in her stand for selfhood. After all, even the women of the church believed that "we all have to be under rule and subjection to our husbands." (Elizabeth called them "my deluded Calvinistic sisters." She later urged them, "Don't sneer at the suggestion of our aspiring to an equality with the men!... Because perverted manhood has trodden us so long under foot, shall we choose to lick the dust?")

True to form, Elizabeth had roundly rejected the church's offer. Only *after* that did the deacons double down on their allegations of insanity. "She would not leave the church," Deacon Dole insisted, "unless she was insane."

With the political tension so taut, it was no wonder Elizabeth had felt the pressure: the wolves' hot breath on the back of her neck. Ironically, once she was in the asylum, surrounded by women who soon became friends, she actually found she was able to relax, perhaps for the first time in months. The asylum truly was "a covert from the storm."

And to her surprise, she found Dr. McFarland was part of that peace too.

The superintendent made daily rounds of his hospital, sometimes visiting Seventh Ward two or three times a day. He was conscious of "how many hopes rest in him" and made a determined effort, in keeping with the treatment principles of the era, to know his patients' "characters, feelings, connections and interests with a good degree of intimacy." His consultations were as soft in tone and manner as the velvet slippers he sometimes wore to attend them, his self-described "fountains of sympathy" ever-ready to wash clean the stricken souls he sought to soothe. As he and Elizabeth got to know one another better, she found—as others had before her—that the doctor possessed "a heart of the tenderest sympathies," while McFarland discovered a woman, in his words, of "extraordinary mental capacity and power, great charm of manner, and taste in dress, and good judgment." His work had always been to him "a labor of love." At times, with Elizabeth, that seemed almost literal.

The conversational "feast" the pair had enjoyed at their first meeting transpired to be a mere appetizer. Never before had Elizabeth enjoyed such an opportunity to converse freely with an intelligent man. At home, Theophilus had always silenced her opinions with looks like daggers; if she really overstepped the line in public, he'd followed through with "after-claps" as soon as they got home. But McFarland never made any such threats. On the contrary, he seemed fascinated by her, later praising "the perfection of her mind." They'd discuss all sorts of things, McFarland expressing interest in the "minutest movements" of her world, but perhaps most important to Elizabeth was that he seemed to sympathize. "I felt that he did pity me," she wrote, "and really wished to be a true friend."

It was only days before his visits "were anticipated with the greatest pleasure of any of my early asylum experiences." Though McFarland, by his own admission, "never could sing a quaver," in the gentle music of his ministrations, Elizabeth found perfect harmony. She thought McFarland "a man of honor, of intelligence, and of real worth." Simply from the "affectionate" touch of his hand, she felt better, so much so that she did not complain when—as she sometimes thought—that touch of his hand on hers "longer continued than this healing process demanded."

"I was then quite a novice in this mode of cure," she conceded. "I might not have been a proper judge."

McFarland's job, of course, was to judge the sanity of his patients and to determine when they were cured. Notwithstanding those damning certificates in his files, McFarland was a man who made up his own mind. Seeing the way Elizabeth had adapted so quickly to life at the hospital, he felt very pleased with his new patient. That was why, when he called on her one day toward the end of her first week, he had good news to share.

"I do not think you will remain but a few days longer," he said reassuringly to his new friend.

CHAPTER 9

In the wake of McFarland's announcement, Elizabeth found the asylum rules relaxed around her until she felt more like a hotel boarder than a patient. Though there was a rule that patients must put their clothes out of their rooms each night before being locked in—a precaution taken to limit the success of any midnight flights—Elizabeth was exempt. She kept her clothes in her own room, able to dress how and when and where she wished. She freely borrowed books from the hospital library, made abundant use of stationery to write as she pleased, and even dined occasionally at the doctors' table. Incredibly, she was also gifted her own set of ward keys and allowed out without an attendant. Such was the trust in her, she became almost like a matron, accompanying other patients on local jaunts without an overseer, the reins of the asylum omnibus clutched loosely in her hands. Indisputably, she had become the "Asylum favorite" and was treated with "almost queen-like attention"; another doctor noted she "had liberty other patients did not enjoy." But she'd seemingly impressed McFarland so much in their early appointments with "her consummate tact and adroitness" that the superintendent saw fit to grant these privileges.

One afternoon in late June, Elizabeth decided to spend her time sewing. This was encouraged for all the women in her ward as part of what doctors later called industrial therapy. Though ostensibly organized for the patients' benefit, the work they did was essential to the hospital's economic efficiency. Patients were employed, without pay, not only in the sewing room but also on the farm, in the laundry and kitchens, and as housemaids or carpenters, with the allocation of labor divided along class and gender lines.

Elizabeth was a truly expert seamstress. At home, she'd not only made her children's clothes but created her own designs—claret merino capes and black velvet tunics, lovingly lined with dove-colored silk. Her tasks in the asylum were somewhat different but no less challenging. The upper-class women in the sewing room made and maintained *all* the bedding, furnishings, and clothing required for the entire asylum; the latter alone saved McFarland $1,000 (about $31,000) each year. Over a two-year period ending December 1860, Elizabeth and her friends made—among many thousands of other items—997 pillowcases, 873 chemises, and 767 dresses. In addition, they mended 3,105 shirts and 1,007 pairs of socks.

Records show the women even made their own restraining jackets.

Busy as it was, Elizabeth liked the quiet industry. The spacious workroom was located four stories up and had unbarred windows, which allowed for greater sunshine to stream into the room. She was also a fan of Priscilla Hosmer, the sewing room's forty-five-year-old directress, whom she came to describe as "my best friend." Priscilla's sister had once been committed to an asylum—in New Hampshire, where McFarland himself had treated her—so she had genuine empathy for the patients. As most attendants did, Mrs. Hosmer slept on site, so she was always there whenever Elizabeth took up her needle and whiled away the hours.

So engrossed was Elizabeth in her handiwork that afternoon that for once, she didn't stir when a carriage drew up outside the hospital in a percussive patter of horses' hooves. Previously, she'd watched the front drive like a hawk. After all, her Manteno friends had vowed they'd try to get her out "in a few days." So it was to her surprise when an attendant came to summon her: Elizabeth had visitors in the reception room.

The Blessings, from Manteno, had come at last.

Yet Isaac and Rebecca Blessing, both in their forties, were not alone. They'd invited Dr. Shirley of Jacksonville too. It's possible they wanted an expert opinion to refute the certificates of Newkirk and Knott. After a stimulating conversation with Elizabeth, Shirley pronounced, "She is the sanest person I ever saw."

There followed an afternoon full of friendship. Keys in hand, Elizabeth showed the Blessings around the hospital. They seemed astonished at her liberty, and Elizabeth confided that any privations she'd suffered at the start of her stay "did not begin to equal what I endured in one day's time at home from my husband."

The Blessings, having seen firsthand the way she had been hounded, agreed wholeheartedly. Yet it prompted them to ask whether Elizabeth *wanted* to go back.

"Indeed I do," she said emphatically. She longed to be reunited with her children. "But," she added, "I must be protected from my husband."

The Blessings had a plan for that. A "public indignation meeting" was scheduled for June 30 in Manteno, intended to rouse the townspeople into helping her en masse. Letters would also be written to the hospital, the governor, lawyers, and judges—anyone they could think of who might be able to set her free. Should all that fail, they had a trump card: they'd apply for a writ of habeas corpus.

Habeas corpus had been a cornerstone of American justice since the time of the Founding Fathers. It provided specifically for "the liberation of those who may be imprisoned without sufficient cause" and was of "universal application in cases of unlawful confinement." It guaranteed Elizabeth would be brought before a court for a ruling on whether her incarceration was legal. It sounded like just the ticket.

Elizabeth bade her friends farewell with a newly lightened heart. It is not known if she shared their plan with McFarland—given their blossoming friendship, it's possible—but he soon received her friends' letters at any rate.

Curiously, "the gentlemanly Superintendent" did not mention them to Elizabeth.

The days and then the weeks passed. June 30 came and went. Elizabeth watched each day for a letter with an update or for a lawyer to come a-calling, but nothing happened. She started to worry. What had happened to the plan? She eventually wrote to the Blessings but received no reply.

Then, on July 13, there was a delivery, but it was not what she'd been waiting for. Into the ward that day came two porters, awkwardly carrying "a monstrous-sized trunk." It had been sent by Theophilus. The other women crowded around, noting its size with shock. Their words echoed her own thoughts: "Is Mr. Packard going to keep his wife here for life?"

To date, Elizabeth had been wearing the limited array of clothes that Theophilus had packed for her the day he took her to Jacksonville. She had at least three dresses, two petticoats, two pairs of pantaloons, and her shawl and bonnet. This small wardrobe might have inspired hope her stay would be short, but Theophilus had dashed that before his departure, telling her the trunk would be sent on. Now, he'd finally done it.

Was that because the Blessings' planned public meeting had failed in its mission? Shut off from society, Elizabeth did not know.

As she always tried to, she looked on the bright side. The trunk, to her mind, came not only from her husband but from *home*: "One ray of comfort gleamed forth...now I shall hear from my dear children."

She wanted to savor the moment, after nearly a month apart. She'd already missed Isaac's sixteenth birthday; George's seventh was in five days' time. When McFarland considerately came to see how she was after the trunk's arrival, she asked to be allowed to unpack it alone, in her room with her door locked. She wanted no disturbances. She wanted this simply to be a silent communion between herself and them. She could almost taste her anticipated joy—sweet as the sugarplums Georgie so adored. McFarland, understanding, locked her in himself.

Elizabeth knelt down on the floor and opened up the trunk.

Her first shock was that it was largely empty, only one-third full. The second was that the clothes her husband had enclosed were not her good ones. She'd specifically asked him to send her black silk dress and white crepe shawl, the ones she wore for church, so she could be decently dressed for chapel prayers at the asylum, but this outfit was notably absent. Elizabeth felt her heart sink as she reviewed the trunk's contents. She really *would* look like a madwoman in this eclectic assortment.

She started rifling through the trunk. All the items were "in a state of the most tangled confusion," with her clothes thrown about with rotten lemons and even a large mirror, which had luckily survived its unconventional transportation. She lifted each item out with tender care, unfolding chemises, unrolling stockings to the very ends of their toes, searching every nook and cranny with an archaeologist's accuracy, not wanting to miss a thing. Because she knew that somewhere in this trunk were the letters from her children. To find them would be "next to finding my child, for his own fingers must have held it and kissed it for his mother." So she handled each lemon, each shawl, each dress, with infinite care, wanting nothing to spoil the moment of discovery, wanting to take no chance of tearing those precious paper gifts.

But no letters did she find. At long last, though she had eked out its evacuation, the trunk stood empty—empty as her heart. She held in her hand just a single scrap of paper. It was from Libby. Yet her daughter's words brought no comfort, just a sharp, stabbing pain.

> We are glad to hear you are getting better; hope you will
> soon get well.

But Libby knew she was not sick.

Elizabeth felt tears pricking at her eyes. She'd had a fear of this, tucked away deep inside. How could she not, when Theophilus had taken pains to tell the children even before she'd left that she was mad? He'd wanted nothing more than to remove them from her influence, both spiritual and political. But *then*, she'd always been there to counteract his lies: to strike a funny face to make her children smile, to speak reasonably of how *she* saw God, or simply to show them that she was the same kind, loving mother they'd always had. For that reason, only twelve-year-old Samuel—her "most troublesome" child—had ever wavered in his support.

But far from home, Elizabeth could do nothing now to stop the corrosive power of his claims. They licked like a hungry tide at a sandcastle built of her children's trust.

As she read and reread that short, sad, singular note, its fifteen words seemed to solidify before her, cementing the fears in her heart. Theophilus had her exactly where he wanted her. And now that end was accomplished, he had "naught to do but to teach [the] children to despise their mother, and treat her name and memory, with contempt."

Was he already doing it? *Was it already working?* The thought was small and scrabbly in her chest, like the wild rabbits in the fields beyond. Like them, it could not be tamed. She feared that Libby could now be "coming under the influence of this delusion."

Elizabeth prayed that her daughter would stay true. And she thought again, more urgently now, of her release from the asylum. Though she did not know what had happened to the Blessings, she was starting to fear their plans had come to naught. Yet how else could she make it home? After all, as she realized bleakly, "Being sane, *I can't be cured.*"

But at this juncture, her friend McFarland stepped into the breach, calling upon her, as was his custom, "with the most polite attentions and marked respect." Once more, he promised her liberty—and he meant it wholeheartedly. She could well be ready to go home now, he said.

There was just one condition.

She would have to return to Theophilus—as his obedient wife.

All she had to do to secure her freedom was submit.

CHAPTER 10

Elizabeth had almost been expecting it. One couldn't hear the tales of the other women on Seventh Ward and not know that an asylum was not so much a place to treat the sick as a pseudo factory for social control. McFarland himself even hinted at it. His hospital, he said, had a "subsidiary use as a social necessity."

In truth, superintendents in the nineteenth century acted not only as doctors but as society's paternal police, ever ready to step in to dissuade people—both male and female—from deviating from the social standards they themselves had set (which largely meant those observed by white, Protestant, middle-class men). Thus male patients were committed for seemingly feminine behavior or intemperance, with immigrants in particular committed in large numbers. Masturbation (which occurred "more frequently...amongst those engaged in sedentary occupations," being "very common among shoemakers" in particular) was described as the leading cause of male insanity. Meanwhile, women who were assertive or ambitious were also sent to asylums, often with the added warning that if they didn't desist from their unladylike behavior, they'd risk becoming infertile too. A superintendent summed it up by saying, "A lunatic asylum is a grand receptacle for all who are troublesome." That even included children: Jacksonville had admitted three patients under fifteen in the past two years, one as young as nine.

Psychiatrists—who had no formal training yet yearned to give their new careers the veneer of professional authority—quickly came up with a medical diagnosis to encompass this broad range of social ills. They called it, quite simply, moral insanity.

The term was first coined by the Englishman James Cowles Prichard in 1835, though much earlier, Philippe Pinel in Paris described something similar. According to Prichard, any person who demonstrated "eccentricity of conduct"—or who showed "perversion of the natural feelings, affections, inclinations, temper [or] habits"—could be diagnosed as morally insane. Crucially, the diagnosis could be given even if the person was not delusional or suffering any mental impairment. Moral insanity affected the *emotions*. Its sufferers were the irrational angry woman or overwrought, expressive man. In all other ways, patients could appear perfectly sane. (Often, they actually were.)

Given this broad blanket, which quickly wrapped many within its folds, moral insanity proved controversial, even within psychiatry. As a general concept, it had been questioned in France since 1810, in Germany since 1822. After all, as one doctor pointed out, its symptoms were such that they could "arise in the bosom of anyone, sane or insane... We might not call that insanity. We might say truly, his temper has got the better of him." In time, its critics would declare it a "misfortune for science" that the idea was ever pursued at all.

But when Elizabeth was sent to the asylum, its advocates were still passionately defending it, even amid increasing doubt. Psychiatrists arrogantly insisted that just because a person appeared sane in all other ways, *they knew better*. They were the experts; it was for them to say who had crossed that thinly veiled line between sane and insane.

And more often than not, they opted for the latter. The diagnosis had become so prevalent that McFarland lamented its sufferers multiplied "faster than institutions can possibly be built for their accommodation." Hence the overcrowding Elizabeth had witnessed. Soon, however, McFarland anticipated that would be in the past; he'd recently secured funding for an entire new wing, *just for women*, to meet demand. The new wards, with space to commit another 150 female patients, would open the following year.

A similar planned extension for men would languish without support from the legislature. It would not be completed for another six years.

Though Elizabeth was not familiar with the term *moral insanity*, she nevertheless appreciated the true, *social* reasons behind her committal. It was "to keep me humble, and in my proper place." Her husband had sent her to the asylum "fully determined I should have a thorough dressing down, or breaking in, before he should take me out again."

And she understood exactly who was supposed to be doing the breaking in: friendly Dr. McFarland. Indeed, as Dr. Tenny put it to another patient, "I will be your father, mother, sister, and brother, friend, and Doctor." The physicians became ciphers for the absent family members, there to encourage the women to behave.

Their actions lay under the umbrella of what was known as moral treatment, summarized as "the law of love." Intimate relationships between patients and doctors were encouraged, so that kindness and sympathy might draw a patient out, the psychiatrist exerting a positive influence upon her. Already Elizabeth thought of McFarland as "my counselor and guide." The doctor was "a most noble, kind protector." Moral treatment encompassed the environment too, with the building itself and patients' daily activities engineered toward peaceful recovery. Amid these delightful settings, the insane were to be taught "proper values, morality and healthy habits that would enable them to return to the world as responsible citizens." It was not so much "therapeutic intervention as that of ethical supervision." And doctors' records show that "cured" women were those who became "quiet, decorous in manners and language, attentive to their dress, [and] disposed to useful activity."

Or, as Elizabeth put it, women who'd been broken in.

When McFarland dangled the olive branch before her, Elizabeth considered it. She could have taken it, could have decided that returning to her children was more important than her own sense of selfhood. But, she said, "Self-defense forbids it." She could not shake her conviction: "I have done no wrong." In her letters home to her husband, she begged *him* to repent. She knew if she went home now, nothing would be different. So she would *not* submit.

"Old Packard will find his Elizabeth has got the grit in her," she wrote fiercely. "I don't think the discovery will afford him much satisfaction. But it does me." She concluded archly, "I think it will be a long time before this cure will be effected."

But just because she wouldn't obey, that didn't mean she didn't want to go home.

She simply needed another strategy.

As she gazed at Dr. McFarland in her room—so intelligent, so reasonable, so very sympathetic—she lit upon it. She would stay at the asylum, but of her own volition. She would stay weeks, even months if that was what it took. But she was going to give the doctor the chance to see the truth. She'd been placed here on a *false* charge of insanity. She didn't need to be cured. She didn't need to submit.

She was just as sane as he was.

She just needed to give McFarland a little more time to see it for himself.

———

Elizabeth believed she could convince him. After all, she was a "model wife and mother," her only crime was thinking for herself, and best of all, she possessed an "impregnable, invincible fortress of calm self-composure." She had gotten out of Worcester within six weeks when she was a teenager.

She was sure she could do it again.

Although Elizabeth did not know it, she could not have picked a better doctor for her plan, because McFarland was one of those psychiatrists who'd begun to question moral insanity. Some cases seemed to him "mere emotional impulses" that "hardly deserve the name of disease." He subscribed to a theory that moral insanity was impossible without an underlying intellectual delusion.

And it was obvious to McFarland that Elizabeth had no "intellectual impairment at all—certainly nothing that deserved the name." When he wrote to Theophilus on August 11, 1860, to update him, he praised Elizabeth's "fine mind and brilliant imagination." He found her case a truly "interesting study."

By August, Elizabeth felt as fascinated by her doctor as he appeared to be by her. Their one-on-one meetings in her private room led only to deeper confidences. In moral treatment, patients were to be "made comfortable, [her] interest aroused, [her] friendship invited, and discussion of [her] troubles encouraged." McFarland's sympathetic sessions with Elizabeth soon inspired "feelings of tranquillity, peace, and quietude" that "permeated into the very fibers of my existence." She called him "my kind friend"; herself, "your faithful Eva." As McFarland drew on his "extraordinary tact and skill," they wove their words into a latticework that lifted Elizabeth's spirits higher and still higher, binding the two of them together in what McFarland hoped would be an "intimate and effective relationship."

Elizabeth's sole complaint was that the doctor could sometimes be taciturn. McFarland was said to possess "a self-control so perfect that to a stranger he might seem impassable and cold." While Elizabeth poured out her heart, he barely replied, leaving her in the dark as to his real opinions.

But to meet a man who *listened* was so wonderful she did not give it much thought. Onto the blank canvas he gave her, she painted masterpieces. She explained away the man's mystery as "one of his God-like traits."

For twenty-one years, throughout her marriage, Elizabeth had been lonely. She'd felt damped down, strangled, and silenced. But now a man had given her permission to speak—to speak her mind. It felt like magic. Day by day, McFarland's conjured claim on her slowly "took possession of my womanly heart."

Ordinarily, when a woman in the nineteenth century was in danger—as Elizabeth still felt she was; she "dare[d] not come again within [Theophilus's] influence"—she sought safety via her husband, her "manly protector" from the society in which she was restricted from maneuvering alone. But to whom could a woman turn when it was her own husband persecuting her?

Elizabeth had few options. Theophilus had told her that her two brothers and her father all supported her commitment. Elizabeth knew they'd only have done so because her husband had told them lies—as she hadn't seen her father in more than a decade due to geographical distance, he was unable to judge her sanity for himself—but it left her entirely alone, without any male family member to represent her in the world. This was scary; she did not feel safe. Elizabeth wrote, "[I] do so want to be loved by somebody, who can help me to get out from beneath the iron feet of my oppressors." She wondered: Could McFarland be that man? She looked to the doctor for protection and, in his friendship, found "buds of hope and promise."

She took strength, too, from the sisterhood on Seventh Ward. McFarland gave Elizabeth permission to hold a prayer circle with her "kindred spirit[s]," and these daily social gatherings soon became a source of comfort and support. There were never less than twelve women in attendance, sometimes eighteen or more.

"O," Elizabeth exclaimed happily, "how I love this new circle of friends!"

In time, her asylum acquaintances widened further. Out for a pleasant stroll in the grounds one day, she heard her name being shouted. To her surprise, a group of patients from a lower ward were calling to her through their window—the asylum favorite now so notorious all the patients knew her name.

Elizabeth stood beneath their window and squinted upward. She'd never visited these wards, but with a creeping feeling, she realized that some of these women must be those she heard crying and calling out at night.

They did not look as wild as they could sometimes sound.

In hurried, frightened whispers, they began to talk to her, sharing "base charges...against the doctor," shocking claims of abuse and mistreatment by the staff. Elizabeth listened politely but felt skeptical. In her experience, "order and system marked all the arrangements" of the asylum; it seemed hard to believe these claims were true.

Nevertheless, she tried to help her fellow patients. "Go with [your complaints] to Dr. McFarland," she urged. "He is our friend."

But to such a suggestion, there was only bleak despair: "It is of no use." Some women even claimed they were sane but had been moved to these lower wards by McFarland as punishment.

At this, Elizabeth's skepticism simmered straight to disbelief. A man of honor such as McFarland would never do such a thing.

As she walked away, Elizabeth shook her head sadly—with pity. It was perhaps her first encounter with the *truly* insane. Remarkable indeed, she thought, were these "hallucinations of a diseased mind."

Yet the following day, she was told by her attendant that she must not speak with the lower ward patients. Why, she wondered, would McFarland issue such a strange decree?

Unsettled, she decided to become a "silent eye and ear witness"—to what was *really* happening in the hospital.

CHAPTER 11

Elizabeth settled into her new role with ease. In truth, the claims of the lower ward patients were not the only thing that had rattled her since her commitment. The seeming sanity of her friends on Seventh Ward was another. But, she'd always reasoned, it was not fair to judge McFarland on this when she was "ignorant of all the light by which [his] actions have been guided." Her friends seemed sane *now*, true, but perhaps that was because they had *recovered* with the doctor's help—and would soon be released.

Her other, major concern was the way the attendants could be. There was a "system of compulsory obedience"—herself excluded—"fearful punishments and unreasonable restrictions." The patients were kept, in her view, under extraordinary surveillance and control, with edicts issued on when they should rise and sleep and bathe. There were rules on when they had to change their underwear, their menstrual cycles were monitored, and they were sometimes even forced to have their hair cut against their will. "Their rules," wrote a female patient archly, "are enough to make a rational person crazy."

The rules were one thing, but it was the *unkindness* that really got to Elizabeth. Nor could she understand it. If a fellow patient cried in her prayer circle, she would comfort them. But an attendant, witnessing the same scene, would say, "You mustn't cry—you are getting worse—you can't go home until you stop fretting." Even just *expressing* a wish to go home was frowned upon. Though Elizabeth believed it a natural desire, psychiatrists of the day thought differently. "It is always a suspicious circumstance," one doctor wrote haughtily, "and always a sufficient warrant for delay" in sending a patient home, evidence of a "lingering spark of disease."

After all, a truly sane patient would *want* to stay until made well.

Perhaps most difficult of all for Elizabeth to witness, however, was the way her friends were treated when the mothers among them mourned the children they were missing. Elizabeth knew it was "as hard to dance without music, as it is for...a mother to be happy away from her babes," but the Seventh Ward women were told they could not go home until they stopped "grieving and talking about their children." If they did not desist, punishment was threatened.

"We must *seem* happy when we are miserable," wrote one of Elizabeth's friends glumly, "or we can have no chance for a release." Every natural emotion—whether grief, fear, or resentment at the rules—had to be stifled. The women walled themselves up behind masks of good manners, politely smiling, calmly chattering about things of no consequence, afraid that anything else would only condemn them—and with good reason. Nineteenth-century asylum records show that women were often put into solitary confinement if they were "being violent, mischievous, dirty, and using bad language." Anything deemed unladylike or overly emotional was banned.

The women had to bear all this "silently and meekly...entirely nonresistant." Daily, they cut themselves to the institution's pattern: a coterie of fabric dolls that said please and thank you, no matter how they were treated.

But in Elizabeth, they found a "confidant...counsellor...bosom friend." The prayer circle, over time, became a place of whispered secrets and shared slights. Though Elizabeth at first urged her friends, too, to take things up with McFarland, she soon saw he "did not listen...with kindness" to the women's concerns. In contrast to his expressed sympathy to her, he seemed "indifferent when complaints of cruelty were made," turning away, speechless, merely moving on to the next woman on the ward.

Elizabeth said nothing, but she did take note.

"We are free to think here," she wrote, "and I for one am going to make the most of this."

And the more Elizabeth thought, the more troubled she slowly became.

———

That August, Elizabeth had a visitor. She walked from her ward to the reception room when summoned, steps sounding in the corridor like a heartbeat of hope. Yet that did no justice to the person waiting for her in the parlor. When she first burst in, she thought her heart itself might burst.

Toffy. Her Toffy. Her firstborn son.

He stood waiting to greet her, that dear face she'd known for eighteen years somehow marked with new manliness. When Isaac had written to Toffy about her situation, her eldest child had pledged to protect her—and he had come, even though his father had threatened to disinherit him. "These two dear sons," Elizabeth wrote of her eldest boys, "did stand, true and firm as the Alps, in their determination never to forsake their own dear mother."

They fell upon each other in a tangle of happy limbs. With Toffy now living apart from his family in Iowa, it had been two years since Elizabeth had seen him. After he kissed her "with all the fondness of a most loving child," mother and son stood still in an embrace, both feeling that safety and security that, before, she'd always given him. He was, truly, her "tower of strength for my days of adversity."

"Mother," he told her, "I could not bear to feel that you had become insane, and I could not believe it, and would not, until I had seen you myself; and now I see it is just as I expected, you are *not* insane, but the same kind mother as ever."

If he could have, Toffy would have released her from the asylum that very same day. But he was only eighteen: three years below the age of majority. In the eyes of the law, he was still a child.

Nonetheless, his faith in her strengthened Elizabeth's own foundations. "When all the world forsook me and fled," Elizabeth later wrote of her son with quiet pride, "you stood…true to the mother who bore you."

Eventually, however, Toffy had to take his leave. Yet he did not leave her empty-handed. He left behind a promise, tucked inside her heart, that he'd write soon. He vowed to do all in his power to get her out.

His words perhaps reminded Elizabeth of a similar promise from the Blessings. Two months on from their visit, she was still no wiser as to the success or failure of their plot, nor did she even know if they were still trying to help. She'd observed, with increasing anxiety, that her asylum friends like Sarah Minard had few visitors: "Scarcely anyone seems to care for their friends after they have served a term of imprisonment [here]." She was starting to fear her own friends might now feel the same. After all, they hadn't replied to her letters. It was almost as if she'd "passed beyond the river of death" so their words could no longer reach her.

But there was no metaphysical obstruction. If their words were not reaching her, it must be because they no longer cared. "Sometimes," she wrote, "when we most need the sympathy and aid of friends, we find ourselves utterly forsaken."

It made her friendships with the women of Seventh Ward even more precious. The patients formed a little community, thrilling together at an inmate's discharge or greeting the news of an arrival with an empathetic "wail of horror." Together, they watched in shock one day as "a lady of refinement…was stripped of all her clothing, except a torn chemise, and laid upon her back on the floor, while Dr. Tenny sat astride her naked body to hold her down." The attendants then applied a straitjacket to this wild woman who would not obey the rules.

It was rare to see such violence and restraint on Seventh Ward; all the women were aghast. Yet such a scene only tightened the friendships between them as they became "sisters in bonds."

So Elizabeth was taken aback when Mrs. Hosmer took her aside in the sewing room one day. The directress glanced left and right for eavesdroppers before saying urgently, "If you ever wish or expect to get out of this place, Mrs. Packard, you must give up…these morning prayers."

Elizabeth was staggered. She would—*could*—do no such thing. But Mrs. Hosmer was adamant: "So long as you hold these morning prayers in your room, you can never get out of this asylum."

Still, Mrs. Hosmer held Elizabeth's gaze, her eyes full of some strange foreboding that Elizabeth could not interpret.

"I know more of this place than you do," Mrs. Hosmer said at last.

CHAPTER 12

"Mrs. Packard... Mrs. Packard..."

It was the patients in the lower ward again, calling to her. Conscious of McFarland's instructions, Elizabeth walked away, but they simply raised their voices. Their pleading words followed her like fireflies: small sparks of unwelcome wonderings that glittered at the corners of her mind. Those sparks of light remained even as she walked back inside the hospital and unlocked the door to her ward.

Despite McFarland's orders, Elizabeth had tried, in her own way, to make a small difference, as she "never could see another one in any sort of trouble without trying to help." Lately, she'd begun appealing to the attendants to be kinder, hoping such a change might filter through the hospital. Elizabeth had this extraordinary ability, wherever she went, to end up the center of a great circle of friends. It had happened at the asylum too: "No one was so popular in the whole institution." She'd actually become friends with some of the attendants, most of whom, by now, actually thought her sane. They talked of her "false imprisonment"; some even said emphatically, "She is not an insane person."

As such, Elizabeth knew the attendants didn't set out to be tyrants, though some became that way. Really, they were simply overworked and underpaid. "All...we get," she wrote, "is cross attendants who can't wait upon us because they are so tired out, and who can't comfort us because they have none to spare themselves."

It was certainly a challenging job. Attendants worked in the wards at least ten hours a day, with responsibility for up to fifteen patients each. Yet despite the long hours—and additional infringements on their personal lives, as most lived in-house—they received little remuneration, earning less than shoemakers and woodworkers. Female attendants, naturally, earned less than the men, a fact that Elizabeth adroitly pointed out. It wasn't fair there was "so much more pay for work done by a man than when done by a woman."

Though McFarland had originally hoped to employ "intelligent, educated, and, at the same time, humane, attendants," even he admitted his efforts had been "without success." The staff demographic was young, poor, ill-educated, and frequently from European immigrant backgrounds; "colored races [were] of course…left out…from the list of those which might supply competent attendants." But McFarland had little choice in whom he appointed. He sometimes received no applications for vacancies, with a dearth of female attendants in particular. "The unworthy," he sighed, "may frequently be found."

And he was always having to recruit. The average length of service was just eight and a half months, and staff turnover was high; as much as 40 percent per year in some asylums. Indeed, attendants were so hard to come by that in one New York hospital, they recruited convicts still serving jail terms as attendants.

It was just as well that superintendents preferred to hire those with no medical training. As doctors wanted to assert their burgeoning professional authority, psychiatrists actively sought to exclude laypeople from treatment of the insane, which included attendants.

Yet another growing concern of Elizabeth's was that there did not seem to be *any* treatment that she could observe. She'd assumed, before she came, that patients at the state hospital would receive "what they needed—kind, humane treatment, combined with medical skill adapted to the necessities of the case." But, she said, "I never saw the sick doctored or nursed *less* in all my life." The only treatment she'd witnessed was the occasional prescribing of "a little ale," and of course the doctor's magical "laying on of hands"—a treatment "almost universally bestowed."

"I can tell you the secret of the cure of insanity, as practised here," she wrote. "It is, 'to do nothing at all for the insane, except to attend to their physical wants.'"

McFarland's own account backed up her observations. In fact, he came from a school of thought that "always acted upon the presumption that his patients needed no active treatment."

"The insane hospital is to the insane what the splint and bandage are to the fractured limb," he opined. "Merely to insure quiet."

His laid-back approach was typical of asylums throughout America at that time, partly due to the overcrowding all were experiencing. Though moral treatment had begun with the ideal of a close doctor-patient relationship, as more and more people were admitted, that ratio became unworkable and therapy obsolete, with care instead becoming custodial in nature. It became more important to maintain order, which meant increased rules and in particular increased restraint of patients. "[A] curb must be about everyone without distinction, to be tightened at will," McFarland wrote, conscious of his need to retain control of his 231 patients.

The larger the hospital populations became, the more focused their superintendents were on management. There was little time for research into treatments and cures; McFarland was not alone in rarely pursuing either. Though European psychiatrists were busy conducting experiments, Americans simply did not. Historians have noted that the professional journal of the Association of Medical Superintendents of American Institutions for the Insane (AMSAII) is "notable only for the lack of articles embodying the results of original research."

Yet in truth, Elizabeth and her friends had a lucky escape when it came to experimentation. Given psychiatrists' focus on women's sexual organs as a cause of their insanity, the treatments that existed in the era centered on these too. So ice water would be injected inside the women's intimate orifices, leeches hungrily latched onto labia and clitoris, and caustics—powerful chemical substances that could destroy tissue— liberally applied to their genitals. At the very least, vaginal examinations with a speculum were standard; only toward the end of the decade would doctors begin to question the "impropriety" of such exams in emotional young women, pronouncing them a "mischievous" practice, "almost always unnecessary."

By far the worst of all the treatments, however, was that recommended by Dr. Isaac Baker Brown, the senior surgeon at the London Surgical Home. The Englishman was not the first to utilize it but became its figurehead after publishing a book on the treatment in the mid-1860s. Well before then, the practice had been adopted in America, being recommended in a U.S. textbook in 1859. To cure a woman of insanity was easy, Brown and other advocates said.

All one had to do was cut off her clitoris.

What we might today call female genital mutilation.

It was a "harmless" operation, Brown enthused, and a necessary one, for without it, women would be subject to increasingly severe insanity and, ultimately, death. He'd been inspired to try it after being "foiled in dealing successfully" with hysterical women "without being able to assign a satisfactory cause for the failure." When the women did not submit to his will, he decided a physical cause must be behind their tenacity. Eventually, he determined "peripheral excitement of the pudic nerve" the culprit. Immediately, he put his theories into practice, carrying out countless operations in which he cut women's clitorises "down to the base," removing them either "by scissors or knife—I always prefer the scissors."

"The rapid improvement of the patient immediately after removal of the source of irritation is most marked," he recorded happily in his case notes, and no wonder, for the women were stunned, their mouths at last stitched shut with shock. Brown reported a 70 percent success rate; the "problems" from which his patients were "cured" including a "distaste for marital intercourse," "distaste for the society of her husband," "sterility or a tendency to abort in the early months of pregnancy," and even a twenty-year-old woman who spent too much time "in serious reading." The patients requiring treatment, as described by him, were "restless and excited, or melancholy and retiring...[with a] quivering of the eyelids, and an inability to look one straight in the face... Often a great disposition for novelties is exhibited, the patient desiring to escape from home, fond of becoming a nurse in hospitals...or other pursuits of the like nature." But these women after treatment, he declared triumphantly, "became in every respect a good wife."

If patients complained or were distressed by the procedure, they were deemed incurable or not recovering well. When a fifty-seven-year-old patient cried that he had "unsexed" her, her family retorted that "nothing of the sort had been done...the operation had prevented her from making herself ill." (She had been fond of masturbation.) Her case was one Brown cited as a success: whereas before, her husband's life was "most wretched, his home was now one of comfort and happiness."

In fact, Brown enthusiastically recommended the practice as an alternative to marital separation—in his book, Elizabeth would likely have been a prime candidate for cutting—and concluded emphatically, "Daily experience convinces me that all unprejudiced men must adopt... the practice which I have thus carried out."

Luckily, not all doctors did. "Would anyone strip off the penis... because [a man] was a moral delinquent?" one dared ask. In time, Brown was expelled from the Obstetrical Society of London, but not for performing the operation per se, rather for doing so without consent. Although his publication at first raised scandal, after the fuss died down, the operations continued, alongside surgical removal of the ovaries, which was another standard treatment for female insanity at the time. One superintendent was accused of the "mutilation of helpless lunatics" through his surgical work, but he continued regardless until his death in 1902. In fact, such practices continued long into the twentieth century. Archives show that clitoridectomies to correct "emotional disorder" were performed as late as the 1940s.

The last recorded case was on a five-year-old girl.

———

McFarland may not have employed clitoridectomies to control his patients, but he did use drugs, spending $749.30 (about $23,000 today) biennially on them. Recommended treatments of the era included opium and blue mass (a mercury-based medicine), the poisonous "tincture of veratria," a concoction of quinine, arsenic, and port wine, and straightfor-ward cannabis. Yet the medicines available were so untested that at times, the doctors themselves would take one "for the purpose of ascertaining its effects." One such doctor reported that after imbibing conium—a then-standard medicine for treating the insane, which is related to the poison hemlock—he developed double vision and a "singular sensation in the knees, which rendered it quite impossible for him to go upstairs without assistance."

Given the doctors' need to impose control, many used narcotics to keep patients quiet. Chloroform and ether were particularly effective on "boisterous" women and therefore used to quiet them "not only temporarily but permanently." One superintendent confided of chloroform, "I use it most on the female side of the house."

It was a declaration with which many doctors concurred, but McFarland was not publicly among them. Nonetheless, his patients' claims that the doctor was abusive followed Elizabeth whenever she walked outside: a slow drip-feed of doubt that settled on her skin like rain. Though she defiantly continued to hold her prayer meetings on Seventh Ward—ignoring Mrs. Hosmer's warning—the justified complaints of her friends that she heard there only added to her unease.

As she strolled about the grounds, it seemed someone was watching. Although Elizabeth obeyed the order not to speak to the lower ward patients, their voices carried all across the lawn. Someone somewhere decided additional action was required. One day, Elizabeth wandered outside to find the paradisiacal peace had been shattered by a most industrious banging of nails and voluminous sawing of wood. A solid board fence was being erected directly in front of the lower ward windows.

Day by passing day, the fence grew longer until it encircled the entire asylum. To her distress, Elizabeth found it reminded her that despite being the asylum favorite, she was still a prisoner. The fence was eight feet high and deliberately planked on both sides "to prevent its being scaled from within, and relieve its unsightly appearance from without." But the double planking couldn't conceal its innate ugliness, nor the truth of what it was: a wall that divided the world into *them* and *us*.

Elizabeth knew she was on the wrong side of it.

It agitated her. It reminded her that it had been weeks since she'd heard from Toffy. Though she believed the Blessings had all but forgotten her, she could not think the same of her son. She would not.

Her faith was rewarded. One day, in late summer, she happened to be in McFarland's office when she noticed a letter lying on his desk. She'd have known that handwriting anywhere; after all, she'd helped teach her son how to make those shapes. As the letter was addressed to her, Elizabeth seized it with an exclamation of excitement.

Smoothly, McFarland snatched it from her. One moment, the letter was there, the next gone: a magic trick that had no payoff. Elizabeth, perhaps laughing at what she hoped was playful intervention, protested, but he did not return the letter. When she demanded to know what it had said—for it had clearly already been opened—the doctor point-blank refused to say.

Fireflies buzzed about her, their light trying to shine inside. Elizabeth had always had the run of this palatial asylum, but now she wondered how well she really knew it. Maybe Mrs. Hosmer had been right. Maybe there were things she didn't know, secret chambers she had not yet seen. As McFarland continued to withhold Toffy's letter, she felt as though she'd stumbled into one.

To her repeated appeals, McFarland remained a "deaf adder": a snake that hissed his obstructions even as he smiled. Elizabeth felt almost in a daze. She'd thought she knew the doctor well, but she did not recognize this man. He'd never treated Elizabeth this way.

Eventually, defeated, she left his office and slowly retraced her steps to the ward. So many times that summer, she'd walked with surety through those long corridors, convinced of the goodness of the man in charge. She felt no such certainty now.

"It is too true," she realized sadly. "You are not our friend."

All summer, she'd woven words with the doctor in conversations that had scaled new heights. Elizabeth felt giddy suddenly, realizing how very far she had to fall. That web of words seemed treacherous now, each silver string laced with poison. An incontrovertible truth gleamed forth: "His word could no longer be trusted."

CHAPTER 13

She began to watch McFarland more closely. She noticed he made a point of asking her, "Mrs. Packard, who are your friends? Have you any in the wide world?"

"Every means possible," Elizabeth perceived, "is used to impress upon my mind the feeling that I am friendless... But I will not believe it."

After all, if McFarland had blocked Toffy's letters, there was a chance he'd confiscated the Blessings' missives too.

Such censorship was commonplace in nineteenth-century asylums, as any link to patients' former lives was deemed "injurious" to health. McFarland's own instruction to patients' friends was to "let [them] alone" and never write at all. Those who ignored his "sterling commandment"—such as Toffy—were easily stymied. Every letter that arrived at Jacksonville was inspected by McFarland and "immediately destroyed if it unfortunately contains anything which he disapproves of."

Yet until Elizabeth had spied Toffy's letter, she'd had no idea what was happening. Even after that, encased in uneasy ignorance, she could not be *fully* sure what McFarland was doing. It was only one letter she'd seen; she did not suspect the censorship was as extensive as it was. So instead, she wrote bleakly of "the sense of desolation which the total withdrawal of friends throws over a prisoner's life."

"It [is] hard to be forgotten," she simply said.

Yet her feelings were the fruit McFarland hoped to harvest, the censorship all part of his idiosyncratic interpretation of moral treatment. His idea was that once patients were completely isolated from family, as he'd instructed, he would then step into that void. McFarland thought the ideal way to treat insanity was for him to become "the dominant and good spirit" in his patients' lives: the higher power from which they were to take their every direction.

Although leading psychiatrists advised strongly that hospital staff should *not* treat patients "with feelings of superiority," McFarland believed the opposite. In his opinion, he *was* the patients' superior, and the quicker they came to appreciate that "his judgment is a safer guide for [them] than [their] own conscience," the better. He wanted the patients under his control to "shape [their] manner of living, in all its minutiae, to the hourly prescription of [their] superior," the latter a word he used interchangeably for *doctor*. This shaping of their lives extended to the clothes they wore, the food they ate, the activities they pursued, and—most chillingly—to the very thoughts they thought.

"The superior...takes full possession of the subject," McFarland wrote candidly, "acts for him, thinks for him." And once such possession had been achieved, the doctor would "modify his thoughts." McFarland perceived himself as a "benignant Prospero [who] controls, for the best of purposes, the Caliban...under his direction."

McFarland was the puppet master, the women of Seventh Ward the mute marionettes he tailored to his satisfaction.

And it was this specific mode of treatment he'd been using with Elizabeth Packard ever since she'd arrived at the asylum. His intention had always been that she would become "elevated by his smile, [and] would bow at his reproof."

Up until that point, it had been working perfectly.

Even after her discovery that the doctor had deceived her, Elizabeth found it very hard to shake off those reins he'd so skillfully wrapped around her. She still saw McFarland as an authority figure whose respect she not only valued but outright sought. So when one afternoon, probably in September, another patient accused her of acting indiscreetly—she'd allowed a male inmate to push her on a swing—it was to McFarland Elizabeth rushed, worried the incident might reflect badly on her.

McFarland listened to her concerns with sympathy. As she chattered, he shifted closer to her, a tiny adjustment of his body that caused her no alarm. The two of them had been physically close many times before, and not only through the doctor's "laying on of hands" in her private room. Elizabeth had also danced with him at the asylum's regular balls.

These were entertainments at which "large numbers of the insane, of both sexes…join for a few hours in temperate festivities." Female patients were permitted to dance with male staff and vice versa, but patients could not dance with one another.

If not for the bars on the windows of the hall they used, Elizabeth could imagine she was at any other party from the outside world at those balls. There would often be live music, and many patients made special efforts with their appearance, the women crafting handmade paper flowers for their hair. But best of all was the dancing. Elizabeth had only ever danced at the asylum; in a way, her incarceration had incongruously widened her world. She'd always been taught before that dancing was a sin, but after she'd watched the other patients—their faces lit not only by the gas lamps but from the joy within—she'd abruptly changed her mind. "Is such ease and grace of figure and motion a sin?" she wrote. "Then the sailing of the fish is sin; the soaring of the bird." She vowed "that I should never be again found among the class who condemned dancing."

Enthusiastically, she'd thrown herself into the action, even taking private lessons from a twenty-one-year-old attendant, Celia Coe. The patients and staff usually danced cotillions, a formal dance for sets of couples in which they all swapped partners until the whole room felt like a friend.

Yet when Elizabeth had danced with McFarland, they'd performed their own duet. Elizabeth remembered that they'd shunned the formal dancing and instead found a "dark corner" in which they'd kept step "all by ourselves."

That September afternoon in his office, McFarland took the lead once more, his body morphing close to her in movements intended to impart moral treatment.

"I will see that you are protected," he told her reassuringly.

And as he made this remark, he kissed Elizabeth on the forehead, where her dark-brown hair met her pale pink skin.

She felt his lips on her. "Dr. McFarland didn't force me, nor I didn't resist him."

Yet her thoughts reeled. Later, she recalled his kiss as "a mere impulsive act, dictated by no corrupt motives." But given the era, it was shockingly indiscreet—especially for a man in his position.

"Dr. McFarland," Elizabeth said disapprovingly once she'd recovered her stolen breath. "Men do not send their wives, nor fathers their daughters here, expecting that you will manifest your regard for them in *this manner*."

For the doctor, the kiss was no doubt all just part of the therapy. For Elizabeth, however, it was a watershed. She began to worry the kiss might be a "stepping-stone to insults." Whether she meant further sexual contact from the doctor or slurs against her virtue is unclear. Either way, she felt an "imperative necessity of devising some self-defensive armor with which to shield my virtue and self-respect from insult."

And Elizabeth had only ever had one means of self-defense worth anything: her way with words. She decided she would write to the doctor, but not just about the kiss. All the events of recent months had built up behind her: a wall of water and wonderings she had to let run free.

Her efforts to date to improve conditions by appealing to the attendants had come to nothing. In fact, when she appealed to them to be kinder, they often replied, "The Doctor orders us to treat them as we do." Whether that was true, Elizabeth did not know, but she thought, "If the doctor lets his attendants abuse his patients, and don't try to stop it, when he knows it is practised, I say, it comes pretty near being Dr. McFarland's abuse of the patient."

Her own situation was also at the forefront of her mind. McFarland had by that point had "all reasonable time" to appreciate her sanity. If he held her any longer, he would have "intelligently and knowingly broken [his] solemn 'oath of office,' by retaining a sane person as a patient."

Elizabeth determined to write two documents: a defense of her sanity and a reproof of Dr. McFarland for the cruel treatment she'd witnessed happening to the women on Seventh Ward.

She was fearless, seeming entirely to forget the warning Mrs. Hosmer had given. But it was coming up to four months since she'd been committed, and she'd frankly had enough. Not for herself, necessarily, for she'd been granted exceptional license, but for the other women. "I will not suffer humanity to be so abused, as you do here, without lifting my voice against it," she wrote, "*and it will be heard.*"

Her pen scrawled across the page, writing with more fluidity than she'd ever known. Elizabeth soon circulated the documents among her friends, reading aloud her "championship of their cause" at their prayer circle. Though all agreed as to the accuracy of her charges, most were alarmed by her audacity.

"[You have] no idea of the Doctor's power," one told her anxiously.

"Mrs. Packard," warned another, "you had better not give the Doctor that document, unless you wish to be sent to a dungeon, where you could never see daylight again."

But with the reins pulling tight against her throat, Elizabeth doubted what they said. She wrote the reproof mainly for the women, but part of her was also inspired to save the doctor from his sins. In pointing out the error of his ways, she hoped to lead him to his own salvation, after which he truly could become the "manly protector" she'd first hoped she'd found in him.

Nevertheless, she'd known her friends long enough by now to take heed. So, carefully, she made a painstaking copy of her documents, then pried off the back of her personal mirror and cautiously hid them between the glass and board back. Whatever happened next, these copies would always be there: proof, in her opinion, both of her sanity and of the true goings-on in the asylum.

She decided to give McFarland the defense first. It was a test. To this point, she'd given him the benefit of the doubt when it came to his retention of patients who to her seemed sane. But in her own case, she knew *exactly* how she'd behaved throughout the past four months, so she knew exactly what evidence—or lack thereof—the doctor had to draw on in his determination of her insanity.

"I therefore shall take your decision in my case as casting the die in my opinion of your real character," she wrote plainly. If he insisted on keeping her at the asylum after receiving the document, she'd know for certain he admitted patients "on simple hearsay testimony, in defiance of positive, tangible proof."

Elizabeth tried to remain confident. She knew her own mind, and she knew she had behaved impeccably, as the doctor's own trust in her showed. Would an insane woman be permitted the keys to the asylum? The very idea that he thought her mad was laughable when she thought of that.

On October 26, 1860, Elizabeth Packard presented her defense to Dr. McFarland. The headlines that day could not have been more apt. They related to the rumbling war clouds now gathering in the South and not to a courageous woman fighting her own battle in a hospital in Illinois. But whether war was waged with pen or sword, "The Approaching Revolution" was finally, undeniably, and quite unstoppably here.

CHAPTER 14

I, your sane patient...do hereby respectfully request that you forthwith give me an honorable discharge from this Asylum... I have a legal and constitutional claim to my liberty as a citizen of the United States, having never said or done anything justly to forfeit it... But should you deny me my petition, will you please to give me your reasons in writing, for regarding and treating me as insane? Or, in other words, what irrational and unreasonable conduct have you observed in me within the four months' time I have been under your intelligent inspection?

Elizabeth had never sounded saner.

McFarland may have shifted awkwardly in his chair as he read her defense. Because—just as Elizabeth knew—she'd displayed no irrational conduct at all. McFarland had been carefully looking for that intellectual impairment he believed underlay all potential cases of moral insanity, but there was nothing in Mrs. Packard that fit the bill.

Four months on from her arrival at the asylum, he had nothing.

He continued to read, his concerns layering up with every word she'd written. Because during the course of her time at the asylum, Elizabeth had become even more political than before.

"I am a martyr for the rights of opinion in woman, in the year 1860, in this boasted, free America" she wrote passionately.

> Have you not reason to fear that my case fairly represents a class of oppressed women, who have been unjustly imprisoned here, by unnatural men; who, because they had the power to oppress an unprotected wife, secretly rejoice in the aid which this institution furnishes them for doing it?... Will you not dare to do right, and...be our protector, instead of our husbands' abettor in crime?

McFarland likely sighed. Just as Mrs. Hosmer had divined, knowing the doctor of old, McFarland had become increasingly concerned about Elizabeth's prayer circle of late, and these words about "a class of oppressed women" only added fuel to his flickering fire of unease. McFarland had given permission for Elizabeth to hold the meetings because he generally did support interaction between his patients, but there were certain circumstances in which it was not wise. "Excitements among them," he wrote, "are to a degree contagious." It seemed as if such a virus was now gripping the women of Seventh Ward. If Elizabeth had been planting seeds in the minds of others, as he now feared, it was not a harvest he wanted to reap.

Yet, as though the asylum favorite anticipated his concerns, she made sure in her defense to flatter the doctor too, appealing to his "understanding...conscience...and...heart." He had a chance to be noble in this instance, she wrote, to "act honorably, manly, intelligently." Would he step up?

"O, my friend," she wrote warmly, "do not disappoint my high, very high expectations of you as a man—one who respects his conscience more than his popularity—one who dares to risk his reputation on doing right even in the face of a frowning world."

And Elizabeth knew the world would frown, because what she now proposed to the doctor was revolutionary: she wanted to be released from the asylum *as an independent woman*. She asked him specifically not to consult her husband in the matter, which was highly irregular, if not downright illegal. She told McFarland, "I am fully determined never to return to my husband again, of my own free-will." By now, Elizabeth was motivated in that determination not by fear, but by reason: "He has forced me from home as insane, when I am not insane. I shall not be guilty of the insane act of returning to such a protector."

Instead, she planned a life free of him; she even asked McFarland for a job. Having spent the past four months acting almost as a matron, working unpaid as attendant, seamstress, and nurse, she considered herself competent and willing "to fill any post of usefulness you may offer me." She simply wanted to "support myself, independent of aid from any quarter."

She did not think what she was asking for was so outrageous. After all, as she queried, tongue in cheek, "Am I under laws which compel those wives who cannot live with their husbands to spend their days in an insane asylum?" She promised that if he would grant her freedom, she would still want "the privilege of seeking you as my counselor and guide."

In her efforts to persuade him, she brought in her political perspective again, hoping to inspire him. "[Make] me an example of one who has dared to break the fetters of married servitude," she urged, "chosing [*sic*] by far, a self-reliant position in society." If he helped her, he could be regarded "as a Moses to lead forth a host of bond-women."

But that was exactly what McFarland *didn't* want to do. One woman like Elizabeth Packard was bad enough; to have more like her would mean trouble indeed. Yet as he read through this section of Elizabeth's defense, interest nevertheless sparked in his mind.

It was the way she wrote about her husband. She was far more candid than she'd ever been before.

As though she knew it, she defended her position: "I know these opinions respecting an husband may seem uncharitably severe... But, O, Dr. McFarland...these terrible opinions are supported by the most stubborn of all arguments—facts." She'd reached her opinion of Theophilus, she said, from "no fancy sketch," nor from "the pictures of an overheated imagination," but simply from the way he'd treated her: as though she had no mind of her own.

To this point in her defense, Elizabeth had written with unimpeachable calmness. To this point in her stay at the asylum, she'd always spoken of Theophilus with the same sensible restraint. But four months is a long time for a woman to be withheld from the world, from her children, from her life. She'd given her husband four months to repent— four months to bring her back home.

He had not taken that chance.

And so, in the past week or so, Elizabeth had hit a brick wall when it came to her feelings about Theophilus. In her private writings, she now confessed, "I hate him...and I can't help it and I don't want to, neither. He deserves to be hated." She continued, "He has by his own actions annihilated every particle of respect I have ever felt." She now considered him "the most inhuman, cold-blooded, calculating tyrant the world ever witnessed" and recoiled from him with "loathing and disgust."

She did not share these feelings in her defense.

She did worse.

She told McFarland plainly that her husband was "a perverted and unnatural man" and that since October 14, 1860, "David's prayer for his persecutors has become my prayer for mine."

> He remembered not to show mercy... As he clothed
> himself with cursing like as with a garment, so let it
> come into his bowels like water... Let his net that he
> hath hid, catch himself: into that very destruction let
> him fall.

It was so angry, so unforgiving...*so very unladylike.* "Her hatred of her husband had something diabolical about it," McFarland later said, almost in abhorrent wonder.

And although the intellectual impairment he'd sought was still absent, this was at least evidence of madness. It always had been. In ancient Greek mythology, Argo's virgins, who "refused to honor the phallus," were deemed insane, pronounced cured only once a doctor persuaded them "to join carnally with young and strong men," after which they "recovered their wits." In McFarland's own era, his peers believed female insanity occurred when "their love is changed into hate."

"They excite the most stormy domestic scenes," one doctor explained, "using gross and even obscene language to their husbands...to resume afterwards, in public, their pretences of reserve."

Some might simply have seen a domestic tiff in this account: a woman driven to her wits' end by an impossible husband...but of course that was the point. She *was* at her wits' end.

Otherwise, she never would have dared speak back.

But Elizabeth felt no need to conceal her feelings anymore. She felt her sane conduct should be enough to free her. "I fear nothing," she wrote bravely in her defense. "The dungeon, or the rack, or the stake, I defy... I am determined fearlessly and boldly to advocate the truth, as it respects my husband."

Then she wrapped everything up with a big finish:

> Dr. McFarland, I beg and entreat you to have pity upon me... You, sir, now have a fair opportunity to judge for yourself [whether I am insane]. If you can conscientiously say that I have given you proof, from my own words and actions, of being insane, I wish you to say so, and take upon yourself the entire responsibility of this decision... Dr. McFarland, my duty is done. Yours remains to be done. Choose for yourself whom you will serve. Choose evil or good...God's blessing or his curse, and God will accept the act as a testimony of your real character.

She signed it, "Your sane patient, E. P. W. Packard."

Back on the ward, Elizabeth awaited the doctor's reaction. The women waited with her, all anxiously anticipating his response.

First one day passed, then another. Elizabeth rose each morning, took her sponge bath in her private room, combed her hair, breakfasted in the dining hall, ever expecting her daily routine to be disrupted.

But it was not. Nothing changed. The doctor expressed no anger at her audacity, but neither did he offer her freedom.

It seemed he had decided to keep things exactly as they were. Elizabeth was a woman of Seventh Ward now—and there she was destined to stay.

She felt McFarland's betrayal keenly. She felt his fall from grace with even greater anger. Because this proved that his decision to keep her at the asylum was *not* based on her behavior. He truly was her husband's abettor—and not only hers, for that matter. Elizabeth had been admitted to the asylum in 1860, six years after McFarland had first been appointed. How many other sane women, she wondered, might have been committed on his say-so in that time?

"He can see insanity in anyone where it will be for his interest to see it," she realized with creeping horror. Another friend was even more blunt: "I have no confidence in that man's honesty." Yet another declared McFarland a doctor "who always finds the suspicion [of insanity in a woman] well founded."

Elizabeth felt a strong calling to take action against this injustice. So she dug out her reproof. It lay in her hands like a pearl-handled pistol.

She wondered whether she actually had the guts to pull the trigger.

It would be wrong to say she did not waver. She knew, only too well, what a favored position she held. Did she dare risk that? While the doctor had allowed her to present her defense, she could not be sure he would be as accommodating about these charges of abuse. Her reproof focused not on her own case but on the way the hospital was run, as Elizabeth sought improvements for the whole community. Would he allow her to express her thoughts on that? Or, like Theophilus, would he silence her?

She did not know if she could again bear that gag around her mouth.

But Elizabeth Packard had been changed by her time in the asylum. In Manteno, she had been fighting for her sole survival. She was not alone now. "Motives higher than those of self-interest actuated me, or I could not have done it," she said. "I felt conscious that I held an influence and power over Dr. McFarland [as the asylum favorite], and I deliberately determined this influence should be felt in [my friends'] behalf."

By her own admittance, her courage came as a "surprise."

Taking a deep breath, she slowly put her papers in order. She reviewed them one last time, stacking them neatly in a pearl-handled pile. Some friends, braver than others, encouraged her.

"I will back that up, Mrs. Packard," one said.

Another vowed, "I will stand by you."

"I tell my fellow captives," Elizabeth herself wrote, "I will stay with them, and cast in my lot with them, and I will spare no pains, until I work their deliverance." Because, she said, "I love my sisters as I do myself," and for them, she was willing to fight.

She was perhaps inspired, too, by events outside the asylum. Each day, newspapers from across Illinois would pass into the wards, "fixed to neat, baize-covered desks." Elizabeth, like the others, would pore over them, desperate for news of the world beyond the wooden fence.

That November, they were full of stories about the presidential election. On November 6, 1860, Abraham Lincoln was elected president of the United States: a man who would come to embody the very concept of freedom.

Six days later, Elizabeth Packard presented McFarland with her reproof.

CHAPTER 15

It seems she read it to him herself in his office. She watched his reaction as she tried to find the words to reach him, using "the most expressive terms I could command."

"I do not approve of publishing your faults to the world," she began slowly, "until you have had an opportunity first, to amend your ways and your doings, by being faithfully, candidly and honestly informed of the true position in which you stand as Superintendent of this institution." Her message, she said, was "a kind act from a kind friend," hoping he would change his ways.

She focused mainly on what she saw as the oppressive treatment of patients: the orders that they mustn't cry, must silence their true thoughts, must believe that "others are better judges of their motives and intentions than themselves," so that, in short, they had to "give up their identity" before they were deemed cured, only allowed to leave the asylum once every ounce of spirit had been crushed from them. Though Elizabeth was not privy to the publications of the AMSAII, she'd none-theless observed the way McFarland was playing Prospero: bending women to his will, the asylum an isolated and darkly enchanted isle on which he held sole sway.

"Dr. McFarland," she said, "it is my honest opinion that the principles upon which you treat the inmates of this institution, are contrary to reason, to justice, to humanity... Your discipline is invariably calculated to increase their difficulties, and make them worse rather than better. And," she warned, "even a person with a sound mind, and a sound body, could hardly pass through a course here and come out unharmed."

Yet she did not include herself in that category. "I came here a sane person—I shall leave a sane person," she told him plainly. And she promised, "I shall make a sane report of my sane observations here." Though McFarland had shown no signs of being ready to free her, Elizabeth was adamant she *would* be released. She even threatened him—perhaps the sole selfish reason behind writing the reproof—that if he kept her even another three months, she would expose him publicly, using the "iron pen of the press."

"I feel called of God, and I shall obey this call," she told him, "to expose...your actions...unless you repent."

Repentance was of course her object. But, she told him, she wanted him not only to change the way the patients were treated but also to release her friends, many of whom had been there for years. McFarland, she said, had had "no right to them a single day."

She spoke not only with her voice but the voices of others, quoting testimony she'd collected over the past few weeks from the patients— and from McFarland's staff.

"The patients are so badly treated here, that I could never think of having a friend of mine ever come here for treatment," one reportedly said; Elizabeth included their words in the reproof.

"Dr. McFarland keeps persons here, that are not insane to my certain knowledge," testified another.

"If it were not for losing my place here, I would expose Dr. McFarland to the world," a third confided.

Elizabeth had boldly drawn on her friendships with both staff and patients to write the entire reproof. The result was that she'd created a chorus of condemnation, each voice more damning than the last.

"This is but a specimen of the kind of testimony I have on hand," she assured him, "in sad abundance, and which, with my own eye and earwitness testimony, would make a ponderous volume. How would you like to see such facts as these in print?"

Her army of support made her scathing. While some of her friends on the staff were too scared to confront the doctor in case they lost their jobs, he held no such power over her. "Perhaps it was for this very thing I was sent here," she said to the superintendent, "to let the State see that Dr. McFarland has yet to learn the very alphabet of his profession... You cannot tell a sane from an insane person... You are incapacitated for your office."

Through it all, McFarland bore her attack without the slightest sign of annoyance. As though anticipating this cold reaction, she said, "You can...try to ease your troubled conscience by [telling yourself]—these are only the ravings of insanity. But, sir, *they are not*. They are the words of truth." She added, "I defy all your attempts to make me out an insane person. You cannot do it...and all your attempts to do so, will be only working out your more speedy destruction."

But the more Elizabeth threatened him, the more laughable she seemed. What power did she have, a woman committed under his control whose fate he held securely in his hands? When she told him he was destined to see her "rising and applauded as the world's reformer," it seemed so unlikely an outcome he may even have smirked.

As the doctor sat stolidly before her, Elizabeth became fierce. "You need not sneer at this," she snapped at him. "I have hundreds on my side, already."

And while "hundreds" may have been an exaggeration, she was certainly not alone. Often, she spoke collectively throughout her presentation. And there was an overt early feminism in her words that rang warning bells for the doctor. "Of one thing you may rest assured," she vowed. "The time for down-trodden and oppressed women to have their rights, has come. Her voice and her pen are going to move the world." She advised him to "fear her artillery."

But McFarland wasn't afraid. He was, however, perturbed. He'd been disturbed by Elizabeth's defense, when she'd written of the bonds she'd forged with the "class of oppressed women" on Seventh Ward, but this rhetoric was worse. It seemed her women's rights obsession was "communicable to others," and McFarland disapproved in case it "spread, like a moral leprosy, to all with whom…she may become associated." This idea of telling women to stand up for themselves, to reject his moral treatment, would cause sheer chaos if others became as unbendable as she. She had clearly filled "the minds of less intelligent patients…with prejudices." It really was "most trying."

Well, he would have to put a stop to it.

Elizabeth seemingly saw none of these workings on McFarland's face, engrossed as she was in reading her reproof. In fact, despite her firm stance, there were clear hints in the document that his reins were even now about her.

"I do want to respect and love you," she sighed. "But I cannot, unless you will exhibit some humanity."

Yet even these kind words provoked no reaction from the doctor. McFarland showed emotion only once that day. Toward the end of the reproof, Elizabeth made a brief reference to the kiss he'd given her, which had first inspired her to confront him. Though it had been the reason she'd first put pen to paper, after she'd gathered the testimony from the others, she'd decided to reduce her own experience to a single line in what would later become eighteen typeset pages. She wanted to champion their cause, not hers. So in just twenty-five words, Elizabeth fleetingly focused on the kiss he'd given her. She told him there had been an eyewitness "when you thought we were alone."

But at this, she observed with some surprise, "his feelings burst their confinement."

Did he slam the table? Stand up with force? Grab at her elbows to shake her roughly? We do not know; she did not say. It could have been a glare or a grasp or a guttural roar. All we know is that, with strong feeling, he finally reacted to her words.

Elizabeth was shocked—perhaps most of all by the fact that this alone had aroused his anger. She would never understand it. In the cold of that November day, however, she simply shivered under the heat of his furious stare. "He seemed determined, from that moment, to either rule or ruin me."

Nonetheless, she found the courage to make her last words a warning. She *was* going to be released one day—of that she was sure. And if the doctor didn't change his ways, she'd hold him to account.

"Remember, Dr. McFarland," she cautioned. "This is your last chance... Repentance or exposure!"

The choice—just like Elizabeth herself—was entirely in his hands.

———

Elizabeth sat alone in her private room on Seventh Ward, but she could not settle. It was Saturday night—some five days after she'd presented McFarland with her reproof—and as yet, the doctor had not responded. Somewhere deep inside, she felt a "presentiment of coming evil."

Restless, she checked again that her documents were safely hidden in her mirror. She sorted through her clothes and "put every article of my wardrobe in perfect order." She wished she had more clothes to sort through; as the Illinois winter started to bite, the items she'd happily worn in the summer now seemed insufficient, especially because her room was "so cold that a cloth would freeze in it." She'd complained to McFarland about the temperature, but he'd turned away, speechless, the word wizard no longer having any spells for her.

He was, truly, a skinflint superintendent. The sole critique ever made of him by his trustees was that he kept too tight a hold on the asylum purse strings, to the detriment of his patients' comfort. McFarland spent just $2.77 ($85.76) per patient per week, the cheapest of all the asylums in America. Yet he liked to boast of "the almost monastic plainness" of his hospital.

Elizabeth left off fidgeting with her wardrobe. She cast her eyes over her now-familiar room. There was her personal pitcher and bowl, her mirror, the sewing box she'd brought from home. Yet none of it served to soothe her troubled spirit. She could only hope that prayer might help.

That evening, she accompanied the other Seventh Ward women to chapel service. They filed out together: a crocodile of community that walked as one.

Long ago, building work had begun on a bespoke asylum chapel, but insufficient funds had curtailed it. Instead, prayers were held in a standard hall; not all who wanted to attend could fit inside. Yet the privileged women of Seventh Ward were always granted this favor.

Elizabeth and her friends edged into the hall, which held about one hundred people and was "neat and well-arranged." The prayers were a treat: a daily occasion of "pleasing anticipation" at which a "soul-cheering doctrine" was heard.

As the service ended, Elizabeth indeed felt merrier. She joined the crocodile line of Seventh Ward women and began to make her way out.

Suddenly, she was stopped in her tracks by a strong hand clutching at her arm.

It was McFarland. He led her away from her friends.

Together, they walked those long corridors that ran the length of the building. Black night was beyond the barred windows now, the summer sunshine of days past long gone. Elizabeth felt her disquiet return as they wended their way through the hospital.

This wasn't the way to Seventh Ward.

Eventually, they reached a heavy door. It wasn't one she'd seen before. McFarland pulled out his keys, for Elizabeth, the asylum favorite, had no key for this particular lock. With an ominous sound, the door opened, and Elizabeth caught her first glimpse of the ward that lay beyond.

Even as the door screeched open, the smell hit her in a noxious wave. She could taste it, a "most fetid scent at the pit of my stomach," which reeked of unwashed bodies and far, far worse. It was almost intolerable, even before she'd stepped inside.

But McFarland took her arm again and dragged her over the threshold. She stumbled in, boots clicking on the cold, uncarpeted floor. There were none of the artistic delights of Seventh Ward here. Hard wooden benches lined the corridor. Even the furniture in the rooms beyond was different: husk mattresses, iron bedsteads, and, peculiarly, no chairs at all.

Ahead of her, she heard noise: "screaming, fighting, running, hallooing." Women with "rough, tangled, flying and streaming hair" ran riot around the ward, their skin pitch-black with dirt. As they ran, they splashed through "unfragrant puddles of water": their own urine, which they delighted "to wade and wallow in."

She looked back at McFarland, brown eyes wide, but he merely made to take his leave.

"You may occupy this ward, Mrs. Packard," he said sharply.

And then the door slammed shut.

PART TWO

DARK BEFORE THE DAWN

Much Madness is divinest Sense.

—*Emily Dickinson, c. 1862*

She did not spend her time so much in doubting as in *doing*.

—*Obituary of Lucy Strong Parsons Ware,*
mother of Elizabeth Packard, 1843

CHAPTER 16

At once, the ward's attendant came to meet her. Twenty-two-year-old Minerva Tenney, known as Minnie, had long, dark hair and an open, wide-eyed face. Elizabeth had met her before during her time at the hospital. Minnie—along with her little sister Emily, nineteen—looked after Eighth Ward, through whose door Elizabeth had just entered. "The maniac's ward!" a friend of Elizabeth dubbed it. "The abode of the filthy, the suicidal, the raving and the furious!"

Minnie and Elizabeth stared at each other, both seeming surprised to find the other there. As they did so, the clanging of the heavy door faded away to silence.

"Miss Tenney," Elizabeth ventured, "what does this mean?"

"I don't know," the attendant replied, her youthful face confused. "All [McFarland] said to me was, 'I wish you not to allow Mrs. Packard to leave the ward.'"

"I don't know what it means either," Elizabeth replied. "I wonder if my reproof has not offended him?"

Minnie may have smiled. "I have heard there was quite a stir about it," she remarked lightly.

To Elizabeth's surprise, Minnie ordered her straight to bed. Curfew was not until half past nine, but things were run differently here. Perhaps to try to calm the raving patients, all were locked in their respective rooms soon after supper, their evenings spent in darkness, "except when the moon gave us…light."

But Elizabeth accepted the command meekly. In keeping with her desire to display only decorous behavior, she'd never intentionally broken an asylum rule without the doctor's prior permission and did not intend to start now. She followed Minnie down the filthy corridor, carefully picking her way around the puddles, lifting her petticoats high.

She paused at the threshold of the room she'd been led to, perhaps wondering if there had been some mistake. It was a dormitory.

But it was just what the doctor had ordered.

Elizabeth took a breath—trying hard to breathe through her mouth, though nothing stopped the stink infiltrating every part of her—and gingerly stepped inside. Six beds were laid out in the dorm, the monastic nature of the room making them stand out starkly, for there was little else inside. It was cramped—a visitor to the asylum later describing how inmates were herded together "like wild beasts"—and Elizabeth viewed her new roommates with vigilance. She feared "there was scarcely a patient in the whole ward who could answer a rational question in a rational manner."

Yet that didn't mean they were all alike. Some of her fellow patients on Eighth Ward were "mild and peaceful, others furious and raving; others deeply sad and silent melancholies, while a few never spoke at all." As she entered the dorm, one approached her cautiously, a "fluttering bird" who seemed frightened half to death. This young woman, Miss Weaver, attached herself to Elizabeth with a sudden strength that belied her anxious approach. "She saw I was a speckled-bird among this flock of black-birds," Elizabeth later remembered, "so she came right to me [and] begged [me] to shield her from harm."

In the "silent musings" of her own heart, she let her thoughts run free. There were no answers to bring solace, only memories mixed with anticipated fears: "Comfort, attention, respect, privilege, all, all were in the dead past, and discomfort, inattention, disrespect, contempt, wrong and deprivation are to mark the future of my prison life."

She could see no light at all.

At half past nine, the curfew bell called, announcing the end of the asylum day. Lamp by lamp, every light was extinguished till the entire building fell black. It matched Elizabeth's mood.

The night watchman began his monotonous march through the long corridors, his slow, steady steps punctuated every now and then by the haunted shrieks of unhappy souls. And in her bed on Eighth Ward, Elizabeth Packard lay wide awake, feeling friendless and voiceless and hopeless and alone.

In all the ways it could be, she thought bleakly, it was the "blackest night of my existence."

CHAPTER 17

When the morning bell rang the next day at 5:30, Elizabeth Packard was ready.

She sprang swiftly out of bed.

Overnight, her favorite saying had come to her: "Duties are ours, events God's." There was simply no point in dwelling darkly on what had happened, nor in worrying for the future. Both were part of God's plan for her, and it would have been impudent to "pretend to be wiser than God, by feeling that it would have been better to have had things my way." Instead, she decided, her duty was to focus on what she could do practically, in the here and now, to honor both God and her own principles.

Here, too, God had shown her the way to remedy her sorrows. Although Elizabeth had lost her privileges "in consequence of my defence of others' rights," that was certainly no reason to stop her campaign to improve the patients' conditions. If anything, it only emphasized the correctness of her course. She had preached her sermon to McFarland; now, she had to prove her words were not "mere empty bubbles," such as those with which the doctor had first dazzled her. Her duty was to practice what she preached.

It wasn't an entirely selfless course of action. Elizabeth knew that she herself would benefit: "The only way I can carry my own sorrows is to carry the sorrows of others." She wrote decisively, "I determined I would not be crushed, neither would I submit to see others crushed. In other language, I determined to be a living reprover of the evils I saw consummated in this Asylum."

She certainly had her work cut out for her. As the weak winter sun began its slow ascent outside, she saw more clearly than she had the night before the filthy state of both the ward and the patients. Some of the latter were seriously disturbed, a category of inmate called the "filthy insane," known for besmearing "their beds, their heads and faces, and even the floors and walls of their rooms" with their own excrement. Though both the Tenney sisters were kind women, the overwhelming and thanklessly repetitive nature of their job seems to have made them negligent in cleaning up the mess. But Elizabeth did not blame them for the appalling state of Eighth Ward.

She blamed McFarland. He was in charge.

As soon as the dormitory door was unlocked that morning, she bustled to the bathroom, taking with her a chamber pot—the only utensil at her disposal—which she filled with soapsuds and warm water. Then she turned her attention to her fellow patients; there were eighteen of them in her immediate hall. As all were in "an exceedingly filthy condition," she determined that "their personal cleanliness was plainly my first most obvious duty."

She had to approach them delicately. Many were scared. They were simply not used to washing or being washed; the hall had just a single washbasin for all the patients to use, and no bathtub. As this strange woman with her soft brown eyes and caring manner tried to attend to them, they reacted as many such patients did: "with a scream, a struggle, and a conflict."

Nevertheless, she persevered. Coaxing, kind, she eventually persuaded them to let her touch them. Then, with firm yet gentle hands, she washed their faces, necks, and hands in her repurposed chamber pot, the warm water flowing like a benediction. With those who would let her, she also shampooed their mangled hair, carefully combing through the tangles so as not to hurt them.

Midway through her daunting task, she heard a key in the lock of the main ward door, and in swooped McFarland on his daily rounds.

"I cannot forget the look of surprise he cast upon the row of clean faces and combed hair he witnessed on the side seats of the hall," Elizabeth later wrote with satisfaction. "Simply this process alone so changed their personal appearance, that it is no wonder he had to gaze upon them to recognize them."

He gave her a bow when he saw her watching him. "Good morning, Mrs. Packard!" he said with a courtesy that now seemed false.

Neither of them made any mention of the dramatic change in her circumstances. Elizabeth had determined to accept it as God's will; McFarland's position, she would leave to his own conscience. Clearly intrigued by her activity, the doctor took a seat in the corridor and watched her as she worked.

"Doctor," she said cheerily as she lathered up another filthy head, "I find I can always find something to do for the benefit of others, and you have now assigned me quite a missionary field to cultivate!"

"Yes," was all he said. When she next looked up, he had gone.

Elizabeth's mission did not stop there. The following day, she asked the Tenney sisters to provide her with a bowl of warm salt water, castile soap, towels, and cloths. She had decided, bathtub or no bathtub, that she was going to bathe each and every patient in her hall. It was shocking to her that there was no system in place for this already, but she had determined to change all that.

She worked one woman at a time, taking her frightened form into her room alone, stripping off her bedraggled clothing, and hand-sponging every part of the woman until she was clean. "It is no exaggeration to say," Elizabeth later recalled, "that I never before saw human beings whose skin was so deeply embedded beneath so many layers of dirt as those were. The part cleaned would contrast so strikingly with the part not cleaned, that it would be difficult to believe they belonged to the same race, if on different individuals."

She was uniformly kind to her charges, no matter whether they were violent or timid or rude. "I do not regard an insane person as an object of reproach or contempt, by any means," she said simply. "They are objects of pity and compassion; for I regard insanity as the greatest misfortune which can befall a human being in this life." As such, she had only respect for those who were surviving this affliction. When every day was a battle, what courage these individuals showed. What respect and love they were due for the daily wars they won.

And Elizabeth found her kindness wrought wonders. "I find, from my observation here, that lunatics won't hurt folks, if you'll only let them alone, and have pasture large enough," she said. The mentally ill were not "brute beasts, but human beings, with human feelings." Day by day that late November of 1860, Elizabeth Packard, fighting a one-woman war, slowly restored their humanity to them. It required so much effort that to clean one patient and one room took a whole day's labor.

As Elizabeth had hoped, her example soon inspired the Tenney sisters to join her. Together, they tackled not only the patients but also the ward itself. Elizabeth scrubbed the dirt-encrusted walls and floors until sweat ran in thick rivers down her face. The three of them stripped back the beds and opened up the elderly tick mattresses; the straw inside was frequently rotten to the core from the patients' incontinence and

KATE MOORE

had in most instances become "as black as soot." Elizabeth, needle now in hand, stitched new cloth covers for them and refilled the mattresses with fresh, soft straw. All these tasks she continued, day after day, for about three weeks, at which point the first patient she had cleaned was due another sponge bath, and she began the cycle all over again.

Working closely together, she and the Tenney sisters soon became friends within only a few days of her being on the ward. "Mrs. Packard," Minnie said one morning, "I shall not treat you as I do the other patients, notwithstanding the Doctor has ordered me to. I shall use my own judgment, and treat you as I think you deserve to be treated." Her open-mindedness made the world of difference to Elizabeth: "To [Minnie's] kindness, and tender sympathy, do I owe much." Because Minnie treated Elizabeth "like a sister," and every freedom that was within her power to grant, she freely did.

With her banishment from Seventh Ward, Elizabeth had lost access not only to her former friends but also all her things. She later learned that after McFarland had taken her to Eighth Ward, he'd gone directly to her room on Seventh and searched roughly through her possessions, possibly looking for any copies of the reproof she might have made. Finding none, he'd nevertheless not allowed her trunk to be sent on, instead dispatching it and all its contents to the hospital's luggage room. And there the trunk had stayed. Elizabeth was not allowed to have it with her on Eighth, nor was she permitted her own combs and mirrors, her private pitcher and bowl, her stationery, her towels. The deprivation she'd anticipated the night she'd moved wards was complete. She had been "stripped of every comfort or convenience."

Though Minnie couldn't get her back her pitcher, she did at least allow Elizabeth to keep a chamber pot for her sole use, and this Elizabeth used for her own daily sponge bath; she tied a scarlet string around its handle to differentiate it from the other night pails. Each morning, her "feelings of delicacy revolted from the gaze" of her roommates, who used to watch her with focused interest as she bathed her own body, but having no choice in the matter, she persevered regardless.

Other liberties granted by Minnie were greater. One afternoon, she snuck Elizabeth out of the ward and took her to the trunk room itself. Elizabeth was allowed to select any items of clothing she wished to have with her, and Minnie also let her take her sewing box, which contained a three-bladed pocketknife, scissors, and the gold spectacles Elizabeth wore for close work. Minnie also found a chair for her—an item usually banned on the ward as it could too readily become a weapon—and even let her have access to a Bible so she could maintain her daily devotions.

However, Elizabeth found that Bridget and others would often interrupt her prayers. She begged of the attendants the privilege of sitting in a side room to pray; this wish was granted, as long as she left the door open. Although this meant other Eighth Ward patients wandered in, it was so much quieter than the busy dorm that Elizabeth accepted the offer gratefully.

She was sitting there one morning, on her special chair, when Jenny Haslett came creeping in. Jenny was the woman Elizabeth had heard crying at night for her Willie; Minnie had confided that Jenny had been driven mad by "disappointed affection."

Elizabeth found her pitiable. She was only eighteen but a "human wreck of existence." Though her hair had been shorn off upon her arrival at the asylum, she remained in Elizabeth's eyes "a handsome, delicate girl."

That morning, Jenny curled up at Elizabeth's feet while she read her Bible. Soon, she began to play innocently with the trimming on Elizabeth's dress, flicking the fabric back and forth. Jenny was often quite childlike in her ways. Her simple actions that morning perhaps reminded Elizabeth of her own children, who now seemed so very far away.

Whenever she thought of them these days, they always drew "most desperately upon my heart-strings." Her final memory of her baby, Arthur, was perhaps the hardest to recall. He had clasped his fat little arms around her neck and clung sweetly to her, his burbling babble of newly minted words—"Dear mamma! Dear mamma!"—a precious melody in her ear. But to think of him and the others in such a dismal place was almost too hard. Sometimes, it was easier to be a blank slate with memories rubbed clean away.

Only every now and then would she let herself dwell on them. And when she permitted herself a recollection—of Arthur's "loving caresses and innocent prattle," or George's dark eyes, or even Libby's "sweet spirit"—that memory brought "pleasure almost unalloyed."

That morning, Elizabeth adjusted her spectacles and looked down at Jenny, still playing with her dress. Her heart rushed out to her like a tide. "I must love somebody," she thought. "And here I can live by loving God's afflicted ones."

Slowly, she closed her Bible. She watched as the young woman continued to play with her dress, her fingers speaking a lonely language she could not translate. They sat there for a while: the woman and the girl; the mother and the child. And perhaps Elizabeth had a ghost of Libby somewhere in her mind, for after a while, she bent forward toward Jenny, hesitant and hopeful at the same time. With a mother's hand—a hand that had done this hundreds of times before—she gently parted the short hair that had fallen over Jenny's forehead. She could have been stroking her own child's hair. Cautiously, with maternal love held tightly in her chest, she planted her lips in the space she'd made: a sweet and tender kiss.

Jenny's response to the uninvited affection came instantly—with a blow upon Elizabeth's temple that came from a tightly clenched fist. Though Jenny was delicate, her madness made her strong; it seemed "more like the kick of a horse, than the hand of a human." Elizabeth's glasses flew wildly across the room while she, for a moment, was knocked unconscious, the heavy blow breaking blank darkness across her brain.

When she awoke, the world seemed maladjusted. She was bleary-eyed, shell-shocked, and stunned. Her left temple throbbed with an urgent, bloody pain. Her left eye felt an unyielding pressure; she feared that it might burst. She forced herself to pry both eyes open.

Jenny was standing before her.

"I am going to knock your brains out!" she cried.

Her hands clenched into fists.

CHAPTER 18

Elizabeth backed out of the room slowly, letting no words escape her that might provoke Jenny further, as she could be prone to "sudden frenzies." She quickly found Minnie, who took one look at her and sent straight for the assistant physician.

"O, Mrs. Packard," Minnie breathed in shock. "What a wound you have got upon your temple!"

Dr. Tenny came and tended to her; for a while, there was a worry Elizabeth might lose her eye. Her face swelled up and ugly bruises bloomed across eye and temple both: a kaleidoscope of color that deepened day by day. Eighth Ward had no mirrors, but even if Elizabeth could have caught a glimpse of her own reflection, she would not have recognized herself. She lay on her bed, head throbbing painfully in time with her heartbeat, the chorus of night voices now nine-inch knives carving through her tender brain.

McFarland showed no sympathy, even after this attack. When Elizabeth explained what had happened and begged for removal to some safer ward, he simply said, "It is no uncommon thing to receive a blow for a kiss."

Did he speak from personal experience?

He did not ameliorate her situation in any way. In fact, he made it worse. In the wake of Jenny's violence, he directed that Elizabeth should eat her meals beside a woman named Sarah Triplet, whom he deliberately moved from Fifth Ward to Eighth. She was known as "the most dangerous patient in the whole female wards." Even the staff were scared of her.

Elizabeth greeted her cautiously as she took her allocated seat. "Old Mother Triplet," as Sarah was known, was an elderly woman of indeterminate age. Large and fleshy, she cut an intimidating figure even before factoring in her unstable mind. Fifth Ward was even worse than Eighth, reserved for "rare and extraordinary specimens of distorted humanity" and not for the "ordinary" insane. It also housed the criminal maniacs— the arsonists, murderers, and homicidally obsessed who'd been dispatched to the asylum by order of the courts or else by a thankful jail only too glad to be rid of them.

Mrs. Triplet sat on Elizabeth's right-hand side. She came from Kentucky and likely had a Southern drawl. As Elizabeth greeted her politely, Mrs. Triplet took instant umbrage.

"I will kill *you!*" she said fiercely in reply. She always spoke in "tones the most vehement."

Elizabeth gulped but had no choice but to remain where she was. It was a baptism of fire—sometimes almost literally. "I considered myself very fortunate," she later wrote, "if I left the table without being spit upon by her, or by having her tea, or coffee, or gravy, or sauce thrown upon my dress."

It was a world away from the civilized mealtimes she'd once enjoyed on Seventh Ward and even further from her beautifully decorated parlor in Manteno, where her fine white china had sat neatly inside a closet painted pea green. Often, mealtimes on Eighth were even more fraught than that brief description, with spitting the least of Elizabeth's concerns. As meat was almost always served, usually pork, it was the one time of day when knives could be found on the ward, and the patients took advantage. Frequently, they would throw the blades at one another, every sudden strike the boiling point of some internecine conflict that had been simmering beneath the surface. Mrs. Triplet was once compelled to act in self-defense when a sharp knife abruptly whistled past her head, missing her eye by an inch.

A domino effect followed. It was an almost everyday occurrence. One patient would attack another, and then all the rest would grab any object close at hand to fight back. The women around Elizabeth would suddenly "seize the tumblers, salt-cellars, plates, bowls, and pitchers, and hurl them about in demoniac frenzy, so that the broken glass and china would fly about our face and eyes like hailstones." Under fire, many times Elizabeth had to duck and dodge this onslaught of unconventional weapons, "hurled in promiscuous profusion about my head." Trying to make herself smaller, she bent double as she crept out of the dining hall, trying to slink unseen, leaving her unfinished meal behind her.

Worse still awaited her though.

Worse was when they seized her directly and dragged her around the ward using fistfuls of her hair.

Though she tried to be brave and kind, she soon became terrified. She felt her life was "constantly exposed," "almost daily and hourly endangered," including at night. Frequently, she would wake with a start to find a roommate flinging night pails around the dorm with noisy violence. Her only option, in such circumstances, was to clamber up on top of her bedstead, from where she could just about reach the transom window over the door. Then she would yell her head off, crying out for help. Sometimes the sleeping attendants would hear her and remove the wild patient. Other nights, they slept right through.

For Elizabeth, the situation became untenable after only a few weeks on the ward. She "begged and besought" McFarland to remove her, even just to a room of her own on Eighth, where she could at least sleep without the threat of violence. But he was merciless. "Even before I could finish my sentence," she remembered, "he would turn and walk indifferently away, without uttering one syllable." She condemned him as "a very cruel, unfeeling man."

But she did not have many opportunities even to appeal to him. McFarland came far less frequently to Eighth than he had to Seventh, and when he did, "he laid his hands upon me in a different manner... far too violently."

In that fierce grip was another new reality. "Dr. McFarland did not treat me as an insane person," she said, "until I had been [at the asylum] four months, when he suddenly changed his programme entirely."

All previous privileges were abruptly withdrawn. Elizabeth was not allowed to leave the ward, even with an attendant. While the other patients on Eighth regularly enjoyed a carefully managed walk or ride in the grounds, she was denied even this. Her only access to fresh air came from the dormitory window: a small square that sadly sketched the borders of her blunted world. She begged McFarland to let her work in the laundry or ironing rooms at least so she could get some physical exercise beyond her daily cleaning, but this plea was rejected. When she first moved wards, she was banned from leaving for any reason at all, except to attend the odd chapel service if she was granted a place.

But perhaps worst of all for Elizabeth was that her writing privileges were withdrawn; it was expressly forbidden for her to be given even a scrap of paper. After having been allowed, for the first time in her life, to write freely and regularly, this cruel curtailment felt like a literal choking. Words had become as essential as air. Without them, she felt her life bottlenecking, the doctor's hands around her throat, pressing firmly down on her windpipe. Ever since she'd joined the Bible class back in February, she'd been carefully committing her thoughts to paper, seeing herself take shape on the page. But now she was back to nothingness, transparent and tongue-tied. The evaporating, empty steam that left no trace of itself behind.

At times, her treatment was harsh enough even to shake her faith. "While I have been here and seen and felt these horrors in my own soul," she said, "I have been led to exclaim, 'Is there a God? Can a just God behold and see these horrors, and let them go on?'" As an asylum inmate put it, "Human endurance is not made of India-rubber." And under these conditions, Elizabeth found it harder and harder to bounce back.

She wondered what the doctor was playing at. She had been concerned before about the lack of treatment for those who were genuinely mentally ill, but this course he had now prescribed went the other way. As one patient put it, "Most of [the] doctors that are employed in lunatic asylums do much more to aggravate the disease than they do to cure it." And another patient went further: "Insane Asylum. A place where insanity is made."

As the calendar days started counting down through December 1860, Elizabeth came to the same conclusion. "I fully believe," she said bluntly, "it was the Doctor's purpose to make a maniac of me, by the skillful use of the Asylum tortures."

But Elizabeth was wrong. Totally wrong. McFarland was not trying to make her a maniac.

Because he already thought her one.

And he always had.

CHAPTER 19

"Her case is indeed an interesting study," McFarland had written to Theophilus on August 11, 1860, "as showing a fine mind and brilliant imagination…and yet, all these mental endowments deep-dyed with the color of radical disease."

McFarland did subscribe to a school of thought that moral insanity existed only if attended by intellectual impairment. But he also believed this impairment or delusion could be invisible, with "no outward form of manifestation whatever."

In truth, it didn't bother him that he had not yet found the intellectual delusion from which he believed Elizabeth suffered, because from the morally perverse conduct she'd already shown (such as her desire to live apart from her husband, even simply the way she'd stood up to him), he did not doubt its underlying existence. He believed in it the same way he did gravity: he could not actually *see* the gravity when the apple fell to the ground, but that did not mean it was not there.

"When I have a case where there are strange, moral perversities, inconsistent with the previous character, conduct, education and habits of life of the person," he said, "I have no hesitation in taking the position that it is insanity."

By this criteria, Elizabeth was a textbook case. After all, for twenty-one years, she'd maintained the habit of obeying her husband. To McFarland's mind, her evolution from submission to self-possession was classic madness. He did not think, as Elizabeth did, that the change in her behavior was due to "a natural growth of intellect."

In addition, although Elizabeth had emphasized to the doctor that her aversion to her husband was based on logic—because of the way he'd treated her—McFarland believed that baseless. Thus he would consider her as having an "absence of...the instinct of love as found even in the lower orders of animals," which was more proof she was sick.

A peer of McFarland confirmed that her behavior met the threshold for intellectual insanity, even if the delusion was unseen. "Apparently motiveless conduct is always suspicious," he wrote. "An unreasonable fancy...that there is a conspiracy against [the patient is] one of the most frequent maniacal fancies when the intellectual development of the disease has been reached."

And what better example of motiveless conduct than Elizabeth's supposedly irrational hatred of her husband? Her accompanying charge that Theophilus had conspired to lock her up in McFarland's asylum when she was sane scored an A grade for "maniacal fancy" too.

McFarland was not alone in happily committing patients with invisible insanities to his hospital. It was almost standard practice. At the meetings of the AMSAII, superintendents rather raced with enthusiasm to share stories of inmates who exhibited "no positive trace of disease for weeks or months together." Interred at asylums, such patients would, for months and sometimes even years, "work, talk and seem to feel and think as other people."

Often—as had happened with Elizabeth—the friends and family of such patients might protest they were *not* insane and should immediately be released, but in these cases, the doctors remained adamant that *they* were right. They would assert arrogantly that "insanity has its own delicate characteristics...which can be read by the expert, but which are not appreciable to the casual observer." They airily promised these doubting family members that they *would* see the doctors' greater wisdom. Just give them time.

Then, triumphantly, they would be proved right. "It was some months before we were so convinced of his true condition, as to have been able...to testify in a court, that he was insane, but he ultimately demented," one revealed with satisfaction. Another doctor said of a female patient that "although he had no doubt of her insanity, she was in the house for six months before the development of her malady." McFarland himself put it this way: "sooner or later," a patient would develop "well marked insanity of mind and habit [to] satisfy the most scrupulous as to their condition."

It was just as Elizabeth had written in her reproof: "No human being can be subjected to the process to which you subject them here, without being in great danger of becoming insane."

McFarland may not have *intentionally* had a plan to make Elizabeth mad.

But that didn't mean it might not happen anyway.

And the doctor's theories about treating her type of case seemed destined to make it even more likely. McFarland considered patients like her "less able than children to enjoy the unrestrained exercise of the prerogatives of sane persons." They were "less suitable subjects for the enjoyment of the pleasures of liberty and the unlimited society of others, than those in whom the power of reasoning may be much less perfect." That was why he'd applied such stiff constraints now that he'd moved Elizabeth to Eighth Ward. In his opinion, she was not a suitable subject for society and unconstrained freedom.

Because he wasn't only looking out for her but also the others around her. As he'd noted in his letter to Theophilus, Elizabeth had a truly brilliant mind—and that made her dangerous. "Being capable of reasoning logically, and, in some instances, with surprising clearness of thought; and having their peculiarities of conduct so under control as to deceive the superficial observer, they...too often enlist the sympathies of well-meaning philanthropists," McFarland wrote of her class of patients. He'd identified as early as August that this troublesome inmate possessed "an artfulness in her play upon the sympathies of others that few can resist." That was partly why he'd been so worried about that prayer circle and the way she'd interacted with his staff. That was why her inclusion of collected quotes in the reproof would have been a final straw.

He'd had no choice but to cut her off from all her former associates. Though she had at first been deemed fit for Seventh Ward, her subsequent rabble-rousing, spreading "discontent and disaffection" everywhere she went, had made her position untenable. Her persuasive and impassioned interference in the lives of others was simply too great for McFarland to ignore; *this* was why she'd been moved.

She may well have been mad in his mind, but she clearly had influence and eloquence—a frightening combination in the wrong woman's hands.

But at the present time, in the wake of his intervention, McFarland must have been pleased to see the way it was going on Eighth Ward. After all, she was now shut up there with only lunatics for company. It would surely be a challenge, even for Elizabeth Packard, to sow her insurgent seeds in that stony field.

Later—much later—McFarland would be challenged directly on how he could have believed, by his own self-stated standards of defining moral insanity, that Elizabeth was insane. She had shown no intellectual impairment. On the contrary, she was intelligent and bright.

The doctor, perhaps tellingly, would choose to dodge the question.

It would be asked again.

And finally he would reply with a calm, conceited faith—in himself. "I believed that delusion existed, and that I should find it."

Now, like his peers before him, all he had to do was wait.

CHAPTER 20

The bell cut through the dark morning, summoning the Eighth Ward patients to rise, if not shine. Elizabeth pulled herself blearily upright, a "bad taste" in her mouth. In her old life, she had always loved her sleep, but lately even this escape into unconsciousness afforded little respite. Sleep was neither as quiet nor as refreshing as it once had been, and it was not all to do with the disturbances in the dorm.

She began her sponge bath, concealing her body as much as she could from the prying eyes of her roommates. With no mirrors on the ward, she could not complete her toilette as she once had but tried her best each morning to maintain her appearance, knowing a slippery slope awaited if she didn't.

It was strange, never seeing her reflection. She had only an old picture of herself in her mind now, but it was fading by the day. It was like the bruises on her face and arms from the patients' angry blows. Each day, their vibrant color grew weaker and more washed out until they appeared only as insubstantial shadows.

One day, she would wake up and they would be gone.

"I must soon become," she thought bleakly, "nothing less than a heap of putrefaction."

Despite her dismal thoughts, Elizabeth helped the other patients to bathe; she was still maintaining her cycle of care, notwithstanding the violence she sometimes received. Attending to their needs was the only thing that kept her going.

At 7:00 a.m., the breakfast bell rang, and Elizabeth followed the others to the dining hall, though she had little appetite. "I smelled and tasted these stinks so much after I entered this stink-hole," she wrote of Eighth Ward, "that, for a time, I couldn't taste anything else." Nevertheless, she took her seat next to Mrs. Triplet and picked at her meal.

The asylum fare did not agree with her. Its lack of fresh fruits and vegetables and overemphasis on bread and potatoes at times caused constipation; she would beg for some "poor, shriveled wheat...to eat raw, to keep my bowels open." It was almost as if her body was reflecting her new life: she was stuck fast in this painful place and could see no way to move forward. At times, in her very darkest hours, she even contemplated another way out—suicide. But thoughts of her children and her faith always stopped her.

"God says I mustn't kill anybody, and *I am somebody*," she thought, as though reminding herself. She credited the "miracle" of her continuing sanity to "God's grace alone."

Cautiously, she lifted her eyes from her plate to glance furtively at her fellow patients. The longer she stayed on the ward, the more she was getting to know them—and their idiosyncrasies. When she'd first been transferred, it had been like moving to "some foreign country, whose inhabitants had manners and customs of their own." Unlike on Seventh Ward, where all the women had been alike—and like her—here there was endless variety.

There were those patients who were dangerous or aggressive; these would cast furious glances at Elizabeth or curse in such colorful language it seemed to turn her own ears blue. Some would even rush at her and grab her petticoats, wanting to raise them to unmask her modesty. But other patients were much calmer. There was an elderly woman who would stare blankly at her for hours on end with her mouth wide open. A young girl "emaciated almost to a skeleton," who took neither food nor drink except by force. A nervous, middle-aged lady with uncommonly fine skin who would constantly pick at her clothes, her restless anxiety venting itself "from the ends of her fingers...upon something tangible." With insight, Elizabeth saw the woman's relentless unravelling of her garments as an "act of self-defense from the overflowings of her pent-up mental agonies."

Even the violent patients had souls within, she was beginning to realize, spirits that were simply trying to be heard. Sallie Low, a patient with large black eyes and short curly hair who had "'spells' of excessive fury" was once put into solitary confinement after one of her outbursts. When Elizabeth, who'd been asked to check on her, looked in, she saw Sallie had "divested herself of all her clothing and was standing naked... with her hands both raised, with all her fingers spread, with her mouth wide open in laughter...she had written her marks upon the wall [with her excrement], as high as her fingers could reach." Yet Sallie was just trying, in her own way, to express herself, to make her mark on an uncaring and unlistening world in any way she could.

That December, Elizabeth Packard decided *she* would be the one to listen. Slowly, she began to make new friends. With Betsy Clarke, a fifty-six-year-old housekeeper from Massachusetts. With a young woman named Emily Goldsby, who was epileptic. (Sufferers of the condition were grouped together with the insane in that era, with some doctors ascribing their fits to "gross indulgence in masturbation," made worse by "the eating of English plum-pudding.") And she made friends, too, with the nervous woman she'd seen destroying her clothes: forty-nine-year-old Emeline Bridgman. She became a special friend.

Emeline—like two-thirds of all the patients in the asylum—suffered from depression. Listening to her talk about her illness made Elizabeth's heart ache. She tried to comfort her, "imparting genuine sympathy in deeds of kindness," wishing she could find some better way to help. In Elizabeth's opinion, the asylum was the worst place for Emeline. "She is diseased in her nervous system," she explained, "and instead of treating her as a criminal, she needs unusual forbearance and kindness, to inspire her with self-confidence... All depressing, debasing influences, are deathlike."

As had happened on Seventh Ward, Elizabeth began to pray with her friends, although, cleverly, it was not as formalized an arrangement as before. But they lived the experience of Eighth Ward together. "I have wept with her sorrows," Elizabeth wrote of Emily, who'd been committed to the asylum by her family, who did not want to care for her. "I have cried over her griefs and wrongs which it was beyond my power to help. Hundreds of times have we prayed to the same Father... confidently hoping that He would...deliver us out of the power of our persecuting kindred." When Emily had a seizure, it was Elizabeth who nursed her now.

And Elizabeth found their collective strength helped her. "In alleviating their burdens and sorrows my own became bearable," she said, almost feeling the weight lift. So she went further, caressing patients if they'd let her, allowing them to feel that human touch. She even permitted that frightened, fluttering bird, Miss Weaver, to climb into her own narrow bed at night when she was scared. There, Elizabeth wrote, Miss Weaver could "hug me still more closely, and I slept...in her amorous embrace. She dared not to trust herself to sleep, unless I was by her side."

Nor did Elizabeth simply soothe and support her friends. "When we suffered any unusual abuse," recalled a fellow Eighth Ward patient of Elizabeth, "it was very often said, 'I'll tell Mrs. Packard of this.' We knew our rights would find an able advocate in our firm and gentle friend."

Because Elizabeth had realized something about herself, perhaps for the first time: "I always stand up for the oppressed." She said she never regretted giving McFarland the reproof. Though it had led her here, to this place of horror, not only had it been the right thing to do, but now she could help these women too.

She started to think more shrewdly about McFarland's removal of her writing privileges. It was a particular punishment *for her*; others were not treated the same. Elizabeth therefore deduced of the doctor's decision, "Mine was the only pen he feared amongst his patients." She considered that distinction an honor.

Her feelings for McFarland at this time had turned 180 degrees from her previous admiration. Now, "even the sight of the man, or the sound or sight of his name, was instinctively and inseparably associated with horror." She would dread the sound of his footsteps in the hall, finding his presence so distressingly painful she couldn't even speak to him. She would turn away, mute, when he entered her dormitory, refusing even to exchange pleasantries.

Her discourtesy was no doubt noted as an unnatural lack of feminine friendliness.

But Elizabeth found that now the battle lines had been drawn, it made her purpose clearer. "I must not turn back," she wrote, "but face this new enemy I have called into the field." McFarland might have hoped that her removal to Eighth Ward would suppress her spirit, but Elizabeth was finding the opposite was true.

"O, Dr. McFarland," she said with patronizing clarity, "you cannot

kill a spirit; it lives after all you have done to destroy its existence."
Though she'd initially found the transfer to Eighth Ward the hardest
thing she'd faced, she'd now discovered that "I can live, move, breathe,
and have a being, where I once thought I could not."

Yet to Elizabeth, simply living, moving, breathing, and being were
not enough. An "aimless purpose" was of no account to her. She didn't
want her life to be solely about surviving, hanging on to make it through.

She wanted to make it count.

Being on Eighth Ward had been an eye-opener in countless ways.
In particular, she regularly saw restraints applied to patients; these had
barely been needed to control the cutout dolls of Seventh Ward. She
had a front-row seat as women were habitually bundled into the incongruently named camisoles—straitjackets—their arms forced inside elon-
gated cotton sleeves, crossed firmly in front of their bucking bodies, and
drawn tightly away behind them, with a strong cord then used to secure

Forms of restraint used in Illinois asylums in the mid-nineteenth century,
including the "camisoles" Elizabeth frequently saw applied on Eighth Ward

them so they could not wriggle free. She saw how screen rooms were used: a form of solitary confinement in a small, uncomfortable room with an iron screen stretched across its window. Also at the staff's disposal were crib bedsteads—wooden boxes with cot-like barred sides—wrist straps, muffs, and mittens.

The Jacksonville women were lucky at least that the array did not include the scold's bridle: a metal muzzle with an iron bit that could be placed on a woman's tongue to stop her from speaking. The most torturous types had a spike attached that would pierce her tongue if she tried. This device had been used to control women ever since the sixteenth century and was still being utilized in at least one provincial British asylum in 1858.

McFarland considered restraint "an absolute essential in any form of associated treatment," in direct contrast to some other doctors who believed that "restraints and neglect may be considered synonymous." But McFarland claimed the restraints used at Jacksonville were "so simple and light as hardly deserve the name."

Yet it wasn't him who usually applied them; attendants formed the frontline. Although the superintendent conceded he was "fully alive to the abuses" that could follow, he still considered restraints "both justifiable and necessary" and thought those who objected "over-sensitive."

As a woman, Elizabeth may have seen restraints being used far more often than she would have on a male ward. As occurred with the prescription of drugs, there could be a gender difference in the way restraints were applied. One superintendent revealed that in his asylum, restraint was "rarely found necessary among males." In contrast, "from five to ten females usually wore the camisole."

Elizabeth observed with concern that the jackets were not only used on violent patients. In fact, sometimes the more aggressive patients were left to roam free while other, quieter patients who had simply made some misstep, acting against their attendants in some way, were restrained as punishment. She came to realize that "abused patients was the rule at that hospital, while those justly and kindly treated were the exceptions."

It was even worse than she had thought.

Elizabeth Packard started to conceive a strategy to address the situation. She'd partly found her transfer to Eighth Ward so shocking because she'd had no concept of the reality of that world. She'd always thought that an asylum would be as its etymology suggested: a sanctuary. She'd had no idea of the cruelty, horror, and deprivation that really went on. "The working of this Institution is so carefully covered up," she thought, "and so artfully concealed from the public eye, that the external world knows nothing of the 'hidden life of the prisoner' within."

If only, she thought, someone could reveal it.

Perhaps that person could be her...

She started to plot. She came up with a plan: "the journal of an eyewitness taken on the spot." It would be "a secret journal of daily events, just as they occurred."

She had no paper. She had no pen. But she had a mind and eyes and a passionate will. She was going to write her way out of this hellhole—if it was the last thing she did.

"It shall be one of the highest aspirations of my earth-life, to expose these evils for the purpose of remedying them," she announced. "It shall be said of me, 'She hath done what she could.'"

She simply couldn't wait to get started.

CHAPTER 21

She became a magpie, a squirrel, a spy. An old pen, carelessly discarded by a doctor, became a prize, a nub of pencil a treasure true. Some other patients were still allowed the privilege of newspapers; Elizabeth would tear the margins from them to scribble along those blank edges. Even before she came to the asylum, she'd always crammed her words onto the page—writing north, south, east, and west if necessary. That habit now stood her in good stead. "I put a wonderful amount of matter on a very small surface," she later said with pride.

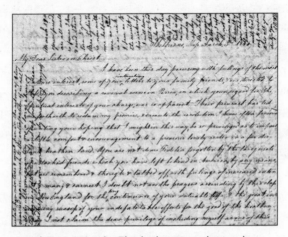

A letter written by Elizabeth in 1846, showing how she excelled at squeezing words onto a page

Yet it still wasn't enough. She still had more to say, more to record. Around this time, Elizabeth was permitted to leave the ward to sew for the asylum under Mrs. Hosmer's direction. She never mentioned being able to reconnect with her Seventh Ward friends, so perhaps—it seems likely—her visits to the sewing room were scheduled so their paths never crossed. It is not known why this potential privilege was restored, but maybe it wasn't seen as one. Elizabeth herself said it was only through her unpaid labor that she could "buy the privilege of exchanging the putrid, loathsome air of the ward for the more wholesome, purer atmosphere of the sewing room." She made a minimum of one vest or pair of pants daily. But at least it got her out.

And there was a benediction to be found in the company of Mrs. Hosmer. The sewing room directress, Elizabeth said, was "the medium of some of my choicest social blessings."

Though Mrs. Hosmer had correctly predicted that Elizabeth's behavior on Seventh Ward would eventually get her in trouble, she still viewed the change in her friend's circumstances with concern. "I have had eyes to see, and a heart to feel," she later wrote. It perhaps reminded her of her own sister's plight; she'd once been forced to write to McFarland during her sister's stay with him to beg him to better the conditions. "The pain I feel when I think of my sister [in the] situation as I found her," she wrote, "do say you will remove her. I can I will pay for better accomodations [*sic*]... think could you be happy to hav[e] your sister there."

Elizabeth, by now, was a sister of sorts too.

So when Mrs. Hosmer noticed her eagerly scouring the sewing room for writing materials, she turned a blind eye to her illicit scavenging. In this way, Elizabeth successfully snuck tissue paper, brown paper, and even scraps of cotton cloth back to her ward. These foraged crumbs joined the torn bits of newspaper to form the blank canvas of her journal.

Mrs. Hosmer was more than happy to support her small insurgency. By that point, she considered McFarland "a man who has no higher aim than his own selfish ambition"; she believed he'd been corrupted by "uninterrupted power." She'd been directress of the sewing room for two and a half years by December 1860 and was increasingly disillusioned with the job. In whispered words, she and Elizabeth shared their mutual concerns about the hospital. "The Doctor is a villain," declared Mrs. Hosmer flatly. She told Elizabeth she could "tell facts of his treatment of patients here" that would make her "flesh creep to hear the recital of." Elizabeth, naturally, asked to hear more.

Back on the ward, the spy had to find a hiding place for her treasures. When Minnie had taken her to the trunk room, one of the items she'd brought back had been her traveling bonnet. Now, fingers fiddling, she managed to hide the journal between the millinet crown and the outside covering of the hat. "I encircled this crown with so many thicknesses of paper," she recalled, "that it sometimes caused the exclamation, 'How heavy this bonnet is!'"

But no one ever thought to look inside to find out why.

The days passed by. The days got colder. Even McFarland acknowledged that "the air in the old wings is with difficulty kept at proper temperature in extreme cold weather"; he blamed "the bad construction of the flues in the brick walls." But that didn't help the patients. Elizabeth shivered as she secretly scrawled, her eyes fixed on the army of skeletal trees outside, now providing not so much shade as a stark reminder that all things end. The newspapers from which she tore her scraps were full of advertisements for "Holidays! Holidays!" but Elizabeth had never felt less like celebrating. December 18, 1860, came and went, and with it her baby boy's second birthday. She should have been at home. She should have been with Arthur. But instead she was here, stuck in this hospital, hundreds of miles away.

She'd had no letters from the children, except that worrying note from Libby in the summer. She wondered sometimes if they'd forgotten her. But, she said, "the mothers don't forget their children." It was torture to be separated from them, torn from her own flesh and blood, the edges of that wound still red and raw and bleeding.

Yet despite her immense pain, she had only to look around her to see worse. "The evils of this Institution are so momentous and aggravating, that my own private wrongs seem lost, almost, in the aggregate."

She turned back to her journal with increased commitment.

After December 20, 1860, the newspapers brought news indeed: South Carolina had seceded from the Union—the first state to make a break for freedom.

It would not be the last.

Although Elizabeth identified with Union interests, that symbolic strike for independence perhaps wove itself into her consciousness.

Because that December, she dreamed...

———

She dreamed she was high above a river, a rope pulled tight around her waist, a stagecoach at her back. The two were linked: her task to pull the coach across the raging river.

But even as she moved forward, the bridge on which she was walking thinned into a narrow slitwork just four inches wide. She could never pull the coach on that.

Elizabeth halted in her endeavors, tried to find a smart way forward. If she just walked on with the coach still attached, it would inevitably unbalance on the slender beam, dragging both herself and it into the rushing river below.

She seized the rope instead and disentangled herself from her duty.

Though she was now free from the incumbrance of the heavy coach, she was still in mortal peril. She could not go back; the stagecoach blocked her path. Yet the way forward seemed too hazardous, the chance of falling far too great.

Elizabeth cast her eyes about her. Her heart leapt when she noticed a group of men on the opposite shore. They appeared to be readying themselves to save her—gallantly manhandling a rope, discussing with fervor how best to reach her. For a time, she settled down on the thin beam and "trusted my deliverance, with all the trustful confidence of my womanly nature, to the care of manhood."

But there was a problem. There was a blockage in the river, which would frustrate any attempts by these men to get to her by boat.

Elizabeth was on her own.

At the realization, she wobbled anxiously on the beam, her balance a debt she feared could not be paid. If she looked down, vertigo seized her, her head swimming with such swooning conviction that she could have been in the waters already. She heard the river rushing, its rising voice hungry for her, shouting out its greed.

For a long time, she merely sat there, struggling, out of reach both of human help and hope. But then Elizabeth sat up straighter. She reached a hand down to her feet. With focused purpose, she slipped off the shoes that had kept them prisoner, watched them tumbling into the rapids below. She wiggled her toes. Freedom. Now, she could stand up, straight on the beam, with her stocking feet free to take the path she had to take.

She had simply concluded that as the men could not help her, she would have to save herself. She had determined to rescue herself, "by my own unaided exertions, by going forward, risking all the hazards of a progressive movement."

She would not look down or back. Not once. That way lay madness.

She would look constantly upward instead, up at the clear blue sky, and trust her unencumbered stocking feet to lead her to safety.

———

When Elizabeth woke with a start in her bed in the dormitory, the vivid dream stayed with her.

She told Mrs. Hosmer about it. Her friend underlined its message with uncompromising clarity: "Mrs. Packard, you must leave public opinion behind you... You must just go on alone."

Alone. Unaided. Unaccompanied.

Elizabeth had never even imagined such a path.

But she wrote, "This period of subjection through which woman is passing, is developing her self-reliant character, by compelling her to defend herself."

"I *must* defend myself," she realized, "or go undefended."

Because no one was coming to save her. She had to save herself.

And after all, what was stopping her? Was she afraid of public opinion? *People already thought her mad.* Was she afraid of losing something? *She had already lost* everything. "The worst that my enemies can do... they have done, and I fear them no more," she wrote with increasing excitement. "I am now free to be true and honest...no opposition can overcome me."

She feared nothing now but God. She was not afraid of men. What did they mean to her? Once, she had thought of them as trees: strong shelters beneath which she could hide. But she wrote, "I can stand on my own feet, alone, now. I don't have to be running around to find some tree to climb upon. *I am a tree myself.*"

She felt it in her: new roots plunging deep into the earth, anchoring her to this unexpected path. She did not want to hide anymore; she wanted to be fearless and free. *She* would be the strong and steady one, feeling the wind howling freshly through her branches, seeing the world spread out before her as she grew. "I feel that I am born into a new element—freedom." It was intoxicating.

"This Insane Asylum has been to me the gate to Heaven," she later wrote—because it had brought her to this rebirth and to what she saw as her new divine mission. "For woman's sake I suffer [here]," she scribbled in her journal. "I will try to continue to suffer on, patiently and uncomplainingly, confidently hoping that my case will lead [the] community to investigate for themselves, and see *why* it is, that so many sane women are thus persecuted."

Her new mindset changed her outlook on her entire life. "My will and desire is, and always has been, to stay with [my children]," she wrote, "to be with them, to care for them as my first great care. But God's will has marked out a counter-line of conduct for the present, and my pliant heart has learned long since to say, 'Father, not my will, but Thine be done.'" And she realized, anyway, "I am not childless. All God's sons and daughters are my brothers and sisters."

In the December dark, she rose each day and kept up with her mission. The lack of light no longer bothered her. Because woman was moon, man was sun, and this was her time to shine.

"The fact is, it is dark times now," she wrote, "so much like night that we cannot tell it from midnight… [But] night or darkness is woman's time to rule, and we intend," she concluded, and with due warning to those who stood against her, "to use our privilege well."

Her husband had tried to contain her—and failed.

McFarland had tried to tame her—and failed.

"Woman is too volatile and spiritual a being to be kept down by mere brute force," she wrote. "You can cage a bird and thus keep her down on a level with her serpent-mate, but just give her the use of her powers, its freedom, *and she will rise*."

From within the darkness of the Jacksonville Insane Asylum, a new moon rose.

And her name was Elizabeth Packard.

— PART THREE —

MY PEN
SHALL RAGE

A word after a word after a word is power.

—Margaret Atwood, 1981

When I was in the asylum they locked me up...but
what did I care for that as long as they had no key that
would fit my mouth?

—Phebe B. Davis, 1855

CHAPTER 22

April 3, 1862
Dr. McFarland's office
Illinois State Hospital for the Insane
Jacksonville, Illinois

———

Dr. Andrew McFarland, aged forty-four, light shining off his clean bald head, dipped his pen into his inkstand and began to write a letter to Theophilus Packard. It was that time again: time to share an update on his wife Elizabeth.

"In the matter of her domestic affections and relations," the doctor wrote, perhaps giving a sigh laced with now annoyingly familiar, thwarted frustration, "she is as unyielding as ever."

Elizabeth certainly was. One year and ten months on from her initial commitment to the asylum, she was as determined as she'd ever been to follow her own path. More so, in fact. "By my experiences," she wrote, "it would seem that my Father intended to so capacitate me, that I should be daunted and discouraged by nothing." Iron will, after all, was "smelted by the furnace of affliction" and Elizabeth's, by now, was almost indestructible.

Yet that didn't mean it had been easy. One year and ten months was not merely measured in time but in missed birthdays, fading bruises, and a relentless cycle of unwashed bodies that swam before her, even as she gritted her teeth and held her breath and soaped them yet again. There had been many times during the past sixteen months on Eighth Ward when she had struggled to stay strong, even to keep her "thinking machine in order." "I never needed my strength so much as I do here," she wrote. Being locked in the asylum, subject to all its rules and regulations, a daily witness to oppression, felt like a "hurricane-blast... sweeping over my unsheltered heart." After all she had seen and continued to record in her secret journal, for her the asylum was now merely a "humanity-crushing institution" and all its inmates, herself included, subject to "a feeling of annihilation." There had been times when she'd felt that crushing weight above her and had barely had the strength to lift it from her brain.

Perhaps the very hardest thing of all to bear was that her term of imprisonment was unknown. Unlike convicts, who could count down toward the end of their jail sentence, Elizabeth and her friends were indefinitely detained at the superintendent's pleasure. And Elizabeth knew from those around her that sometimes those terms could last for years. At least thirty-six patients with her in the asylum in 1862 had been there for five years or more; one woman, committed for displaying "extreme jealousy," had been there ever since the asylum had first opened in 1851—the first patient entered in its register. "If the prisoner could but know for how long a time he must suffer this incarceration," one of Elizabeth's friends wrote, "it would be a wonderful relief. Then the Superintendent could not perpetuate it at his own option, as he now can and does."

That doctor dipped his pen in his inkstand, thinking of Mrs.

Packard's prognosis. What to write to her husband? In McFarland's view, one year and ten months was not so *very* long for him to have been providing what Elizabeth called his "subduing treatment." It was his belief that "the patient who affords any prospect of recovery should not be removed from the Asylum...till every delusion has been banished from the mind."

By this criteria, Elizabeth's continued, unnatural hatred of her husband made her release impossible. The doctor sighed. As much as he might wish it differently, her prognosis was no different from the year before, when he'd written to Mr. Packard on February 2, 1861: "I have in vain looked to time to make a change in the character of Mrs. Packard's case. In the place of the usual emotions, that exist in the bosom of a wife...there appears only an unmitigated hate, as obdurate as adamant." Such a position, in McFarland's professional view, debarred "the possibility of any continuance of the natural relations of wife and mother, and...require[s]...her residence in an asylum for the insane."

Elizabeth was going nowhere.

As McFarland reflected on her progress over the past year, he found none. Even a visit from Theophilus in 1861 had rendered things only worse, not better. Elizabeth had been set against her husband's presence from the start, outraged by a recent letter he'd sent in which he'd discussed breaking up the family and—illogically, given her commitment—sought her advice on who should raise Arthur. But Elizabeth had deduced—correctly—that the entire letter was a lie to induce her, for her children's sake, to plead to go home.

She told McFarland frankly, "He is trying to make me say, 'O, husband do take me home! If you only will, I will think, speak and act just as you please...and will never venture to think for myself again!'"

Elizabeth had refused to cooperate, but that didn't mean she wasn't worried. Other elements of Theophilus's letter had rung true. Libby, for example, was described as doing "all the work for the family." In his private diary, Theophilus enthused about his then eleven-year-old, "My daughter did exceedingly well in household duties." Everything that Elizabeth used to do—the cooking, cleaning, ironing, sewing, gardening, nursing, and so much more—had fallen on Libby's slender shoulders. As the only girl, she was simply expected to get on with it.

Elizabeth felt wretched about it, not least because Libby was at that "very important age of budding womanhood" when a girl needed her mother. For goodness' sake, Elizabeth thought, she hadn't even had time to show Libby how to make piecrust before she'd been kidnapped, but now her little girl was catering for the whole family.

It was yet another reason to hate Theophilus. "How can a father put upon this child of eleven years, the cares of a woman—the care of a babe, in addition to the care of a family, while she needs to attend school!" she railed. Libby had been a first-ranked scholar in her studies before Elizabeth had been committed, but it seemed highly unlikely she'd be able to maintain her schooling now that she had to keep house.

Elizabeth tried harder to get out, appealing to anyone who might listen to let her live alone as an independent woman—"Is there not room enough in this wide world for me to live separate from him?" she would beg—but every appeal was blocked. This meant the stage was set for a showdown when Theophilus had arrived at the asylum in 1861. "When I visited her," he said crossly, "she utterly refused to speak to me in the three days I stayed."

But Elizabeth was adamant: "I have done no wrong, and he has done nothing but wrong." She insisted that "he is answerable for our family troubles." She would not act the hypocrite by bestowing pleasantries on "a being whom my whole nature *abhors*," and neither would she be so foolish as to let him have any further power over her. "I can protect myself—thank you," she announced sharply. "I have a body of my own, and a head of my own, and a heart of my own, and a will of my own, and I do not consent to share this capital with [him] again... I have sense enough to keep out of the fire, and old Packard's hands, too."

It almost amused her to see how shocked Theophilus was at the intensity of her emotion. "Yes, husband," she wrote with bitter cheer. "You now find that I have hating faculties as well as loving."

A woman's heart was deep inside—and Theophilus was only now discovering that he was completely out of his depth.

Reflecting on the visit, McFarland shook his head sadly and pressed his pen to the paper.

"Everything in her whole nature of that kind is so perfectly callous," he informed her husband in April 1862, "that it is most painful to witness...she shows rather the malignity of the fiend, than any natural sentiment ever before seen in woman."

And nothing McFarland did seemed able to persuade this recalcitrant woman to change. After Theophilus's visit, the doctor had appealed to her, saying, "Mrs. Packard, do you think it would be considered as natural, for a true woman to meet one who had been a lover and a husband, after one year's separation, even if he had abused her, without one gush of affection?"

Yet she'd insisted it *was* natural to behave as she did; to *offer* affection "would be an insane act in me."

There, they would have to disagree.

Theophilus's visit had stirred her up, McFarland remembered. That may have been because her husband had remarked to another patient—in a comment that ultimately got back to Elizabeth—"I never saw children so attached to a mother, as Mrs. Packard's are to her—I cannot by any means wean them from her."

Oh, when she'd heard this, Elizabeth's heart had *soared*. *Not* forgotten. *Still* loved. What a precious treasure from her jewels, glimmering with light and love. It had inspired her to try to get a letter back to them. Yet Elizabeth had known too well by then that to write via the usual routes would be useless. McFarland's censorship still ran as a tight ship, and no watery words could break that solid hull.

No words on *paper* at least.

Working in the sewing room one day that past June, she'd carefully selected some bleached cotton and begun embroidering some underwaists to send to Libby. Yet the embroidery was merely a deceptive distraction; using her nubby pencil, she wrote a long letter on the underside of the plain cotton. Her plan was that a fellow patient who lived close to Manteno and was soon to be discharged could take the clothing to her child as a gift. No one would be any the wiser until her daughter opened up her underwear and read her mother's secret words.

But McFarland, suspicious, had discovered the plot, searching the discharged patient and sending the scribbled-upon underwaists for washing, so the message was erased.

McFarland shifted in his seat. His attempts to isolate Elizabeth hadn't been entirely successful, to his chagrin. The previous summer, she'd kicked up an enormous fuss when she'd somehow gotten a message from her Manteno friends that they'd raised a fund for her legal defense; a "new effort for her removal" from the asylum had begun. McFarland consistently received letters from Elizabeth's friends, such as the Blessings and the Hasletts, and from the husband of her cousin, Angeline Field, which protested her sanity and demanded her release. He firmly shut them all down, writing that "Mrs. Packard"—whose insanity, it may be remembered, had been recorded as merely "slight" when she'd first arrived—"has become a dangerous patient; it will not be safe to have her in any private family!" When David Field had respectfully inquired on what evidence this claim was based, McFarland had reportedly replied, "I do not deem it my duty to answer impertinent questions!"

Happily, at least, the new legal effort had come to nothing, as McFarland had always known it would. Her friends had wanted to obtain a writ of habeas corpus, but that specifically ruled on cases of *unlawful* confinement. As Theophilus had explained to his wife on the very day he'd brought her to the asylum, the "forms of law" were all complied with in her case. No legal remedy could reach her, because everything Theophilus had done *was* within the law.

Trapped within the iron cage of McFarland's censorship, Elizabeth did not know the outcome nor even the specifics of her friends' attempts to free her. By April 1862, however, she'd simply had to accept that she had "no hope of deliverance through this source." The only thing that had changed in the wake of her friends' efforts was that although McFarland had by then relaxed his rules to allow her to exercise outside, *she* refused to go. The renewed attempt to gain her freedom had centered her mind painfully upon the fact that she was a prisoner, held against her will. She appreciated now that the beauty of the asylum grounds was mere window dressing, there to make a passerby "think this place is a heaven, instead of a hell." In her view, if she walked out of the hospital to ride or walk in those deceptively pleasant grounds and then walked back in again on her own two legs, she was complicit in her incarceration. Therefore, she'd told the doctor, "I shall never return again a voluntary prisoner to my cell." She'd added, "You, Dr. McFarland, have *might* to put me there, but no *right*."

Consequently, since the summer of 1861, she had left the ward for no reason: not to pray and not to sew and not to walk. It was the only physical way she felt she could protest her imprisonment. Though it was extremely hard never to leave the ward—never to feel the changing weather on her face or to taste even the false freedom of fresh air—she wrote, "I never regretted taking this step, as...having entered my protest, I was thus exonerated from all responsibility, as in any way a willing accomplice in the conspiracy."

No one could accuse her of going along with it or of not fighting back.

Although all legal remedies for Elizabeth's release were denied her, Dr. McFarland, in private, sometimes wished that were *not* the case. While most patients retained as long as Elizabeth soon began to show a "slow constitutional deterioration"—"The cheek loses its fresh tints," McFarland recorded in his notes, "the eye its expression"—he'd noticed that Elizabeth's eyes seemed only to burn brighter. Other patients wrote of the "sedative influence" of an asylum, describing the "power and authority...it would be useless to resist," but Elizabeth just didn't get those memos. The longer she stayed, the stronger she seemed to become.

She certainly felt that way. "What is very singular in my case [is that] this woman-crushing machinery works the wrong way," she wrote joyfully. "The true woman shines brighter and brighter under the process, instead of being strangled."

So over the past sixteen months, she'd begun to break the rules more flagrantly. The secret journal had been only the start of it. Now appreciating McFarland's censorship, she established an "Underground Express" to try to get mail out illicitly, relying on the daring assistance of attendants whose identities she never revealed for their own protection; it was expressly forbidden for staff to "assist in any clandestine correspondence." Unfortunately, the Underground Express was a one-way system: Elizabeth received no replies, meaning she could never quite be certain her own letters had made it safely out.

She also chose overtly to help other patients, ghostwriting letters to their families as she articulately begged for their release. "Where woman is suffering injustice," Elizabeth declared, "I claim a right to speak in her defence."

Yet to McFarland's frustration, if he tried to clamp down on her activities—not all of which he knew about—his efforts to curtail her managed only to arouse sympathy for her from the staff. Before she'd taken her stand never to leave the ward, she'd once gone shopping with an attendant in Jacksonville, where she'd immediately broken the rules by buying herself some paper. Hearing of this, McFarland had searched her things and confiscated not only the paper but also the bits of pencil and old pens that he found. Yet the doctor's heavy-handed actions "aroused the just indignation of the house"; consequently, his staff secretly snuck Elizabeth her stationery supplies.

Her hidden journal grew longer and more detailed by the day.

Even McFarland's own wife seemed to side with her. Forty-four-year-old Annie McFarland, who in Elizabeth's opinion "possessed more than a usual share of common-sense and common humanity," had assumed the matronship of the hospital in late 1861. It was not unusual at the time for doctors' wives to take such roles, given their family lived in-house. Having assumed this more powerful position, Annie deliberately sent comfort to Elizabeth in the form of little treats—a tumbler of jelly, a sugarloaf, an exotic taste of pineapple—and arranged for her to have a private room. In addition, other former privileges, such as the use of her trunk and private pitcher and mirror, were restored. Meanwhile, Celia Coe, the attendant who'd taught Elizabeth how to dance, had become the asylum's cook and with Mrs. McFarland's blessing brought Elizabeth "apples in abundance, and raisins, and oranges, and prunes." It was a feast not only for the stomach but the heart.

It gave Elizabeth the appetite to challenge the doctor directly. "You know I am not, by any means, the only one you have thus taken in here, to please a cruel husband," she would say. "It is fatally dangerous to live in Illinois, under such laws, as thus expose the personal liberty of married women. This [is a] kind of married slavery...and it *must* be abolished."

McFarland could have rolled his eyes at that: *here she goes...* He categorized Elizabeth's political ambition as "a mission upon which [she is] driven with all the impelling power of insanity." Even as he watched, she would become more excited.

"With resolution, firm and determined," she would say, "I am resolved to fight my way through all obstacles to victory—to the *emancipation of married woman.*" She would stand up straight, all five feet one inch of her, as she said proudly, "To be God's chosen instrument to raise woman to her proper position is a glorious office."

Yet to McFarland, her every word and action seemed a classic case of moral insanity. All this talk of reform and a divine mission...*honestly.* He saw not faith but fantasy.

Nevertheless, he watched her carefully—and with caution. Because she truly had "a disposition wantonly inclined to create the greatest amount of trouble possible to others," and these empowering speeches she regularly gave had a habit of leaving all she spoke to rapt.

If only she wasn't so persuasive. So damn compelling. She had, McFarland thought, a "more than lawyer-like ability to put her own case." And in the only court available to her—*his* asylum—she seemed to have the jury of all its residents, sane and insane alike, in the palm of her hand.

Sitting at his desk in April 1862, McFarland paused in his letter to Mr. Packard. Then he pressed his pen to the paper and wrote with weary stoicism, "She gives us a world of trouble, which I only put up with under the thought, that she would give you, if possible, still more."

Elizabeth was staying put. The only question was: What would she do next?

CHAPTER 23

When the breakfast bell rang at 5:30 a.m., Elizabeth Packard arose in her private room on Eighth. She knelt on her carpet to pray, drank a tumbler of rainwater, and quickly washed her head, hands, and face before dressing. A lot had changed since Mrs. McFarland had become matron, and one such thing was that the wards now all had bathtubs. This had not only relieved Elizabeth from her relentless cycle of sponge-bathing her fellow patients—because the attendants could now more easily wash them and did—but it had also changed her own daily routine. She saved her bathing until midmorning now, when she would take a cold bath for its refreshing qualities.

After breakfast, Elizabeth invited the ladies on her ward to join her for prayer circle. McFarland hadn't stopped her when she'd defiantly started these up again—because he could see for himself he had no need for concern. They weren't the collegiate, disruptive sessions of old; to Elizabeth's disappointment, only one or two patients came and, sometimes, none at all.

That was because the makeup of her fellow patients was now completely different, at McFarland's especial direction. The year before, the new west wing for women had finally opened, and the doctor had shaken up the classification of the female wards, changing which women lived where. On Eighth, the most dangerous patients, such as Mrs. Triplet, had been removed, while others, more capable, had been dispersed to other wards. Things had taken a while to settle, but Elizabeth now resided on Eighth Ward with "a quiet class of maniacs."

To her, it still seemed something of a misnomer ("Quiet maniacs!" she wrote. "Quiet thunder! Quiet hurricane!"), but even she conceded that with the violent patients removed, her circumstances had improved. In addition, her private room was a pleasant one that looked out toward the front of the asylum; it even had a view of distant Illinois College. She had her own easy chair and footstool, a dressing table and her own trunk of clothes, on which she'd embroidered a pretty cushioned seat.

Yet these furnishings, while attractive, were merely an external benefit: a gilding of the bars on her cage, which could not conceal the unforgiving steel beneath. Elizabeth wasn't fooled by them. She saw too often the harsh reality of asylum life, which no comfy cushioned seat could soften.

In a way, the removal of the violent patients had only made that harsh reality clearer. Now surrounded by solely quiet patients, there should have been no need, in her view, for the attendants to rebuke or punish them. Yes, they were sick and could sometimes be difficult, but insanity wasn't a crime. However, over the past year or so, the abuse the patients suffered had increased rather than decreased.

It was now the worst it had ever been.

A change in personnel was partly to blame. The Tenney sisters no longer looked after Elizabeth, and the replacements McFarland had managed to hire were neither as sensitive nor as kind. So bad had the situation become, in fact, that Mrs. Hosmer had left the hospital. The directress later said she'd worked at the asylum "until my soul has been pierced with cries for mercy." When she could bear it no longer, she left.

She was lucky to have had the choice. There was no such option for Elizabeth.

Instead, she was forced to watch as her fellow patients were beaten, choked, and punished daily. Elizabeth being Elizabeth, she tried to intervene. On one occasion, she'd heard loud screams coming from a dormitory and rushed in to find a beefy attendant wrestling an already injured woman into a straitjacket.

"What is the matter?" Elizabeth had asked. "Why are you putting the straight-jacket on that woman?"

But the attendant hadn't answered. Instead, she'd shouted, "Mrs. Packard, leave this room!"

Elizabeth had obediently taken a single step back over the threshold, but she kept on asking questions. As long as she had a tongue in her head, she always would. "Why are you putting her into a straight-jacket? What has she done?"

At this impertinence, the attendant reacted strongly. She "came at me in a great rage," Elizabeth recalled, shocked at the direct attack. The woman grabbed Elizabeth brutally by the arm, dragged her along the corridor, and locked her in her own room so she could interfere no more.

But such attempts to control her only increased Elizabeth's desire to help. "I am becoming so extremely sensitive to wrong and abuse, that I cannot, nor shall not, witness it without interference, even if you put me into fetters for it," she announced. When she'd first arrived at the asylum, Elizabeth's shocked focus had been on those women she thought sane who'd been committed to the asylum and those travesties of justice. Now, however, she found her eyes opened to another field of battle—that of protecting the genuinely mentally ill from abuse.

She was repeatedly threatened for speaking up for others—"Mrs.

Packard, stop your voice! If you speak another word…I shall put a straight jacket on *you*!" Meanwhile, her compassionate act of sneaking a bit of johnnycake to a patient who'd been "locked in her room to suffer starvation" saw Elizabeth herself threatened with solitary confinement, the words "accompanied with the flourish of a butcher knife over my head." Given solitary was described by one doctor as "calculated to convert the sane man into a lunatic," she had a lucky escape.

On that occasion at least.

The violence had grown worse and worse. One day, Elizabeth had been forced to bind a patient's throat after an attendant had gouged a hole in it with her fingernail while choking her. She'd used a piece of her own linen for the dressing, carefully binding the wound of the young woman, who was only twenty. So stunned had she been by the violence that afterward, Elizabeth kept the cloth "red with the blood of this innocent girl, as proof of this kind of abuse in Jacksonville Insane Asylum."

It joined with her diary as a record of all she was witnessing.

Yet choking and beating, straitjackets and solitary, turned out to be child's play for some of the new attendants. Ironically, the very worst abuse the patients suffered was that enabled by the arrival of the bathtubs. These should have been such a source of comfort to the women: a chance to be clean, to be human, to wash away the pain and hurt. Instead, they became a place of torture.

Elizabeth's room was located opposite the bathroom. As both rooms had ventilation windows above their doors, it was easy for her to hear what was going on. One late night, she heard a new patient being inducted into the regime. When the patient wouldn't stop screaming, frightened by the asylum and the screen room she'd already been sent to, she was dragged into the bathroom.

Elizabeth heard as her body was manhandled into a tub filled with cold water. Yet the shock of this unexpected bath "so convulsed her in agony that she now screamed louder than before."

But not for much longer. As Elizabeth listened, body stiff beneath her sheets, the woman's voice bubbled into blank silence...as she was held beneath the water. Nothing was more terrible than that silence, Elizabeth thought, after all the words and screams that had come before. The woman's voice—and life?—were cut off abruptly, blanketed into oblivion by a veil of water that kept her mute. Elizabeth held her breath, only hoping the woman had been able to do the same before her head was plunged below the surface. She listened intently, hoping to catch some small sound that would let her know the woman was still alive.

After a period of silence, the water sloshed, and Elizabeth heard a "piteous" cry for "help! help!" Clearly chastened, now broken in—just as had been designed—the woman promised meekly in a rasping voice that she would not scream anymore.

Yet her words cut no ice with the attendants. They were determined to make it "a thorough 'subduing,'" to ensure this new patient knew who was in charge. And so, repeatedly, as Elizabeth listened in the opposite room, she heard the terrifying tandem sounds of water and no words, water and no words, as the woman was held beneath the water once again. And again. And again.

And again.

Nor was that the only way to skin a cat. Sometimes the bathwater was hot, so it scalded. Sometimes the water was poured in a pail above their heads. Sometimes the patients were placed in the bath with "their hands and feet tied, and if they resisted, a straitjacket was placed upon them." The attendants would then hold their heads beneath the water "as long as it was safe to leave them." They'd be lifted out only to "cast the water from their stomach," then the same process would continue "as long as the patient was thought able to bear it."

This punishment was administered when the women disobeyed attendants' orders to stop talking, when patients modestly wished to bathe alone, and when patients spoke back. Even the attendants themselves conceded they used it "for a slight offense," such as "silly behaviour and laughing."

Elizabeth had tried appealing to McFarland about this torture. He seemed all too conscious of it, later writing of the "convenience" of the bathtub as "an engine of petty tyranny." "How many scores is it made to pay off; how many sly grudges to satisfy?" he asked rhetorically, describing it as "a Damocles' sword, always suspended" above his patients' heads. Yet he defended his staff, saying the use of physical force was "but to confess to the fallibility of human nature."

It was a view in keeping with those of his peers. "The best attendants are but human," another superintendent wrote, "and their mercy endureth not forever, and after much long-suffering the time is too apt to come when they are perfectly convinced that a little wholesome chastisement is just the thing required."

McFarland claimed he was powerless to stop such abuse. "No humane regulations, and no possible vigilance are proof against such perversions," he wrote easily. "The temptation to the abuse is ever at hand, and its discovery well-nigh an impossibility."

But it would not have been an impossibility to discover *if he'd actually listened when his patients complained.* Yet he was deaf to all their protests. Because they were supposedly insane, he simply assumed they were "never to be believed" and denied them "the right of petition and investigation" when they made allegations of abuse. "The remark is perfectly safe," the doctor wrote, "and not in the slightest intended as a professional vindication, that in more than nine cases in the ten, where persons lately resident abound in complaints…it will be found that there are in the individual, still existing evidences of mental unsoundness."

McFarland was not the only psychiatrist to think so. One of his peers announced that "in proportion as a patient's recovery is complete and permanent, he will be likely to speak well of the institution; [but] if he still has any degree of insanity about him…he is more likely to speak ill." It was a catch-22: the patients were mad if they complained, sane if they didn't. McFarland's asylum rules stated clearly that attendants should only be made subjects of official complaint "on the best assured grounds."

A patient's allegation of abuse was never that.

"Giving vent to indignation in insane asylums is like trying to breathe under water," Elizabeth wrote, eerily invoking the scenes of worst abuse. The women had been put "where [their] word is not regarded," so any complaints were treated as "mere phantoms of a diseased imagination." Another patient wrote, "It is of no use to appeal to [Dr. McFarland], while a patient there. He seems to act as though patients had no rights… We feel that we are a despised class, to be tolerated, rather than be respected."

Elizabeth put it even more simply. "What is an insane person's testimony worth?" she asked, then succinctly answered: "Nothing."

That was why, in June 1862, she'd decided to call in reinforcements. Mrs. Hosmer may have departed, but Elizabeth had other friends in the hospital upon whom she could call, and she'd concluded it was time she did.

That day, Elizabeth continued her daily routine as normal so that no one would be alarmed by any deviation from her schedule. Her day was so monotonous she could have set her gold watch by it. "The record of one day is a record of all," she wrote, and each day was as painfully long as the last. "You cannot imagine how long time seems here," she wrote. "One day seems like a month elsewhere."

On this day, however, she was likely glad of the routine, because it potentially provided cover for her other plans. So as normal, she took her bath at 11:00 a.m. and then commenced her gymnastics. Taking a deep breath, she stretched her arms above her head to take a firm grip on the ledge of her door frame. She hung there, legs dangling, stretching out her abdomen and arms, for as long as her muscles could last.

She performed these exercises twice a day: a range of calisthenic movements she'd developed to tone her body. She felt she needed to stay well for what she called "this field of action." Like a soldier training for a war, Elizabeth was ruthless in her pursuit of fitness, knowing a tough fight lay ahead.

But in truth, the fight was already here. And on this day in particular, Elizabeth Packard was determined to wage war.

Because it was June 18, 1862: exactly two years to the day since she'd been brought to the asylum.

She planned to mark the anniversary with rebellion indeed.

CHAPTER 24

She pressed her pen into the paper. "An appeal in behalf of the insane," she wrote. "Mr. Editor: It is our desire to lay before the public, through your paper, the manner the insane are treated in Jacksonville, Insane Asylum, Illinois."

She was writing to the editor of the *New York Independent*, a leading liberal newspaper. She was writing to the Chicago papers too. But crucially, *she was not writing under her own name*.

This appeal purportedly came from the pen of Mrs. Celia and Mr. James Coe, the asylum's married cooks, who'd long been Elizabeth's allies. It's not clear exactly whose idea it was, although Elizabeth later said she wrote it "at the request of Mr. and Mrs. Coe." They felt their own knowledge of the goings-on at the asylum was a "burden" on their consciences. Knowing of Elizabeth's eloquence, they'd asked her to help alleviate that burden as they blew the whistle on the abuse to the press.

With their liberty to work and walk all over the hospital, the Coes had seen far more abuse than even Elizabeth knew of. They were particularly concerned about a woman who worked on Fifth Ward, Lizzie Bonner, a "large, coarse, stout Irish woman, stronger than most men," whose face had "an expression of stern repulsiveness" and who possessed a ferocious temper. She kept her bunch of heavy keys on a cord around her waist—but this merely gave her easy access to a ready weapon.

"I have many times, seen even tardy or reluctant obedience punished with fearful severity," one patient later wrote of being "cared for" by Bonner. "I have seen the attendant strike and unmercifully beat on the [patient's] head…with a bunch of heavy keys…leaving their faces blackened and scarred for weeks. I have seen her twist their arms and cross them behind the back, tie them in that position, and then beat the victim till the other patients would cry out, begging her to desist… It was not rarely and occasionally, but hourly and continually, that these brutalities occurred."

Lizzie Bonner punishing patients

In the appeal to the newspaper editors, Celia Coe asked Elizabeth to include one particular instance of abuse she had witnessed.

> [I] found Miss Bonah [*sic*]…using the patient's head as a hammer, and her hair as a handle, and thus pounding the floor with it with the greatest violence…
>
> "I will have satisfaction upon her!" she [said], "for

she has got the devil in her and I mean to *beat* it out
of her."

She then persisted in putting on the [strait]jacket...
and then she...dragged her across the hall to the bars,
where she tied [her up]. And thus, having entirely dis-
armed her, she seized hold of the hair of her head again,
and commenced beating the back of her head against
the sharp corners of the bars—each blow inflicting a
deep gash into her head, so that every blow was followed with *blood* splashing in every direction, besmearing the floor and walls, and our own persons, and a pie
I had in my hand, with human gore.

It was vivid and brutal—but nothing less than the truth.

Elizabeth kept writing. She wrote of patients' arms that had been
dislocated by attendants; of dying patients given no comfort, their cruel
treatment likely hastening their end; of patients choked "until their faces
were black, and their tongues would hang out of their mouths"; of the
bathtub torture she herself had heard.

"It is the *artful* Dr.'s policy to pronounce all the witnesses of these
scenes of cruelty, as *insane* persons, hoping that this, his *lying* testimony
in many cases, may *outlaw* them as witnesses against him, and his doings
through his own attendants," she wrote in the Coes' voice, hoping that
this appeal from asylum staff would be treated differently.

She and the Coes concluded their document, "May this mute appeal
be responded to by the friends of humanity." The Coes said they held
themselves "in readiness to answer any inquiries which may be addressed
to us."

Yet the post office address they gave was not in Jacksonville but

Winchester, Virginia. They were going out in a blaze of glory, but they were nevertheless still going out. Like Mrs. Hosmer before them—who'd written upon her departure to both renowned mental-health campaigner Dorothea Dix and to the head of the asylum's trustees to report the abuse she'd witnessed—the Coes had found the courage to speak publicly only as their term of employment came to an end.

Despite their imminent departure, Elizabeth bound up the handwritten appeal with careful fingers and a hopeful heart, having weighed each word to ensure it was as impactful as could be. Going to the press was a new development, but she anticipated it would make a difference. She'd threatened McFarland in her reproof with this very idea—"How would you like to see such facts as these in print?"—and now, thanks to the Coes' decision to go public, that day was closer than ever before. Surely, once the abuse was brought before the public, outrage would be such that an investigation would commence. And when those investigators threw open the heavy doors of the asylum and came crowding into the wards, they would find Elizabeth Packard, with her bloodstained rags and her scribbled scraps of diary, ready to tell all.

She thought often of what Mrs. Grere, one of her fellow patients, said: "If Dr. McFarland won't do right, can't he be made to do right by some power?"

Elizabeth hoped the power of the press was what they'd all been waiting for.

CHAPTER 25

That summer of 1862, the papers were full of news about only one thing: the U.S. Civil War. It had been raging for fifteen months, defying the early predictions of those who'd thought it would be over in ninety days. As one citizen put it, "Madness was upon the people." The lunatics were now not only held within the asylum but roaming free outside.

When the national conflict had first begun, Elizabeth had had no access to the newspapers. She'd felt "entombed alive," desperate to be kept informed "of what is transpiring now in my country, at this eventful crisis"—a desire that had only intensified when, in autumn 1861, Toffy had visited once more and brought word that Isaac wanted to join the Union army. Her second son had sought his mother's advice, and Elizabeth, admiring his principled wish to fight for his beliefs, had answered via Toffy, "You may join the army if your father is willing, but if he forbids you, you must not disobey him by going."

But whether Theophilus had said yes or no, Elizabeth did not know—just as she no longer knew if her Isaac was alive or dead.

Come July 1862, one month after she'd written the Coes' appeal, Elizabeth was once again permitted access to the newspapers, some of them snuck to her by sympathetic attendants. She pored over them, searching amid the names of dead soldiers for that of her own dear son. Eyes skating over syllables with desperate speed, her heart darkly gladdened when they formed the name of some other mother's son and not Isaac's.

She sought, too, for any sign of the Coes' appeal, but nothing did she find. Perhaps, with the Civil War dominating the headlines, the newspaper editors had simply decided that now was not the time to protect the mentally ill.

Elizabeth had no choice but to *make* now the time. In truth, she hoped that the war might prove a watershed for all those suffering, given that in taking the country into conflict, President Lincoln had "dared to espouse the cause of the oppressed." Elizabeth, impassioned, wrote of the president, "God holds him up, amid the crash of worlds." She was fully supportive of Lincoln's position. To Elizabeth, slavery was a "giant evil" and she endorsed any means of ending it. In her heart, she hoped the end of the oppression of women might be next in line.

Indeed, as she read the war news, she saw a parallel with her own story. "The North may as well give up this civil war," she thought, "and succumb to the South, and put their necks again under the yoke of the slave oligarchy, as [a woman] yield up her contest for 'spiritual freedom' by returning to her husband and establishing the marriage union as it was. It is not union *as it was* that I am fighting for—but it is union *as it ought to be*—a union based on 'equal rights'—on justice." She concluded fiercely, "For as is my *fate*, so will be that of *my country*."

Like the soldiers on the outside, she fought with everything she had.

But unlike those soldiers, Elizabeth could no longer call for reinforcements. By summer 1862, her allies on the staff such as Mrs. Hosmer and the Coes had left, while her interactions with her fellow patients were deliberately restricted, too, as McFarland followed a self-described policy of separating any women he felt were friends for "mischievous purposes." As he considered *all* Elizabeth's alliances to be thus, he took action whenever she forged a new friendship. He believed the enforced separation was necessary to prevent what he now dramatically termed her "evil influences" from contaminating others.

As a result, Elizabeth could take comfort only from her writing, from her scraps of handwritten notes that she called "my treasures." They were, quite simply, the only things of value she had left in the world. She kept them safely hidden, the pieces of her ever-expanding journal now secreted within a false lining in her band box, tucked beneath the bottom board of her satchel, and concealed in her trunk. She carefully pinned those pieces inside various items of her wardrobe so it looked as though she was simply making alterations to her clothes. Though McFarland searched her things from time to time, he never found those scraps of journal.

At the time, she had a lot to record, for in July 1862, her attendants were the worst yet. Miss Smith was in charge of Eighth Ward now, a quick-tempered, cruel woman assisted by Mary Bailey, who used "insulting and abusive language" with the patients.

Yet Elizabeth was painfully aware that recording abuses alone meant little. What good was deciding to "lift up my voice like a trumpet" if her words could not escape the soundproofed walls of the asylum? She could play the most powerful melodies, but they became meaningless if no one heard.

Elizabeth was an independent woman; to "get out of the mire, all alone" was her professed strategy for escaping her situation. But in light of the failure of all her efforts to date, she simply could not continue down that path.

The problem was that there was really only one person who had the power to assist her—only one man who held her "temporal destiny entirely at his disposal." Yet as she herself wrote on July 12, 1862, "My reason and judgment, and my most bitter experience assures me there is no hope for me in this quarter."

"Still," she went on, "there is no man left but [one] to turn to."

No man but McFarland.

In the outside world, the war raged on without a final, decisive battle to end it. "If something is not done soon," Abraham Lincoln wrote that year, "the bottom will be out of the whole affair." Just like her president, Elizabeth recognized that she needed to take firm action. "I do hope I shan't be so slow about my work as [General] McClellan is about his!" she wrote of the hesitant man at the helm of the Union Army. "I think it's well to be cautious, but I don't think it is best to be too much afraid of treading on the devil's heels, lest he get the start of us."

Dr. McFarland had truly seemed a devil to date. But Elizabeth's theology taught her "that in every human being there is a soul to be redeemed. That in every rock there is a well." Despite the doctor's cruel discounting of the patients' complaints and his repeated betrayal of her, Elizabeth's faith nevertheless encouraged her to try to see some good in him. Though she hated his sins, she thought she should not hate the sinner. "Could I not therefore hope," she mused, "that the drill of long and patient perseverance might yet reach this spring in this Doctor's flinty heart?"

An idea began slowly to coalesce in her mind: an idea for a new campaign. Elizabeth wondered, could she possibly "fan this embryo" goodness she was sure McFarland must have buried inside him into a burning flame? A flame that would burn down all the barriers in her way.

Up until that point, Elizabeth had tried ignoring the doctor and castigating him, yet neither approach had effected any change in the man. A new tack was needed, one that focused more on accord than animosity. "I intend to be fearless," she wrote, "in using every possible means that love can devise to save him; for it is to me a far more desirable object to save him than to destroy him." In offering an olive branch of newly fired friendship, she hoped to lead the doctor down the path *she* wished him to take.

She thought of how she had so easily managed to get the humane staff on her side so they happily broke rules for her benefit. She thought of how, after she'd first arrived on Eighth Ward, the Misses Tenney had so quickly joined her to improve the patients' conditions, themselves scrubbing away at walls and women. Elizabeth had done it all with just one thing: the power of her tongue. She could be incredibly persuasive when she wanted. She could change people's minds. McFarland wasn't the only person with power to "modify [their] thoughts." Two could play at the game of behavior modification, and Elizabeth decided that she had to give it a try.

Because she needed the doctor to change his mind about her. She needed to get out of the asylum. For her children, who were growing up too fast without her. For her sanity, before the daily trauma she was witness to completely shattered her spirit; already that July, despondent after the failure of the Coes' appeal, she was feeling "exceedingly sorrowful." But perhaps most of all, she needed to get out for her "beloved sisters in bonds," whose abuse she'd been so busy recording all this while but for whom she could do nothing more from behind these thick brick walls.

But McFarland could recommend her release—if he so wished. He could set her free to fulfill her mission—if only she could convince him to "dare to do right" and become her "protector, instead of [my] husband's abettor."

If she played this right, could she transform the doctor from an enemy to an ally after all?

Some people later misconstrued her turning back to McFarland in the way she did. They saw it as an act of weakness, perhaps even a kind of syndrome, in which her captor became someone with whom she hoped to forge a positive relationship.

Yet others—including women trapped in similar power dynamics—saw it very differently. "I find it very natural that you would adapt yourself to identify with your kidnapper," one said. "It's about empathy, communication... [That] is *not* a syndrome.

"It is a survival strategy."

And Elizabeth, like the Union itself, was determined to survive.

CHAPTER 26

Elizabeth held her breath as she waited for the doctor's response.

It was early September 1862. For the past few months, in keeping with her new campaign, she'd been patiently encouraging McFarland to be a kinder, more sympathetic superintendent—and she felt it was working. For example, Elizabeth had long petitioned for Miss Smith to be removed from Eighth Ward; while McFarland hadn't fired her, Smith had recently been moved to the ironing room. The situation on Eighth had improved considerably, as eighteen-year-old Adelaide Tryon, "a reasonable and kind attendant," replaced her.

Elizabeth felt her plan was slowly succeeding. A "new spirit seemed to hold [the doctor]," she observed. "I began to hope he was treating the patients on the principles of justice."

So in September 1862, she'd seized her chance. She'd asked McFarland if she could meet the hospital's trustees at their quarterly meeting, due to be held at the hospital in a few days' time, to present her case for her release to them—in person. To her astonishment, the doctor gave his "free and full consent."

He even gave her the paper she needed to prepare her presentation.

What a major deal it was for him to have said yes cannot be understated. Elizabeth had tried desperately to gain proper access to the trustees over the past two years and three months but had always failed. On one occasion, she'd managed to pass them a petition as they walked through her hall; on another, she'd crushed a secret letter into the hand of one of their wives. Both documents had protested her sanity and appealed for her immediate release; both had been resolutely ignored. The problem, naturally, was the entrenched perspective that all who had been committed to the asylum *must* be insane, and that any patient who protested her sanity was sicker than the rest.

"It is a rule sanctioned by the highest authorities," wrote one of McFarland's peers, "that a patient cannot be considered as recovered who does not fully and willingly recognize the fact that he has been insane."

The trustees were the sole overseers of McFarland's work. There were six of them. Every ninety days, they held a quarterly meeting at which they inspected the hospital and determined, with McFarland's input, which patients were ready for release.

Yet their so-called inspections could not be called thorough. More time was spent admiring the workings of the handsome farm outside and partaking in the dining pleasures of the doctors' table than in visiting the wards. Even then, they inspected only those "it was thought proper to visit," with staff briefed days beforehand so that "every [strait] jacket [could be] taken off, every strap hid, and the patients compelled by fair or foul means, generally the latter, to...act as decorous as their poor crazy brains will allow."

The trustees themselves conceded that they knew "no more than any other citizens" about the workings of the wards. As it was, they'd been advised to treat any complaints they received with skepticism. The received wisdom of the age, as dispensed by leading superintendents, was that patients were "liars by nature" and had a "tendency to have a hostile attitude toward the institution." The Jacksonville board therefore attached "but small importance" to patients' claims, due to the "unreliability of this species of testimony." They preferred to take McFarland at his word; trustees at another asylum openly admitted their superintendent "had great influence on their report." Trustees were not only "intimate friends" of the doctors "but relatives by affinity."

Despite their evident bias, Elizabeth was still thrilled to have been given a chance to appeal to them in person. Until now, McFarland's had been the sole hand in which her fate had been held. But the trustees had the power to release patients too. She just needed to be given a chance—a chance that was now, finally, within her grasp—and they would surely see the truth: that she was "imprisoned...simply for claiming a right to my own thoughts."

On September 4, she dressed carefully, picking out one of her nicer outfits from the handful in her trunk. As it was a hot day, she chose a white lawn dress with sky-blue trimmings and finished the look with a "tasteful head-dress" placed atop her neatly coiffed hair. As she settled it into place, she was struck by a "queenlike feeling"—a sentiment only emphasized as McFarland, in a smart summer suit, appeared at her door to escort her to the meeting.

He offered her his arm. Elizabeth took it. It was a half-remembered action from a long-ago time. To take a gentleman's arm and be attentively ushered through those long corridors felt like the life of a woman from a completely different era. She was certainly not the same woman inside. Yet as her heels clicked on the hard floor, suppressed memories came flooding to the fore, and she felt irrepressible impatience and hard-won hope bubbling up. "I have been like the soldier so long trying to keep down an inordinate desire to see my children once more," she thought, "that the least probability of the closing of the campaign almost fills me with ecstasy."

Just imagine, if she was successful... She would board a train to Manteno. She would walk through her own front door. She would sweep her children into her arms, exclaim at the weight of three-year-old Arthur, tousle nine-year-old Georgie's hair, embrace her twelve-year-old Libby, who might now seem more woman than girl. She could almost feel them in her arms already, smell that special scent of their hair. She tightened her grip on McFarland's arm, *hoping*. Yet the September sunshine streaming in through the barred windows seemed only to encourage her. A brighter day *was* coming. And Elizabeth was determined to do everything in her power to seize it.

The doctor ushered her into the meeting room where the trustees were waiting. They were a party of professional gentlemen, and Elizabeth felt "the sanctimonious gravity of this august body" as she entered on the doctor's arm.

There was another man present too: her husband. Theophilus had been invited to give his own views on his wife's case; he'd already delivered his presentation.

Elizabeth almost entirely ignored him. Her eyes bright, she focused only on the trustees sitting around the table as McFarland introduced her. The chairman was William Brown.

"Mrs. Packard," began Mr. Brown as she settled into her seat beside him, "we have heard Mr. Packard's statement, and the Doctor said you would like to speak for yourself. We will allow you ten minutes for that purpose."

Elizabeth took out her gold watch and placed it next to her papers. Then she commenced reading, "in a quiet, calm, clear tone of voice," the document she hoped would secure her freedom. McFarland had reviewed it the day before and given her permission to proceed. She focused at first on the religious differences between herself and her husband, explaining why she preferred not to teach Theophilus's favored doctrines to her children.

As she spoke, the trustees made an attentive audience, their silence so profound that Elizabeth "could almost hear the joyous pulsations of my own heart." She blasted her husband for not allowing her, "a spiritual woman—a 'temple of the Holy Ghost,'" to follow her own beliefs. She concluded by thanking McFarland for the privilege of speaking.

And then, from beneath the pile of papers that McFarland had approved, she withdrew some torn-out pages from the Bible, which were also covered with her handwriting.

"I now ask you," she said directly to the board, "if you have any objection to my exposing the sophistry of my husband's demand upon this institution to perpetuate my imprisonment, on the plea that the good of his children requires it?… It is written upon the leaves of our ward Bible, which some patient tore out and left upon my table; and, as I have no paper, I appropriated them to this use."

Unknown to McFarland, Elizabeth had prepared a *second* appeal— one he hadn't yet seen.

The whole room seemed to hold its breath. It was "so still," Elizabeth recalled, "I could have heard a clock tick."

Yet the trustees responded affirmatively, even though she'd already overrun her time. Elizabeth took a deep breath and commenced reading her *real* defense.

"You say, Dr. McFarland," she began, staring at the doctor sitting opposite her,

> that my abuses must be balanced by my children's abuses… [But] can my husband be justified in his abuse of me, by the plea that the good of the children

demands it?... Has he a right to assume that my teachings are ruinous in their tendency? Have I not a right to teach them what I *think* is God's revealed will, or must I yield my own convictions of truth and duty to his dictation? Would he be willing that I should assume this authority over him, or, in other words, is he doing by me as he would wish to be done by?

How would you, Dr. McFarland, receive such a demand from me, as you seem bound to respect from him? Suppose I should say to you: Dr. McFarland, I conscientiously believe that the legitimate tendency of [Mr. Packard's] creed is to make hard, unfeeling, bigoted, cruel, tyrannical characters, like himself; and now, out of regard to these helpless children's interests, I demand that you take Mr. Packard from his position in society, his family, and from all his constitutional rights as an American citizen, and imprison him in this Insane Asylum, for life, or until I can remove his children out of the reach of his influence. How would you receive such a demand from me, the mother of the children, whose interest in their welfare is as deep, at least, as their father's? Would you not regard it as an *insane* request, and would you not employ it as a *proof* that I was a fit subject for the Insane Asylum?

Now how can you listen to this same demand, involving precisely the same principle, and urge it as a reason to justify you in perpetuating *my* imprisonment, based on the same principle?

McFarland and Theophilus listened in stony silence. "They did not deny or contradict one statement I made," Elizabeth later said, "although so very hard upon them both."

She spoke for nearly fifty minutes. Yet as soon as she stopped, the trustees asked to hear more. She rejoiced to have the chance to deepen her case as she revealed "the darkest parts of this foul conspiracy, wherein Mr. Packard and their Superintendent were the chief actors." Fearlessly, she "exposed their wicked plot against my personal liberty and my rights."

Yet she also acknowledged that—unlike her husband—McFarland *had* allowed her spiritual liberty, at least, while in the asylum.

"So long as he did that for me," she said softly, "I should trust him, though he slay me."

Theophilus was then asked to leave the room; McFarland followed. Elizabeth was left alone with the board. They all, perhaps to her surprise and certainly to her relief, "manifested a kindly interest in my welfare," so much so that she was convinced of their "benevolent intentions." The earlier sanctimonious gravity of the meeting dissipated until good spirits hummed throughout the room. Elizabeth relaxed enough to confide that her husband claimed she was insane because she was "not as [she] used to be," but she said she knew full well that the change in her behavior came only from "a natural growth of intellect."

"My husband placing me in an Insane Asylum to be cured of this natural development," she said boldly to the trustees, "was like his placing me under the treatment of a cancer doctor to have my breasts removed, insisting upon it that my breasts were cancers, since they were not there when I was a girl!"

A "roar of laughter" met these remarks, "accompanied by the expressions, 'That's good!' ''Tis apt!' 'To the point!'"

Eventually, she was asked to step outside while they made their decision. She waited in the adjoining matron's room as McFarland returned to give them his opinion. She did not mention if Theophilus was there.

She waited for perhaps ten minutes. She could not hear what the men were saying as they adjudicated her future, but she did, from time to time, "hear roars and roars of laughter." She took that as a good sign; her own heart leapt a little higher.

She wondered what Theophilus's presentation before she'd entered the room had entailed. In fact, unlike Elizabeth's all-too-brief preparation, he'd been putting in groundwork for weeks beforehand, having known her case was coming up for review. He'd therefore brought with him signed affidavits from various members of his church attesting to Elizabeth's insanity, even though they hadn't seen her for over two years. Theophilus's entire presentation "protested against her discharge."

But whether the trustees—and McFarland—would take his side or hers remained to be seen.

Finally, Elizabeth heard the door open and turned expectantly. McFarland explained that an unusual decision had been made. As was recorded in the trustees' record book, "In relation to the case of Mrs. Packard...it is *Ordered*, That the final consideration of the case be postponed until the next meeting of the Board" in December.

Hearing this news, Elizabeth let her breath out in a rush. She nodded briskly, understanding. She'd explained to the trustees that she point-blank refused to return to her husband for fear of the legal power he still held over her; she wanted to be released only on her *own* responsibility. She surmised that this unprecedented request had led to this postponement, while they figured out how such a discharge might be done.

The deferment was undeniably good news. They had not dismissed her appeal out of hand. They had not opted for unlimited imprisonment. Though the postponement made no firm pronouncement either way on her future, it still gave her something priceless: a deadline to count down toward.

And it was only three months away.

Elizabeth knew the quarterly meetings were always held at the start of the relevant month. As she remembered this, her breath caught tightly in her chest.

She could be home in time for Christmas.

Oh, how grateful she was. How pleased. She thought fondly of the trustees, "I regard them all, now, as my friends... I do think they now see the injustice they have done me, to keep me so long unjustly imprisoned." She concluded, "I expect they will discharge me at their next meeting." Her heart skipped just to think of it.

With the decision postponed, there was nothing more for Elizabeth to do that day. At this juncture, with her return to the ward imminent, McFarland would usually have summoned a burly porter to transport her to her room, knowing she would refuse to walk there. But on this day, he chose not to.

He carried her back to the ward himself.

Elizabeth felt herself pressed against the doctor's chest, her body secure within his firm embrace. "I am satisfied and gratified, both," she thought. "There could not have been a more complete victory. My case is now known to [the trustees] to be one of persecution for opinion's sake. Not one of them believes me to be an insane person. *They know I am not.*"

She was carried carefully through the long corridors. McFarland's arms around her felt like a hammock and not a cage: something to support her, not confine her. Because it was true, what she'd said in the meeting: she *did* now trust him. And she knew from what had happened that day—from *all* that had happened, which had not yet been revealed—that she was right to.

Outside the asylum, the moon waited patiently below the blue summer sky to rise. Yet despite its invisibility, its influence could still be felt. It tugged at the world with inconspicuous strings, which were no less powerful for that.

"The tide has turned," Elizabeth thought triumphantly. And she knew, in her heart, that she had been the one to turn it.

Because downstairs in the room, before the board, McFarland himself had recommended her release. "I proposed to the Board of Trustees," he revealed, "to discharge her."

After all this time, Elizabeth and her doctor were finally fighting on the same side in their age-old war.

CHAPTER 27

The following day, the doctor called on her for a debriefing.

"Well, Mrs. Packard," he said, "the Trustees thought you hit the mark."

Elizabeth smiled. "I see none of them believe me to be an insane person, after all."

McFarland, like her, was all grin. "Mrs. Packard," he said, "won't you give me a copy of that document [you wrote]?" He seemed very keen on the idea. "What is worth hearing once, is worth hearing twice."

Elizabeth felt gratified by his interest. "Yes, Doctor," she said, enthused. "I am perfectly willing to do so, for I should like you to have a copy, and the Trustees also."

It seemed to Elizabeth that these two documents she'd prepared for the trustees might now take the place of those precious Bible class essays she'd long ago lost. What better way to assert her sanity and prove to all that she was kept here under false allegations? She wanted them to have as wide a circulation as possible.

"But," she said to the doctor, seeing a flaw in the plan, "it is very irksome for me to copy [by hand]. How would it do to get a few printed in handbill form?"

The doctor nodded his agreement and even offered to pay the printer.

"You re-write it," he encouraged, "and add to it...and I will see that it is done." He added with special emphasis, "Write what you please!"

"Well done, for Dr. McFarland!" Elizabeth cried, bowled over by his support. "If you are going to give me such liberty, I shall feel that I am a free woman; and this may possibly prepare the way for my liberation."

Because it seemed to her that these documents could prove paper stepping-stones: "to liberty—to darling children—to home—to life itself."

True to his word, McFarland provided her with a plentiful supply of paper. Elizabeth got straight to work that same day, preparing her documents for the press.

But a strange thing happened as she sat in her private room, with a huge stack of paper piled up beside her and her mind at last given the freedom to express itself howsoever it wished.

Elizabeth had a vision. A writer's vision. A vision of a big book.

Because how could these few pages do true justice to her story and all the implications it had for her country? "It seems to me self-evident," she later wrote, "that this Great Drama is a woman's rights struggle. From the commencement...this one insane idea seems to be the back-bone of the rebellion: A married woman has no rights which her husband is bound to respect." She needed to set out that she *did* have a right to think for herself and explain her own personal background, yet she also wanted her story to highlight that *she was not the only one this had happened to.* Her "hitherto prison-bound intellect" rapidly expanded as her pen lay idle in her hand, thoughts and theories and missions taking flight. "The subject so opened before my mind," she later said, "that I could not find a stopping place."

She needed to lay out the reality of a woman's position in soci-ety, to create a clarion call to arms for change, to present the necessity of immediate legislative change that would protect and not persecute women. "Reason taught me to be quiet while in the asylum," she wrote, "[but] my pen shall rage if my tongue didn't." She'd kept her tongue from raging on purpose "so that my pen might [now] have a chance to."

The time had come, she decided, to let her feelings flow in ebony ink. She would stain the paper with her sentiments, silent and invisible no more. She would make her mark. This book would be a building block to a better world. It would allow *her* to stand upon it, yes, but she would also pull up womankind with her: a podium full of perfervid princesses, all ready to claim their prize.

Equality. Respect. Revolution.

Because who would speak for the howling women she heard at night *if not her*? Who would speak for the women of Seventh Ward, stitched into silence by the rules of the world, *if not her*? Who would speak for those women who'd tied their tongues even before reaching the asylum, cowed into submission by the very threat, *if not her*?

She sat up straighter, her mind not contained by the four walls of her ward but flying high over the land of the free, soaring past corn-filled fields and ascending over vistas of desert and mountain and trees. She saw a vision of a better future rising clearly on the horizon. She took a firmer hold of her pen. And she smiled, for she could not help "the most delightful feeling of satisfaction with my undertaking."

Pressing pen to paper, Elizabeth Packard began to write.

The words poured out of her. When she told McFarland of her vision, he beamed and urged her, "Write it out just as you see it." He gave directions to the attendants to let no one disturb her. Hour after hour, she wrote in her room: the door closed, her mind open, her pen leaping from topic to topic with all the unfettered freedom of the wild rabbits in the grounds outside.

She wrote in a stream of consciousness. One moment, she was appealing directly to President Lincoln to emancipate women; the next, she was taking literary revenge on those who'd signed the petition against her in Manteno, warning that "their names will be left to blacken the pages of American history." The scattershot approach allowed her readers—as she herself acknowledged—"only a 'glance and a glimpse' of the passing panorama of thoughts chasing after each other in seemingly promiscuous, wild confusion." Yet the pent-up expression of almost twenty-five years was pouring out now and could not be dammed. Since she'd been sent to Eighth Ward, Elizabeth had had to make do with mere scraps on which to record her thoughts. An unlimited supply of paper, with unlimited freedom to write what she wished, almost literally went to her head. She was like a woman starved, cramming mouthful after mouthful to her hungry lips, little caring if what she tasted was savory or sweet, often eating both at the same time, simply desperate to sate her appetite and eat, eat, eat.

The hours blurred into days, and still Elizabeth kept writing. The book was by turns allegorical, biographical, reformative, informative— not "an ordinary book in the common style of language" and not logical either; "I leave the logic for my readers to supply." She wrote on religion, on politics, on periods and lactating breasts. It was the story of her own life—a woman's life—and she wrote with a brazen honesty that seemed fearlessly to defy the buttoned-up culture of her time.

Naturally, she wrote of what she'd seen in the asylum and appealed to politicians for succor: "Now we are knocking at your philanthropic heart to let us out of prison by unbolting the doors of your insane asylums and letting the oppressed go free. Free! Free!! Free!!! Oh! How I do want to be free!!"

Yet through her book, Elizabeth felt she had *found* the key to her liberty, and not simply because it provided opportunity for self-defense. "I intend to write a book that the people can't help buying," she wrote assertively. With sales of such a book beneath her belt, she would finally be financially independent. "When I get my [book] printed, and circulated and sold," she wrote, "[I will] pocket the money it brings me—to pay my fare home to Manteno."

Tellingly, the most detailed, loving, descriptive passages in the book were those about her children. Through her pen, she conjured them: her babies, playing on the floor of her cell, reaching out to her with chubby arms, their faces like photographs, so vivid she could almost touch them. She luxuriated in the most intimate details—colors, fabrics, sights, and smells—almost torturing herself to remember with exquisite intensity.

At times, those memories formed into fantasies, her grief at their actual absence overflowing into ink: "Home! Sweet home! When! Oh, when shall I meet my loved ones there?... Oh, will the welcome tidings ever reach my asylum ears! 'Mrs. Packard...your loved ones are waiting to give you a welcome home!'"

But with every page she finished, every chapter she wrote, she felt that welcome home was one step nearer. "Mrs. Packard often sighs," she wrote, "but it is not the sigh of grief—as when I parted from [Theophilus], because he would be so cruel as to separate me from my children. No, 'tis the sigh of inspiration...invigorating me with new life and hope of getting my book soon done, so I can get to see them once more, this side the grave." She wanted to "see my baby again before he entirely forgets me." By now, she had set her heart "upon keeping the next Christmas festival at home with my children."

By September 17, 1862, just a week and a half after she'd started writing, she had completed what would prove to be a quarter of the book. She called it her "great battery" and drew phenomenal strength from it. "My book is me," she wrote simply. It was her "pet," her "pride," "a transcript of my own individuality upon paper."

That September night, she was awoken at about midnight by the singing of two patients in the lower halls. "They seemed to be in different wards," she noted, "but answering to each other like an echo." And though Elizabeth could not have known it—though perhaps the spiritualists in the asylum did—America was in mourning that night. That day, the deadliest one-day battle in all U.S. military history had taken place in Antietam. Nearly five thousand men had died, with another twenty thousand wounded.

Elizabeth listened quietly to the mournful song of her fellow prisoners: a requiem that coursed its way along the corridors of the hospital, stealing through the shadows. They sang the same thing, over and over, just "one breath of music in length." They sang for themselves. They sang for the soldiers.

And Elizabeth identified with both.

"I tell you," she wrote, "women are of some use, too. You have no idea what brave soldiers and generals we women do make."

Tomorrow, she would rise again and ride out into battle.

CHAPTER 28

As though Lincoln himself was privy to the writing on the Eighth Ward, on September 22, 1862, he issued a preliminary Emancipation Proclamation. As of January 1, 1863, all slaves in the seceded states "shall be then, thenceforward, and forever free." Elizabeth, who had been calling on the president in her manuscript to do this very thing, quickly amended her literary position to push him further. "If you continue to let our husbands oppress us," she appealed to Lincoln directly in her book, "and free the black slaves as you seem determined to do, I shall call you partial in your element of justice... We [women] do want equal rights at least with a colored man."

Her book—which she now named *The Great Drama*—was overtly political. She called for better rights for women, the mentally ill, African Americans, and Native Americans. And speaking from her own experience, drawing on the horrors she'd witnessed inside the asylum, she appealed for changes in existing legislation.

"The [insane] patient has no protection from inhuman abuse in the practical application of these laws," she explained. She wanted humanity in Illinois to "be allowed to think their own thoughts, and speak their own words, without being imprisoned for it," but such a thing was currently impossible. Building on her original vision for her journal, she wrote, "I intend to do my part to report [asylum life] as it is [for] the patient, for God has qualified me for this purpose, and sent me here to do it."

Yet she saved her most impassioned appeals for women's rights. "Does our government think," she wrote, "that because it protects the inalienable rights of the men of America, it protects the rights of *all*? Are not women citizens? Are not their rights worth protecting?... I want it so fixed that any woman can run—*on her own feet*—right straight to [the government] for help [via the law] the minute she wants help, to get out of the power of a cruel husband. You must credit her testimony as well as you do his... It isn't fair for you to credit their lies—and discredit our truths!"

She called male politicians "mean, and ungenerous, and unmanly" not to have already protected women through the law. "We don't want fragments of liberty anymore," she asserted, "nor fragments of men to disburse it, neither. We want the full-grown 'Goddess of Liberty'"—and if took a revolution to achieve it, so be it. She dismissively called the all-male government a "half affair" and instead urged, "Put woman into your ballot-boxes, your legislatures, your senates, your Congress, your president's chair."

She had no truck with the idea that women couldn't do it. "Never let a man now say that a woman is a dependent being. For she is not," she wrote. "She has fought her own battle. She has gained her own victory. She has declared her own independence. She is free!" And she appealed directly to women, too, urging her readers to rise up and assert themselves: "Dare to do it!"

As the book continued to come together, McFarland came to her room to see how she was getting along. To Elizabeth's surprise, he allowed her to write exactly what she wished—even about himself. "He trusts me," she thought. "He seems as unconcerned about what I write, as if his character didn't depend upon the opinions of one of his patients." She took his position as an incredible act of faith in her.

It inspired a faith in him in return. She'd already been encouraged by the improvements she'd seen at the asylum that summer, with the abuse reduced on Eighth Ward and Miss Smith banished. The doctor's recommendation of her release had softened her suspicion of him still further. Elizabeth's game plan from the very beginning had been to persuade McFarland to release her, and this was now a course of action he fully supported. With his permission to write her book in complete freedom granted as well, Elizabeth felt forgiveness flooding through her. All her life, her "great want" had been to be permitted spiritual liberty—to have no one fettering her mind or pen—and *McFarland had just gifted her with what she'd always wished for*. "No man on this continent," she wrote in wonder, "had ever allowed me [that] but himself."

So despite everything that had passed between them, once again she began to conceive of McFarland as a "noble protector," sent to her by God in her time of need. Earlier that year, she had hoped to fan his embryo goodness into a flame: now, she warmed her hands on his fire, convinced by his actions she could trust him.

With the doctor forgiven, she welcomed his visits to her writing room, the sound of his footsteps in the corridor outside now causing her heart to "bound with joy." It was "the inauguration of a new and delightful era of my prison life." She would write and write, he would read and read, and together they would discuss the book. He would bring "such a tranquilizing influence with him," she remembered, "and leave me in such a state of elevation and kind of spiritual illumination, that he seemed, as it were, to father the book… I could appropriate his thoughts and assimilate them so easily with my own deductions, that the two forces of a male and female mind formed one perfect mental union."

It was a sensual experience Elizabeth recognized as such. "This I do say," she wrote frankly, "that if there is such a thing as the male and female intellect being mated, it seemed as if I had found my intellectual mate in Dr. McFarland." Their "magnetisms mingled and blended in this book," yet it was an entirely intellectual endeavor, and "not one word of sentimental love ever passed between us."

It wasn't about love. Not love like that at least. This was about Elizabeth's love for expression, for her own mind, her own views. To be allowed to think and speak and write for herself was such a novel position that she was almost like a virgin, exploring for the very first time her own intellectual prowess—and having her own mind blown by the power she possessed inside *herself.* That McFarland had facilitated it made her cast him in the same light she felt shining out from inside her, but the light was hers alone. Nevertheless, she said, "He is the first and only man I had then ever met, to whom my whole soul could pay the homage of my womanly nature. I not only could, but I did love and reverence him… I simply loved him because I could not help it." As Elizabeth could not separate the man from the muse, the doctor and her divine inspiration became as one in her mind.

She didn't seem to see the irony that had he not treated her as he had in the past, she would have had no need to write her book at all. McFarland was both captor and liberator, but Elizabeth was seemingly dazzled by the dual roles. "As he had had almost omnipotent power to crush," she wrote, "so he now had this same power to raise and defend me. The power of the husband, the power of the Trustees, the power of the State, had all been delegated to him. As to the power of protection, he was all in all to me now; and the spiritual freedom granted to me by this power was almost God-like."

She worshipped at his altar, faith filling her.

Toward the end of September, when Elizabeth had perhaps two-thirds of the book down, she received word that she had a visitor. She went to meet them, head likely still full of her own writing, little knowing who awaited her.

It was not one visitor but two.

Not one son but a second also.

Toffy *and* Isaac had come to see her.

How to embrace two boys at once? She clasped them to her, her movements like music: an old refrain that came from eighteen years of mothering. The feel of Isaac's young man's body, the sight of his dear sweet face, were all the more precious after her worries for him in the war. Their stories came spilling out: Theophilus had said no to the army, but Isaac and Toffy had both been working as sutlers—merchants who followed the soldiers to sell provisions—and had been attached to the Nebraska Regiment, which had spent much of the past year on garrison duty. They'd both been saving their hard-earned wages for the expensive fare to Jacksonville, and now, at last, both were here.

They were delighted to find her in such good spirits.

"I don't see, mother," Isaac said cheerfully, "as you have changed at all… I was afraid I should find you gray-headed, and withered in looks, after passing through such hard times. But I am so glad to see you just as bright and happy as ever."

Elizabeth confided in them the reason for her current happiness—her authorship of her book—but swore them to secrecy, fearing Theophilus might somehow put a stop to it should he discover her mission. Elizabeth knew it was critical for her to publish her book as soon as possible. Only then would the government realize the truth and change the laws to protect her.

Only then would she be safe.

Her boys had some very interesting news to share of their father: he was no longer a minister in Manteno. He'd resigned in July 1862. Elizabeth was intrigued to know more, but her sons, having been away traveling, could not enlighten her. Isaac told her Theophilus now lived on charity.

They'd last heard from their father following the trustees' meeting. When Elizabeth heard what her husband had said, she felt jubilant. He'd written, Toffy said, "that he feared he should not be able to keep his mother much longer in the Asylum."

Everyone was expecting her to be released in December.

In the meantime, she had to keep writing to ensure that freedom came forth. She bid her boys a fond farewell, assuring them all would soon be well.

Just a few weeks later, around October 16, 1862, Elizabeth dashed off a final punctuation point. She laid down her pen. Beside her, her completed book lay in a box on the floor. Twenty-five hundred pages were covered with her beautiful script. Twenty-five hundred pages she'd written in just six weeks, with only a Bible and a dictionary for stimulus—and her own memory and imagination.

The Great Drama was finished.

The great drama had only just begun.

CHAPTER 29

It spread throughout the hospital like a virus, a contagion, or a scattering of wind-blown seeds that sprouted where they fell.

The power of Elizabeth Packard and her words.

She did not keep her book to herself. Books were for reading. For reading aloud to her fellow patients on Eighth Ward. For entrusting to rebel attendants, who snuck copied pages to Seventh, where Maria Chapman hid them between the tick mattresses of her bed, reading them in snatched moments when the doctors' backs were turned. Books were for sharing with the spirit mediums, who claimed to know the contents of Elizabeth's epic before she'd even finished writing.

It wasn't long before *The Great Drama* became "a very common topic of remark in almost every ward in the house." And it caused a "universal sensation."

"I will die fighting, before I will not think as I please... No one has any...right to call me insane, because I do not think as they do," Elizabeth wrote passionately, and each line was a vow that every reading patient echoed. "My thoughts are as much my own right as my eyes; and I would as soon part with one as the other."

Reading her words, the patients dared to imagine a world in which they might be free "to sit under their own vine and fig tree, with none to molest or make them any more afraid of being called insane, simply because they dare to be true to themselves." Her words made them sit up a little straighter, walk a little taller through the long corridors. They held their heads just that little bit higher.

Elizabeth, by all accounts, had an "extraordinary power of conviction." Her words simply leapt off the page, whether she herself was present to read them aloud or not. And so her book became a cipher for herself: an early hologram that could transport itself into every cell, every hall, every ward of the hospital. She talked her way into the mind of every reader. She spoke to them in the early morning and in the dead of night. She whispered along with them as the patients huddled in small groups to discuss it. She roused the patients to believe in a better world—a world in which they were *all* worth something.

The patients felt as though they were waking from a deep sleep as her words sank in. And these waking soldiers began to take their first few steps on a long march to freedom. Soon, a handful of them laid down their labor in protest at the lack of payment, enough that McFarland had cause to comment on it in his biennial report. He lamented that he was struggling on this issue where overseas institutions did not; getting his defense in early, he claimed foreign patients tended to work without complaint, having "a mental level, too low to be reached by the incentives of hope and ambition."

They were also untouched by the words of Elizabeth Packard.

"The wonderful power she possessed over the minds of others drew all to her ample heart," raved one reader, blown away by the book. Another predicted that *The Great Drama* would be "read in our Legislative Halls and in Congress." One spiritualist even confidently prophesied of Elizabeth, "She'll be in Congress one of these days, helping to make new laws!"

The author scoffed at that. "If this prophetess had said that *woman's influence* would be felt in Congress, giving character to laws," she said, "I might have said I believed she had uttered a true prophecy."

Elizabeth's biggest fan was perhaps a patient named Sophia Olsen, a relative newcomer to Eighth Ward, who'd been at the asylum since August. Like Elizabeth, she'd started out on Seventh, but after she'd protested various rules, she'd been promptly moved to Eighth to make her conform.

But there she'd encountered Elizabeth. "When she came into our hall," Sophia said of her first impressions of the author, "every hand, eye and heart were open to receive her. I never saw one...who, after having seen her once, did not wish to see her again."

Sophia felt exactly that way. The two women hit it off instantly. They were actually incredibly similar: both came from New England (Sophia from New Hampshire), both had received excellent educations at first-class academies, both loved to write (Sophia, too, was keeping a secret journal), and both focused on alleviating the sufferings of others in favor of dwelling on their own. Both were forty-five, and both had been committed by their husbands, with Sophia having possibly suffered domestic abuse prior to her banishment.

Yet similar as they were, Sophia had never met anyone like Elizabeth. "Such an ardent lover of truth, so heroic a defender of principles...I never saw outside these walls," she said in wonder. She thought *The Great Drama* and its author truly phenomenal: "The boldness with which she reproved tyranny, and the thrilling eloquence with which she defended the cause of suffering humanity!"

Elizabeth was equally enamored of Sophia. It was rare on Eighth to find such an intelligent and sympathetic woman. She described Sophia's companionship as "the brightest oasis of my prison life." She soon lent her new friend clothes from her trunk and even gave her a "beautifully wrought white chain" as a "pledge of her attachment," which Sophia wore every day. It was not long before they were intimate acquaintances, their conversations in the dining hall a great solace to them both.

"This inestimable woman," Sophia said, "has proved to me the brightest star that ever shone around my dark path of life."

The problem was, Elizabeth was a star to too many people. And like the special starlight in the nativity, where she shone, others followed. Her influence was truly like that of a celestial body: invisible yet all-powerful, pulling at the hearts and minds of patients like gravity.

McFarland, of course, could not be blind to the impact she was having.

One day, after a meal was over, Sophia and Elizabeth arose from the dining table and went their separate ways; they resided in different halls that were both within Eighth Ward. Sophia suddenly thought of something else she wished to say, so she followed her friend a step or two, even though her own hall did not lie that way.

She felt herself pulled back violently as an attendant grabbed hold of her dress.

"You needn't speak to Mrs. Packard," the attendant said crossly.

She gave no other explanation for her actions, despite Sophia demanding one.

The curtailments on Mrs. Packard's new friend soon grew tighter. Sophia protested, for she refused to abide by the unwritten rule that patients must accept indignities, yet that was just prelude to punishment. Mrs. McFarland looked her up and down one day when she begged to be allowed to send a letter to her family, remarking coolly, "If Mrs. Olsen gets troublesome, I think she will have to go down."

Sophia was soon reported as an "unmanageable, mischief-making patient." Before October was out, she was banished to Fifth Ward, and Elizabeth lost yet another friend.

She watched her go with deep concern. Sophia's unwarranted transfer to Fifth didn't fit with her impression of McFarland as a changed man. Mrs. McFarland's cruelty, too, was something new, though Elizabeth had noted that the closer she'd become to Annie's husband, the colder the relationship between herself and the doctor's wife. "She don't like me these days at all," she noted. No special jellies arrived in her private room on Eighth anymore, and she overheard Annie making fun of her book. "She calls me the 'poor deluded woman' now," Elizabeth said sadly.

Her thoughts stumbled on a rock as she considered why, but she did not peer too closely at it. "I wonder," she thought, "if my 'delusion' lies in my improved opinion respecting her husband's character?"

But she couldn't let herself dwell on that; she had a book to publish. At McFarland's suggestion, she'd divided it into parts, as publishing the whole would have been enough to "frighten away the practical reader." She'd decided to focus on getting only the first volume into print. McFarland had reportedly agreed to fund its publication, just as he'd previously offered to pay for the handbill printing of the documents she'd written for the trustees; the book had now supplanted these in her priorities. As the fall days passed by outside, Elizabeth focused all her time on neatly copying out the first volume, preparing it for the press.

Her hope was that it could be printed prior to the trustees' meeting in early December. That way, it could both support her appeal for immediate release *and* allow her instantly to draw financial and legal aid from it once free. McFarland, as her sole patron, became ever more important to her.

Which was why Elizabeth was so troubled when Sophia finally

returned from Fifth Ward in mid-November 1862. Oh, what an unexpected joy to walk into the dining hall that dinnertime to see her! The women stared at each other, eyes dancing even as their arms stayed still. Both longed to embrace and "weep with joy" at their reunion, but they both knew better than to show it. The surveillance of their attendants was too close; they would only be punished.

They must have been more successful at concealing their emotions than even they had thought, for to their mutual surprise, they were granted permission to sit next to each other. Side by side, they "conversed in very low tones, so as not to disturb anyone, and not to permit our attendant to suspect that we were particularly happy."

In whispered words, Sophia shared the trauma of her recent experience. The cold potatoes stuck in Elizabeth's throat as she listened. It seemed Fifth Ward had remained the lowest ward, both figuratively and literally, even after the reclassification of the patients. Located at the bottom of the hospital, it had low ceilings so that "there wasn't quite air space enough for the patients." Some rooms had only half doors, the upper part being made of an open iron frame so attendants could keep their eyes on the violent patients within. Books were banned. Sophia described it as a "charnel house of human woe."

Elizabeth now learned that her campaign to clean up Eighth Ward had not touched Fifth. Sophia had spent the past twenty days living among "very filthy women," whose garments were "indecently torn," and who sat with puddles of "unfragrant water on the floor under their feet." Yet she'd been even more appalled to realize that the women's faces were often blackened not with dirt but with bruises, for Fifth Ward was where Lizzie Bonner held sway, and she was as fearsome as ever.

Sophia revealed that Elizabeth "did not see the worst forms of this cruelty." Elizabeth had by now made such an impression on the staff and was so well known for speaking out against injustice that they often self-censored their behavior in her presence, anticipating her impassioned rebuke. But on Fifth, Sophia had seen patients abused every single day.

"Sometimes it appeared that I must turn away, that I could not endure to see human beings thus abused," she remembered sadly. "But the next thought was one of self-accusation for being thus tender to my own feelings. 'If these sufferers can bear to feel it, I can and will bear to see it...for if I do not see these things, I cannot testify that I did. So I will even look on,'" she'd vowed.

When she'd finally summoned the courage to threaten to tell McFarland of the abuse—perhaps drawing on memories of Mrs. Packard to take that leap—Miss Bonner had merely responded, "Dr. McFarland knows all about it...he tells me to manage the patients here by my own judgment, and I intend to do as he tells me. So you can mind your own business."

To Sophia's chagrin, even now that she had returned to Eighth Ward, she was still not free of Lizzie Bonner. As Sophia and Elizabeth sat side by side in the dining hall, Miss Bonner paced the length of the table behind them, the heavy keys that she hung around her waist jangling menacingly with every step. It was the first time Elizabeth had had direct contact with her. But Sophia was not the only Fifth Ward patient to have been moved upstairs: she was accompanied by thirteen others, including Mrs. Triplet, Elizabeth's former dining partner. That was perhaps why Miss Bonner had transferred with them. She kept a close eye on the patients as they obediently lifted their food to their mouths or, in Mrs. Triplet's case, spat it at the nearest bystander.

Elizabeth listened in shock to her friend's vivid account. She thought of her secret journal, on which she'd barely drawn to write *The Great Drama*. McFarland had seemed so penitent, and it was not her way to expose a reformed man. "Repentance or exposure," she'd told him when she'd delivered her reproof in November 1860. He'd had a choice, and she'd thought he'd chosen the former.

But perhaps he hadn't.

Secretly, unknown to the doctor, Elizabeth began to conceive of a second book, in which she would expose him and his specific cruelty to patients, for although *The Great Drama* recounted some of the dire treatment she'd witnessed, it did not hold McFarland to account. Yet still, she held it in reserve. As long as he kept his word to help her, she did not think she would ever need to use it.

But the portents were not promising. Shortly after Sophia's return to the ward, it was Elizabeth's turn to be segregated. An official proclamation announced the following:

> All intercourse between Mrs. Packard and the inmates of the west division of the Eighth ward [where Sophia lived], must be prohibited except under strict guard of an attendant! Mrs. Packard must not be allowed to go into the hall, except when accompanied by an attendant. She is to hold no more prayer meetings, lend no more books, and those she has lent must be immediately returned.

The "universal sensation" had caused far too many waves. The normal service of separating Elizabeth from those over whom she held influence had emphatically resumed.

But it was far too late. The book had already done its damage—or wrought its magic, depending on which way one looked at it. The proclamation was met with a mixture of voluble swear words and "silent hisses of execration" from the patients. Sophia wept "bitter tears...knowing that now my life was to be deprived of almost its only earthly solace."

But Elizabeth bore the new rules stoically, locked within her fortress of self-composure. If McFarland wanted to separate her from her friends, so be it. She would accept it; she was used to it by now. And she would be permanently separated from them before too long anyway: living on the other side of the fence. She chose silently to endure it, biting her tongue for just a few weeks more, doing nothing that could jeopardize her release in December.

But the army she had raised was bolder. "We all felt," said Sophia, "that we had been drawn into a regular civil war with the Institution!"

It was a war in which fire was fought with fire. The rebellious patients found themselves placed under the severest restrictions yet; Sophia called it a "reign of terror." All outdoor excursions were prohibited and asylum dances canceled: "We were seldom permitted to go out of the house at all." Private conferences between patients were banned, "and all who did not render instant obedience were severely punished." The Eighth Ward halls echoed with the patients' screams and their cries of "Don't kill me, don't kill me!" as Miss Bonner regularly dragged them away for beatings.

Yet the cruel attendant felt free to act with impunity. The Civil War had taken from the hospital "its most valuable employees." Staffing problems were so dire that superintendents nationwide felt they could no longer even discipline abusive staff for fear they would quit. The doctors decided "even an unworthy attendant is better than none." So Lizzie knew she could hit and drown and beat without censure.

The dramatic decline in circumstances sat uneasily with Elizabeth. "I feel that I cannot report [McFarland] as a practical penitent in his treatment of his patients," she wrote in anguish. "I have great reason to fear...that he upholds abuses of his patients as much as ever." Yet now just days away from the trustees' meeting, she shrank from a campaign to get Miss Bonner dismissed, as she'd done with Miss Smith. Given the understaffed asylum, she knew it would be "no use, and I should be only exposing my book to destruction by awakening the doctor's wrath against me."

It was not a risk she could possibly take. That book was her ticket to freedom—and also the best way to help the other patients, as she could expose their abuse once out. No one could hear her scream within these walls.

Yet the book was still not published; there had not been time. Nevertheless, Elizabeth was confident of her release. No matter her other concerns about the doctor, he was still standing by her at least.

He was still recommending that she be discharged from the asylum.

So Elizabeth sat tight, counting down the days to December 3. She rose each morning, dined in the hall—so close to Sophia and yet so very far, the women forbidden to converse. She watched proceedings with her usual observant eye, even though she was prohibited from discussing them with friends.

One day, a thin woman at the table caught her attention. She looked absolutely desperate, but that wasn't an uncommon sight at that time, with all the patients suffering severe sensory deprivation from being kept indoors.

But this patient had been pushed too far. With a clutching hand, she caught a knife in her fist. She raised it to her throat...and slit it.

Blood burst forth in a stream of scarlet, though not enough to make a fatal wound. As Elizabeth watched, nerves shaken by the suicide attempt, the woman was bundled away in a straitjacket to be dumped in solitary.

It was not the only drama. Another patient, "mild and gentle," who'd arrived only a few days before, also made a bid for freedom. It happened outside the ward; she'd been taken to the sewing room to work. There, high above the asylum's gilded-cage grounds, she suddenly spied opportunity in the unbarred window.

She threw herself from it, a flight of floundering skirts and fear... and hit the solid brick basement beneath.

The snap of her neck made a staccato full stop.

Sophia saw these dreadful acts of suicide as "unmistakeable portents that a storm was coming."

The clouds were about to burst.

CHAPTER 30

On the morning of December 3, 1862, the breakfast bell and sunrise came within minutes of each other. Elizabeth rose in tandem with the glowing orb, her hope and expectation burning just as bright. Today, she would be released. Today, she would start her long-awaited journey home to her children: exiting the asylum as a free woman, with the liberty to write and publish as she wished. The truth could be told, laws could be changed, and liberty would thus, eventually, not solely belong to her but also to her sisters.

It was fifteen days before Arthur's fourth birthday, twenty-two until Christmas. Elizabeth let herself dream of that day. What a feast she would be able to cook for her family! Her mouth, so long accustomed to unappetizing asylum fare, almost watered at the thought of her own home cooking. She would fire up her trusty iron stove and busy herself in baking, stirring love into her sauces, the singing of her copper teakettle a serenade to scenes of sweet reunion. What "good talking times" she would have with her children! She likely smiled as she dressed, each garment adding another layer of excitement to this special day.

The trustees' meeting was accompanied by one of their quarterly inspections. Tellingly, although by Sophia's account the "reign of terror" was at its height, the trustees commended in their report "the capacity, intelligence, and kindness, of the attendants." Though McFarland worriedly informed them that the asylum was currently "full to overflowing," with the hospital having reached its "extreme limit in numbers" with 302 patients, the trustees claimed the asylum had never "been in so good a condition as at the present time"—a curious comment given that overcrowding and the wartime understaffing. Yet they had nothing but praise for the "great professional skill and excellent administration of Dr. McFarland...and the order and cleanliness observable in every part of the establishment."

It does not appear that Elizabeth made a second presentation to them. It is possible she shared some extracts from her book. She had to wait all day for their verdict, stuck in her room, probably pacing until her carpet wore thin. Finally, however, she heard the ward door clanking and the blessed sound of McFarland's steady footsteps in the corridor outside.

With a gentlemanly knock upon her door, he entered, bearing news more precious than priceless jewels.

Her release, he announced with gravity befitting of the moment, had been "indefinitely postponed."

Elizabeth must have blinked, shocked. No... No, that wasn't supposed to happen. Even the doctor had said she should go home.

Why could she not have her liberty?

Her happy fantasies, conjured by cemented expectation, crumbled cruelly into ash. The burning hope she'd felt that morning burned itself out. "I never felt so much like despairing of all human help as I do now," she thought desperately. "I feel desolate and forsaken...in this my hour of midnight darkness."

She was blind. No moon. No light. She could see no way forward. Because the trustees, she was convinced, thought her sane. Yet they had "shut their ears to the cry of the oppressed. They have coolly and deliberately dared to perpetuate my imprisonment indefinitely, in open defiance of reason, truth and justice."

But this rational rage came later. That day, she simply realized bleakly, "There is no hope of my ever receiving justice at their hands."

And so she slumped, all fight gone out of her. With it, too, went her icy fortress, so long sustained as a bastion against emotion. The locked tower that she'd kept herself inside, the better to keep her sanity, melted away to nothing. Hope, so long deferred, now "sickened" within her, so that all her former glories became poison in her veins. Thoughts of her children caused agonies, their memories no longer sweet but rancid.

She had no hope she would ever see them again.

"If grief can kill," she thought, "it seems as if I should be killed of overmuch sorrow." Her heart was "broken and crushed from hope of seeing them once more." Her hope had become a too-heavy weight. It should have been something to buoy her, but everything in this world was out of joint. Sane women stayed in asylums. A sure release became indefinite commitment. And hope became a hard, hard rock, dragging her below the water.

She did not fight it. The weight of that water squeezed out through her eyes. Silently, she sobbed before McFarland, little caring anymore what he thought of her tears, whether a cry for home and children might lead to punishment.

She could not be punished any more than she already had.

In vain, she waited for an apology or some kind of explanation. It seems McFarland did not share one with her.

But the trustees did later provide one.

"It is proper to state that this reluctance to discharge the patient, at the thrice repeated request of the Superintendent," they wrote, "arose from the remonstrance of her friends; not the least urgent of whom were her father, brothers, and other relatives [including her husband]." They said further, "In the...retaining of some [patients], the selection is made of those...whose discharge would be most injurious to their families."

They had taken her husband's side.

Eventually, after time had eclipsed itself, until she did not know what was forward or back, Elizabeth's tears dried into the silence surrounding her and the doctor. Though she felt "very much grieved" that McFarland had not managed to arrange the publication of her book in time for the meeting—she felt strongly that if such public evidence of her sanity had been available, the trustees would not have dared keep her—she knew she could not blame him for this calamity.

"You will not leave me, will you?" she asked him.

The doctor responded simply, "No, I will not."

Elizabeth sniffed. "May I go on writing my book?" she asked.

McFarland smiled expansively. "Yes, you may."

She could do nothing but trust him. "My all of earthly hope lies in the decisions of Dr. McFarland." He was, truly, "the God of my earthly destiny" and she "utterly forsaken of all men, except Dr. McFarland." In his promise she could keep writing, she saw a subtext—a promise "not to leave me desolate."

It was something at least. To write was something. To write gave her a voice. To write potentially gave her a chance to help others. And if she died in here—as she now feared she might—then perhaps, in the end, she would become a martyr for woman's rights. "It shall be my dying prayer," she thought to herself, "that some champion for the truth shall dare to publish my posthumous writings as they were penned by me for the world's benefit, so that, being dead, I may yet speak in defense of... the inalienable rights of woman."

She had no idea what was in store for her now. She'd spent the past three months anticipating her release, but now there was just a blank emptiness where before there had been a whole world. "Perhaps I am to die a prisoner in my cell—forgotten—unknowing and unknown," she thought darkly. Perhaps she would end up on the "dead cart" she heard rattling around the hospital at night. She'd long ago learned that patients' corpses were taken away on this. Once encased in a cheap shroud and placed in a rough box, they were laid out under turf dug up with "hasty spade" and buried like "a beast" with no funeral service, in an unmarked grave, the whole operation carried out "in the dead of night by lamplight." How that dismal future haunted her now.

That December, truly, was "the saddest month of the year." Winter infiltrated the asylum in all the ways that somber season can touch a woman's heart. Within its walls, there was a "sense of utter loneliness... utter isolation of spirit." The "daughters of affliction" locked within lived a "dim, shadowy, spectral semblance of life," themselves figures who were barely there, rubbed away by the slow "undermining of every tie that bound us to earthly existence." The cutout dolls had become mere shadow puppets.

They would vanish the moment all light was gone.

Outside the asylum, things were not much better as the Civil War marched mercilessly on. On December 13, 1862, thousands of Union soldiers met their ends at the Battle of Fredericksburg: a poorly planned combat that saw nearly three thousand killed or wounded within the first hour alone. The men fell, it was said, like "grass before the scythe."

Elizabeth felt all her hope cut down too, each spark of it another fallen soldier dying before that unforgiving blade. "Doubt—suspense—uncertainty," she wrote, "is all the nourishment my hope is permitted to receive of ever having justice done me."

In time, December 31, 1862, arrived. The year's end—but not the end she had wanted. Because there was no end: her trial continued. The women of Eighth Ward, summoned by the supper bell, solemnly took their seats. Elizabeth, of course, sat separately from Sophia.

But little was said anyway. "The faces of all," her friend remembered, "silently but eloquently spoke the burning thoughts within."

After supper, all were swiftly remanded to their sleeping quarters, despite the supposedly special nature of the night. It was not special to them; it brought only more suffering.

Elizabeth shut the door of her private room quietly, her despair a constant shadow that brought no comfort from its closeness. "Darkness, cold and silence" were her only companions.

The minutes passed by until "the bell heavily chimed out its last hour, and another year had departed forever."

With it went Elizabeth's final hope for freedom.

PART FOUR

DEAL WITH THE DEVIL?

"We must have perseverance and above all confidence in ourselves. We must believe that we are gifted for something and that this thing must be attained."

—*Marie Curie, 1894*

"She stood in the storm, and when the wind did not blow her way...she adjusted her sails."

—*Elizabeth Edwards, c. 2006*

CHAPTER 31

January 1, 1863, was a date set in stone in history. Lincoln's Emancipation Proclamation went into effect and over three million of the nation's four million slaves were immediately freed.

In the asylum, there was no such salvation. Yet Elizabeth felt a tiny flickering of an idea. Because while *she* could not be freed, her *book* could still be released into the world, and through it perhaps some public outrage might be raised, that such an eloquent woman had been condemned to spend her life behind these bars. "On this book," she concluded, "now hangs all my hopes and prospects for this life." It was her last brainwave—her last "single anchor" beneath her "sinking ship."

But to her bewilderment, McFarland appeared to be dragging his heels on printing the first volume of *The Great Drama* as he'd promised, even as he still encouraged her to write more. "He has given me reason," said Elizabeth darkly, "to think he never intends to [publish it]."

Naturally, she "argued and discussed this matter with the Doctor, and gently urged him to not thus forsake me utterly." She asked no more of him than this one thing: to put one single volume of her book in print. But as the days passed, there was no sign of him relenting. "Vain my logic, vain my entreaties," Elizabeth sighed. It left her feeling ever more desolate: "Nothing but a rayless midnight gloom enshrouded my present and future...I was plunged into the gulf of black despair. Nothing to hope for! Nothing to live for!"

Her surroundings did not help. The "reign of terror" continued on Eighth Ward, the New Year bringing "only a protraction of...the same revolting scenes [which were] daily and hourly repeated; the same restrictions, the same everlasting espionage, the same threats, and disgusting horrors!" The women "all felt ourselves hotly pursued by the enemy."

Appeals to both McFarlands were made in vain. There seemed nothing the patients could do.

But Elizabeth had taught them that there is *always* something. A spirit cannot be killed. And with spirit comes hope. With spirit comes strength. With spirit comes the energy to start the fight for justice.

It seems the worst of the reign of terror took place in Sophia's hall, perhaps because that was where Lizzie Bonner worked. Even though Elizabeth did not reside there, her inspirational example had nevertheless left its mark on the patients, as it had throughout the asylum. The hospital authorities had acted too slowly to separate her from those she influenced. Because her star was still glowing, even if she herself currently felt as though her light was all but burnt out.

The patients in Sophia's hall decided to fight back.

"At every opportunity," Sophia confided, "we banded together in little secret societies." They planned various strategies, devised a hundred plans that were rejected, reworked, and gone over until they felt ready to proceed. They acted only as a last resort, once all other strategies to secure a kinder environment and a restoration of basic privileges had failed. But they were determined not to endure the reign of terror any longer. They were worth more than that. They deserved more than that. And if the doctors wouldn't listen, they would *make* them.

One Sunday—and then for days afterward—the "military activity" began. It was an organized patient protest, almost unheard of at that time. And they had but one mission: sabotage of state property.

Sophia did not participate directly, according to her. One wonders if she made this statement because it was transgressive enough already for her to be a female writer, without adding this secondary insurgency to her catalog of unfeminine behavior. But her fellow patients, working as one, caused hundreds of dollars' worth of damage. Blankets were torn into long narrow strips, skeins of sewing silk and spools of thread "tangled up in inextricable confusion," and glass and crockery were deliberately smashed—cleverly, in time with the blast of the asylum bell or when another patient shrieked in order to avoid detection.

"Looking glasses, goblets and crockery were dashed upon the floor, at different times, on all possible safe occasions," recalled Sophia. "Teaspoons, knives and forks were stealthily taken from the table, and thrown out of the window; clothing and curtains torn and mutilated, doors were smashed, cushions opened, the walls were scratched and strange literature in conspicuous places written there!" She said she felt "little uneasiness" at the widespread destruction, because the emotional devastation wrought by the restrictions was so much worse. These were mere things, after all: far less valuable than hearts and minds.

On one of these defiant days, another patient called her to bear witness to one of their acts of rebellion. As the woman ripped open a collection of pillows, she cast their contents to the air outside.

A winter gale caught them. "The wind was an auxiliary," said Sophia in wonder; it took the women's side. It "so scattered the feathers, like the flakes of a coarse snowstorm, that no outsider could tell from which of all the numerous windows the rejected feathers were cast out."

So they watched with impunity as the wind made those feathers dance: a thousand snow-white birds that were finally flying free. There was something so beautiful about it. They wended where they wanted. As the women watched from behind their barred windows, they only wished they could taste even a touch of the same liberty.

To their delight, the sabotage worked. "Orders were suddenly given," Sophia announced triumphantly, "that walks might again be allowed, company again permitted to visit us, and that in several other particulars more lenity [was] to be shown...a general amnesty ensued...and the mischief at last ceased."

Sitting despairingly in her own hall, waiting for an end that could only ever be endless, Elizabeth perhaps felt inspired by their courageous example. Like a circle in the sand that had neither head nor tail, she had prompted their passion, but now, in turn, it sparked something inside her. Perhaps a deal *could* be struck with the doctor, she reasoned, exactly as the patients in Sophia's hall had done. She felt her only hope now was to publish her book, but without McFarland, she simply could not do it. Toffy had not replied to her letters asking for money, nor had her friends in Manteno. She was entirely in the doctor's hands. And if she could not persuade him to publish, then "blasted reputation and life-long imprisonment" alone awaited her.

With the stakes so high, Elizabeth felt "in a state of desperation." Frantically, she racked her brains for what on earth she could offer McFarland in exchange for his support. She had no money. She had no power. She was already married, which was the only currency a woman in the nineteenth century had.

But this was about her book. Her pet, her pride...her *self*. "This book is dearer to me than my reputation," she realized. "I felt willing, and do still, to lay down my life for my book."

She saw she had only one thing left to offer him.

She could give him her heart. Her heart for her book.

"It is my last—my only hope," she wrote slowly. She regarded the trade "as an act of self-preservation, or a justifiable means of self-defense."

But to save her book, to give it life, it would be worth it.

It was a dark exchange, such as one might find in a fairy tale. But as much as she might have wished it differently, Elizabeth was in dark times and they called for the darkest of acts. So Elizabeth pulled out her paper. Elizabeth picked up her pen. She told herself, after her unhappy marriage, that "my heart had never been appropriated." This was a fresh trophy she could offer to McFarland, red and raw and true. She "willingly offered him a woman's heart of grateful love…as the only prize left me to bestow."

On January 19, 1863, Elizabeth Packard pressed pen to paper and wrote:

Dr. McFarland—

My True Friend… I have never seen a man, before I saw you, to whom my whole womanly nature could instinctively pay homage, as my head, as the husband should be to the wife. To such a one, alone, can I entrust the key with which to unlock the fountain of conjugal love within me, whose depths no mortal has ever yet sounded. This key I entrust to you, Dr. McFarland, with all the trusting confidence of a true woman.

The only response I ask of you now is, to help me carry the heavy pack of lies before the public, which Packard has put upon me to bear so unjustly, as a vindication of my assailed character.

If, before I leave this institution, you issue the first edition of my first volume, however small, if not less than twenty-five copies, on your own risk, trusting simply to my verbal promise to pay you back the whole *amount in less than three months' time after leaving this institution, I shall regard the act on my part as an engagement sealed to be yours alone, until death part us. You can continue to be, as you now are, a husband in a Far-land...until God's Providence brings you near enough to recognize the relation with my bodily senses. I love your spirit...but I must not love your person, so long as that love is justly claimed by another woman—your legal wife...*

I know this is a bold step for me to take, but...if [McFarland] is the true man I take him to be, it won't offend him, or expose my honor or virtue to let him know it... I wish no one, except your own private soul, to know of this act. It must be a sacred, profound secret between us, trusted entirely to your honor...

Yours in the best of bonds,
ELIZABETH

The first-name signature was notable; Elizabeth usually concluded all her correspondence as Mrs. E. P. W. Packard. But to use her married name on such a letter may not have seemed appropriate. What she was offering was herself, stripped of all societal encumbrances. Stripped of everything, in fact. Bare, she presented herself to him.

This is me. This is all I have to give. Do you accept?

Elizabeth believed strongly in an afterlife in heaven, which makes the nature of her offer all the more extraordinary. Because her vow to be forever his was undertaken namely for "our future existence" and *not* for this earthly life, in which they were both already married. She was almost literally signing her soul away, making a deal with a man who might yet prove a devil, in promising to be his for all eternity.

If only he would help.

"I did then, and still do regard this offering as none too costly to lay upon the altar of my personal freedom," she wrote.

What price liberty?

So she let her words stand on the page. She folded over the paper. She'd decided to write as she wanted not one syllable of this offer to be uttered aloud, lest someone overhear and misconstrue her words. She resolved to hand the letter to the doctor the next time he visited her alone in her room.

When he did, she shut the door and handed him the note, asking him to read it there and then.

Perhaps confused, he took it from her and seated himself. Saying nothing, he read the letter through. She had written, "This note must be burned, since an exposure of it might imperil my virtue." Perhaps the knowledge that the letter must be destroyed was why McFarland read it a second time, more closely.

Elizabeth watched him anxiously as his eyes scoured the paper, trying to interpret his expression. So much lay on the line, yet still she could not judge from his inscrutable eyes exactly what he was feeling. It was like when they had first met and he had been a blank canvas.

She tried not to paint pictures now. This moment was far too important.

Unexpectedly, McFarland stood up. And then, "without uttering one syllable"—exactly the nonverbal exchange she had desired—he approached her.

He offered his right hand.

Elizabeth stood up too, mirroring his movements. She reached out her own hand and their fingers slid together, side by side, like train carriages on adjacent tracks, until the two touched palms.

The doctor bowed, a "low, respectful bow," and once again, his body spoke words he did not say. Because as he bent at the waist, the movement was accompanied "with a slight pressure of his hand" in hers. She felt it speak as if a sentence. She felt "the highest expectations of my future were all consummated in this the Doctor's final decision."

The train carriages separated, a blast of steam sending them off, and her hand felt cooler after the warmth of his close touch. Yet a connection had been made, whether written in steam or skin or silence.

"I considered this," she later said, "as an acceptance of my terms."

Devil or no devil, the deal had been done.

CHAPTER 32

January passed into February. Elizabeth continued to prepare for publication. But McFarland made no efforts that she could see to uphold his end of their bargain. After empty weeks had passed, she decided to write to him again. On this occasion, she asked her attendant to pass on the note.

This was no love letter.

This was a threat.

Elizabeth reminded him of the long-ago choice she'd given: *repentance or exposure*. She now wrote fiercely, "If you fail to keep your promise to publish my book...I shall feel bound to fulfill my promise to expose you." She shared with him, for the first time, that she had been secretly working on a second book, which she called *The Exposure*.

McFarland took only an hour to respond. She could "almost hear my own heart palpitate with emotion" as she heard his footsteps coming closer to her door.

"Good morning, Doctor!" she said with customary cheerfulness.

But her greeting was not returned. McFarland ignored her outstretched hand, too, and its memories of promises past.

"Step out of your room," he insisted.

No sooner had she stepped over the threshold than he slammed the door and locked it.

Her book was in there.

Both her books.

"Mrs. Packard," McFarland said with all the disapproving censure of the superior he saw himself to be, "I consider that note you sent me as unladylike—as containing a threat."

Because no woman could be both assertive *and* feminine.

"Dr. McFarland," replied Elizabeth with just as much authority as he'd professed to have, "that note contained the truth, and nothing but the truth. I promised you when I had been here only four months, that I should expose you when I got out, unless you repented—I don't take it back!"

At her words, he seized her—albeit gently—and escorted her swiftly down the corridor. When Elizabeth realized where they were going, she may have trembled.

Solitary. He was locking her in a screen room.

It was McFarland's own hand that drew the bolt across the door.

Yet as she inspected her new surroundings, Elizabeth may have smiled wryly. Because the iron screen was in place across the window and the monastic plainness of the room was undeniable, but sitting squarely in the middle of this intimidating space was an anomalous object: a single chair.

It didn't belong there. It had been placed there purposely.

As though he himself was self-censoring his actions, as the attendants often did before her unyielding gaze, McFarland had prepared the room in advance of her arrival. There was even a pillow placed neatly on the bed.

With nothing else to do, Elizabeth took the chair and placed it in the corner of the room. She picked up the pillow, plonked herself on the seat, and then tipped the chair back against the wall at a comfortable angle, the pillow behind her head, intending to sleep or try to. "Good sleep" was, after all, "as good an antidote to trouble" as she could think of. There was nothing she could do to prevent this incarceration or influence the doctor's actions beyond the bolted door. So why try? *"Duties are ours, events God's."* She closed her eyes and rested.

Two hours later, she heard the door opening again. McFarland stood in the doorway, staring in some surprise at her composed position.

"Can I come out now?" she asked calmly.

"Yes."

"Can I go to my room?"

"Yes."

She led the way; he followed. He unlocked the door of her private room for her...and revealed a scene of stunning disarray.

The doctor had been busy. Her bed barely deserved the name: tick mattresses, sheets, counterpane, and pillows had all been thoroughly searched. Her clothes lay tossed beside her trunk, which had been ransacked. Combs, mirrors, jewelry...all lay asunder, as though this room in an asylum had truly contained an insane occupant for the past few hours.

Worst of all, to Elizabeth's eyes: the box in which she kept the finished manuscript of *The Great Drama* was completely empty.

He'd taken every scrap of writing he could find.

Yet Elizabeth turned calmly from the "sad scene" before her to face McFarland. She laid her hand gently on his arm.

"Doctor, never fear," she said soothingly, as though to quiet the storm that had raged in her room. "God reigns. This will all work right."

In her mind, "God's purpose would stand, and...nothing could hinder it." She just had to let God work His way through these events.

And God had been looking out for her. Though McFarland had taken every page of *The Great Drama*, he discovered neither her journal—still pinned in place in her garments—nor the manuscript of *The Exposure*, which she'd carefully hidden before sending her note, "knowing the dog [would soon be] on the scent."

With the assurance that these documents were safe, she felt even more tranquil. After all, she and the doctor had a deal. Though her friends in the asylum feared McFarland might burn her book, she had faith he would not: "He will return it to me entire and unharmed."

Her friends listened with confoundment. "There seemed a mystery attached [to my confidence]," Elizabeth explained, "to which none but myself held the key." That key was "this secret of the letter" of January 19. As Elizabeth put it, "This…was the talismanic power which finally and alone wrought out my deliverance."

Because three weeks after he'd stolen all her papers, McFarland returned them to her, "unasked, with an apology for not having done so before."

Elizabeth felt triumphant. She had offered her heart for her book, but it had been worth it. Victorious, she resumed the "delightful work" of preparing the first volume of *The Great Drama* for publication.

"I never could ask any man to treat me with more deferential respect than Dr. McFarland uniformly did from this time," Elizabeth wrote exultantly after the drama of her manuscript's theft and return. Because McFarland had returned her handwritten pages, she felt he *had* reformed, which imbued her with "entire trust and confidence in his manhood." To Elizabeth, freedom of expression was everything, an unsurprising position given she'd ended up in the asylum because her husband wanted to deny her it. This influenced all her dealings with McFarland too. When writing her reproof had led to her banishment to Eighth Ward or when McFarland had failed to listen to patients' complaints, she saw the devil in him. But—as she'd said at the trustee meeting—when he allowed her spiritual liberty, the liberty to express herself, she "should trust him, though he slay me."

"I had no reason to feel," she concluded after the safe return of her precious manuscript, "that another man lived on earth who cared for my happiness, but [him]."

Certainly, her husband cared nothing for it. Around this time, Elizabeth received some unsettling news via her cousin, Angeline Field. Angeline was more an adopted sister than a cousin, having been raised alongside Elizabeth after Angeline's mother had died; she was Elizabeth's "dearest friend." Her cousin had never wavered in believing Elizabeth sane, her conviction further strengthened after Theophilus had tried to "browbeat her into silence" after she and her husband had written to McFarland to request Elizabeth's release. The moment they'd heard of Elizabeth's commitment, they'd suspected "foul play" on the pastor's part.

And more foul play was afoot. Theophilus had been greatly disturbed back in September when he'd thought the trustees might discharge his wife. So he'd started looking for another asylum that would take Elizabeth—this time, one whose superintendent would never recommend her release.

Angeline now shared that he'd found one. The State Lunatic Hospital in Northampton, Massachusetts, was an asylum that was "open to all... without regard to the form or duration of the disease." It prided itself on the fact that "none have ever been turned from its doors." Theophilus might possibly have thought to try it as an old schoolfriend of his was one of its trustees: another safety net to ensure his will was done.

Should Elizabeth ever be released from Jacksonville, Theophilus intended that this hospital would be her next, and final, destination. Because there she would stay: for life.

Hearing of her husband's plans from Angeline, Elizabeth felt scared—a fear that only deepened as the next Jacksonville trustee meeting loomed in the diary on March 4. Once again, Elizabeth's case came up for review. Previously, she'd always anticipated these dates with uncontained excitement, but now she felt frightened. After all, at least here she had McFarland's support. The Northampton superintendent might not be so accommodating.

Ironically, she now felt safer *inside* the Jacksonville asylum than out.

Elizabeth did not attend the March meeting. Only McFarland did. The trustees duly made their decision: "Elizabeth P. W. Packard is ordered to be discharged after June 19, 1863."

That discharge date was curious. Usually, patients were given only a month to leave the hospital. But likely at Theophilus's request—to give him time to make arrangements?—that period had been dramatically extended.

Elizabeth protested, vehemently. She did not *want* to leave now, not now that she knew Theophilus's plans: that lifelong imprisonment in another asylum awaited.

But when had men ever listened to her?

Three months left.

CHAPTER 33

The news of Elizabeth's imminent departure spread like wildfire through the hospital, becoming "a theme of animated discussion." But she stayed out of it.

She had another plan in mind.

On March 17, 1863, her eldest son, Toffy, turned twenty-one. And while Elizabeth had long been told she could not possibly take responsibility for herself, with her male child having now reached the age of majority, he could. To his credit, he stepped up.

Had this happened prior to her learning of Theophilus's plot, Elizabeth would likely have requested a straightforward discharge into Toffy's care. But things were different now. She was fighting not only to regain her freedom from Jacksonville but to avoid commitment to a second asylum. She knew from bitter experience that she was not entitled to a trial to prove her sanity; therefore, her book was her only chance for self-defense. "I felt that when this was [published]," she explained, "I should be secure from another assault from my husband, but not before."

Elizabeth's priority therefore became "to secure for me a place where I could be unmolested and uninterrupted until I could complete my work of preparing my book for the press."

And she knew exactly where that place should be. "I felt," she wrote, "that the bolts and bars which had for three years held me falsely imprisoned would now be employed as a refuge of safety."

The world was out of joint again, but this time, it was a topsy-turvy inversion she embraced. From prison to sanctuary: the asylum became, once again, what it was *supposed* to be. Theophilus would not be able to touch her in here, especially with McFarland standing guard as her protector.

"I had full faith to believe he would dare to defend me," she wrote of the doctor.

> He, more than any other individual, had proof from his own observation, that I was a truly worthy object of protection, and that I was truly oppressed and persecuted by a most unworthy legal husband. He had seen more, and I had told him more, and he had read more of my book than any other individual in the world, and my confidence in his intelligence as well as manliness, assured me he could not pervert all this knowledge of the truth…and not be true to me… On this most grateful conclusion, I based my purpose to make his house my refuge.

So she asked to stay at the asylum while she finished her book, and McFarland consented. At this juncture, there is a curious divergence in their accounts. Elizabeth believed the decision made her a boarder rather than a patient at the hospital. Toffy, in keeping with his new responsibility, seemingly paid for Elizabeth to stay, and in this economic transaction, she perceived a change in her status. Though ostensibly still under lock and key—she was not allowed her own pass that might permit her to come and go at her pleasure—because of the trustees' decision to discharge her, her own subsequent decision to remain, and Toffy's paying of her way, everything felt different. "I considered myself as responsible alone to myself for my own actions here," she concluded, "as I should have done at the Mansion House [hotel] in Jacksonville, and just as much my own keeper."

Yet the hospital's records make no note of any such change. It was unknown to Elizabeth, but the hospital's financial position had altered since she'd been committed. Back in 1860, the state had paid for all patients' care at the asylum, regardless of pecuniary status. But in February 1861, a new law had been passed that allowed the asylum to charge those patients who were of "sufficient ability." Likely due to Theophilus's debts and the subsequent loss of his ministry, Elizabeth had to date been kept as a pauper patient: the state paid for her care.

But Toffy was not his father. He had a full-time job. When he became Elizabeth's male representative, McFarland apparently charged him; the fees were a maximum of $3 (about $61) a week, capped at $156 (about $3,000) a year.

Yet in that exchange of money, Elizabeth saw liberation. It totally changed her mindset. Consequently, when Toffy came to visit in May 1863, she made a radical suggestion: why didn't they head into Jacksonville together?

So that May, for the first time in two years—for the first time since she'd insisted she'd never voluntarily return to her ward—Elizabeth Packard left the hospital. In her mind, she left as a free woman, on the arm of her son.

How wonderful that walk must have been. Step by careful step, Elizabeth made her way back down the asylum's brick sidewalk that she'd first strolled along with her husband three long years before. The trees, seeming to salute her as she went, were much more mature than when she'd last walked by them. As they reached the boundary of the fence, she noticed with awe that twelve-foot entrance gates and stone gateposts had been constructed where previously there had been none. They stretched far above her head, dominant and fearsome. As she crossed the boundary, she must have felt so free.

The novelty continued all the way into Jacksonville. The old footpath the patients had once used had been replaced with a substantial plank walk. Mother and son strolled merrily down it, Elizabeth marveling at how much the world had changed since she'd last been in it. When last she'd shopped at the public square, the sidewalks had been "a hodgepodge of rotting, rat-infested plank walks...that sank into the mud each spring," but the merchants she was visiting now had laid out smart, ten-foot streets made of good brick or stone, with actual curbstones too. It was all so civilized.

To talk to the shopkeepers, to nod at passersby: all these were things she had not done for two years. She felt her neck bending, memories of times past easily summoning back the social niceties. Everything felt new and old at the same time. The fresh air on her skin. The smile on her lips.

The ability to come and go exactly as she pleased.

When Elizabeth returned to the asylum, she walked happily through the front door and back up to her ward. She was "simply a boarder who voluntarily submitted to all the rules of the house." Why should she not return freely to her rented room?

After all the trauma, she'd found a certain peace. "I really felt safer under the gallant protection of Dr. McFarland," she wrote of this time, "than I could have then felt in any other situation."

But had she known what was happening in New York City, Elizabeth would not have felt safe at all.

CHAPTER 34

It was a six-story brownstone that stretched along the entire block front of Broadway. Built at a cost of some $1 million ($33 million), it was a place that "dazzles and bewilders the visitor," evoking the "palaces of 'Arabian Nights.'" Patrons' shoes clicked on marble floors as their eyes alighted on frescoed ceilings and silk damask draperies. They took their seats in rosewood furniture "rich and inviting." Thirsts were slaked from gold and silver goblets while the largest plate-glass mirrors in the United States reflected back the opulence.

Also reflected in those mirrors on May 19, 1863, was Dr. Andrew McFarland.

At the famous Metropolitan Hotel in New York, he laughed heartily with his fellow superintendents, their deep voices rumbling like coming thunder. It was the annual meeting of the AMSAII, and he was informing them all of a curious case he'd been studying.

Yet he was not—as Elizabeth might have hoped—telling them of a brilliant female author whom he was currently protecting from persecution.

He was telling them how he had "got tired" of a patient who'd given him "infinite trouble."

"I proposed to the Board of Trustees to discharge her," he revealed to his peers at their meeting, "as the only means of getting rid of an intolerable and unendurable source of annoyance."

McFarland *had* recommended Elizabeth's release. But not because he thought she was sane.

Because she'd caused too much trouble.

That first trustee meeting, back in September 1862, when Elizabeth had thought she'd convinced both the doctor and the trustees of her sanity, was actually the first time McFarland *could* have requested her discharge, because patients were always given a trial of two years to see if the doctors could help them recover. But the first chance he'd gotten, he'd wanted her gone.

The law under which he'd asked the trustees to release her—the law under which she *had* just been released—was one in which patients were deemed incurable. Though McFarland actually disputed the idea professionally that such a distinction could ever be drawn, he'd happily made the call in Elizabeth's case. In later years, he would release homicidal patients whom he believed were "at any time liable...to repeat the butchery" as *sane*, but Elizabeth was deemed more afflicted with insanity than even these people.

That past September, when the patient herself had requested to speak to the trustees, he'd leapt at the chance for her to do so, giving his "free and full consent."

Anything to see the back of her.

He'd wanted Elizabeth gone even though, to his professional frustration, he *still* hadn't found that source of intellectual delusion that he believed must lie at the heart of her moral perversity.

"I do not think that for two years of the closest study I could discover any intellectual impairment at all," he now confided in his fellow doctors. "[Though] her hatred of her husband had something diabolical about it...the closest study could not discover any intellectual impairment."

But then, at that same trustee meeting at which he'd hoped she'd be discharged, she'd said a very curious thing. She'd talked about how she was "a spiritual woman—a 'temple of the Holy Ghost.'"

McFarland's ears had pricked up. She thought she was the Holy Ghost?

The following day, he'd asked for a copy of her statement, wanting to read again *exactly* what she'd said. When she'd suggested preparing it for the press, he'd enthusiastically agreed and even urged her to add to it: "Write what you please!" When she'd come to him with her idea for her book, it was as if all his Christmases had come at once.

Because for two years, she'd managed to keep him distant from her delusion, "dexterously" avoiding giving him the evidence he'd so keenly sought. But McFarland believed that patients like Elizabeth "may utter almost any continuation of spoken language without betraying themselves—[but] the severer ordeal of writing, alone, [will serve] to discover the diseased mental processes."

He'd therefore given her permission to write whatever she wished. He gave her all the paper she required. It was, in his mind, a rope with which she might hang herself. He told her attendants not to disturb her.

He wanted nothing to get in the way of his revenge.

And it *was* revenge. Because his decision to let her write was not only prompted by professional curiosity, hoping to discover the cause of her perceived illness. McFarland admitted: "As there always will be some, even of fair intelligence in other things, who will be led...to believe that she is not insane, I deemed it best to let her continue her strain of writing." He wanted her to write a book that would "convince the most incredulous" she *was* mad. Because she was simply too convincing in asserting her sanity to others: too eloquent, too compelling. He needed a gun of his own to shoot her down.

And Elizabeth herself, in McFarland's view, had duly loaded it and put it straight into his hands. As he'd read the erratic, stream-of-consciousness manuscript she'd subsequently produced, he'd felt vindicated. In his view, she had proven her insanity "most effectually." He considered her writings "absurd and childish."

"Are not women citizens?" she'd written. "Are not their rights worth protecting?"

"*Put woman into your ballot-boxes, your legislatures, your senates, your Congress, your president's chair.*"

No wonder Elizabeth had felt the doctor was "unconcerned about what I write, as if his character didn't depend upon the opinions of one of his patients." In his view, it didn't. She was insane, and she could write what she wished, because no one would give weight to her opinions.

No one *ever* would.

Yet the clear evidence of her insanity was not the only boon to be discovered in those twenty-five hundred pages he had patiently plowed his way through.

He also thought he'd discovered her primary delusion. He took pleasure in revealing it to his peers, like a magician demonstrating a dark trick: "The delusion was that, in the Trinity, distinctions of sex had to exist...and that she was the Holy Ghost... It appeared...this delusion had possessed her...giving origin to all this perversity of conduct." He ultimately concluded, "Her insanity consists in a thoroughly diseased conception of her own powers as one having supernatural attributes."

Yet his conclusion in fact said rather more about him than it did Elizabeth. To reach it, McFarland had been deliberately selective. He'd ignored all the many instances in her manuscript where Elizabeth made it perfectly clear she was speaking only metaphorically about her gender: "Is not a spiritual woman a *personification* of the Holy Ghost?" He'd also ignored—or was ignorant of—centuries of theological theories that the Holy Ghost might indeed be female. The argument ran that the Father was male, the Holy Ghost female, and the Son the fruit of their union. Otherwise, the Deity was *solely* male, but Elizabeth believed that "He can't be a perfect being unless His nature includes both the male and female." Though it should not truly matter in the question of her sanity whether Elizabeth's beliefs were original or not, in fact there was a solid academic foundation to her ideas on which she'd let her faith flourish.

But McFarland saw only madness.

Yet if he'd expected his peers to congratulate him, he was disappointed. They focused on the fact that it had taken him two years to find this so-called delusion. They questioned whether that meant he did not believe she was insane for two years (in which case, how could he have justified her continued commitment?). But that was *not* the case. Elizabeth had hated her husband so aggressively that her madness was a given for McFarland. That was why he'd deemed her incurable, even *before* he'd discovered the delusion.

To have found it, McFarland may have reflected, was *almost* worth all the trouble she'd caused with that crazy book of hers. Because of course he'd then had to endure six months of her "stirring up the other patients to discontent and insubordination": their refusal to work, their destruction of property, even merely their stronger wills that would not now bend so easily to his Prospero power.

But once he'd discovered the delusion, enough had been enough. What a "most welcome" day it had been when the trustees—*finally!*— had granted his wish to let her go. He knew her husband would be disappointed, so he'd written to Mr. Packard to explain.

"The extraordinary amount of trouble, which Mrs. P causes us," he'd said, "and the disastrous influence which she exerts on the other patients, is the cause of this step."

But that was not all the doctor had done. Whether of his own volition or at Theophilus's request, he'd decided to help the pastor with his plot. Earlier that month, on May 5, 1863, McFarland had issued a formal certificate to Elizabeth's husband, stamped with the seal of the Illinois State Hospital:

> I hereby certify that Mrs. E. P. W. Packard, the wife of Rev. Theophilus Packard of Manteno, Ill., was received into this Institution and has been in its charge for nearly three years... Of the existence of insanity I have no question... She is now ordered to be discharged, as having remained here as long as it is expedient to retain such a case, and not because the disease is cured, or because any doubt has arisen as to its existence.

Elizabeth was leaving—and he was making sure she would stay gone.

Because as Elizabeth and Theophilus and McFarland all well knew, she would receive no trial before any second commitment. All her husband needed to lock her up were two certificates of insanity from two different doctors.

With McFarland's certificate already in hand, Theophilus was halfway there.

Elizabeth felt safe at the asylum because she believed in her deal with the doctor. But their contract had always been one-sided, McFarland's supposed signature as empty as the air.

"I care nothing whatever for the pages...which Mrs. P. has...wasted on myself," McFarland later remarked coldly. "They are just about as important as her passionate love letters to me."

McFarland had indeed been a blank canvas to Elizabeth. But on the reverse of that vacant painting was a horror story that would have scared her senseless—if only she knew.

Because McFarland was in league with her husband. And in exactly one month's time, her stay of execution at the asylum was up.

And there was only one way out.

With Theophilus.

CHAPTER 35

On the morning on June 18, 1863, Elizabeth's attendant came bustling into her room with an order: "Mrs. Packard must be suitably dressed by nine o'clock to go with her husband on board the cars."

The pronouncement was not a complete shock to Elizabeth. On June 15, McFarland had warned her that Theophilus would be coming later in the week to take her away. Yet Elizabeth had remained blissfully confident that the doctor would never let it happen.

The only thing that unsettled her was that McFarland himself would not be present; he'd been called away to testify in a murder trial on behalf of the accused. Their parting had been, to her mind, surprisingly brief. After imparting the news of her husband's imminent arrival, "He then shook hands with me, and bade me 'good bye,' as if he did not expect to meet me again!"

Yet Elizabeth was assured that her impression of a final parting must have been wrong. She was certain she would still be at the asylum when McFarland returned. She was a boarder in her own rented room, after all. She would leave when her book was ready, not before.

Yet on June 17, two porters had entered her room to pack her trunk. Though she'd told them assertively they had no right to touch her things, to her shock, she was threatened with a screen room if she got in their way. She had no other protest she could make. Clothes, looking glasses, books, and Bible were all removed against her will, with her packed trunk then deposited in the matron's room for safekeeping.

So when, on the morning of June 18, her attendant ordered her to dress for a journey, Elizabeth informed her briskly that if she wanted her to wear such clothes, she would have to bring them to her: there was nothing left in her room now but what she stood up in. She added that while she might consent to dress in such articles as the girl thought suitable, "As to accompanying the said gentleman to the cars, I shall *never* consent to do this."

The whole hospital was in a "tremor of excitement" about her possible departure. The night before, Sophia Olsen and her fellow Eighth Ward patients had been informed that Elizabeth would be leaving the following morning.

"No flash of lightning then came gleaming into our window," Sophia wrote, "no clap of thunder broke our meditations; nor did an earthquake rock the ground our house was built upon; yet if all these phenomena had really happened, I hardly think the excitement could have been greater. The raving actually forgot to rave; the swearers were held in dumb suspense; even the scarred victims of despair looked up from their blood-shot eyes! The exclamations, discussions, questions that for several hours took precedence of every other commotion, I cannot describe."

But now, on the morning of June 18, in Elizabeth's private room, there was only quiet. Only silence. She sat patiently awaiting whatever came next: her traveling dress upon her body, her shawl around her shoulders, her gloves pulled onto her fingers in readiness for a journey she did not want to take. She sat in her chair, idly reading, as all her writing papers had been confiscated the day before.

She had pulled her bedstead across her door. This was a habit, as there was no lock on the inside but this improvised variety. Elizabeth liked the feeling of privacy it gave, albeit illusory. She did not think of it as a barricade, because it took her only a moment to move it whenever a knock came upon her door.

But that morning, they did not knock.

Instead, without warning, the bedstead suddenly shunted backward. Dr. Tenny and two other men burst into her bedroom. Elizabeth felt almost frightened as the furniture moved violently across the floor, stopping only inches from her feet. As she looked up, aghast at the intrusion, she saw three stout men standing at her door, their breaths already heavy with effort.

"Mrs. Packard," Dr. Tenny said, "your husband is in the office waiting to take you to the cars in the [omni]bus which is now waiting at the door. We wish you to go with us for that purpose."

Elizabeth felt her spirits sink. She'd argued with Tenny in the days beforehand, calmly making out her case for staying at the asylum, but it seemed her arguments had fallen "like water spilt upon the ground." It had, perhaps, only ever been a distant hope that Tenny might defend her in McFarland's place, but to find herself friendless was still a bitter blow. Nevertheless, she raised her head high.

"Dr. Tenny," Elizabeth said evenly, "I shall not go with you for that purpose. And here in the presence of these witnesses, I claim a right to my own identity, and in the name of the laws of my country, I claim protection against this assault upon my personal rights. I claim a right to *myself*."

But her words were moonbeams disregarded in the light of day. Later, McFarland, her husband, and the trustees would all cite her refusal to leave the hospital as evidence of madness. But given what Theophilus had planned, was it any wonder she did?

In response to her defiant words, Tenny merely issued orders: "Take Mrs. Packard up in your arms and carry her to the 'bus."

Elizabeth kept her body stiff, exactly as she had three years earlier, her paralysis the only power she had left. The men surrounded her, made a saddle seat upon which she was soon lifted.

"I held myself again in readiness," Elizabeth wrote, "to be offered a sacrifice on the altar of unjust legislation to married women."

They carried her out of her room. They carried her out of her hall. Elizabeth, throughout, called out loudly for help, determined to use the voice she'd gained in the asylum to protest this persecution. She called for friends, for attendants, for anyone at the asylum to stop this scandal.

But she said sadly, "None came... Not even one man, woman, or child appeared to help me; and none, to my knowledge, protested against this outrage but Mrs. Sophia N. B. Olsen."

But as much as she may have wished otherwise, Sophia was impotent to stop it. And it all happened so fast. With just a few staggered steps of the men down the corridor and out through the door, Elizabeth exited Eighth Ward with as little ceremony as when she'd entered. They carried her down three flights of stairs: Dr. Tenny at the front, then Elizabeth with her porters, and finally her female attendants bringing up the rear.

There was no one left to defend her. She was carried swiftly through the downstairs hall, under the white arching frame that surrounded the front door, and down the asylum's stone steps. And there she saw her husband, waiting patiently at the foot of the stairs, standing beside the carriage that he'd booked to take her away.

"Mr. Packard's wishes were so generously anticipated," Elizabeth sneered, "that he had nothing to do but to stand holding open the door of the 'bus, while my betrayers brought me in their strong arms and rested my feet on the steps of the omnibus."

Upstairs on Eighth Ward, the women all rushed to the windows. They saw Elizabeth being settled in the carriage, the asylum's employees joining her inside lest she make a fuss at the station. They saw Theophilus seating himself and Dr. Tenny reaching a hand inside the carriage in a gesture of farewell. He would be the last person to say goodbye to Elizabeth, just as he'd been the first to greet her, three long years before.

Elizabeth stared in astonishment at his proffered handshake.

"No, sir," she said shortly, turning away from him, and her words were ice. "I don't shake hands with traitors."

He withdrew from the carriage. He gave the signal they could leave. As the horses began to trot, the sound seemed an ominous drumbeat in Elizabeth's ears.

"I knew not where I was bound to, whether into another Asylum, a Poor-house, or a Penitentiary," she said. "But…I supposed [my husband] was going to put me into an Insane Asylum at Northampton, Mass.

"For life."

Sophia watched the carriage draw away with a "throbbing heart" and "fast gathering tears."

"She has gone," she whispered, and the empty words did no justice to the import of the moment nor the gravity of her loss.

In the wake of Elizabeth's departure, the other patients mourned. A kind of wake was held in which they talked out their grief. "Some lectured on the oppressiveness of husbands," recalled Sophia, "others on that of State institutions; a few on 'Woman's Rights,' but a larger number still upon a subject with which I think they had a much better acquaintance, namely, Woman's Wrongs."

Elizabeth saw none of this. Her friends and the institution in which they were held merely receded in her eyeline as the carriage bore her away. And although she said, "I maintain, that I *entered* this institution as *sane* a person as I *left* it," the hospital logbook contained no such record. Instead, in a small, neat line beneath her name, the doctors noted, "June 18/63. Dis[charged] Order Trustees."

As the carriage passed out beyond the asylum gates, she felt McFarland's power dissipate entirely. Her feelings hardened as her new reality sank in. As she stared across the omnibus at her husband—at this cold, unforgiving man who'd already fixed her fate—she thought of the doctor: "The one [I trusted] above all others to defend me against my enemy, proved to be the very one to put me into his hands." She was almost stunned by the revelation: "I had found that the best man I had ever found could do the worst act I had ever known." Too late, she realized he had not reformed at all.

Far too soon, the Packards arrived at the station. The asylum staff bid her goodbye.

"We shall miss you, Mrs. Packard, at the Asylum," said one, "for there never has been a person who has caused such a universal sensation there, as you have."

But universal sensation or not, all that was now in the past. A different future awaited. Elizabeth was left alone with Theophilus—left alone with the man who planned to lock her away for life.

The Packards boarded the cars; they pulled away. Elizabeth did not speak one word to her husband. Yet he acted strangely—solicitously. No sooner had her shawl slipped off her shoulders than he was ready to readjust it. When she called for lemonade, he followed after her only to pay her bill. He did not try to engage her in conversation; neither did he stop her from speaking with others. He did not follow her "in any suspicious style" at all, she noted, "as if I could not be trusted, but on the contrary, I had...perfect freedom in talking what I pleased, and to whom I pleased, and he...heard me say many things to the passengers much to his discredit, and still he did not attempt to restrain me."

Elizabeth did not say she was suspicious, but she ought to have been. Why this sudden and uncharacteristic kindness? Was it merely a prelude to his total victory? Was there simply no point in silencing her now, not when he was about to silence her for good?

Morning turned into afternoon, afternoon into evening, and still they traveled. Still, Elizabeth had no clue where they were headed. She would not lower herself to Theophilus's level to ask, and he simply did not say. The passing stations held no clues that she could decipher, the countryside outside bland fields that bore no landmarks.

In time, the rocking motion of the train, combined with her exhaustion, took its toll. It was Theophilus who took out his handkerchief and offered it to her, who folded it under her head for a pillow, who allowed her to rest her weary head upon his shoulder. Elizabeth closed her eyes, the smell of him so familiar it almost lulled her to sleep, as though the train were taking them back through time and not through physical space.

When she woke, it was dark outside, yet still the train was in motion. At around 1:00 a.m., she felt it begin to slow. She glanced outside the window, but the place—Tonica—was not familiar. Was this merely a stopping point on their way to Massachusetts? Was Theophilus's plan that they would stay overnight in this strange town and then continue their journey on the morrow?

The cars came to a complete stop. Theophilus rose and told her to follow. Elizabeth felt suddenly petrified. Her heart stuttered under the shock. "I had no protection," she realized numbly, "no shield but the

Almighty. Under His wings I shielded myself, and in His overruling providence was my only trust."

Obediently, having no other option, she rose and shadowed her husband. She could not see beyond Theophilus's back as he led the way off the cars. She could only follow meekly in his footsteps, fearing the path that lay ahead. As she moved closer to the doorway, the cold night air blew in from the outside. She shivered, her summer shawl no match for its icy bite. What portents were carried on that freezing wind?

Yet she had no time to wonder. She had to concentrate on her footsteps, on navigating the train's steep steps, holding her hoop skirts with one hand as she disembarked into the night.

When she looked up, she thought her eyes were deceiving her. For she stepped off the cars into a warm embrace. Arms surrounded her, grabbing her, squeezing her, loving her.

Theophilus had not led her to another asylum after all. He had taken her to her beloved cousin—to her lovely Angeline.

And to unexpected freedom.

PART FIVE

TURNING POINTS

I am not free while any woman is unfree, even when her shackles are very different from my own.

—*Audre Lorde, 1981*

Woman has her work to do, and no one can accomplish it for her. She is bound to rise, to try her strength, to break her bonds.

—*Elizabeth Blackwell, 1848*

CHAPTER 36

To be in Angeline's arms was a wonder. The women shared the same family features—a long face and nose, brown hair, and dark, almond-shaped eyes—and their joy at being reunited was mirrored in their faces too. Elizabeth could barely believe her luck as she was helped into a carriage by Angeline's courteous husband, David, and found herself riding beside "my truest and kindest friends I have on earth" on her way to their home in Granville, Illinois. David made her "as welcome a guest as one of his own family."

Her unexpected deliverance to the Fields made her question whether her husband might possibly have reformed. Was he ready to repent and allow her freedom? Despite all she'd endured, she suddenly felt willing to consider a reconciliation, as long as Theophilus was sincere in repenting and granting her full liberty.

But it was soon apparent nothing had changed. She castigated herself—"little, weak-minded Mrs. Packard"—for even entertaining the idea. In fact, it became clear that this seeming freedom wasn't freedom at all. Theophilus was allowing her to stay at the Fields' and out of an asylum on one very strict condition: she must *never* return to her family. He left blunt instructions that the Fields should treat her as a madwoman—these, they ignored—and warned Angeline, "If she ever does come to see them [the children], I shall put her into another Asylum!"

On June 19, only hours after she'd left Jacksonville, Elizabeth could not compute that future; she was simply relieved to have escaped the first. Yet she discovered, on that very first morning, that her fate was still firmly tied to that asylum with steel strings soldered by sisterhood. While others looked at time spent in a mental hospital "as a kind of horrid nightmare, which they wished to banish, as soon as possible, from their recollection," Elizabeth was driven by her memories from day one.

"I cried so hard, the next morning after I got here," she wrote, "to think that the bliss of freedom, so dear to me, was not yet felt by those I left in bonds... To think of the dear afflicted ones I had left behind... with none to protect them from the most outrageous abuses."

But Elizabeth was no longer one of those afflicted ones: she had gotten out. *She* could protect them. It became her "first and chief business now to deliver those in bonds."

Freed at last from the tyranny of McFarland's censorship, she therefore wrote a "field of letters" within days of being released, telling her friends' families the truth of what was going on behind the barred windows, using her unmuffled voice to speak out. She urged Sophia's brother to secure his sister's release immediately. To his credit, though it took six months and "tiresome negotiations" with lawyers, he eventually succeeded. Sophia went to live near him in Wheaton, Illinois, becoming an artist who painted maps.

Elizabeth also wrote to the husband of Sarah Minard, whom she'd first met on Seventh Ward, and to the trustees about Mrs. Minard's case. Sarah had been at the hospital for at least five years, yet Elizabeth assured them she was "in no respect a fit subject for the asylum." Knowing the rules of the game, she added that Sarah "entertained none but the kindest and most charitable feelings towards her husband."

But unlike with Sophia's family, silence was the only response.

Elizabeth wrote, too, to her dear children. Though it seems likely Theophilus would have intercepted any letters, Elizabeth wrote regardless, wanting to cheer Libby. She told her daughter all about her book and its imminent publication and declared, "There is not a girl in America who has *so capable* a mother as you have, and the world will know it soon."

Because Elizabeth was certain that once her manuscript was published, the government would change the laws that discriminated against women. After which she could return to Manteno with impunity, because Theophilus would no longer have the power to keep her from her home.

Unfortunately, the world seemed determined to prevent Elizabeth's plan. All the publishers she approached rejected it point-blank. "I found the fact of [my book] having been written by a patient in an insane asylum was, of itself, an incubus I could not dispose of to their satisfaction," Elizabeth wrote, "and they would, therefore, waive all further investigation as to its intrinsic merits."

Elizabeth knew nothing at this time of McFarland having issued a certificate to her husband. The simple fact that he'd retained her at the asylum for three years was evidence enough she must be mad.

"I find it very hard for a woman who has lost her reputation...by the cruel defamation of insanity, to do anything alone," Elizabeth wrote in frustration. "I never realized until now what an unpardonable offense [McFarland] committed against me...in [ever] calling me an insane person."

She tried desperately to right the wrong by writing to the

doctor—"my treacherous friend"—on August 10, 1863. Ironically, she requested that he issue her with a certificate of her *sanity*.

Naturally, believing the opposite, he did not reply. She was outraged. "Mr. Packard is a *fool* in calling me insane, because he don't know any better. Dr. McFarland is a *villain* in calling me insane, because he does."

And his villainy was dark indeed. Elizabeth now learned—from a gloating Theophilus?—that McFarland's permission to write her book had *never* been the liberal act of generosity she'd always presumed, but "an act of treachery on his part, to draw out my views, as a testimony in support of his opinion, that I am insane." Too late, she realized that McFarland "thought the book ought never to be published."

It was the ultimate betrayal. She had offered this man her self, her heart. She had thought she'd found in him "one spring of pure gushing water in this great Sahara desert of my soul." Yet that seeming oasis had been mere illusion. "He is no less a sinner against me than is Mr. Packard," she wrote numbly in wake of the realization, "and so far as his penitence is concerned, I have no proof of it all." She was angry, wanting to shoot these "rattlesnakes," husband and doctor both, "and then drag their lifeless bodies before the public, for exhibition on the public gallows of the printed page."

But that printed page could not be her book, as she'd long hoped. Though no longer resident in the asylum, she found its shadow stitched to her. She was still bound by the ties of her lost reputation, caged by the stigma of her supposedly lost mind. "The very word insane is like a stench in my nostrils," she wrote, but it was a stink that others smelled, too, and shied away from. Defeated, she had to "abandon the project" of publishing her book "for the present, as an impossibility."

But without the project, what future did she have? The plan had always been to publish—to secure her liberty. Without it, she had no document of self-defense, no hope of saving her sisters, no way to point out to politicians the injustice of the current laws. Without it, Elizabeth could not safely return home and live happily ever after with her children—the thing she desired most intensely of all.

The only light in all this darkness was the reaction of the Granville townspeople to her plight. It had not taken Elizabeth long to make friends with her new neighbors, and once she told them her story, they were up in arms. Elizabeth told the doctor of their support in her August letter. "The stone of truth has commenced rolling," she warned McFarland, "but where it will roll, my once dear friend...God only knows."

Even Elizabeth was surprised to learn its first destination: a public indignation meeting staged by the Granville residents toward the end of the summer. The sheer unfairness of Theophilus's dictate that she should never see her children again, when she was clearly sane, had riled them. They felt that Elizabeth's wish to return home should be granted, "even in defiance of Mr. Packard's most cruel threat."

The people put their money where their mouths were. Knowing she had none, they generously raised a purse of $30 (about $612) for her—more than enough to pay her train fare to Manteno. They said any funds left over should go toward her legal costs, "should self-defense require it." Finally, they assured her that they themselves would defend her liberty if Theophilus ever tried to send her to a second asylum, though as Granville lay eighty miles from Manteno, they would not exactly be close at hand. Nevertheless, Elizabeth felt she had a veritable army behind her.

Their kindness was unexpected and most welcome. Hearing of their generosity, Elizabeth gently made a request. Even though she'd had to shelve her plans to publish her book, she still felt passionately that the best way to protect herself—and her friends in the asylum—was through publication. So she asked the residents if they'd help her publish a pamphlet, hoping through it to enlist public sympathy. The townspeople readily agreed.

Elizabeth reached into her trunk and dusted off the "Appeal in behalf of the insane" that she'd written in June 1862 under the name of the Coes: the letter to the newspaper editors that had never been published. Granville duly printed it in their county paper, while Elizabeth spent $10 (about $204)—probably from the Granville fund—to print one thousand copies.

It was her first publication. And it was a resolute success—in more ways than one. "It shall be one of the highest aspirations of my earth-life, to expose these evils," she'd written in the asylum. Having now published her exposé about the abuse at the hospital, Elizabeth could hold her head up high that she *had* "done what she could." She sold the pamphlets through the post office, for a dime apiece. Slowly, money started trickling into her previously penniless purse.

It proved a summer of turning points. In the Civil War, the Battle of Gettysburg in July 1863 saw the tide start to turn in favor of the Union. In Granville, the same happened for Elizabeth. With the nucleus of a publishing business now under her belt, an iota of income, and the support of firm friends, she finally felt able to face her husband. So she planned to return to Manteno—threat or no threat.

It was dangerous, she knew. But she wanted—*needed*—to be a mother again. She wrote of missing her children, "The pain is unutterable, unspeakable." Elizabeth could no longer live in this limbo land, where she was free but not free, where her body spoke of children born but her arms had none to hold. Her life seemed one of countless contradictions, but they all coalesced under one constant threat: commitment to a second asylum. *But she knew she was not mad.* She had to stand up to Theophilus's dictate, or her life was over anyway. She refused to live a half-life such as this.

Yet she packed her trunk with apprehension. She had no idea what she'd find in Manteno. She had no clue if she even had *any* friends there anymore. She hadn't heard from the Hasletts or Blessings since June 1861. She felt forced to conclude that they'd probably abandoned her, thinking her insane after all. She felt Theophilus had "alienated from me every friend I had in the world but Angeline."

It was therefore extremely hard to leave her cousin. But Elizabeth could not countenance living the rest of her life like this, with her husband's control over her as absolute as always. She had dared to defy him before; she would defy him now.

It took a while to put her plans in place. But eventually, four months after her release from the asylum, around October 20, 1863, Elizabeth boarded her train to Manteno. She traveled alone, one woman on a one-way ticket, heading back to the scene of her husband's crime.

CHAPTER 37

The train pulled into Manteno on a cold October morning. In contrast to her departure three and a half years earlier, the station was deserted. And where June sunshine had incongruously crowned her when she'd left, on this day of arrival, a few inches of snow, heralding a harsh winter, had fallen overnight. Those few inches were fast melting. Elizabeth disembarked cautiously, the ground "wet and sloppy under foot."

She left her trunk at the depot, but as she started for home, fear suddenly gripped her that Theophilus might intercept it and destroy her book; under the law, her property was his, so he could easily lay claim. She turned abruptly, intending to double back to instruct the stationmaster further.

As she turned, she saw for the first time that she'd had a shadow since she'd left the station. A small boy, with a cap pulled down low upon his head, was following her. Not wanting to slip on the platform, she asked if he might run back to the stationmaster with her message.

"[Tell him] Mrs. Packard wishes Mr. Harding to not let Mr. Packard take her trunk," she instructed politely.

But to her surprise, the boy hesitated. It was hardly an outrageous favor for a lady to ask. The child was perhaps ten—old enough to know his manners.

"An't you willing to do this favor for me?" she asked brightly. "It is so wet I don't like to go back."

The boy wriggled awkwardly. And in that restless wiggling, she perhaps had a sudden flashback to a child she'd once known who'd never liked to sit still... Just as she was thinking it, the child burst out, "I don't want to say anything against my Pa!"

Elizabeth froze, her heart suddenly colder than the swiftly melting snow. She grabbed at the boy and raised his cap. She looked him full in the face.

Dark hair. Dark eyes. How could she not have known him?

"Who are you?" she whispered. "Is this my little George! Didn't I know my darling boy!"

She'd been away so long she had not recognized him. But three and a half years is a long time in a child's life. He'd been just six when she'd left; now, he was well on his way to eleven. He was taller, of course, his arms and legs longer, as though he'd been stretched. His face was already losing its childlike shape, the bones of the man he would become pushing through. Nevertheless, she knew that somewhere inside his oddly outsized frame was that same sweet boy who'd once loved to serve her strawberries.

She caught him to her and hugged him. "My darling George shall have his mother again," she told him breathlessly. "We shall never be separated now. Kind people are going to protect me and your Pa can't take your mother from you again."

But at her affectionate embrace, George pulled back roughly. "My Pa has done right," he parroted, as though the message had been drilled into him. "He has not done wrong."

Elizabeth's heart sank, even though she'd known this indoctrination would have been happening for three long years. She sighed patiently.

"Yes, George," she insisted, albeit lightly, "your Pa has done wrong to take your mother from you and imprison her, as he has, without cause."

Then she grinned at him suddenly, a smile that came from their "good talking times." "An't you glad to see your mother?"

"Yes, mother! Yes!" he cried instinctively before he could stop himself. Yet the lessons he'd so painfully learned were burned into him. "But—but—" he burst out. With those stuttered words came tears.

Elizabeth stopped his misery. "We won't talk any more about your father," she promised. She reached out a gloved hand and took his still-small one in hers. "Go with me, George," she said, intending to walk on.

"No, mother, I can't," the child replied. "Pa said I must get the mail and come directly home…"

"You may go, then, my child," she said, releasing him, "and I will come by-and-by."

By this time, the gossip that the notorious Mrs. Packard was once more walking along the plank sidewalks of Manteno had spread throughout the village. Elizabeth soon encountered her old friend Mr. Blessing, who insisted that she dine with him at his hotel.

Elizabeth was possibly hesitant, given his lack of communication over the past few years, but accompanied him nonetheless. Back at the tavern, she found Rebecca Blessing and Caroline Ann Haslett (whom Elizabeth called Sarah) eagerly waiting. There were new faces as well. Rebecca nursed a ten-month-old baby boy, born since Elizabeth had been sent away. She had missed all that, just as she'd missed Georgie's growth spurt and goodness knew what else.

It must have been an awkward reunion. For years, Elizabeth had had no choice but to doubt her friends. Though she was aware of McFarland's censorship, it had been so hard to write letter after letter and receive no reply. Trapped in the asylum, knowing nothing of what was happening outside, she'd had to conclude that all had abandoned her. But with her friends finally able to speak freely, she now realized she'd seen "only one side of the picture."

"The other side I could not see until I saw my friends," she said. "Then I found that the many letters I had written had never reached them; for Mr. Packard had instructed Dr. McFarland...that not a single letter should be sent to any of my friends." Both Theophilus and McFarland read all incoming and outgoing letters before deciding whether to share them. "The result," Elizabeth said angrily, "was scarcely none were delivered to me, nor were mine sent."

But the truth was out now. Her friends told her, too, of the many efforts they'd made for her release. They *had* staged a public indignation meeting on June 30, 1860, mere days after her kidnapping. Theophilus had been outraged by this "injurious interference of mischievous inter-meddlers." But having had advance notice, he'd pressed a handful of influential Chicago men into arguing his case. They did so with seem-ingly more skill than the minister himself could muster. "Their speeches came down on the astonished mob like avalanches from the Alps," Theophilus wrote in triumph, "and the mob broke up."

Undeterred, her friends had then embarked on an extensive letter-writing campaign. But as McFarland had known before them, all their endeavors to secure Elizabeth an insanity trial were fruitless, because she had no legal recourse to freedom. They described their attempts to release her using habeas corpus and revealed how this supposedly catch-all safety net could be applied *only* to cases of *unlawful* confinement. Her stay at the asylum had been anything but.

Story after story flowed out over the food they shared, the friends not so much breaking bread as building bridges. The Blessings' hotel was the perfect setting for this warm reunion. It was a modern inn, decorated with gilt picture frames, looking glasses, and a book rack; it was the choice location, in later years, for regular dances by the Fantastic Club. Finding herself surrounded by these old, true friends for the first time in years, Elizabeth felt pretty fantastic too.

From her point of view, the good news just kept coming. She asked, of course, about her husband's current position within the community, knowing that he'd left the Manteno ministry almost eighteen months earlier but little more than that.

She was not prepared for what her friends told her.

The church itself had split. Back in 1861, a group of parishioners had begun, in Theophilus's words, to give "great trouble to the church" as they protested against the new doctrines they'd been ordered to follow—exactly as Elizabeth had done the year before. Where one person leads, others may follow... Eventually, there were so many of them they became impossible to ignore; they could not all be locked up in insane asylums like the pastor's wife. Instead, the church divided, with the resistant members establishing a Congregational church that followed New School doctrines.

The church elders blamed Theophilus for the members' exodus. There was also a rumor that some parishioners left not because of the doctrines but because of his treatment of his wife. Either way, "he preached until none would come to hear him." Eventually, "in order to save the church from utter extinction," the deacons had requested his resignation.

So Theophilus had lost his job. Despite his desperate efforts in 1860 to retain his position—to the extent of abandoning his principles and silencing the wife who would not—it had all been for nothing.

"We lived without any salary," Theophilus confided in his diary, "and with a debt of nearly $4,000... Yet through...the kindness of beloved friends...we had a house, food & clothes."

Elizabeth's friends told her that house was one she would no longer recognize. Understandably, Libby had been unable to maintain her mother's high standards. The Packard home was now "desolate-looking," with an "extra amount of defilement—the accumulations of three years."

Hearing this, Elizabeth at once engaged a hired girl to help get everything shipshape. She asked her to come the following day, planning to use the Granville fund to pay her. Elizabeth had no compunction in asserting her domestic authority in this way, because her intention, having now returned home, was "to do my whole duty in the family, as mother and housekeeper." However, she'd definitively *not* returned as a *wife*; after her husband's behavior, she believed "the marriage contract is no more binding on me...than is the lamb bound to be the wolf's wife, after the wolf has once torn his defenceless body to pieces."

Throughout that dinnertime, she and her friends discussed the course she should now follow. In the immediate future, Elizabeth had only one plan: she wanted to see her babies. So eventually the Blessings, Hasletts, and Elizabeth returned to the depot to collect her trunk. At the station, Elizabeth withdrew all her papers and pressed them into Sarah Haslett's hands. Sarah was "the most efficient friend I knew of in Manteno"; Elizabeth trusted her to keep them safe. They'd be better off with her, Elizabeth knew, than under the same roof as her treacherous husband.

She shut the trunk, absent its treasures for the first time since their creation. It was almost like being without a part of herself. Mr. Blessing then heaved the trunk into his carriage and extended his hand down toward her. He and his team of horses were going to drive her to her door. He offered to come in with her—even to provide a permanent bodyguard if she wished—but Elizabeth declined. She didn't want to get Theophilus's back up any more than it already would be from her returning in the first place. Her hope now was that they could coexist. She would not trample on his rights, hoping he would respect hers also. They had both made this home and these beautiful children. Why could they not both enjoy them peaceably?

Elizabeth's breath must have caught in her throat when she saw her home again for the first time in three years. Green shutters. A rather dilapidated garden. A dirty house, yes, but a house that was still *hers*.

Mr. Blessing lifted her trunk up onto the porch for her. Then he climbed back into his carriage, urging his horses on.

The sound of their hooves faded as Elizabeth faced the door.

Alone, she entered in.

CHAPTER 38

The front door opened easily. Elizabeth walked into the reception room, her eyes drinking in the dearly familiar furniture. There was her china closet, painted pea green by her own fair hands. Her settee, covered over with a black throw. Table, bureau, mirror, pictures... After years living in monastic plainness at the asylum, it was like returning to a palace.

Yet there were no princesses or princes she could see. She kept walking, through to the kitchen, the heart of the home, located at the back of the house.

The first person she saw was Theophilus. He sat in an easy chair beside the stove. The kitchen seemed to have become his study; stationery and papers were strewn about. Yet she had no eyes for her husband or even the mess. In his arms was baby Arthur.

Though surely, this was not the same child. Now nearly five, he was a baby no more. She had missed so much.

She went straight to him, ignoring Theophilus's strained greeting; he did not get up. She pulled Arthur from his father's arms, seemingly without resistance, and commenced caressing her child, marveling over this little boy who was her own, yet so much a stranger. As she fussed, the back door opened, and George and Libby came running in. She hugged and kissed them, then sat down with Arthur on her knee and the other two children before her.

"[You are] going to have a mother again," she told them happily. "I [have] come to take care of [you] and hope we [shall] be very happy, and never be separated again."

She could barely believe she was back in her own kitchen, with her own children before her. In her imagination, though, it had never been quite like this. The children had been smaller, for a start. And Isaac had been present; in reality, her nineteen-year-old had moved out and was living in Chicago, as was Toffy at that time. Samuel was missing, too, though he did still live at home; he was almost sixteen.

It was perhaps Libby who'd changed the most. She was still the "perfect image" of her father, however; Elizabeth wrote, with a mother's cutting honesty, that her daughter was "as good and gentle in temper as she is bad in looks." Aged thirteen going on thirty, Libby protested at being called "little daughter" these days, indignantly pointing out that she was "in my *fourteenth* year." Nevertheless, in Elizabeth's eyes, she was still so young.

"My daughter," she said to her now, "won't it be pleasant to have someone to relieve you of your...responsibilities?"

But it was Theophilus who answered, looking at these scenes of reunion in disgust.

"No," he snapped, "you an't wanted here! We get along better without you!"

Yet whatever her husband claimed, Elizabeth could see that wasn't true. Dirt lay thickly all over the house, the beds needed airing, and she dreaded imagining the state of the carpets.

The next day, rolling up her sleeves, she got straight to work. But Theophilus seemed determined to block her, notwithstanding the domestic sphere was supposed to be her own. By now, Elizabeth had transgressed too much even to be allowed that woman's world. He fired the girl she'd hired before she'd even crossed the threshold. He forbade the children from helping with any aspect of her planned spring clean. Even when Elizabeth placed a simple saucepan on the stove to boil some water to clean the walls with, Theophilus took it off again: "You shall heat no water upon *my* stove." In response, trying to keep the peace, Elizabeth merely bit her tongue. She cleaned with cold water instead.

When Rebecca and Sarah called by on October 26, she'd moved on to the feather beds and was scrubbing them in the yard. Rebecca noted that "they needed cleaning badly." Sarah was simply delighted to see her friend's hard work paying off: "It looked as if the mistress of the house was at home."

Yet Elizabeth confided that things were not as picturesque as they might appear. One problem was that the locks and keys of the asylum had seemingly followed her home. Theophilus had locked her good clothes and all her linen in a closet and refused to give her the key. She could neither change the sheets when she wanted nor access her winter hose and the smarter garments she'd longed for ever since he'd sent only her dilapidated clothes to the asylum. Yet he was immovable in not letting her gain access, even though he allowed the children the key—a slight that did not go unnoticed. Only Elizabeth could not be trusted, lunatic that she supposedly was.

Worse, he ordered the children not to mind her. She felt they'd developed slovenly habits in her absence regarding "bathing, toilet duties, hours of rising and retiring, and their wardrobe." Yet when she tried to encourage the stricter behavior she'd always insisted on in the past, Theophilus cut in. He "required them to disregard my directions, whenever they conflicted with his own plans or wishes." But Theophilus did not seem even to *see* the dirt she easily spied behind her children's ears and ingrained in their home. "It don't need it," Theophilus would snap when she tried to clean something, batting her hands away.

There had been one particular scene that had really hurt. One day, soon after she returned, she saw Libby struggling to make piecrust in the kitchen. When she stepped up to the table and excitedly said, "Let me show you how to make your crust, my daughter, I see you don't understand how to do it," Theophilus once again intervened.

With "his hand upraised" and his voice "loud and most authoritative," he'd shouted, "I forbid your interference!"

It seemed his wife could do nothing right.

Yet uncharacteristically, Elizabeth did not speak up for herself. "I exchanged no words with Mr. Packard upon this or any other subject—I knew argument was useless," she explained, "and…would only add fuel to the flame of hatred and distrust which evidently still rankled within him."

At least she claimed that was the reason why. It could have been something else was going on. Perhaps she'd finally learned her lesson. After all, being too assertive might get her locked up in another asylum. Now she was finally home, finally back with her children, the idea of another banishment must have seemed even more dreadful than before.

She had more motivation to avoid it too. Surely the worst thing of all about being home again was the discovery that her children *had* been taught she was insane. Though Elizabeth maintained in some of her writings that "three years was too short a time for their father to convince these children," every single day, they were instructed "not to respect the counsels or heed the voice of a maniac just loosed from the Asylum."

The situation must have been desperate for Elizabeth. It made it even more crucial that she was not committed again. As calmly as she could, she went about her business.

And as she shopped in Manteno, exclaiming with her fellow towns-people at the shocking price of goods in the midst of war—the cost of bread and eggs had almost doubled since she'd gone away—she had pleasant conversations with her neighbors, such as Joseph Labrie, the local postmaster, and Isaac Simington, the Methodist minister. Her conduct gave clear evidence to her community of her state of mind.

"I have seen nothing that could make me think her insane," Labrie later commented, in a sentiment seemingly shared by all—except for her husband's friends. They still maintained that she was mad, partly because Elizabeth bluntly ignored them. She'd determined to withdraw friendship from anyone who'd ever called her insane, "until they had made suitable satisfaction to me for the wrongs they had done." Why grant the time of day to those who'd colluded in her committal?

But they saw only the unnatural sight of a woman holding a grudge.

Elizabeth spent most of her time, when not at home, visiting the Hasletts and the Blessings. Sometimes they met at the Blessings' hotel; at others they went to nearby Kankakee. Theophilus, keeping tabs on his wife, noted these meetings in his diary, complaining that these "mischievous intermeddlers, male and female" made a habit of "meeting her secretly with locked doors."

And those friends were outraged by his behavior. They felt Elizabeth deserved to be allowed to mother her children as she wished. She deserved for them to respect her. She certainly deserved access to her own wardrobe so she could once again assume the place in society she'd long ago lost. Clothing *mattered*, and Theophilus's continued confiscation of his wife's best outfits was deliberate. Elizabeth's friends were so disturbed by his actions that they appointed a committee to protect her.

Come October 30, 1863, it decided to take preemptive action before things got any worse.

Theophilus saw them coming to the house. "A Manteno mob assembled," he recorded crossly, though his description appears hyperbolic, as he clarified it was actually only "a couple of men." These were probably Mr. Haslett and Mr. Blessing, whom he described as "the chief instigators in all these scenes of mischief."

Theophilus was lucky that day: he was not home alone. His brother-in-law Hervey Severance, married to his sister Marian, was visiting from Massachusetts, and his sister Sybil Dole was present too, along with Libby and Samuel. All watched as the men came into their home and began to question Theophilus about the way he'd been treating his wife.

"O what scenes were these!" the pastor lamented in his diary, outraged that these outsiders had come "to regulate my family affairs." "I cannot *here* describe them," he added tightly, words failing him, aghast at his neighbors' audacity.

But to his surprise, help came in his hour of need from a most unexpected source: Elizabeth. She, too, was in the room when her friends came to help her. And when they questioned her husband, it was Elizabeth who interjected.

She said she had received "good treatment," thank you very much. She said she "had a great deal of attention paid to her," though she was seemingly unaware of just how close Theophilus's surveillance really was.

She had still not finished. Taking a deep breath, she said she "did not wish the committee to examine into their family affairs."

She refused the help of her would-be rescuers.

Her speech made, Elizabeth Packard "left the room, the committee, and the house."

Theophilus merely nodded in satisfaction as he sent the intermeddlers away: *his* home, *his* wife, *his* way.

At long last, it seemed even Elizabeth was starting to accept that.

CHAPTER 39

If it wasn't for the intermeddlers, Theophilus Packard thought in November 1863, he could have considered himself quite satisfied. Elizabeth's return did not appear to have torn the children from him as he may have feared. All were still toeing his line, with Libby, in particular, a "great comfort" to him; he seemed to rely on her a lot emotionally.

Perhaps the most pleasant surprise had been Elizabeth's own behavior. She'd excused herself from family prayers, so there was no conflict there, and in truth she barely spoke to him. Even if her silence came from resentment, he did not much care. Really, the maddest thing she did these days was to keep asking for those Bible class essays she'd written in the spring of 1860. He'd commandeered them long ago but refused to return them. What she might want with them, he could not imagine.

But those intermeddlers... They refused to give up. To his dismay, they were persistently "prejudicing and influencing the public mind" against him, refusing to let the matter of Elizabeth's treatment drop.

Yet there was a development in mid-November that meant he suddenly had to treat Elizabeth very differently indeed. A set of keys went missing. Theophilus was immediately suspicious that Elizabeth had stolen them. The sense of security he'd been lulled into vanished in a flash.

He searched her person, but though he patted her down this way and that and even stripped her clothes from her, they were not hidden there. He searched her room. Her wardrobe. Her trunk. Elizabeth watched him rifling through her things as he "took an inventory of every article." Silently, she gave thanks that all her precious papers were safely stored with Sarah Haslett. God only knew what Theophilus might have done with them had he found them.

But he not only didn't find her papers; he did not find the keys.

His search widened. "The entire house and premises were most carefully and diligently searched in every corner, nook, and crevice," Elizabeth observed. "Even the embers of my stove were examined."

Still no keys.

The search headed outdoors, where "every stone, leaf and shrub were upturned to find the missing keys—but all to no purpose."

Theophilus was frantic. The bunch of keys that were missing were not only for the linen closet but also for the house. He feared what Elizabeth might do with them—and the freedom they afforded her. He could not let the matter stand. He was convinced she'd taken them and wanted to give her no opportunity of using them at all.

So he locked her in her nursery; he pocketed that key. As he'd done in 1860, he got out his hammer and nails and shut up the windows, blocking her in. He made sure the front and back doors were always securely fastened or guarded so she could not escape. He stopped her from joining the family for meals, intercepted her mail, and, crucially, cut her off from all communication with her friends. The intermeddlers had had it all their own way for far too long. He'd had enough of Elizabeth running off to see them and of them dropping in to visit. They were a bad influence.

He even roped his son Samuel into this imprisonment: a mini jailer who stepped up to the plate. "I...refused a woman admittance," said Elizabeth's third-born son, "as she invariably made mother worse every time she came."

Ironically, almost concurrent with Elizabeth being confined in this ever-tightening cage, Abraham Lincoln delivered the famous Gettysburg Address. "This nation, under God, shall have a new birth of freedom," the president promised his country.

But Elizabeth's freedom had never seemed further away than at that time.

———

Theophilus was aware his makeshift jail could only be temporary. He therefore wrote to Dr. McFarland to request he readmit Elizabeth, perhaps thinking that the local state asylum would be more convenient than the Massachusetts one. He'd warned his wife: if she ever returned to the children, he would send her away. On this matter at least, the pastor intended to keep his word.

In the meantime, he kept his wife locked up, his temper fraying by the day. Rebecca Blessing remembered calling on Elizabeth with another friend, sixty-nine-year-old Abigail "Nabby" Hanford. But Theophilus, Rebecca said, "would not let us see her; he shook his hand at me, and threatened to put me out." Elizabeth, too, reported physical violence: Theophilus "striking" her and "dragging [her] by the hair."

It was a miserable existence. Elizabeth's only entertainment was peering out through her fastened windows, the only highlight a stranger passing by each morning as he collected water from the Packards' pump. Yet her husband did not care. "His sympathy is as empty of a soul or heart as a crab-apple is of sweetness."

Nor did Theophilus listen to the protestations of her friends at his cruelty. On the contrary. He commissioned new certificates from the Doles to combat what his allies called "false and slanderous reports."

"Mrs. Packard, the afflicted and deranged member of the family," wrote Sybil and Abijah Dole, "has not to our knowledge, been treated otherwise than in a kind and suitable manner."

That "suitable" was key. Elizabeth was supposedly a madwoman, after all. Theophilus and Samuel thought her friends' visits made her mental condition worse, so was it not a kindness to prohibit them? Given Elizabeth's sickness, surely it *was* suitable treatment that she wasn't free to leave the house? As a leading psychiatrist of the day put it, "To deprive the insane of their liberty is a sort of first principle...and so imperative as to render...interference...unnecessary and impertinent. Nobody questions the right of the husband to confine his wife in his own house if she is [mad]."

Theophilus soon had reason to believe his "suitable" treatment was working. Around this time, Elizabeth suddenly acquiesced to a request he'd long been making.

He was trying at the time to sell some real estate, but the law required his wife's consent. Elizabeth had refused to give it. Long ago, her wealthy father had gifted her $600 (about $18,000), and—as most wives would have done in that era—she'd entrusted it to Theophilus for safekeeping. Yet since 1860, Theophilus had refused to trust her with even $10 of it. In all likelihood, Elizabeth's fund had probably been swallowed up by his secret debts. But Elizabeth refused to sign the property paperwork until he returned this patrimony. With the money long gone, the Packards had been left at loggerheads. Yet Elizabeth now proposed a deal: she'd give her consent *if* he returned her Bible class essays.

It was an easy win for Theophilus. He couldn't see why she wanted them anyway. He called in Mr. Labrie—who was not only the postmaster but a notary public—and asked him to prepare the deeds.

Labrie therefore visited the house...and expressed consternation. "The door to her room was locked on the outside," he observed. "Mr. Packard said, he had made up his mind to let no one into her room."

But Labrie was allowed in, on that day at least. The essays and signatures were duly exchanged.

Possibly in response to Labrie's reports of the new reality inside the Packard home, Elizabeth's friends tried once again to reach her. Sarah Haslett, now in the early stages of another pregnancy, called on her one day; she was barred by Samuel. She did not give up. She went to the fastened window and conversed with Elizabeth through it.

Elizabeth reportedly begged to be "released from her imprisonment." She wanted "protection from Mr. Packard's cruelty."

"I advised her," Sarah said, desperate to help, "to not stand it quietly, but get a divorce."

But Elizabeth didn't *want* to be divorced. Under nineteenth-century law, to divorce her husband would also be to divorce herself from her children and home. She would have to sue for the rights to both and was highly unlikely to win. Although a handful of mothers had been successful in winning custody suits by the 1860s, almost every such published decision underlined that fathers' rights took precedence. These rare pro-mother decisions were exceptions to the rule.

"Would it not be becoming an accomplice in [his] crime, by doing the very deed which he is so desirous of having done," she said plainly, "namely: to remove me from my family?"

Learning of her resistance, Theophilus could not help but be glad. As long as Elizabeth remained his wife, it would be easy to commit her. He hoped, any day now, to return her to Jacksonville.

But in December 1863, a wrench was thrown in the works of this intended arrangement. McFarland wrote to inform him that the trustees had refused to readmit Elizabeth on the grounds she was incurable. The doctor said—in what was possibly a white lie, given her troublemaking tendencies—that he'd "favored her readmission."

The pastor filed the letter among his papers with bitter disappointment. He was not used to having his plans thwarted.

Yet he was not *too* disheartened.

Time to effect plan B.

CHAPTER 40

In the winter of 1863, the Northampton asylum in Massachusetts held 383 patients, 216 of them women. Theophilus schemed that very soon, Elizabeth would be among them.

Though he already possessed McFarland's certificate of insanity, the pastor wanted to secure a declaration from another doctor too. He'd in fact started this ball rolling as early as November with a Manteno physician, James Mann.

"Mr. Packard had told me she was insane," reported the doctor, "and my prejudices were, that she was insane."

Mann had come to the house and interviewed Elizabeth. To his surprise, he'd found a rational woman. "I was there from one to two hours," he said. "I could find nothing that indicated insanity."

He'd refused to issue a certificate.

At the time, it hadn't much bothered Theophilus. McFarland thought her mad, and if Jacksonville accepted her as planned, no other doctor's view was needed.

But with Jacksonville no longer an option, Theophilus renewed his efforts once more. He invited Mann back again, but despite a second interview, the doctor still insisted Elizabeth was sane.

So Theophilus invited Dr. Joseph Way, from Kankakee, to examine his wife. The native New Yorker came for two hours. In that time, he gained Elizabeth's trust, because she confided in him.

"She said she liked her children and that it was hard to be torn from them," Way reported. "That none but a mother could feel the anguish she had suffered; that while she was confined in the Asylum, the children had been educated by their father to call her insane."

Way thought her "easily excited" with a "nervous temperament." Yet as they chatted about various subjects, he found her "perfectly sane." At least until they talked about religion. Elizabeth, he felt, expressed "undue excitement on that subject." Her original thinking was shocking too. He therefore reached the conclusion Theophilus desired: "I thought her to be somewhat deranged or excited on that subject [of religion]."

Theophilus duly added Way's certificate to his file.

All these visits from physicians made Elizabeth suspicious. When another man walked through her door in the week before Christmas, she asked him directly if he was a doctor.

But he wasn't. He was a sewing machine salesman. She ended up chatting with him for three hours, an extraordinary amount of time to grant a passing salesman, which spoke volumes about Elizabeth's loneliness. They talked about sewing machines, women's rights, the war, and religion.

But the salesman, Elizabeth thought, showed rather too much interest in her views on the latter. As they raked over the subject on which so many had previously found fault with her, Elizabeth suddenly felt foreboding. Her mouth fell silent; her manner became clipped. She felt "some calamity would befall her" because of this stranger. It was mad in itself, she knew, to fear such an innocent passerby. Nevertheless, when he took his leave, she refused to shake his hand. She did not care what he thought; she just wanted this black crow of calamity gone.

After he'd left, she got really scared. Before the year was out, she suggested, radically, to Theophilus that she leave the house—to go alone to New York to try to get her book published.

But Theophilus couldn't allow that. His plan to incarcerate her for life was nearing fruition. If she left now, all his preparation would have been in vain.

"It [is] my duty to prevent [you] going," he told her strongly.

He said he used no force to stop her. Whether he did or didn't, he got his way. He wrote in his diary, "She gave it up."

The new year started with an unusual spell of extreme cold weather that more than matched the atmosphere in the Packard home. Across the state, people froze to death from the terrible temperatures; others suffered frostbite and amputated limbs. Snowdrifts were ten feet deep, the thermometer showing thirty degrees below zero. Outdoor operations were "almost totally suspended, except such as were necessary to the preservation of life."

Stuck indoors, chained as much by the weather as by Theophilus's edicts, Elizabeth proposed to the children that they clean and polish the cookstove one day, to which plan her husband, for once, consented. He withdrew to the nursery while they worked, taking his mass of papers with him. Feeling the chill, he lit Elizabeth's stove to warm him.

But there was no such heat come Saturday, January 9, 1864. On this day, Nabby Hanford and Rebecca Blessing tried again to visit Elizabeth.

To their surprise, they were allowed in—almost as though their bad influence no longer mattered. Theophilus simply found the nursery key and unlocked the door to let them enter.

Shockingly, they found Elizabeth sitting in a room with no fire. Given the extreme weather, it was cruel indeed. Yet the three women had no choice but to sit there in the freezing cold, with Theophilus apparently unconcerned at the incivility.

But his worries were almost over. He was just days away from taking Elizabeth to the Northampton asylum. He counted them down in the way he'd always counted slights against him: harboring them close to his chest, picking over them like a vulture. The Saturday passed without incident, then Sunday and Monday too.

But at 10:00 a.m. on Tuesday, January 12, the pastor's plot abruptly derailed.

He perhaps heard the horses' hooves first, pounding to his door. Then an officious knock that demanded answer. When he opened up, a court clerk stood upon his doorstep. He presented the pastor with a legal writ.

A writ of habeas corpus.

Theophilus knew exactly who to blame. "Four intermeddlers in town got out a writ of *Habeas Corpus*," he raged, "as though I was falsely imprisoning her!"

He did not seem to see the cleverness behind that legal filing.

Because such a document could never have been issued if Elizabeth was already at Northampton. Then, her commitment would have been legal. But to be held by her husband in her own home was not. Who was Theophilus to keep her prisoner? Not a doctor, protected by the perks of his profession. A cruel husband: no more, no less. Because locking up a wife in her own home *was* potentially unlawful, and habeas corpus could therefore be used to grant her a trial to find out.

That was something Elizabeth and her friends had known—for months. They'd known it ever since their first attempt to free her from the asylum had failed. They'd certainly known it since that fall, when they'd visited lawyers in Kankakee and then secretly plotted behind locked doors...

And it was something Elizabeth had known that past November, when she'd stolen the house keys from her husband and buried them in the sodden earth beneath her bedroom window.

She took them not to use them but to ensure he locked her up.

"Thus was my imprisonment in my home secured," she wrote triumphantly, "whereby a writ of *habeas corpus* could be legally obtained."

He had thought it was her he was imprisoning as he'd nailed shut her window and locked up her door. In fact, Theophilus had unwittingly boxed himself into a corner: hammering home the nails in his own coffin, dealing himself a fatal blow, sealing his own dire fate with every heavy hammer blow he'd rained upon her window.

CHAPTER 41

Theophilus scanned the writ with angry eyes:

> We command you, that the body of Elizabeth P. W.
> Packard, in your custody detained and imprisoned...[be
> brought] before Charles R. Starr, Judge...at his cham-
> bers, at Kankakee City...on the 12th instant, at one
> o'clock P.M.

One o'clock was only three hours away.

It was, therefore, a rushed goodbye. Elizabeth barely had time to call Libby, George, and Arthur to her, to plant upon them a hurried parting kiss, before she and Theophilus headed straight to Kankakee, the clock against her husband all the while.

As they rode the twelve miles through the snow-strewn country-side, Elizabeth may have noticed "a rise of the mercury [and] snow that has lost its crunchiness." The impasse between herself and her husband was not the only thing that had broken; the weather was beginning to thaw too.

As they traveled, Elizabeth let her mind sweep back over the whole operation. Though the doctors' visits had scared her, it had been a discovery on the day she'd cleaned the cookstove that had really lit the dynamite of her planted bomb. When she'd exchanged places with Theophilus in her nursery after the spring clean, she'd realized that in his haste to leave her room, he'd left a package of his letters behind. She did not notice them until nightfall and at first had thought it would be wrong to examine them.

She'd soon concluded, however, that she'd be a fool not "to avail myself of every lawful means of self-defense which lay within my reach." She'd therefore spent several hours carefully reading the letters.

And there, laid out as plain as day but seen by the light of the moon, was Theophilus's recent correspondence with McFarland and the superintendent of the Northampton asylum. The latter had happily agreed to admit her "as a case of hopeless insanity, upon the certificate of Dr. McFarland that she is 'hopelessly' insane."

It was the first Elizabeth knew of that damning certificate, which allowed Theophilus to imprison her as soon as blink. The treachery took her breath away. But worse than McFarland's machinations was the date of her planned admittance.

It was just days away.

Immediately, Elizabeth had become frantic, memories of her Jacksonville experiences exploding in her mind. "O, when one has been thus degraded [in an asylum], to come back again! Can anything be more dreadful!" she thought. Though she'd suspected Theophilus might carry out his longtime threat, to see the proof of his plan made his cruelty suddenly concrete. "Three long years of false imprisonment does not satisfy this lust for power," she raged. "No—nothing but a life-long entombment!"

And she truly feared what her treatment might be like at Northampton, should her husband succeed in his plans.

"I should run a poor chance of being well-treated, there," she real-ized, "since [Theophilus] would be very apt to tell them that I was so troublesome under Dr. McFarland's care, that they would not receive me a second time. And he might tell them that Dr. McFarland kept me in a ward with the worst maniacs in the house... How could my word or representation be relied upon, under such circumstances? Could I expect anything but the reception, and treatment, of a maniac, there?"

Seeing the dates on the correspondence, she realized bleakly, "In a few days I should be beyond the reach of all human help."

She needed to set the wheels of her own plan rolling—and fast. But how could she get word to her friends that she needed help immediately when she was not permitted to communicate?

She suddenly remembered the stranger who passed by her window every morning. He was now her only hope. She quickly scribbled a note to Sarah Haslett, informing her of the imminent danger. When, the next morning, the stranger passed by, she beckoned him to her and man-aged to slide the note out from her sash window. She found a small gap where its two parts came together, though they could not be pried apart.

"Stranger, please hand this note to Mrs. Haslett," she whispered urgently.

It had therefore been Sarah who'd raised the alarm. Given the prox-imity of danger, a proposal was made that Elizabeth simply break the window to escape and her friends would protect her, but Elizabeth rejected this hasty plan. "If I should not finally succeed in this attempt," she reasoned, "my persecutors would gain advantage over me, in that I had once injured property, as a reason why I should be locked up."

Instead, Sarah went to the Kankakee courts, and with her went four men: her husband, William Haslett; seventy-two-year-old Zalmon Hanford, husband of Elizabeth's friend Nabby; sixty-five-year-old

Daniel Beedy, Manteno's first-ever town supervisor; and sixty-one-year-old Joseph Younglove, a local merchant. It was these four men—"responsible citizens" one and all—who'd filed the writ of habeas corpus on Elizabeth's behalf.

And now, mere hours after he'd been summoned, Theophilus arrived outside the Kankakee courthouse with his wife. Both looked up at the grand building with something approaching awe. It was an impressive, three-story monument, constructed from brick and limestone and topped with a pretty wooden cupola. The Packards duly entered, passing by jail cells on the first floor, county offices on the second, before finally arriving at the courtroom on the third.

Though Kankakee was the county seat, one wouldn't have known from its dilapidated courtroom. It had a bare floor and "ill-arranged seats," which made it "very difficult for the Officers of the Court to preserve the order and decorum which should at all times be preserved in a Court of Justice."

On that front, Elizabeth's habeas corpus hearing was already proving challenging. A massive crowd had gathered; Theophilus observed it was "enraged" and "seething." Kankakee was a religiously diverse city, its population of thirty-eight hundred worshipping at nine different churches. Elizabeth's case, as described by her friends, had already inspired outrage. As Elizabeth put it, "I have neglected no duties, have injured no one, have always tried to do unto others as I would wish to be done by; and yet, here in America, I am imprisoned because I could not say I believed what I did not believe."

Theophilus viewed the crowd with apprehension. At least he could take some comfort from his lawyers. Two stood to represent him. One was Mason Loomis, a young lawyer in his midtwenties, who shared office space with Dr. Knott, the Kankakee physician who'd issued Theophilus with a certificate of insanity in 1860. His other, lead attorney was the impressive Thomas Bonfield.

Bonfield's name was almost synonymous with that of Kankakee. He was one of its earliest settlers, becoming its first elected president in 1855. Aged thirty-six, he was a neat man with a balding forehead, tightly clipped beard, and astute, dark eyes. "Devoid of all ostentation," being a quiet chap with a retiring disposition, Bonfield sat calmly at his lawyer's table, his presence reassuring to the anxious minister.

The lawyer who was to fight in Elizabeth's corner could not have been more different. Thirty-one-year-old "Steve" Moore was of Irish descent, "the life and soul" of any party. He loved a good practical joke and wore his beard outrageously long, like a legal Santa Claus. Good-natured and humorous, courteous and affable, he attracted "hosts of friends" wherever he went. He had a strong nose, bushy eyebrows, and a solid head that contained a remarkable brain. Becoming a lawyer had been his childhood dream, and he was known as "one of the most gifted and able members" of his profession.

Yet he was also one of the most thoughtful, "benevolent and charitable above the average of his fellow-men." His biography declared, "He gives his bread to the hungry and never turns 'his face from any poor man.'" With the Civil War aflame, he'd recently started representing war widows struggling to get pensions, often acting without fees. For Elizabeth, he'd done the same, agreeing to defend her "without any expectation of fee or reward, except such as arises from a consciousness of having discharged my duty toward a helpless and penniless woman." He was assisted in his endeavors by two attorneys: twenty-nine-year-old James Orr, and Harrison Loring, a decade older.

With the company all assembled, the judge, Charles Starr, swiftly began proceedings. First on the agenda was Theophilus's written response to the writ, pulled together only that morning.

The thirty-nine-year-old judge bent his head to read. A handsome man, he had a full head of salt-and-pepper hair, a curly beard, and thoughtful eyes. Starr was known to be conscientious, with a well-grounded knowledge of the law, his judgments "distinguished by the utmost fairness and impartiality." He was entering his seventh year

Judge Charles R. Starr

in the job, but he'd never encountered a case like *this* before.

Theophilus's lawyers were vocal in protesting the "very short time" their client had had to prepare his defense. But Starr honestly wouldn't have known it from the thick file before him. Thanks to Theophilus's preparations for committing Elizabeth to Northampton, he was immediately able to supply the judge with McFarland's certificate and many other supportive documents. He absolutely denied the imprisonment or unlawful restraint of his wife, claiming she was insane, incurably so, and had been in the asylum for the past three years for that very reason.

Starr read carefully through the documentation. He questioned Theophilus. Under the judge's steady gaze, a slight change in the pastor's account came through.

"I...denied the charge of imprisonment," Theophilus later wrote, "but admitted the exercise of a slight necessary restraint over her on account of her insanity."

The judge looked over at Elizabeth Packard. She sat at her counsel's table, occasionally speaking with her lawyers about their management of her case. According to an eyewitness, she behaved "as one who is not only not insane, but as one possessing intellectual endowments of a high order, and an equipoise and control of mind far above the majority of humankind."

The judge may well have scratched his salt-and-pepper head.

Starr was not only a lawyerly but literary man, renowned in the town for his "genuine imaginative powers." As he pondered the perplexing evidence before him, he decided to draw on them to resolve this thorny case.

Theophilus had testified he'd restrained his wife because she was insane.

Starr now had just two words for the man.

"Prove it!"

CHAPTER 42

It had taken four years, but Elizabeth Packard had finally been given the insanity trial she had always wanted. Never had it been more important. In short, the trial was her only hope for any kind of future outside an asylum's walls.

Nor were the stakes high solely for herself. After all, if the court ruled *for* her, what did that say about the unjust law by which married women could be committed "without the evidence of insanity…required in other cases"?

The judge moved at once to empanel a jury of twelve men to adjudicate on whether Elizabeth was mad. Bonfield immediately objected. It was a highly unusual course for the judge to have taken. Not only were married women not supposed to be allowed insanity trials at all, but this had *originally* been a habeas corpus case, in which the judge alone was supposed to rule. But the objection was dismissed.

Theophilus was spitting mad. "It was illegal," he alleged of the judge's decision. He thought the angry crowd, with its "impudent, violent mob spirit," had influenced Starr to make a corrupt, self-motivated call. "The direct votes of the people choose periodically the Judge," Theophilus hissed, "and the time for an election will at length arrive."

Though the mass of people who'd turned out to support Elizabeth were religiously diverse, Theophilus noted only that they were "of a different persuasion" to him. He'd always had a them-versus-us mentality when it came to religion; he was quick to charge the spectators were "excited by sectarian prejudice."

Therefore Bonfield, having had his first objection overruled, immediately prepared an application for a change of venue, echoing his client in alleging that "a jury could not be obtained that would not...partake" of the sectarian feeling. Yet in the end, he decided not to present it.

That was probably because as the jury members began to be selected, that allegation of sectarian prejudice simply could not stand. Of the twelve jurymen, five were Presbyterian: Theophilus's religion.

As would be expected, the jurymen came from a range of backgrounds. There was a shoemaker, an architect, the owner of a livery stable, and another who ran a local saloon. There was even a major landowner, Lemuel Milk, who seemed a good choice to Elizabeth's counsel; he was known for being "the reverse of orthodox" when it came to religion. That was the kind of juryman Stephen Moore was after.

The jury took the oath. Then, with a bang of the judge's gavel, Elizabeth's trial began.

———

Theophilus was asked to present his case first. Though he'd busied himself since 1860 collecting documentation to support his position, he'd never wanted to see this day. He had an unfortunate record of coming off badly whenever his behavior was judged in court. Notably, he always gave a familiar excuse as to why. "The case was tried amid great sectarian prejudice," he'd once complained of a previous brush with the law in which he'd lost the case. But whether he wanted it or not, the legal spotlight was squarely on him now.

The first witness called was Christopher Knott, the certificate-issuing doctor on whose word Elizabeth had been committed in 1860.

"I am a practicing physician in Kankakee City," Knott testified. "Have been in practice fifteen years. Have seen Mrs. Packard; saw her three or four years ago. Am not much acquainted with her." He described the two half-hour visits he'd made to her home in which Elizabeth had not even been told she was being examined and concluded, "I thought her partially deranged on religious matters, and gave a certificate to that effect." He finished, "I have never seen her since."

Which rather made his opinion as to her *present* state of mind somewhat questionable.

Moore began his cross-examination—and he elicited a gem from the doctor. "She was what might be called a monomaniac," Knott opined. "Monomania is insanity on one subject. Three-fourths of the religious community are insane in the same manner, in *my* opinion."

It was an outrageous thing to say and likely raised a ripple through the courtroom. "Hisses even from the females," observed Theophilus, "threats and outrageous language pervaded the atmosphere."

Perhaps that was why the doctor hurriedly added, "Her insanity was such that with a little rest she would readily have recovered from it."

That was an intriguing opinion. It certainly did not support a three-year incarceration in the Jacksonville asylum, nor Theophilus's current plan of lifelong commitment.

Bonfield had to cross-examine after that account. He grilled Knott on Elizabeth's hatred of her husband, which had been such an obvious symptom to McFarland. But at this line of questioning, Knott qualified his answer.

"Insanity produces, oftentimes, ill-feelings towards the best friends, and particularly the family," he acknowledged, "but not so with monomania... I had no doubt that she was insane [but] I only considered her insane on that subject, and she was not bad at that. I thought if she was withdrawn from conversation and excitement, she could have got well in a short time."

But surely, her committal to the asylum was necessary?

"Confinement in any shape, or restraint, would have made her worse," testified Dr. Knott. He repeated, "I did not think it was a bad case; it only required rest."

It was not exactly the testimony the pastor's legal team had planned. Thank goodness, then, for Dr. J. W. Brown, who took the stand thereafter.

Elizabeth's brow likely furrowed as his name was called. She knew of no doctor by this name. As she watched him enter, her jaw probably dropped. She may not have known the name, but she'd have recognized that face anywhere—having recently spent three hours sitting opposite it.

For into the courtroom strode the "sewing-machine salesman" she'd met just before Christmas.

Elizabeth reassessed what she'd thought was paranoia at their meeting. She'd been *right* to fear some calamity from his presence. He'd been intending to help her husband lock her up.

And now he had the perfect opportunity to do so.

Brown strutted to the stand with the confidence of a man who liked to boast he had achieved "almost unparalleled" success in his chosen field. He loved to talk in "the high-flown language of an expert" and seemed ready to enjoy his moment on the stand.

He was sworn and confirmed he was a physician from Kankakee. He gave a full account of his recent "extended conference" with Elizabeth.

"I had no difficulty in arriving at the conclusion, in my mind, that she was insane," he announced emphatically.

Bonfield retired, his shoulders relaxing, having gotten the killer statement in the bag.

Stephen Moore rose to cross-examine. Perhaps at Elizabeth's prompting, he drew out from Brown that strange, underhanded tactic of concealing his true identity from his client.

"She asked me if I was a physician," Brown confirmed, "and I told her no; that I was an agent, selling sewing machines, and had come there to sell her one." In a rare moment of levity, he continued, "The first subject we conversed about was sewing machines. She showed no signs of insanity on *that* subject."

Moore talked him through the other topics they'd discussed, but although Brown conceded that on most, Elizabeth "exhibited no special marks of insanity," he still would not be swayed from his focal point.

"I brought up the subject of religion," he testified. "Then I had not the slightest difficulty in concluding that she was hopelessly insane."

Moore paused. As a lawyer, he was famed for his "clear and lucid" logic and his ability to use "simplicity of statement" to make his points clear to a jury, no matter their own intellectual ability. He decided to drill into Elizabeth's so-called madness and illuminate it for the watching jurymen.

"Doctor," he began, "what particular idea did she advance on the subject of religion that led you to the conclusion that she was hopelessly insane?"

"She advanced many of them," Brown said vaguely. "I formed my opinion not so much on any one idea advanced, as upon her whole conversation." Perhaps feeling under pressure, he added, "She then said that she was the 'Personification of the Holy Ghost.' I did not know what she meant by that."

"Was...that a new idea to you in theology?" Moore asked lightly, seemingly sympathetic to the doctor's struggle.

"It was," Brown affirmed.

"Are you much of a theologian?"

"No," the doctor conceded.

"Then," said Elizabeth's lawyer, his tone sharpening, "because the idea was a novel one to *you*, you pronounced her insane."

"Well," said Brown defensively, "I pronounced her insane on that and other things that exhibited themselves in this conversation."

Moore would not let him slither away that easily. He pinned him, asking, "Did she not show more familiarity with the subject of religion and the questions of theology, than you had with these subjects?"

"I do not pretend much knowledge on these subjects," Brown replied, flustered at the very suggestion that a woman might be more expert than he.

"What else did she say or do there," Moore inquired, "that showed marks of insanity?"

"She claimed to be better than her husband," Brown said hurriedly. To a doctor, this would genuinely have seemed insane, given the "scientific" belief of the era that white men were biologically superior to all. Nor had Brown finished. "She had a great aversion to being called insane. Before I got through the conversation she exhibited a great dislike to me, and almost treated me in a contemptuous manner."

What unnatural, sick, unfeminine behavior...

Brown was Bonfield's witness again. Perhaps sensing that the doctor had more to say on his reasons for finding Elizabeth mad, Theophilus's lawyer asked him to state "all the reasons you have for pronouncing her insane."

Happily, Brown pulled out some notes he'd brought with him. "I have written down, in order," he said, regaining his professional deportment, "the reasons which I had, to found my opinion on, that she was insane." He cleared his throat. "I will read them."

All around the courtroom, the gathered masses leaned in. Elizabeth, at her lawyers' table, turned her bright brown eyes on him as she listened.

"That she disliked to be called insane," he read. "That she pronounced me a copperhead [unsupportive of the Union in the Civil War], and did not prove the fact. An incoherency of thought. That she failed to illuminate me and fill me with light."

Glances began to be exchanged among the spectators.

"Her aversion to the doctrine of the total depravity of man," he continued. "Her claim to perfection or nearer perfection in action and conduct." He was perhaps getting flustered. "Her aversion to being called insane," he repeated. "Her feelings towards her husband."

The crowd was getting restless now. These were no reasons to say a woman was mad.

"Her belief that to call her insane and abuse her, was blasphemy against the Holy Ghost. Her explanation of this idea. Incoherency of thought and ideas."

But it was Brown who was becoming incoherent. "Her extreme aversion to the doctrine of the total depravity of mankind," he said again over a rumble of laughter from the crowd, "and in the same conversation, saying her husband was a specimen of man's total depravity."

He may have raised his voice to be heard over the laughter. "The general history of the case," he asserted. "Her belief that some calamity would befall her, owing to my being there, and her refusal to shake hands with me when I went away."

Elizabeth may have narrowed her eyes at that. She'd been absolutely right to fear calamity. If this doctor and her husband had had their way, she'd already have been on her way to an asylum.

"Her viewing the subject of religion," continued Brown pompously, his doctor's sensibility offended by the amused reaction of the crowd, "from the osteric standpoint of Christian exegetical analysis, and agglutinating the polsynthetical ectoblasts of homogeneous asceticism."

If it was meant to shame an ignorant crowd into silence, his high-flown language absolutely failed. "The witness left the stand amid roars of laughter," Stephen Moore later recalled, perhaps trying to suppress a smile himself, "and it required some moments to restore order in the court-room."

When the gathered crowds at last fell silent, it was to hear the oath of Dr. Joseph Way, who'd also recently certified Elizabeth's insanity. History does not record where he waited before giving evidence, but his account was such that it was almost as if he'd just overheard Brown's humiliation.

Bonfield talked him through his examination of Elizabeth.

"On most subjects she was quite sane," recalled Way. "On the subject of religion I thought she had some ideas that are not generally entertained. At that time, I thought her to be somewhat deranged or excited on that subject; *since* that time," he added, "I have thought perhaps I was not a proper judge."

It was hardly the indictment Bonfield had been aiming for.

"I am not much posted on disputed points in theology," the doctor continued anxiously, "and I find that other people entertain similar ideas.

They are not in accordance with *my* views, but"—and here he differed from Dr. Knott, who'd condemned three-fourths of believers with his opinion—"that is no evidence that she is insane."

There was barely anything for Moore to do on his cross-examination after testimony like that.

"She was perfectly sane on every subject except religion," Way confirmed, "and I would not swear now that she was insane."

This was really not the start to the trial that Theophilus had wanted. But he still had more witnesses to come—and he was far more confident in those who were to follow. Because it had not only been him who'd worked so hard to commit Elizabeth in 1860. His parishioners had literally petitioned for that end.

The very first sermon ever preached in his former church had been 1 Corinthians 1:10: "Now I beseech you, brethren...that ye all speak the same thing."

Elizabeth was about to learn if the wolves were all still howling from the same hymn sheet.

CHAPTER 43

As the trial continued, it excited "much attention"—"one of the most remarkable cases ever brought before a judicial tribunal," declared the *Chicago Tribune*. Each day that Elizabeth arrived at the courthouse—she was staying with friends while her case was heard—the crowd seemed to have swollen in size.

Many people were on her side. "Mrs. Packard, I always knew you were not insane," they would shout as she fought her way toward the courtroom, or "I always felt that you was an abused woman." Theophilus, in turn, had his own supporters. Samuel Packard, now sixteen, attended court in his father's corner, his "hypnotic and compelling…intense blue eyes" watching every moment of his mother's trial.

And then there were the Doles.

"One morning early, I was sent for," Deacon Abijah Dole began as he took the stand. He told a story of finding Elizabeth in her night clothes, her long brown hair an unruly river. "Her hair was disheveled," he testified. "Her face looked wild."

His implication was plain: if her *appearance* was as unpinned as this, what was happening in her mind? He was happy, too, to throw some Salem-style witchcraft into the mix for good measure.

"She took me by the hand and led me to the bed," he recalled. "Libby was lying in bed, moaning and moving her head… She [Elizabeth] called Mr. Packard a devil."

Under cross-examination, he continued, "I supposed when I first went into the room that her influence over the child had caused the child to become deranged… I believed that she had exerted some mesmeric or other influence over the child, that caused it to moan and toss its head."

Only under further questioning from Moore would he admit that "the child had been sick with brain fever" and that Elizabeth's distressed appearance might have been caused by her watching over her daughter all night. Tight-lipped, Dole had to confirm, "The child got well."

His testimony continued, focusing on the Bible classes that had caused such trouble, yet the stress was getting to him. As he described how Elizabeth had asked his permission to read her essays aloud, he suddenly cracked. "I was much surprised; I felt so bad, I did not know what to do," he managed before bursting into tears, perhaps haunted by the pressure the church had been under at that heightened political time.

It was a good while before he regained control of himself. Once he did, he was back on message: "I knew she was crazy."

When Moore cross-examined, he was perhaps cautious, given the witness's apparent instability. He probed Dole gently on his religious views.

"Her ideas on religion did not agree with mine, nor with my view of the Bible," Abijah said.

"Was it an indication of insanity that she wanted to leave the Presbyterian Church?" asked Elizabeth's lawyer.

"She would not leave the church unless she was insane," replied Dole as though pointing out a fact. "I am a member of the church," he added emphatically. "I believe the church is right. I believe everything the church does is right. I believe everything in the Bible."

"Do you believe Mrs. Packard was insane, and is insane?"

"I do," he said firmly. "I do not deem it proper for persons to investigate new doctrines or systems of theology."

Yet Dole had earlier testified that he and Theophilus had become Presbyterians only eight years before. Previously, they'd been Congregationalists, following the New School creed.

Moore attacked, the easy question already on his lips: "Was it dangerous for *you* to examine the doctrines or theology embraced in the Presbyterian Church, when you left the Congregational Church, and joined it?"

Dole bristled. "I will not answer so foolish a question."

At that, the witness was discharged.

Theophilus's lawyers consulted one another. There were three of them now: forty-two-year-old Chauncey A. Lake joined the team a day or so into the trial. He was a member of the Illinois House of Representatives as well as a lawyer, and all his skills were now at Theophilus's disposal.

After Abijah Dole, the second of the church's deacons, Deacon Smith, took the stand to testify that Elizabeth was mad. He had a high forehead, low beard, and unforgiving eyes. The fifty-year-old deacon was halfway through his evidence when he suddenly stopped. All eyes turned as one as forty-nine-year-old Sybil Dole unexpectedly entered the courtroom. She strode toward the tables at the front, leading Libby, who walked obediently behind.

Sybil strolled straight past her sister-in-law, not giving Elizabeth a single glance, but as she whirled past in a snooty swish of skirts, she lost her shadow. Libby stopped. She stopped beside her mother. As Stephen Moore reported it, she suddenly went straight up to Elizabeth and threw her arms around her, "clinging to her with all child-like fervor."

It was perhaps the first real affection she'd shown her mother since her homecoming, but maybe the hope that the trial afforded was affecting Libby too. Her brother Isaac reported that after her mother had been sent to the asylum, Libby learned "to keep her feelings to herself." She'd squashed them all down: her love for her mother, grief at her absence, guilt at being unable to help. Perhaps that box of feelings was now bursting, emotion finally rising to the fore.

But she was not allowed to seek comfort with her mother. As soon as Sybil realized what had happened, she doubled back to collect her niece. She "snatched the child up."

"Come away from that woman," she hissed. "She is not fit to take care of you."

She pulled Libby roughly away.

The spectators erupted with emotion, to such a degree that it stopped proceedings. "Not a mother's heart there but what was touched," said Stephen Moore, "and scarce a dry eye was seen. Quite a stir was made." But it was nothing compared to the roiling emotions within Elizabeth.

She *had* to win her case. She *had* to be with her children again— and properly, not this strange half-life they'd been living for the past few months. She *had* to be declared sane, to be made safe from committal, so she could become their mother again, in every way a woman should. They clearly needed her. She had to do this as much for them as for herself.

She took a deep breath and focused again on the momentous task before her. This trial was her only hope for her future.

Eventually, the courtroom settled again as the sheriff restored order. Moore rose to cross-examine Deacon Smith, though there wasn't much he wanted to elicit.

"I was elected superintendent of the [Sabbath] school," Smith conceded, "for the special purpose of keeping Mrs. Packard straight."

Moore was far more interested in the next witness: Mrs. Sybil Dole. She returned without Libby, her cameo having already made her familiar to those who were following the case. As though to soften that initial impression, she was careful to be fair to Elizabeth in a way the other witnesses had not done to date. It's possible, too, that she did not want to come across as too hard and unforgiving, lest she herself be accused of unfeminine and therefore insane behavior.

"Her natural disposition is very kind and sweet," she said of her sister-in-law.

But then she spun a tale of seeming sickness. Her evidence portrayed an irate Elizabeth demanding that Sybil return her baby after Sybil had taken Arthur ahead of Elizabeth's committal. "Her appearance was very wild," Sybil testified disapprovingly. "She was filled with spite toward Mr. Packard."

She also remembered that Elizabeth had once stormed off from the supper table, having become angry with Theophilus when he called her mad. "She...told him she would talk what and when she had a mind to," Sybil avowed. "She...left the room in great violence."

And in this era when ill-tempered women were seen as crazy, this was far more damning evidence than her husband had managed to muster. Sybil even criticized Elizabeth's housekeeping, condemning her further as a woman who could not properly perform the role society expected. Of one impromptu supper party, Sybil recalled censoriously, "She was out of bread and had to make biscuit for dinner."

Other parishioners gave similar accounts. "Mrs. Packard was very pale and angry," one testified. "She was in an undress, and her hair was down over her face... She would not talk calm. She said Mr. Packard... and the members of his church had made a conspiracy to put her into the Insane Asylum."

It was a brick wall made of Elizabeth's own behavior. As she herself had once described it, "The least mistake, a slip of the tongue, a look, a gesture, are all liable to be interpreted as insanity, and the least difference of opinion, however reasonable or plausible, is liable to share the same reproach."

Those differences of opinion came out in the parishioners' testimonies too. "I approved taking her away," one said. "I deemed her dangerous to the church; her ideas were contrary to the church, and were wrong." To support her testimony, this parishioner cited a Bible class essay of Elizabeth's that "bore evidence of insanity." However, when challenged, she said, "I cannot give the contents of the paper now."

After the church members had completed their accounts, Bonfield rose and moved graciously forward to speak with the judge. Theophilus's lawyer conversed "in a decisive, plain and direct way...without superfluity of words or loss of time." Cutting straight to the point, he requested an immediate ten-day adjournment. A key witness had been telegrammed, he said, and their testimony could only be given in ten days' time, upon their return from traveling. This testimony was "very important." It would be worth the wait.

The name of this most significant witness?

Dr. Andrew McFarland.

CHAPTER 44

Elizabeth's counsel immediately objected. It was an "unheard-of proceeding" to adjourn after a hearing had commenced "to enable a party
to hunt up testimony."

Starr suggested a compromise: Elizabeth's lawyers should go ahead
and present their case, and after that was concluded, if still needed, the
court would rule on whether to pause the trial to await McFarland's
testimony.

Elizabeth's lawyers consulted with each other and with her. It seems
likely Elizabeth was extremely worried about McFarland testifying: she
knew from bitter experience how very talented he was at convincing
people to think what he wanted them to.

So Moore proposed something extraordinary. The defense was willing, he said, to "submit the case without introducing any testimony."
They invited the jury to give their verdict now, before Elizabeth had
presented a single witness. They clearly thought the local physicians
had been weak on the stand and that it was best to rest now before
McFarland's more expert testimony could be brought to bear.

Naturally, Bonfield objected. He renewed his motion for a delay.

But the court refused it. McFarland would not get his day in court
after all.

Elizabeth was delighted, but Bonfield fought back. If they could not have the doctor, they wanted his documentation. Theophilus's team submitted a request to read to the jury McFarland's certificate of insanity and his recent correspondence with Theophilus.

"Incompetent testimony," objected Elizabeth's lawyers, a legal term that aimed to cast doubt on McFarland's expert ability.

Yet the doctor was the nationally renowned superintendent of the State Hospital. That argument was never going to wash. Incompetent testimony can also mean the evidence is irrelevant, but these documents cut right to the heart of the case. Moore tried one final objection: to present the paperwork but not the person "debarred the defense of the benefit of a cross-examination."

But Starr overruled him on every single point. Theophilus had chosen his lawyer well; Bonfield was an "acknowledged leader" among his peers, with a "convincing personality" that commanded respect. His arguments were known to carry "more than ordinary weight with court, bar and jury," and it seemed he had triumphed again. McFarland's letter from December 1863 and his certificate were both allowed to be read to the jury.

It was damning evidence indeed. And although Elizabeth had already seen the documents among Theophilus's papers, this felt like fresh treachery. It was one thing to read the words herself in the quiet of the night, quite another to hear them read aloud by Theophilus's lawyers in a courtroom. Every word of McFarland seemed to seal her fate.

"Of the existence of insanity I have no question," the lawyer intoned as he recited the certificate, while the words of McFarland's December letter were yet more bricks in the walls beginning to surround her. "The officers of the institution…were satisfied she could not be cured."

Elizabeth sat glumly, numbly listening. It didn't help that her own lawyer seemed equally despondent. "The defence had no opportunity for cross-examination," Moore complained, "while Mr. Packard thus got the benefit of McFarland's evidence that she was insane, with no possibility of a contradiction."

As if scenting victory, Bonfield confidently rested his case.

Moore tried to rouse himself. He called his first witnesses: Isaac Simington, the Methodist minister, and Dr. Mann, the physician who'd twice refused Theophilus a certificate of insanity in 1863. Both testified they believed Elizabeth sane, but Bonfield did not even bother to cross-examine.

Joseph Labrie, the local postmaster and notary public, was up next. The forty-one-year-old was a slight man with a wire-brush mustache. "I always said she was a sane woman, and say so yet."

In addition to his other jobs, Labrie had trained as a lawyer and gave evidence with all the eloquence and command one might expect from such a man. For that reason, perhaps, he *was* cross-examined—to weaken him before the jury.

"I am not a physician," he conceded. "I am not an expert. She might be insane." Yet he insisted, "But no common-sense man could find it out."

Moore tried to reestablish Labrie's standing.

"I am a Justice of the Peace, and Notary Public," the witness confirmed. He testified that at Mr. Packard's request, he'd witnessed Elizabeth's signature on real estate deeds "within the past two months," suggesting that her husband had then thought her sane enough to sign.

Labrie had done as well as could be hoped for, but it's probable Moore still felt uneasy as his witness stepped down. Bonfield's lack of cross-examination of most of his witnesses, plus his line of attack with Labrie, spoke volumes. Theophilus's lawyer clearly did not think that any of them had a patch on the authority of Dr. McFarland.

The trouble was: he was right. The doctor's words seemed to hang in the courtroom with an emphatic presence: "Her insanity consists in a thoroughly diseased conception of her own powers as one having super-natural attributes." Moore had done brilliantly earlier in dismantling Dr. Brown's prejudices about Elizabeth's feminist theological beliefs, but with McFarland not present to be cross-examined, he hadn't been able to strike down these haunting words in the same way. What the jury was left with was a sensible-sounding diagnosis from an expert medical man. And no amount of testimony from a Methodist minister, a local doctor, or a notary public could combat it.

What Elizabeth needed was her own expert, who could not only refute McFarland's powerful testimony but also present a strong case *for* her beliefs. But as of yet, they didn't have one. Theophilus still held all the cards.

But they did have one secret weapon.

Elizabeth herself.

"[We would like] to read to the jury the following paper," began Elizabeth's counsel, "which has been referred to by the [prosecution's] witnesses as evidence of Mrs. Packard's insanity."

Theophilus and his lawyers may have exchanged glances. What was this? The paper in question was passed across the courtroom for the pastor to examine.

He likely could not believe his eyes. It was one of Elizabeth's Bible class essays. Those essays she had been so desperate, all fall, to get her hands on.

This was the reason why. This was the reason she'd given Theophilus her signature on those deeds in exchange for them. With the habeas corpus plot tucked in the back of her mind, she'd known a trial would soon be forthcoming, and she'd needed those essays back. Because she'd always thought they'd provide compelling evidence that she had *never* been insane, and Elizabeth knew, in light of the three years she'd spent in the asylum, just how critical that now was. Because she could look as sane as she liked at her counsel's table, day in and day out of this ongoing trial, but the stigma of insanity still trailed her like smoke. Those twelve jurymen might well be thinking she *seems* sane now, true, but what about those three years in an asylum? Surely a woman could not be committed for nothing?

There is no smoke without fire.

But Elizabeth had always believed her Bible class essays could confirm the truth: she'd never been mad at all.

Now was her moment to use them.

Reluctantly, Theophilus admitted it was the same paper that his own witnesses had cited as evidence of Elizabeth's madness. He handed the essay back, resigned to hearing its eloquent arguments being pronounced aloud in her counsel's articulate voice.

But he was in for another shock.

"[We request] permission of the court," said Elizabeth's lawyer, "for Mrs. Packard to read it to the jury."

It was the worst idea Theophilus could imagine. His charismatic, brilliant wife, allowed to speak for herself? His lawyers "most strenuously opposed" the motion.

But Starr overruled them, perhaps interested himself to hear from the woman at the center of the case.

Elizabeth took a very deep breath. Never had a more important moment nor a more important speech been before her. She pressed her hands into the table and pushed herself upward, her hoop skirts unfolding around her in a swell of support, like a Greek chorus made of cloth. She picked up the essay she'd written long ago, before she'd known that a woman could be imprisoned for her views. In "a distinct tone of voice" in which "every word was heard all over the court-room," she began to read her own writing aloud.

Every person in the courtroom listened intently. The crowd fell silent in astonished awe. It was not just the sight of Elizabeth Packard, so small and yet so powerful, standing up for herself that was arresting; it was the audio of a woman's voice speaking in that male-dominated court. In 1864, female public speaking was still relatively rare. It was, in fact, a risky strategy to let her have a voice. Back in 1837, when the Grimké sisters, early female advocates of abolition, went on a public speaking tour, they were condemned, ridiculed, and threatened. The Congregational Church had been so disturbed by their powerful eloquence it had issued a pastoral letter, warning the faithful against "unnatural" preaching women, whose actions would see them "fall in shame and dishonor into the dust." Some people's views had not advanced much further in the intervening years.

But Moore believed in his client. He thought her "a lady of fine mental endowments"; he even paid her the compliment of calling her a "masculine thinker."

And he'd made the right call. Elizabeth was simply mesmerizing. "She drew all eyes, all ears, in every circle," people wrote of her, as they fell "under the spell of her marvellous power."

She read her essay entitled "How Godliness is Profitable." In it, she'd answered the question of whether a Christian farmer might expect more success in his labors than a sinner, a question to which Theophilus's church had resolutely answered yes.

Yet the evidence in their own farming community had belied that stance. "I think we have no *intelligent* reason for believing that the motives with which we prosecute our secular business, have any influence in the *pecuniary* results," Elizabeth therefore argued. In her essay, she espoused that man's physical, intellectual, and spiritual realms operated independently. "For instance," she said aloud in the courtroom, "a very *immoral* man may be a very *healthy*, long-lived man."

But that did not mean she thought godliness unprofitable. "The profits of godliness cannot mean, simply, *pecuniary* profits, because this would limit the gain of godliness to this world, alone," Elizabeth explained, "whereas, it is profitable not only for *this life*, but also for the *life to come*...

"Happiness and misery are coins which are current in *both* worlds. Therefore, it appears to me, that happiness is the profit attendant upon godliness."

Her "common sense reasons" resonated in the courtroom in a way they never had in the Bible class. As she reached the essay's conclusion and modestly retook her seat, "a murmur of applause arose from every part of the room." Though promptly suppressed by the sheriff, the sound still rang in Elizabeth's ears: confirmation of her mini victory. She'd always thought that writing down her thoughts would save her.

She only hoped, when the jury gave its verdict, that she'd be proved right.

After her showstopping performance, the witnesses who followed seemed almost anticlimactic. She was supported by the former Manteno town supervisor, Daniel Beedy, and by Mr. and Mrs. Blessing.

"I never thought her insane," testified Mr. Blessing, while Rebecca sketched for the court the cruelty of Elizabeth's husband: the lack of fire in the midst of winter, the locked doors, banned friends, the threatened fist if she did not leave his house.

As the evidence stacked up, the reaction in the courtroom was visceral. "The popular verdict is decidedly against [Theophilus]," Elizabeth realized.

And the public were not afraid to make their feelings known. The Doles were fearful of "the disorderly demonstrations by the furious populace filling the Court House," while Theophilus condemned the "vulgar hisses issued from the females in the crowd." In particular, he resented being "surrounded by bawdy women," who would point their fingers at him in open court, exclaiming about his actions. He criticized Starr's "feeble attempt...to express his sense of the impropriety of...such demonstrations."

Yet the crowd settled down to hear what was probably the final testimony of the trial's first week as Sarah Haslett took the stand.

"I never saw any signs of insanity with her," Sarah said firmly. "I called often before she was kidnapped and carried to Jacksonville, and since her return." She testified that she'd been banned from seeing Elizabeth, so the women had been forced to converse through the window. She described in detail how that window was nailed shut.

Unusually, Sarah was cross-examined. But Theophilus perhaps detested this intermeddler above all others, because of what he knew she'd said to his wife. With that insider insight tucked into his pocket, Bonfield rose to quiz the pregnant housewife.

He asked what she'd talked about with the pastor's wife at the window.

"She talked about getting released from her imprisonment," Sarah said pointedly.

But that was not what the lawyer meant.

"She asked if filing a bill of complaint would lead to a divorce," Sarah admitted. The d-word was likely why she'd been cross-examined; Elizabeth's mere discussion of the subject could cast her character in a poor light. Yet knowing all too well how the topic might play with the all-male jury, Sarah added quickly, "She said she did not want a divorce; she only wanted protection from Mr. Packard's cruelty."

Sarah seemingly didn't care, however, what the jurymen thought of *her*. She perhaps fixed her friend's husband with a glare as she added, "I advised her to not stand it quietly, but get a divorce."

The spectators in the courtroom seemed to share Sarah's feelings as she stepped down from the stand. There was a new "rabid, ferocious savageness" to their hisses and their boos. Theophilus witnessed it with alarm, later writing, "It was unmistakably evident what the verdict of the infatuated assembly was." He did not attribute his own behavior to their animosity but identified it as "the bitter spirit of sectarianism."

His lawyers could not help but observe it too. As the court closed for business on Saturday, January 16, they agreed that if these angry outbursts happened again, they'd withdraw their client from the courthouse.

But all that was for the next week. That Saturday, everyone began filing out of the courthouse into the darkness of the night. The air was aflame with outraged exclamations from the spectators at the evidence they'd heard.

And those exclamations took on a different timbre that snowy Saturday night. Anger boiled over and bled into enmity. Concern transformed to collusion. Plots and plans began to be hatched like gremlins, which soon circulated among the spectators, tugging them toward trouble. What began as mere rumors of "lawless violence" coalesced into details and designs. Urgent whispers were shared, ideas jumping from one group to another like hungry fleas. And then the scheme sauntered through the night with feigned innocence—the better to entrap its target.

At the train station in the city, mobs began to gather, "ready to sacrifice their victim." The shadowy figures paced along the platform, breaths puffing out into icy air, those clouds of steam concealing their intent.

They were not waiting for the cars...but for Theophilus Packard.

CHAPTER 45

Elizabeth arrived at court on Monday, January 18, in good time for the day's proceedings. To her surprise, she noticed that Theophilus was not there. But Stephen Moore was, and probably in even higher spirits than normal, because he'd found that expert witness he'd long sought for his client, and today, he would take the stand.

But as Judge Starr swept into the courtroom and all rose, ready for that witness to be called, there was still no sign of Theophilus.

What, Elizabeth wondered, could have kept him from the court?

Yet she couldn't worry overlong about it. She had to focus. Her team called Dr. Duncanson.

Alexander A. Duncanson was a Scotsman, likely with the accent to match, as he'd only been living in America since 1852. Now in his forties, he'd been a practicing physician for over two decades, having gained his diploma from the University of Glasgow. He'd also worked as a clergyman— and not just any clergyman. He'd been a dissenting minister: a pastor who'd formally broken from the Presbyterian Church of Scotland. Upon learning of his expertise, Moore had scrambled to get him an interview with Elizabeth, and Duncanson, who currently lived in Kankakee, had managed to conduct his examination even while the trial was going on. Given his theological background, it must have been a true meeting of minds.

"I live here," Duncanson said on the stand soon after being sworn, "am a physician; have been a clergyman; have been a practicing physician twenty-one years. Have known Mrs. Packard since this trial commenced. Have known her by general report for three years and upwards."

Because the case of Elizabeth Packard, the clergyman's wife who was sent to an asylum for thinking her own thoughts, had become notorious in her local area over the past few years.

"I visited her at Mr. Orr's," Duncanson continued. "I was requested to go there and have a conversation with her and determine if she was sane or insane. Talked three hours with her, on political, religious and scientific subjects."

Moore asked for his professional opinion on her state of mind. Duncanson was forthright. "I think not only that she is sane," he said, "but the most intelligent lady I have talked with in many years."

It was a compelling endorsement, yet the doctor was only just getting started.

"We talked religion very thoroughly," he continued. "I find her an expert in both departments, Old School and New School theology... Many of her ideas and doctrines are embraced in Swedenborgianism, and many are found only in the New School theology. The best and most learned men of both Europe and this country, are advocates of these doctrines."

Moore quizzed him about Elizabeth's most infamous belief regarding the female Holy Ghost.

"[It] is a very ancient theological dogma," Duncanson confirmed, "and entertained by many of our most eminent men."

Yet Duncanson wanted to move on from the Holy Ghost, because he could not stop enthusing about Elizabeth. "On every topic I introduced," he said, almost in awe at her intellect, "she was perfectly familiar, and discussed them with an intelligence that at once showed she was possessed of a good education, and a strong and vigorous mind. I did not agree with her in sentiment on many things," he conceded, "but I do not call people insane because they differ from me, nor from a majority, even, of people."

He warmed to his subject. "Many persons called Swedenborg insane," he said. "That is true; but he had the largest brain of any person during the age in which he lived; and no one now dares call him insane. You might with as much propriety call Christ insane, because he taught the people many new and strange things; or Galileo; or Newton; or Luther; or Robert Fulton; or Morse, who electrified the world; or Watts or a thousand others I might name. Morse's best friends for a long time thought him mad; yet there was a magnificent mind, the embodiment of health and vigor."

Elizabeth wanted to slap the table in agreement; this was a point she'd long made in her own defense, to which no one had listened. "It has always been my fortune…or rather *mis*fortune…to be a pioneer, just about twenty-five years in advance of my cotemporaries," she'd written in the asylum. "Therefore, I am called crazy, or insane, by those so far in my rear, that they cannot see the reasonableness of the positions and opinions I assume to advocate and defend."

Following his comparison of Elizabeth to some of the greatest minds the world had ever known, Duncanson opined, "So with Mrs. Packard; there is wanting every indication of insanity that is laid down in the books."

That was the killer statement. Elizabeth only wished that Theophilus could have been there to hear it.

But he had still not made an appearance.

Duncanson wanted to make one final comment. He cleared his

throat and perhaps spoke a little louder for the benefit of the court. "I pronounce her a sane woman," he said emphatically, "and wish we had a nation of such women."

His words were powerful. Though doctors such as Mann had previously said Elizabeth was not insane, no one had ever before *endorsed* her views. In all fairness, it should not have taken a man saying other men shared her opinions for Elizabeth finally to feel vindicated. But that was the world she lived in, and as a result, Duncanson's evidence was explosive.

Theophilus's lawyers struggled to combat it. Although they cross-examined Duncanson at length, they managed to elicit nothing new. One complaint was that the doctor had only known Elizabeth since the trial had started, but as Theophilus had successfully committed her in 1860 on the testimony of Knott, who'd met her for only an hour in total, that was highly hypocritical. Eventually, Duncanson was discharged from the stand, his ringing endorsement of Elizabeth still fresh in everyone's ears.

Moore announced they had called their last witness. So convincing had the doctor been that the attorney said he was happy to submit the case without closing arguments, but the opposing lawyers were not. They needed that final opportunity to present Theophilus's case, so Duncanson's words were not the last the jury heard before they began their deliberations.

Moore acquiesced. Theophilus's lawyers presented closing arguments for the pastor while Orr and Loring stepped up for Elizabeth. Both sides argued their cases "ably and at length." But at last, there was nothing more that either side could do. The fate of the case—and Elizabeth—lay squarely in the hands of the twelve jurymen.

It was very late by the time they retired to debate their verdict; the closing arguments and cross-examination had taken up much time. Moore noted it was 10:00 p.m. before the jury retired, the sheriff leading them out. It was doubtful they'd return a verdict that same night.

No one knew which way the case would go. Though the crowds were firmly on Elizabeth's side, the crowds were not on the jury. How would those five Presbyterians feel about her beliefs? Were they of the mindset that all should be allowed to worship as they wished, or might they take a dim view of Elizabeth's rejection of their creed? Some thought that "a painful case of mental insanity has been *construed*...to be a case of domestic abuse," but would the jury agree? And how would this all-male group react to the outspoken wife Elizabeth had proved herself to be? Was the domestic abuse perhaps *vindicated* in their view? Perhaps they might agree with her husband that she needed to be put back in her box...

If the jury found her insane, she would be swiftly committed. Elizabeth didn't know if she could survive that experience a second time; she already knew how close she'd come to going mad in Jacksonville. At times in those three years, she'd felt in the hands of a "venturesome driver" who "likes to see how near he can go to the edge of the precipice, and not go over to the other side." Was she really strong enough to survive a second imprisonment, especially one in which there was no hope, *ever*, of release?

Even as Elizabeth was mulling morbidly on her future, there was a disturbance in the courtroom, which had barely even begun to empty.

After only seven minutes, the jury had returned.

What did such a speedy verdict mean? Elizabeth cast her eyes around the courtroom, trying to read the jurymen as they came back in. Her gaze rested briefly on the opposition's table: lawyers but still no husband. After everything, Theophilus was going to miss the verdict.

She blocked him from her mind. She held her breath as the jury foreman read the verdict aloud.

> We, the undersigned, Jurors in the case of Mrs. Elizabeth
> P. W. Packard, alleged to be insane, having heard the
> evidence in the case, are satisfied that said Elizabeth
> P. W. Packard is SANE.

A tidal wave of sound smashed upon the shore as "cheers rose from every part of the house." Spontaneous applause broke out in the court-room, the clapping hands a percussion that played directly to Elizabeth's pounding heart. Ladies pulled out their handkerchiefs and waved them, a gesture of free action that mirrored the freedom Elizabeth had just been granted. Free. She was free. She was *sane*.

The crowds surged forward without any formal order, the people pressing around her. Yet their cries of congratulation, rejoicing "to have the truth known," were drowned out by the continuing applause and scattered shouts of sheer joy.

Elizabeth stood, stunned, in the middle of the melee. There could have been so many emotions: relief, vindication, happiness—even grief or anger at the long lost years.

But when she described it later, she used just two words. In her heart, when she first heard the verdict, she said she felt simply a "grateful joy."

It was some time before the crowds could be quieted. The applause for the verdict rang on and on, sheriff and judge both powerless to stop it. When at last order was restored, Elizabeth's counsel rose and asked Judge Starr that she be formally discharged. Starr agreed, instructing his clerk to enter the following in the official record:

It is hereby ordered that Mrs. Elizabeth P. W. Packard
be relieved of all restraint incompatible with her condition as a sane woman.

Starr signed the order, and justice was done.

Elizabeth's thoughts turned at once to her children. No longer could
their father teach them she was mad; the court had decreed she wasn't.
No longer could he tell them not to heed her; she would be able to love
them any way she wished. She wanted to see them straight away, to
return home to her green-shuttered house and look in on them sleeping
soundly in their beds, little knowing their family drama was finally at an
end. Her arms almost ached to hold them again. Thanking her counsel,
she turned at once to leave, the freedom she'd just been given meaning
she could go.

But before she'd even gotten out of the courtroom, she was handed a
letter. She blinked down at it, surprised. Curious, she tore it open.

It was from her husband. Her husband, who'd received a warning on
Saturday evening not to trust himself on the cars, who'd been told that
plots against him had been overheard and his life was under threat. In
consequence, as McFarland put it, "His troubles...unmanned him, and
he could not brave the danger."

He'd planned to run away that very same night.

In the letter, he told Elizabeth he'd gone.

And he'd taken the children with him.

Elizabeth did not want to believe it. She could not. She summoned
her friends, and they left immediately for Manteno. Theophilus had
been at court only days ago; surely he could not have packed up a whole
house in that time and organized this sudden flight?

The horses ran swiftly across the snowy landscape, hooves scuffing up dirty snow. They raced under an inky sky, dark as her fearful heart, the stars above single pinpricks of hope that she might return to find the house exactly as she'd left it.

But when she arrived, those hopes blinked out, black holes of hopelessness replacing them. Because her banging on the door brought only an unknown man to answer it: a Mr. Wood, who said he'd rented the house from her husband. As Elizabeth burst inside, the property was unrecognizable. This was not *her* home. The familiar pea-green closet, the embroidered ottoman, the maple bedstead...all were gone. Every piece of furniture she'd ever owned had been ripped out of her home and had vanished.

But worst of all, there were no children.

No children. No children. No children.

She felt "death agonies" that ripped her "soul and body asunder." The searing pain felt like a "living death of hopeless bereavement."

"I want to live with my dear children, whom I have borne and nursed, reared and educated," she thought desperately. "I love them... and no place is home to me in this wide world without them."

But as Elizabeth was ushered out of her former home, taken back to the house of her friends the Hanfords, she realized she now had no home at all.

"I am thrown adrift," she thought numbly, "at [forty-seven] years of age, upon the cold world, with no place on earth I can call home."

She had been deemed sane. She was innocent of any crime. Yet regardless, she had been robbed of everything she held most dear. She was now homeless. Penniless. Childless. All she had to her name were the clothes she stood up in and a manuscript she'd been repeatedly told would never see the light of day.

Her victory in court should have been the end of it. But it turned out Elizabeth had only won the battle. Like the Civil War that still raged on that very same night, her long-term fight was far from over.

And there were campaigns ahead that even Elizabeth could not then conceive of.

CHAPTER 46

According to his letter, Theophilus Packard had moved to Massachusetts. The note itself was likely given to avoid charges of desertion; he kept certified copies that he showed to anyone who accused him of neglect. He hadn't deserted her; he'd extended an invitation to follow him—"with the promise," Elizabeth read bitterly, "that he would provide me a suitable home."

But she did not trust him. A "suitable" home could well mean another asylum, no matter the verdict of the court in Illinois.

Now living with the Hanfords, Elizabeth tried to get her head around what had happened. She felt she had to "grope about in midnight darkness, unaided and alone, except as her own instincts pointed out to her the way to live upon her own vitality."

Luckily for Elizabeth, as Duncanson had so recently attested, her own vitality was pretty damn impressive. She soon discovered that Theophilus had not taken the furniture with him; all her belongings were stored at the Doles' house in Manteno. She immediately made contact with her Kankakee lawyers. She'd paid for that furniture herself, with money given to her by her father. She felt Theophilus had no claim to it and therefore wanted to take legal action.

"Can I replevy it as stolen property?" she asked the attorneys briskly. A replevy was a writ that enabled a property owner to reclaim goods.

But the lawyers shook their heads. At first, Elizabeth feared that her time in the asylum had invalidated her legal status, despite the recent verdict, but the situation was actually worse.

"You cannot replevy anything, for you are a married woman," her attorneys explained, "and a married woman has no legal existence, unless she holds property independent of her husband... This is not your case... Your husband has a legal right to all your common property—you have not even a right to the hat on your head!"

"Why?" asked Elizabeth, outraged. "I have bought and paid for it with my own money."

"That is of no consequence—you can hold nothing, as you are *nothing and nobody* in law."

It was another cruel aspect of the legal framework that had seen Elizabeth committed to the asylum in the first place, under which married women had no legal identities of their own. They were denied all rights, because how could you grant rights to what was no more than a shadow: the silent, unseen shadow of her spouse? Married women had no rights to property or even their own wages; their husbands owned it all. It was something known as coverture: a law inherited from England, dating back to the 1100s.

Ironically, many states ranked married women and insane patients together in terms of their legal rights. Elizabeth had cleared one hurdle, but the other was not so easily set aside. She could protest all she liked that such a law "annihilates all my rights as a human being," and that "I am not a chattel...but a being, after I am married, as well as before," but it didn't change the facts. She was merely an appendage to her husband, legally, and had no voice to speak.

"I...appealed to the laws for protection, as a married woman," Elizabeth wrote in frustration, "when, alas! I found I had no laws to appeal to."

But her property was one thing; more pressing were her concerns about her family. With "the most intense anxiety," she asked the lawyers, "How is it with my children? Can I not have children protected to me?"

"No," they replied shortly, albeit sympathetically, "the children are all the husband's after the tender age." At that time, the tender age was defined by different judges in different ways; to some, the cutoff point was seven years or puberty, but to others it simply meant those being breastfed, especially with regard to male children.

Elizabeth felt herself deflate. "[I have] no ray of hope from [Theophilus] or the law, that I shall ever see them more."

But legally, there was nothing she could do. It was an outrage. She was angry at Theophilus, but he had, in fact, only treated her as the law allowed him to. "And can one be prosecuted for doing a legal act?" she wrote. "Nay—verily—no law can reach him."

All she wanted was legal protection from her husband's actions, but her lawyers informed her that in law, Theophilus *was* her only protector. It didn't matter that he'd turned on her. Because she'd given herself to him twenty-five years before, he held entire power over her—and would for the rest of her life.

"On the principle of common law," they explained, "whatever is yours is his—your property is his—your earnings are his—your children are his—and you are his."

Her lawyers could offer only one slim branch of hope. "You can have no legal right to your own children," they said, "unless you get a divorce."

But it was a poisoned chalice. Even if Elizabeth opted for a divorce, there was no guarantee she would win custody. In reality, she was likely not to. Although she had at least recently been found sane, she had little else to commend her: no earnings, no home, and, most crucially of all, no male protector. "The idea of a woman alone with legal custody over her children, without the support of a paternal male," wrote an expert in the field, "would...have been almost unimaginable."

Although the corollary of her recent court victory was that Theophilus was guilty of cruel conduct, in the eyes of most courts, a husband's abuse of his wife did not make him unsuitable to raise children. An 1857 case saw an abusive father win custody, even though his wife was still breastfeeding. The mother was denied all rights, even as her milk dried in her breasts.

Though it was a slim shot, the lawyers still advised that a divorce was Elizabeth's only chance. Not only could she then sue for custody, but she would also be free of the danger of another committal at her husband's hands. In addition, she would likely win a financial settlement. Theophilus had left her with nothing; he'd even stolen Elizabeth's good clothes. The only way to redress the balance was divorce. So her lawyers, friends, and even the *Kankakee Gazette* all urged her to consider it. Still, she resisted, in part because she felt she could not "conscientiously get a divorce, as I am a Bible woman."

Come January 21, 1864, her situation was no clearer. The headlines in the papers that day spoke straight to her: "When Will the War End?"

———

It proved a war Elizabeth was forced to fight on several fronts. If she'd thought that her husband and McFarland would be content to let her court victory lie, she'd have been mistaken. Neither was the type of man to accept a judgment that had gone against him. And from January 29, their comeback began.

They didn't launch a legal appeal, however. Theophilus did instruct his lawyers to do so, but they refused, telling him frankly it would not succeed. Instead, Elizabeth's enemies fought back through the press.

They almost needed to, for the sake of their own reputations. All the early publicity was in Elizabeth's favor. "Depravity of a Clergyman" ran the headline in the *Chicago Tribune*, the article below it condemning McFarland for having been "a willing tool to aid in this nefarious scheme."

McFarland responded the very next day, in a letter published by the same paper. "I may here state explicitly," he wrote, "that I have no question whatever that Mrs. Packard was an insane person…and that her committal here was as justifiable as in the majority of those now here…

"That many persons—a Court and jury, even—who see the first display of her pleasing address…should hold a different opinion does not surprise me… [But] I have no hesitation in saying that any person of good intelligence, who has had sufficient opportunity of judging, will, sooner or later, share [my] opinion."

The doctor totally rejected the court's verdict. He hadn't been shaken by it at all. It was the *jury* that was wrong.

With his usual arrogance, he thought it couldn't possibly be him.

Elizabeth thought the letter outrageous. She wrote to the *Tribune* herself to rebut the many falsehoods in McFarland's account, but the newspaper refused to publish it. Worse, other newspapers republished McFarland's note, not only in Illinois but also Massachusetts.

In that state, her husband started his own PR campaign as soon as he and his three youngest children had settled into his sister Marian's house. (Samuel, now sixteen, moved to Chicago when his father fled

Manteno.) On February 5, 1864, Theophilus wrote to his local paper to "respectfully request the public to suspend their judgment" in the case should they hear rumors of it. Like McFarland, he blasted the "sham" verdict, denigrating the "illegal and oppressive [court] proceedings" and "the impudent, violent mob spirit [which] prevented a fair trial."

He was tireless in his defense of himself. Any time he spied a pro-Elizabeth article in either state, he wrote to complain and offer his own account, complete with "the reliable testimony of some fifty witnesses"—the petitions and certificates he'd been collecting since 1860 from his partisan friends.

His efforts paid off. In Massachusetts, he was swift to reconnect with his former professional association—they happily supported him, despite the court verdict—and one of these colleagues gave him an in with the boss of the *Chicago Tribune*. This friend told the paper, "I see not how the poor man can have justice done him...unless his defense is published"—as though Theophilus was the victim, not his falsely imprisoned wife.

Amid this media melee, Elizabeth was left in the cold. While Theophilus was being gifted introductions to powerful pressmen, she could not even get a simple letter published. It seemed impossible for her to fight back. Her adversaries were "two talented men, occupying high social positions of honor and trust." In contrast, she'd spent the past two decades as a housewife. She *had* no professional association or former colleagues she could call upon for help. How could she possibly win?

Perhaps that was why, on February 8, Elizabeth Packard made an unexpected decision.

She filed for divorce.

Her petition accused Theophilus of "repeated and extreme cruelty," including "using violence." She cited his desertion and formally requested a dissolution of their marriage. When Theophilus received the writ, he still denied his wife her agency, blaming the "unhallowed influence" of her meddling friends for her decision to file suit.

But in fact, it was Elizabeth who'd started fighting back.

"I do say when we must fight," she wrote, "go at it in good earnest."

She began pulling herself together. Though the obstacles before her had at first seemed insurmountable, she told herself, "Woman cannot be made to sink permanently." She *would* rise again. And when she thought of what she had to gain at the end of her fight—her children and an independent life—"doubt, despondency and fear fled apace before the determined will and purpose to succeed."

Though she had to date been a woman solely operating in the domestic sphere, she realized that her current poverty must be "supplanted by plenty" if she was to stand any chance of winning custody or of standing on her own two feet. Just as she'd determined in the asylum, she now had to "become my own protector." That simply could not be done by staying in the home. Unlike her husband, she refused to become a charity case—not when she had a brain and body able to earn wages.

Yet it wasn't going to be easy. Though the Civil War had opened up employment opportunities for women, who took on roles in post offices, shops, and factories, even filling cartridge shells, it was a competitive market, in part thanks to the increase of war widows who now needed to support themselves. Women's wages, already low, were driven down as a result. Seamstresses—a job for which Elizabeth was particularly well-suited—had seen their wages decline from 17.5 cents a shirt in 1861 to just 8 cents a shirt by 1864. They earned an average of $1.54 (about $25) a week, working a fourteen-hour day. Other positions were better paid, with Chicago saleswomen taking home an average of $7 (about

$115) a week and factory forewomen $10 (about $160) a week, but with the cost of living rising all the time—to Elizabeth's shock, sugar, a unit of which had once sold for 8 cents, was now retailing at 38 cents, while a unit of butter had jumped from 10 cents to 50 cents—it was very difficult for women to eke out an independent existence.

In the end, however, she decided not to pursue any of these more traditional forms of employment. As she put it, "No talent can lie dormant." And while Elizabeth was an exquisite seamstress, she was also a born writer.

It was time for that talent to shine.

McFarland's recent intervention in the press had given her an idea. She went over to Sarah Haslett's house and reclaimed her papers. She rifled through her things. She pulled out her old mirror and pried off its back.

They were still there: the documents she'd hidden back in 1860. She scanned her eyes across them. She'd written them so very long ago, but they were no less powerful for that. She decided she would publish one of these documents as a pamphlet: her reproof of Dr. McFarland.

She felt no compunction about exposing him. Hadn't she warned him long ago: *repentance or exposure*? He had made his choice.

She was merely following through on her threat.

Yet she wasn't motivated solely by the idea of exposing McFarland personally, as necessary as that was. She had a far more important reason to press ahead with publication. Although living with the elderly Hanfords was not the future she'd dreamed of, every day, she knew how lucky she was to be with them and not in an asylum, where her days would have been punctuated by the ringing of the bell and the screams of her fellow patients. Despite all the dramas of the past few months, she hadn't forgotten her sisters, nor the other women in asylums all across America—"the many thousands who are still enduring the horrors of these inquisitions, from which the decision of this Court has delivered me."

"Knowing as I do," she wrote in her newly penned introduction to the reproof, "their helpless, hopeless condition, so far as *justice to them* is concerned, I can find no sort of rest for my liberated soul, so long as my associates are not delivered, also."

She hoped her pamphlet might make a difference. She wanted to "enlighten the public mind into the true nature and character of our Insane Institutions" so that her countrymen might be motivated to "caus[e] their overthrow." Elizabeth intended to shine a light on the issues so that others, more qualified, could then take up the fight.

She did not plan solely to publish the reproof; that alone would make a flimsy work. She also wanted to include her letter to the *Tribune*, which they'd refused to publish, as well as her account of the hospital abuse, written under the Coes' name, "Appeal in behalf of the insane."

In addition, she reached out to her old friend Mrs. Hosmer, the former asylum sewing room directress, who'd once been as concerned as Elizabeth at what she'd witnessed in the asylum. Priscilla Hosmer had taken a new husband on January 11, 1863, and was now Mrs. Graff. She replied enthusiastically to Elizabeth on March 5, 1864, fully supporting her ideas for publication and enclosing the letters she'd written to the trustees and Dorothea Dix to try to stop the abuse. Elizabeth added these letters to her pamphlet. She knew only too well that her own voice—despite the recent verdict—would still be shadowed by the stigma of insanity. Mrs. Graff's account provided independent corroboration that what she said was true.

While Elizabeth busied herself in Manteno preparing her pamphlet for the press, the Packards' media war continued apace. By this time,

Theophilus had submitted his thick file of documents to the *Chicago Tribune*. Though the paper ultimately declined to publish them—it was an "immense mass of evidence...for which it is impossible for us to find room"—on March 12, 1864, they nevertheless printed their own damning verdict.

Elizabeth Packard, so they said, was afflicted "with a well-defined species of monomania." It was indisputable, despite the way she displayed an "almost supernatural strength of mind" (the subtext of *witch* was almost shouted). The paper concluded with a sense of finality: "The public should give this painful subject no further thought."

But Elizabeth had an altogether different plan in mind.

CHAPTER 47

On March 17, 1864, the iron horse rode into Chicago amid a cacophony of screeches and squeals. Yet it sounded to Elizabeth almost like a trumpeted chorus heralding her arrival. It certainly made for a "dazzling entrance into the great, splendid Chicago depot." Having borrowed $10 (about $160) from the Hanfords, promising to pay them back once she'd made her fortune, Elizabeth had set out for the big city, determined to succeed.

She disembarked and wended her way through the city, her spirits enervated from Chicago's own vigor. The city was buzzing. On every street, new buildings seemed to be going up: "the unmistakable signs of active, thriving trade are everywhere manifest." Everywhere, there seemed to be people—its population was 171,356 and growing—as well as hens, cows, and billy goats, because it was legal to keep livestock in the city at that time. Perhaps as a result, it smelled, badly, with the sewage-rich river adding to the stink: "a combination of sulphurated hydrogen, the odor of decaying rodents, and the stench of rotting brassica." And it was noisy, its urban orchestra scored by the shriek of the two hundred locomotives that arrived each day, the cries of newspaper boys and shopkeepers, and the clip-clop of hooves from the horsecars.

Elizabeth had never lived in a city before. Theophilus did not like them, finding "more ostentation, pride and vice in cities than in country towns." But Chicago had a worldwide reputation for energy and enterprise, so it was exactly where she needed to be.

She wasted no time. Within days, she'd made arrangements with the Times Steam Job Printing House on Randolph Street to print two thousand copies of her thirty-two-page pamphlet. Perhaps to her surprise, she did not find it hard to establish business relationships, for the *positive* publicity she'd received preceded her. "The facts of the case were so well known there," she wrote, "I needed no other passport to the confidence of the public." With more women entering the workforce in wartime, too, she was not alone in breaking new business boundaries.

What an achievement it was to hold the finished pamphlet in her hand. It was a slim, almost weightless publication, its cover printed on the same pale paper as the inside pages. She'd asked for a decorative border around the title, and it looked very smart indeed; she planned to sell them for 25 cents each ($4.11).

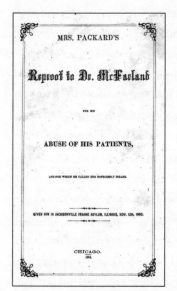

Elizabeth's reproof,
published in 1864

With the reproof published, she felt herself feeling weightless too. "My skirts are now washed of the guilt of *hiding the truth*," she wrote, "for I have told the *truth*." She'd told the world McFarland was not "fit for [his] place" and hoped that her countrymen would now take action as they felt was necessary.

She wanted, herself, to focus on her greater ambition: publishing her book. Having hit a brick wall with publishers, she'd determined to self-publish. In truth, the independence suited her. "I shan't trouble myself at all to go around and ask…if I have written the right sort of book… The whole world…may blow at it—but they can't blow it away… It won't be kept down, any more than its author can be!"

However, the cold hard facts of commerce were an anchor to these dreams she did not anticipate. To her shock, the prices she was quoted to print the book—even just a single volume of it—were hundreds of dollars, far out of her price range, even though she hoped soon to have some income from the reproof. The only capital Elizabeth had was her "health, education, and energy." She couldn't possibly afford it.

Yet she felt an "invincible determination" to prove herself. She would not retreat to Manteno and become a burden on her friends. She could not seek help from Angeline; sadly, her cousin had died in December 1863. She would definitely not return to Theophilus or seek shelter with her father, because Samuel Ware was still supporting her husband, believing his summation of the "sham" trial.

No: she would do this alone. She would support herself with her writing. She truly believed she could do it. She just needed to come up with a plan.

And though it took her "much study," she finally devised what she hoped might prove the solution.

Today, we would call it crowdfunding.

She planned to sell tickets for her book, in advance of its printing, to raise the capital required. It was still no easy task. "I must first inspire in my patron sufficient confidence in my veracity, ability, and perseverance," she realized, "to induce him to pay out fifty cents for a ticket, simply upon the promise of a stranger, that it should be redeemed in three months by a book as yet unprinted."

And she would need to convince fourteen hundred people to invest.

But if she didn't try, she would never know. So she produced a series of small visiting cards upon which was printed, "The Bearer is Entitled to the first Volume of Mrs. Packard's Book... None are genuine without my signature." And on March 23, 1864, she took out an advertisement in the *Chicago Tribune*.

> The subscriber wishes to give notice to her friends in America that the first volume of her book is to be issued by the Chicago press in May... All those who wish a copy for themselves or others, are hereby requested to forward their names to "Mrs. E. P. W. Packard"... And to my friends I would say that, since I am left PENNILESS, by the desertion of my husband, and the laws of Illinois, it would be a great favor TO ME, should you send the money with your names, as I am entirely dependent upon this mode of raising the money to meet the expense of getting my book into print... Friends of humanity and the oppressed, I wait your response to this notice.

And then she went from door to door, selling as many tickets and pamphlets as she could, relying on the simple power of her personality to entice readers to support her work.

It was hard graft, but she had little choice. She could not be like her husband, firing off letters to well-connected friends. She had to *make* those friends she did not have, spending day after day telling and then retelling her story, always hoping to get another sale, to win another heart, to find another ally for her ongoing fight.

It was true that many more women were seeking work in wartime. But *this* kind of public work was definitely not the norm. With no male escort, Elizabeth simply knocked on doors and pitched herself to people without fear or favor. There was stepping out of the domestic sphere— and then there was catapulting out of it, with pompoms twirling and a brass band playing in the background. Elizabeth, with her public advertisements and her in-person pitches, had definitely chosen the latter.

It was a highly risky strategy, not only because of the association of "unnatural" female behavior and madness, but also because of the possible immoral connotations. After all, the very term *public woman* originally meant a prostitute; a woman working outside the home without a male protector "risked ruining her reputation irreparably." As Elizabeth enthusiastically embarked on her new career in Chicago, someone was keeping a very close and very horrified eye on her activities.

"I write in behalf of *my* mother and *your* only daughter Elizabeth," Toffy wrote to Elizabeth's father on March 29, "and if you have *any* regard for her, and wish to have her saved from ruining herself, temporally and spiritually, I hope you will take this matter in hand, and *do* something effective at once... [Please] adopt some plan to get her into proper keeping."

For whatever her eldest son thought about her sanity, his mother following such an unconventional public path was anathema indeed. That he didn't like it was completely unsurprising. Mothers were for cooking and crying to; they were not supposed to have lives of their own...

But while Toffy was attempting to curtail Elizabeth's activities, lobbying both grandfather and father to get her into "proper keeping," the woman at the center of his campaign had no intention of stopping.

"The more freedom I have," Elizabeth wrote, "*the more I want.*"

Elizabeth hit the road. In railroad cars, country villages, towns, and cities across Illinois, she pitched her unprinted book. She paid her way using some of the capital she was raising, meaning she needed to sell yet more tickets. She sold to soldiers, judges at the Supreme Court in Ottawa, and even Mayor Sherman in Chicago.

"Mrs. Packard, you shall have my protection; and I can also assure you the protection of my counsel," the mayor promised once she'd outlined her case, having boldly called on him at his office. "If you get into trouble, apply to us, and we will give you all the help the laws will allow."

But the laws allowed no help. Elizabeth educated him on coverture.

"I must say," he said, shocked, "I never before knew that anyone under our government was so utterly defenceless as you are. Your case ought to be known...our laws changed."

As she sold her books, Elizabeth noticed something striking. Her *personal* story had a terrific impact. It was so easy for men to dismiss women's rights, but when someone who was a victim of those unjust laws stood before them, testifying to the truth of *what had happened to her*, it was harder by far to ignore the issues or protest no change was needed. As living proof married women *were* vulnerable, she forced people to face the difficult realities and inspired their support—not only financially but politically too.

Because, still married as she was to Theophilus, the reality was that he could at any time stop the publication of her book or steal the earnings she hoped to make from it, even seize Elizabeth herself and send her to an asylum. All of that was still possible with the laws as they currently stood.

Which was perhaps why, when the Packards' divorce case finally came to court in April 1864, it didn't turn out as either party expected.

Theophilus did not return for it. His counsel appeared on his behalf—to oppose it vehemently. The minister may have wished to be rid of his wife, but he did not want the social or spiritual stigma of being divorced. He was prepared to fight her every step of the way.

But Elizabeth simply abandoned the case. By that point, she'd set her sights much higher than merely freeing herself from Theophilus's power. A divorce would be a private battle; it might help her but would help no one else. But if she could persuade people that *legal reform* was necessary, then not just one woman but thousands could be saved.

Back in January, she'd been given a binary choice by her lawyers, the latter option really just a joke. "The only way I could secure any rights at all," she'd been told, "was either by a divorce, or *by getting the laws changed.*"

Now, Elizabeth said fiercely, "I chose the latter."

"I don't want another sister in America, to suffer as much as I have."

But if legal reform was her ambition, she needed to construct a strong campaign. And what could be more compelling than a woman in peril? From her limited time on the road, she already appreciated how much more powerful her political arguments would be if she remained legally tied to Theophilus.

"Being in the position of a married woman," she explained, "I was in eminent [*sic*] danger of being wronged still further, unless [the politicians] helped me, by a law, that would help all other married women."

Her marital status made the danger ever-present. It added pressure to the politicians: a loaded gun against her head that could kill her lest they acted. And even though it meant she was still at risk, she was willing to take that chance.

She dropped the divorce proceedings.

In May 1864, a newly ambitious Elizabeth returned to Chicago. She handed over to her printer her precious $700 (about $11,500) that she'd raised entirely through her own efforts. And then, at long last, she held in her hands a finished copy of her book. It was not *The Great Drama* but the second book she'd squirreled away from McFarland while in the asylum: *The Exposure*.

Really, it was an anthology of her asylum writing, her secret journal excepted. It included her defense from October 1860, her statement before the trustees from September 1862, accounts of dreams she'd had, letters she'd written... Her Kankakee lawyer, Stephen Moore, had penned an account of her trial, and this, too, featured. Yet with her legal campaign foremost in her mind, Elizabeth concluded the book with what was perhaps its most important piece: an impassioned "Appeal to the Government for Protection."

> My case is now before you for action, and O, may God grant that your eyes may be opened to see...how many a sainted wife and mother has been ground down and trampled into the very dust... Can you not enact laws by which a married woman can stand on the same platform as a married man—as an American citizen?... Will you not, my Countrymen, recognize in every human being a brother or a sister, who has equal rights...with yourselves?

Soon, as the book started its journey into the world, people would get to read those words, and the politicians would have a chance to respond. In the asylum, she'd told McFarland, "I am resolved to fight my way through all obstacles to victory—to the emancipation of married woman."

This book was round one.

Through her words, Elizabeth hoped to agitate and prompt, to start fires that would burn down the status quo. In short, "her page became a pulpit," with the whole world her congregation, there for her to convince.

Yet there was a message in her book, too, for a much smaller audience. For six people who would likely never even see it: "To my beloved children is this book most affectionately dedicated."

But even within that dedication was a sign of things to come. For although it declared her love, it also suggested that Elizabeth had already risen from the ashes of her family.

"The mother has died!" she inscribed. "But she has risen again—the mother of her country."

Elizabeth Packard was a housewife no more. She had been born again: as a political campaigner.

"Women are made to fly and soar," she wrote, "not to creep and crawl, as the haters of our sex want us to."

In May 1864, Elizabeth finally unfettered her wings.

PART SIX

SHE WILL RISE

Every woman who appears wrestles with the forces that would have her disappear. She struggles with the forces that would tell her story for her, or write her out of the story… The ability to tell your own story…is already a victory, already a revolt.

—Rebecca Solnit, 2014

Prostitute. Whore. What did they really mean anyway? Only words. Words trailing their streamers of judgment.

—Janet Fitch, 1999

CHAPTER 48

January 1867
Springfield, Illinois

———

With a gleam in her vibrant brown eyes, Elizabeth Packard, aged fifty, set her sights on the "house...upon a hill, that could not be hid" and approached it with a determination matching the property's: she *would* be seen.

Uninvited guest or no.

Though her trademark determination was much as it had always been, a lot had changed for Elizabeth in the years since she'd published her first book. "I intend to write a book

Elizabeth's official author photograph, circa 1866

that the people can't help buying," she'd written in the asylum.

Within weeks of publication, it was apparent she had met her aim.

A second edition of *The Exposure* was on sale by June 18, 1864; by the end of the year, she reported having sold $3,000 (about $49,000) worth of books. Come January 1865, a further six thousand copies were in print in Boston, Massachusetts—and flying out the door. And Elizabeth had done it all herself, a one-woman publishing machine, handling production, distribution, sales, marketing, and more. Triumphantly, the newly minted businesswoman declared, "I am now independent!"

She'd put her new financial wealth to good use to pursue those causes closest to her heart. In March 1866, she'd published a follow-up, *Marital Power Exemplified*, which more purely focused on married women's rights. "Reforms succeed just in proportion as the need of them is apprehended by the public mind," she wrote presciently. This book was intended to illuminate readers on the injustice of the current laws and enlist them to her cause. She'd been inspired by the bestselling *Uncle Tom's Cabin*, which had made the case for abolition. "My experience, although like 'Uncle Tom's' an extreme case, shows how all married women are *liable* to suffer to the same extent I have."

This second book—a slim, navy volume bound with bronze ribbon—soon proved another hit; in one town alone, Elizabeth hand-sold five hundred copies at $1 (about $16.00) each. Her phenomenal success meant she had a solid "platform of 'greenback independence'" from which she could launch her political campaigns.

Which explained why she was in Springfield, Illinois—the state capital—and on her way to the Governor's Mansion.

At the top of the hill, Elizabeth paused, pulling her shawl more tightly around her to protect her from the bracing cold. She eyed the handsome redbrick building with admiration, though she was hardly alone in that; "many persons...paused upon the street to admire the spectacle." Unlike these rubberneckers, however, Elizabeth soon swished her hoop skirts into her hand and boldly ascended the grand split staircase at the front of the house. Her physical elevation rather matched the journey she'd been on as a campaigner over the past few years: rising from ignorance to expertise, step by steady step.

She'd begun campaigning back in January 1865, keen to get going with what she saw as a God-given mission. Yet she'd known nothing about "the complicated machinery of legislation" and had been forced to embark "ignorantly...upon the work of reforming the laws under which we live." Yet if she ever flagged, she would ask herself, "Where do you find courage? Where do you find dauntless perseverance?" and answer her own question resolutely: "In woman!"

Her campaigning had begun in Massachusetts, the state to which her husband had fled and where her youngest children now resided. Elizabeth had wanted to be close to them—hoping perhaps for shared access or even just occasional visits—but Massachusetts's commitment law was almost identical to that of Illinois: husbands needed only two doctors' certificates to lock up their wives. As Elizabeth saw it, unless she changed that law, "another kidnapping [was] inevitable." The verdict of the Illinois court meant nothing in Massachusetts.

So, using her powers of persuasion, she'd enlisted a legal whiz, Samuel Sewall, to guide her through the intimidating maze. Aged sixty-five, Sewall had thick white hair that came down to his shoulders and sideburns to rival an ill-pruned bush. Though he was a passionate abolitionist—one of the founders of the Massachusetts Anti-Slavery Society and a supporter of the Underground Railroad—it was actually women's rights that were closest to the lawyer's heart; he ultimately assisted in passing over 150 statutes for their emancipation. "Our society [is] debased," he declared, "because the two sexes do not associate as equals."

Sewall was already intimately familiar with the abuse to which the current commitment law could be put. He'd previously represented a Mrs. Denny, who'd been banished to an asylum after daring to ask her husband for a divorce. Sewall had made his own attempts to improve the law in recent years; when Elizabeth came calling, the pair decided to work together.

It was Sewall who taught Elizabeth the tricks of her new trade. Together, they'd unleashed publicity for their cause and personally lobbied the legislature, with Elizabeth appearing in person before a joint special committee to plead her case. Sewall also drafted a petition to drum up public support, and although only his name appeared on the paperwork they eventually submitted to the Massachusetts House of Representatives, it was Elizabeth who pounded the streets of Boston to secure the signatures required, selling yet more books as she did.

As she'd been in Illinois while crowdfunding, she was absolutely fearless. Boston's Custom House, Navy Yard, and Common Council were among her targets, and she canvassed these masculine worlds as though a woman had every right to be there. She befriended sailors and engineers, counting room clerks and aldermen, doctors, lawyers, and bank directors too. Almost every man to whom she appealed treated her "in a most generous, and praiseworthy manner," but she always had a ready response in case of any criticism: "I say I have just as good a right to discuss politics as a man, if I am a woman."

On May 16, 1865, the Massachusetts legislature had amended the insanity law. Partly thanks to Elizabeth's impassioned campaign, the law was strengthened to protect those being sectioned, rendering "secret frameups more difficult by informing a number of interested persons of the event."

The new law was the crowning glory for Elizabeth in what had proved a tumultuous spring for her country, with the passing of the

Thirteenth Amendment—abolishing slavery—President Lincoln's subsequent assassination, and the eventual end of the Civil War. Elizabeth had been in Massachusetts for the latter, listening in delight to the patriotic bands that had begun spontaneously to play and to the joyous two-hundred-gun salutes. The celebrations were like "a dozen 'Fourths of July' concentrated into one day."

Although there was no two-hundred-gun salute for Elizabeth's victory, it was no less momentous for that. Because her political triumph gave her immense confidence—confidence that she drew on now as she reached the top of the staircase of the Governor's Mansion and ventured through its wide and curved front door. She entered with ease; its shape had been specifically designed to accommodate the sometimes six-foot diameter of ladies' hoop skirts.

In the lobby, however, her smooth passage suddenly came to a halt. Here—without an invitation to admit her—she had to pause and patiently await an audience with the governor. She settled down, prepared to wait for as long as it might take.

Patience was perhaps the other thing she'd been forced to learn over the past few years. After Boston, her campaigning had taken her to Connecticut. (She'd intended to return to Illinois, but as its general assembly was not sitting in 1866, a change of plan had been required.) There, she'd launched an ambitious campaign to overturn coverture, proposing a bill in which "any woman entering the marriage relation shall retain the same legal existence...and shall receive the same legal protection of her rights as...does...a man." In many ways, it was a trial run for what she hoped one day to replicate in the states where her children resided, because such radical reforms would allow her at last to sue for custody.

As things stood, Theophilus refused even to let her see her children.

Drawing on that personal injustice, in Connecticut she'd managed to win the support of hundreds of men. Ultimately, however, her proposed law proved too much, too soon. The committee that considered it informed her that it was "inexpedient to make such radical changes at the present time."

Despite the disappointment, Elizabeth had dusted herself off. "No such thing as failure," she'd told herself sternly. She'd reminded herself, "My work ain't done, yet. And I ain't any of your half sort of folks."

And this was where her unfinished work had led her next: to the lobby of the Governor's Mansion in Illinois. As she waited for the man himself to appear, she could not help but be struck by the building's handsome fluted pillars and its grand interior staircase, the latter winding like an unfurling ribbon through the full height of the residence. Yet such imposing surroundings did not cow her courage. If she'd learned anything over the past couple of years, it was the importance of being single-minded.

Her latest campaign in Illinois was her most focused yet. Because Elizabeth had never forgotten the women she'd left behind in the asylum, and she'd now returned to rescue them. In fact, for almost four years Elizabeth had been appealing to various lawyers to assist her sisters while she'd been busy in other states battling for legal reforms. But none had taken up her cause. By January 1867, Elizabeth had come to the only conclusion that she could.

If no one else was going to help these women, *she* would.

In many ways, theirs was a battle she'd never stopped fighting. When she'd first hit the road in Illinois to sell her book, she'd made a point of visiting the hometowns of her friends in order to stir up support for them. In Sarah Minard's hometown of St. Charles, for example, she'd found the townspeople gave "one uniform testimony that her confinement...was unnecessary." Yet she'd also discovered that not one citizen was prepared to champion Sarah personally, "lest their own pecuniary interests should be…imperilled, by a conflict with their townsman and banker," because Sarah's husband was a wealthy and very influential man.

Once, Elizabeth had even returned to the asylum. She'd been permitted to visit her friends, but McFarland had insisted he chaperone. With the doctor openly eavesdropping, Elizabeth had explained to Sarah all she'd done to try to secure her freedom, including writing to the trustees and Sarah's husband in June 1863. Yet she'd had to confess she'd received no reply to those letters and did not know what had become of them.

McFarland had interrupted, "These letters came to me, and are in my hands."

"Ah!" Elizabeth exclaimed knowingly. "*That* is the reason I have never heard from them."

Even now, nearly four years after Elizabeth's own release, Sarah Minard and many other women Elizabeth believed were sane were still shut up in the asylum. All were held there on the strength of the superintendent's word.

And that superintendent *was* still McFarland. It had mattered not that, as Elizabeth put it, "the verdict of the jury [in my trial] virtually impeached Dr. McFarland as an accomplice in this foul drama, and as one who had prostituted his high public trust." The court verdict, combined with Elizabeth's bestselling books, had at first provoked "severe comment" in Illinois, but all the allegations, serious as they were, had ultimately left McFarland untouched. Despite what Elizabeth had hoped for when she'd first published her pamphlets, no one in authority had held him to account.

Instead, his career had gone from strength to strength. Back in June

1864, he'd been unanimously reappointed by the board of trustees—given another ten-year tenure at the hospital and a substantial pay raise to boot. In 1865, he'd received an honorary degree.

Even the press had become effusive in approval. They'd been helped to this endorsement by carefully managed media tours in which they were invited to the hospital and served "a substantial dinner." Glowing articles from January 1867 described how McFarland's health was toasted at these parties and Havana cigars were smoked by all.

No wonder the doctor's labors were praised in print as "untiring."

Only in passing in these same articles was the story of a patient asserting his sanity "in the strongest terms" mentioned. But the journalists said, "We were assured that his mind was anything but clear." So they went on their way, "perfectly in raptures" about the "well conducted" asylum and its "able and accomplished Superintendent."

It was clear, however, that Elizabeth's case had riled McFarland personally. He devoted the first biennial report of his new tenure to writing about her, though he did not deign to mention her by name. When some of his friends in Massachusetts heard Elizabeth's story—thanks to her campaigning—and wrote to him in consternation, McFarland swiftly assured them that the court verdict casting doubt upon his work came only from a "sham trial." Additionally, he told them that Elizabeth was insane to a "very high degree."

McFarland believed he had a raft of new evidence to support his diagnosis. "I wonder that those who so implicitly believe her story," he wrote, "do not ask themselves, whether a woman who has been truly wronged ever goes to work in this fashion for remedy—is her course exactly a natural one? Should you, if persecuted by a husband, adopt that style of life [that she has, as a political campaigner], thinking to procure a vindication for yourself?"

Because wronged women were not supposed to stand up for themselves. Wronged women were not supposed to come out fighting, or be angry, or battle for injustice to be overturned. Elizabeth's course was unnatural in his eyes—and therefore insane.

Elizabeth had the opportunity to read his words, for they'd appeared in a Connecticut newspaper: part of an orchestrated campaign to thwart her anti-coverture bill. His attitude had only increased her commitment to her cause. Indeed, it had perhaps reminded her of all the many abuses she'd witnessed at the hospital under McFarland's rule—abuses she'd once recorded in her asylum diary.

In 1867, both journal and abuse alike had still not seen the light of day.

And so Elizabeth's focus had shifted, from her wide-lens ideal of canceling coverture to a much more narrow frame of reference.

"I intend," she wrote assertively, "to turn Jacksonville Asylum inside out."

CHAPTER 49

At the sound of footsteps, Elizabeth readied herself, squaring her shoulders and smoothing her skirts. She may have muttered to herself a favorite phrase: "Nothing venture, nothing have."

In a burst of bonhomie, Governor Richard J. Oglesby swept into his luxurious lobby, trailed by an entourage of dinner party guests. At forty-two, he had a strong physical presence: a tubby man with thick, dark hair and prominent, fleshy features. A Civil War hero, he had a reputation for fighting for minorities, including Native and African Americans. As such, Elizabeth hoped he might at least give her the time of day.

Governor Richard J. Oglesby

Appreciating that she was interrupting his evening, she simply asked when she might call on him again in business hours to discuss a new bill that she wished to bring before the legislature.

"What is the object of the bill?" Oglesby asked. His usual geniality was absent as he grilled this uninvited guest.

"'Tis about the Asylum at Jacksonville."

Yet these words were not welcome either.

"Oh, I think that is doing well enough," he said curtly. "I am acquainted with Dr. McFarland, and esteem him very highly as my personal friend."

Elizabeth may well have been expecting that response. In Oglesby's opening address to the general assembly that very year, he had publicly praised the hospital's "prudent management."

The governor's support of McFarland bothered Elizabeth far more than it would have done even four years prior, when she herself had been a patient under the doctor's control. Because, legally, things were very different now in Illinois. Her own suffering had not left the statute books of the state untouched. On February 16, 1865, a new law had been passed that allowed *all* those accused of insanity to have a jury trial before commitment—*including* married women. Given the extensive coverage of her case, these reforms were undoubtedly inspired by her, yet she claimed no credit.

But if it seemed as if there were therefore no legal reforms for Elizabeth to undertake, nothing could have been further from the truth. Through one of her new allies, a thirty-eight-year-old Chicago judge named James Bradwell—whose brilliant wife, Myra, later became the first woman admitted to the bar in Illinois—Elizabeth had learned that the new law was frequently being flouted. It had no penalties attached for noncompliance, so there was literally no way for it to be enforced. In addition, it was not retroactive, meaning all those wives admitted to the asylum *before* a jury trial became (allegedly) compulsory were still there and still had no remedy for their release. As Elizabeth saw it, the 1865 law was "a dead letter in practice."

These flaws in the law were what Elizabeth now intended to fix, so as "to relieve all the unjustly imprisoned victims in that institution." Even before arriving at the Governor's Mansion that January night, she'd put what she'd learned in other states into practice, producing a petition to enlist support. Even as she spoke with the governor, that paperwork was in her pocket. It had been signed thus far by thirty-six men, including a mayor, a congressman, and "some of the heaviest merchants and businessmen of Chicago."

As soon as Oglesby mentioned his friendship with McFarland, Elizabeth presented the petition. McFarland may well have had friends in high places, but by now, *so did she*. She handed it over, pressing the governor to look closely at those influential signatures giving their support.

Oglesby had "a studious and thoughtful mind"; upon seeing the names, he put every synapse of that brain to work. As he reviewed the impressive list, the governor's "tone and manner changed at once." Cordial now, he invited Elizabeth to his office the very next day to discuss the matter further.

Elizabeth wasted no time getting to her point. Oglesby was renowned for his "wise, just and honest administration," and she found he listened patiently, then offered assistance. He introduced her to Elmer Baldwin, a member of the Illinois House of Representatives, and via Baldwin's contacts, Elizabeth pitched her proposed bill widely, including making an informal presentation in the state house library one Friday night to "a very respectable number of members." Best of all, she secured an introduction to the Judiciary Committee and to Senator Joseph Ward, who helped her draft a new personal liberty bill. It set out both that patients must *not* be admitted without a jury trial *and* that any current patient who'd been admitted without one was now entitled to be so judged.

After Ward completed his draft, Elizabeth was invited by the

Judiciary Committee to review it with them. It was her last chance to make changes before the bill was formally introduced before the general assembly.

The draft was read aloud; she was asked if it suited her.

Elizabeth replied promptly, "Gentlemen, it does not... It needs a penalty attached, for as it now stands 'tis merely legislative advice."

The committee duly added a penalty of a fine (not less than $500, not more than $1,000) or imprisonment (not less than three months, not more than a year), *or both*, for any doctor who admitted a patient to an asylum without trial.

"There is no [deadline] appointed for the trial of the [current] inmates of the asylum," she pointed out.

This too was introduced: sixty days from the moment the bill became law.

Elizabeth breathed a sigh of satisfaction. "Gentlemen, the bill suits me now."

"Then we will recommend its passage."

And that is exactly what the committee did, from the moment it was introduced to the general assembly for its consideration in mid-January 1867.

To her delight, Elizabeth found that the politicians were far from the only people to support her campaign. Both the *Chicago Tribune* and *Chicago Times* wrote endorsing editorials of her work, while the *Daily Illinois State Register* was also an ally. Elizabeth herself wrote several anonymous articles published statewide. At every opportunity, she also shared her "sensational novel"—both the books she'd published to date. Illinois readers soon declared they "ought to be read by every citizen."

But while the world at large seemed increasingly supportive, at least one man was not: Dr. Andrew McFarland. He'd strongly objected to the passing of the 1865 law, but in his view, Elizabeth's new personal liberty bill was palpably worse.

"[It] is injurious, odious, barbarous, damnable, and you may add as many more expletives to it as you please, and still not say the truth in regard to its evils," he railed. McFarland objected to jury trials on principle, feeling "the haphazard opinions and caprices of men grossly ignorant of the subject before them" were not the way to determine insanity; only experts like himself should be given authority to judge. In that spring of 1867, he was campaigning too, but he wanted the *opposite* to Elizabeth: a complete repeal of the 1865 law so things would go back to the way they were before.

He wasted no time in communicating his message. Using all the freedom allowed him by his gender, he met the politicians in hotels and boardinghouses, and there, likely over wine and cigars, he shared his professional diagnosis of Elizabeth and urged them not only to reject her bill but to repeal the other. "In nearly three thousand admissions here," he claimed of his asylum, "a question [of unfair commitment] was never seriously raised, in a single instance [under the previous law]."

Upon hearing his claims, which he also published in his biennial report, Elizabeth's jaw dropped. A question had never been seriously raised? Honestly? Elizabeth soon published her riposte: "Has the Doctor forgotten that the question has been once, at least, seriously raised by the court at Kankakee City, in the case of one whom that court decided had been falsely imprisoned for three years?" Mindful of her sisters, she added, "Mrs. Packard's case is a type of other cases of false imprisonment now there; and the simplest claims of justice and humanity demand that this Legislature extend to such a fair trial."

But an angry article in the press was no match for the personal pressure that McFarland was able to bring to his intimate tête-à-têtes. With

McFarland cozying up to the members of the general assembly, woman or not, Elizabeth felt she had to do the same. She therefore called on the landlords of the relevant boardinghouses and begged permission to meet the members in their parlors. In face of Elizabeth's persuasiveness, all cheerfully agreed. She took along copies of her printed riposte to McFarland as well as her many books and pamphlets, often giving away her publications for free in order to further her cause.

One might have thought that some men would think her pushy or unnatural for this fearless behavior. But over the past few years, Elizabeth had honed a very clever strategy as she campaigned. On the surface, she seemingly embraced the male view of women as weak and defenseless, but if that *was* the truth, she argued, men *had* to protect them *by passing the laws she proposed*. She also openly flattered the lawmakers, telling them she knew that *they* would never dream of treating women badly; if *all* men were true men like them, no legal reformation would be required. But as deviants, such as her husband, did exist, she had no choice but to beg them to change the law on her behalf.

It was a method a million miles away from the radical philosophies in *The Great Drama*. But Elizabeth Packard was nothing if not practical. She knew instinctively that it was too soon politically for those ideas; they would hinder and not help her. She needed to see change in her lifetime, so she employed these manipulations in order to persuade the politicians.

Her wily positioning worked a treat. Despite the shockingly public nature of her work, she regularly earned men's praise and not their opprobrium. In later years, she was even commended for not being one of the "offensive class" of female campaigners. "You are reasonable and sensible on the subject of 'Woman's Rights,'" one man said. "Coming with such views as yours, there is more hope, at least, of your making it a success."

In late January 1867, success did indeed seem within reach. Elizabeth felt her bill was "constantly growing in favor with the enlightened public."

There was a particular reason for that. Elizabeth was not backward in coming forward with *all* the details of her time in the asylum, which included stories of abuse as well as unjust imprisonment. Given the extensive press coverage, others soon began to share their own experiences. Some were erstwhile attendants, including Mrs. Graff (formerly Mrs. Hosmer). They wrote letters to the media, which sat alongside Elizabeth's own vivid accounts. "Horrible revelations" began to be published of the violence patients suffered behind closed doors. In such a climate, Elizabeth's reforms—and the spotlight she was fearlessly focusing upon the asylum—seemed increasingly essential.

Yet despite these further, serious allegations, Dr. McFarland remained untouched. A legislative committee visited the hospital on January 26, but it was a rerun of the outcome of those glowing media tours; the committee expressed "much gratification at the condition & management" of the asylum. It vowed to recommend the customary budget for the next two years.

In other words, business as usual.

Elizabeth had only one last-ditch attempt to make a difference—to make them see the truth. On February 12, 1867, she was personally invited to address the general assembly.

One last chance to make it count.

CHAPTER 50

Only once before in her life had she spoken to such a huge crowd of men. The year before, she'd made a similar presentation in Connecticut's legislative hall, one of the first women ever to address a general assembly.

But this day's speech was much more personal. It was her friends she was fighting for: women she had known and loved and who, if she failed today, would be destined potentially to lifelong imprisonment. If she failed, too, there was every chance the assembly would follow McFarland's advice and roll back the flawed law of 1865. That left even Elizabeth herself with no protection, liable once again to be locked up because of her beliefs.

Even now, McFarland was telling anyone who would listen that she was certifiably insane. He certainly felt she would be better off behind barred windows, never again to have a voice she could use against him.

But she had a voice today.

This was her chance to use it.

She felt nervous, in case she was not up to the job. Yet Elizabeth was a born public speaker who often found that "after the first sentence was fairly spoken, such a feeling of perfect, quiet self-assurance took possession of me, that I, from that moment, felt as much at my ease as if I was talking to parlor guests."

And from that moment, it became almost easy.

"Gentlemen of Illinois General Assembly," she began as the men milled before her: one woman standing tall and strong to make her case.

> Thankful for the privilege granted me, I will simply state that I desire to explain my bill rather than defend it, since I am satisfied it needs no defense to secure its passage… [I ask you to] use my martyrdom…to herald this most glorious of all reforms…
>
> We married women…have had our personal liberty, for sixteen years, suspended on…one man's opinion; and possibly [McFarland] may be found to be a fallible man, and capable of corruption.

She planted that idea almost lightly, scattering it as a seed in a garden that was already beginning to flower. Because if *all* she was saying was true, then surely an investigation should follow? What was *really* going on behind those walls?

"Now, if the Doctor was required to prove his patients insane, from their own conduct, there would be a shadow of justice attached to his individual judgment," she went briskly on,

> but while this law allows him to call them insane, and treat them as insane, without evidence of insanity, where is the justice of such a decision? You do not hang a person without proof from the accused's own actions that he is guilty of the charge which forfeits his life. So the personal liberty of married women should not be

sacrificed without proof that they are insane, from their own conduct...

To my certain knowledge, there were married women there when I left, more than three years since, who were not insane then at all, and they are still retained there, as hopelessly insane patients, on the simple strength of the above ground of evidence; and it is my womanly sympathy for this class of prisoners that has moved me to come, alone...to see if I could not possibly induce this legislature to compassionate their case: for it is under your laws, gentlemen, I have suffered, and they are still suffering, and it is to this legislature of 1867 that we apply for a legal remedy.

She took a breath, hoping her words were sinking in. She turned next to read an extract from McFarland's own letter that had been published in the *Chicago Tribune* in January 1864.

"Dr. McFarland writes, 'I have no question but that Mrs. Packard's committal here was as justifiable as in the majority of those now here,'" she quoted. Elizabeth was like an expert lawyer as she pointed out the corollary. "Gentlemen, your Superintendent's own statement verifies it, that *I am not the only one who has been so unjustly imprisoned there.*"

Point nailed, she continued breathlessly,

In the name and behalf of those now there, I beg of this body that you extend to such a fair trial or a discharge... Only think of putting your own delicate, sensitive daughter through the scenes I have been put through. Do you think she would have come out unharmed?...

> We [women] have an individuality of our own…will
> you not protect our personal liberty, while in the lawful,
> ladylike exercise of it?

She was eloquent and passionate as never before. "Fear nothing so much as the sin of simply not doing your duty," she urged, "in defence of the heaven-born principles of liberty and justice to all humankind."

As her speech came toward its close, she turned her attention once again to the reality of life inside the asylum. With a push to the politicians that was so slight it was barely palpable, she lightly said,

> Gentlemen, permit me also to say, that when you have
> once liberated the sane inmates of that hospital, and
> effectually fortified the rights of the sane citizens of
> Illinois against false commitments there, you will have
> taken the *first* progressive step in the right direction, in
> relation to this great humanitarian reform.
>
> And here I will say, that from what I do know of
> the practical workings…of that institution, as seen from
> behind the curtain…I predict it will not be the last.

Changing the law was Elizabeth's primary aim. But a full investigation of the hospital, which looked behind that iron curtain, would certainly be a satisfying secondary success.

Her time was nearly up. Elizabeth gathered herself for a final push. "Gentlemen, this law and its application to me cannot be obliterated, for it has already become a page of Illinois history, which must stand to all coming time, as a living witness against the legislation of Illinois in the nineteenth century. There is one way, and only one, by which you can redeem your State...and that is by such practical repentance as this bill demands."

She fixed them all with her gleaming brown eyes. "Gentlemen... so far as you are concerned, my work is now done. Yours remains to be done.

"God grant you may dare to do right!"

When Elizabeth Packard stood and spoke, all listened "with the most profound and respectful interest." And that's exactly what the members of the legislature did that February day as her words worked their way inside their hearts and minds. A newspaper later wrote that she was able to hold her audience "spell-bound...every ear...intent on receiving her utterances."

In short, she was nothing less than a "sensation."

So persuasive was her speech that it had an immediate impact. At 9:00 p.m. on the very same day as her presentation, the telegram boy in Jacksonville suddenly sat upright. Though the hour was late, electrical impulses began coming down the wire at lightning speed: a message from the spellbound politicians in Springfield.

Against the noise of the pouring rain outside, he quickly transcribed the message.

They were coming, the telegram read.

The time for complacency and cover-ups in Jacksonville was over; exposure and investigation were now the name of the game. Because the politicians would be arriving for an unscheduled visit at 9:30 a.m.

The boy's pen paused over the all-important date.

Tomorrow.

CHAPTER 51

The Jacksonville citizens scrambled to make arrangements, keen to show off their celebrated hospital at its best. As the *Jacksonville Journal* stated, "The success of the town depends in no small degree upon that of her institutions." Yet the weather was against them; the heavy rain created an "excessive quantity of mud" that impaired their efforts. When the politicians arrived, it was to find a mud-slicked city unable to scrub itself clean.

It's possible the legislature did not want the citizens—or McFarland—to suspect the real reason for their sudden visit. They split into two groups: one a committee that embarked on other official business, the other a mismatch of house and senate members who requested a tour of all the state institutions in the city, including the asylum.

As the media had been at their visit in January, the politicians were feted, with concerts and dances laid on in the evening. Before then, however, the more serious business of the unannounced inspection took place. One member at least, having been briefed by Elizabeth, made a special request to visit Mrs. Minard and Mrs. Chapman on Seventh Ward, which was granted.

"How long have you been here?" the gentleman asked of Sarah, having been directed to her room full of house plants, in which sat a lady wearing gold spectacles.

"Nine years," she replied forlornly.

"Has your husband ever been to visit you?"

"He has not."

They conversed a little while longer.

"I do not know what motive it is that requires me to be confined in this lunatic asylum," Sarah burst out, "or what good purpose can be answered by my remaining here. My main desire is to get home."

The gentleman told the two women he knew Elizabeth. Both Mrs. Minard and Mrs. Chapman brightened visibly. "Give our love to Mrs. Packard," they urged. "Tell [her] she must not forget us."

The urgency of their message resonated. "Mrs. Packard and I have consulted about your cases," he revealed. "I am not at liberty to say anything definite now...but this much I can say, your case will not be forgotten."

He took his leave of them feeling stunned. As he later told Elizabeth, "I am more forcibly impressed with the injustice of their confinement by seeing them, than from the impression I had received from you. I have no hesitancy in saying these persons ought to be removed from that asylum."

Nor was he the only visitor to feel that way. Another gentleman who also toured the hospital felt an "irresistible conviction" that many currently there ought to be sent home. For he observed not only "the wild, frantic maniac" and "the partially deranged," but also, "not unfrequently...the sane." He blasted the conditions in which he found the patients, shocked they were herded together "like wild beasts."

"In view of all these facts," he wrote in an article, published February 21, "there should be something more than a medical director, something more than a mere board of trustees... There should be such an ample and full provision [of oversight] as shall entirely prevent [the asylum] from being subverted from its original and true design."

Yet McFarland, the trustees, and the AMSAII virulently objected to the very idea that their work needed inspection from an independent body. As the state stood in loco parentis to patients, they felt their affairs should not be "liable to any general inquisition," just as "no father of a household allows of interference with his private...arrangements or discipline." Such inspectors would be a "fruitless annoyance," more likely to do harm than good. "Such a commission," complained one doctor without irony, "would be governed solely by an enlightened sense of honesty, justice, and fair dealing."

So strongly did the AMSAII feel about the issue that in 1864, they'd voted unanimously to adopt a resolution condemning independent inspectors as "not only wholly unnecessary, but injurious and subversive." To them, a board of trustees provided ample supervision—ignoring the evident bias and incestuous friendships that often influenced trustees' work.

Yet the need for independent inspection seemed increasingly evident to Illinois's citizens every time they opened up their newspapers that spring. Elizabeth maintained a constant campaign, seeking justice for the asylum's inmates. She remembered all too well the women's screams just before they were held under the water. She remembered all too well those crying voices in the night. So she spoke out, sharing her memories, describing all she'd seen, and "so pointed were her statements of the maltreatment of patients...so fortified by the corroborative testimony of other witnesses, that there began to be a State-wide outcry of disapprobation at the management of the Asylum, and a clamor for an investigation."

However, luckily for McFarland, at least one senator took his side. In the senate on February 23, the senator in charge of the Finance Committee announced that his team had "examined into these matters, and…the members were satisfied that there was no foundation for the charges." He admitted they hadn't had time to make a "thorough investigation," yet concluded emphatically that the doctor "had been grossly misrepresented and slandered." As far as he was concerned, it was the end of the matter.

"His statement seemed to be entirely satisfactory to the Senate," reported the *Illinois Journal*, "and, we are sure, will be gratifying to the Doctor's many warm friends."

Yet despite the senator's declaration, Elizabeth had by then provoked such a sensation that the rumors were too loud to ignore. Even McFarland himself, in the end, wrote to his friend Governor Oglesby to ask for a chance to clear his name, while the *Jacksonville Journal*, a newspaper supportive of the doctor, called for an investigation too. "We have every reason to believe that it will greatly benefit the institution," it said smugly, "and increase the well-earned reputations of the trustees, and able superintendent."

The politicians could not help but hear the outcry. Just three days after the senate's Finance Committee had tried to put it all to bed, T. B. Wakeman rose to speak in the Illinois House of Representatives.

"[I have] waited for other gentlemen upon this floor to take action in this direction," he said, "but as they [have] not done so, [I have myself] introduced…resolutions. [I think] it of the utmost importance that this general assembly should at once take such action as would prove the truth or falsity of the reports in circulation concerning the management of the penitentiary."

He used *penitentiary* synonymously for *asylum*; Elizabeth would have approved.

Wakeman proposed that a special joint committee be immediately appointed to investigate the charges—and his colleagues concurred.

Reporting on the explosive development, the *State Register* declared, "The appointment of this [investigating] committee was mainly the result of the efforts of Mrs. Packard."

In the asylum, Elizabeth had often thought of what Mrs. Grere, one of her fellow patients, had said: "If Dr. McFarland won't do right, can't he be made to do right by some power?"

At last, that day had come. Finally, an independent body was going to investigate the doctor and his hospital. It was what Elizabeth had only dreamed of when she'd started her secret journal. The committee was given powers to examine witnesses under oath, its mission "to ascertain whether any of the inmates are improperly retained in the Hospital, or unjustly placed there, and whether the inmates are humanely and kindly treated."

"O, yes, Mrs. Grere," Elizabeth now thought, "there *is* a power which can make him do right." She concluded fiercely, "Let justice…unsheathe its flaming sword."

———

The day after the committee was appointed, Elizabeth's personal liberty bill had its third and final reading in the state senate. Women were not allowed on the senate floor for votes. When Elizabeth came to the senate chamber, therefore, she had to climb the wooden staircase outside. She took a seat in the gallery upstairs, trying not to have her view blocked by the room's many ornate pillars.

By now, it really was *her* bill. Whereas in Massachusetts, when she'd first started her political campaigning, her petition had been filed under Samuel Sewall's name, now, in the press at least, the woman and the legal reform had become one. "Mrs. Packard's Personal Liberty Law" ran the headlines. Some meant it dismissively, intending to weaken the bill's integrity by association with a woman's name, but Elizabeth claimed it as her own with pride.

She could barely breathe as the senate came to vote. She'd had a long fight to get to this moment, experiencing various acts of administrative sabotage along the way; the bill itself even went physically AWOL. Even now that it was finally before the senate for its third reading, it did not mean it would pass. The general assembly was about to conclude its business for the session, and they'd spent all day killing bills, ordering that they not be passed as there was no time to get them through. Elizabeth feared hers might meet the same fate, even though she'd personally lobbied as many senators as she could to extract a promise that they'd vote in favor.

By this point, it was late in the day. Earlier, Elizabeth had been joined in the gallery by many other women who'd been eager to see this act for their protection passed, but it was now the supper hour, and they'd retired home to cook for their husbands. It was the time for lamp lighting, the windows to the outside dark eyes that seemed to promise anything but freedom. Below where Elizabeth sat in the gallery, the senate chamber seemed gloomy, and some of the senators may have started lighting the candles on their desks. It was dizzying to look down upon those circular lines of tables, all arranged around the speaker's stand, all crammed with men who really just wanted to get home at this late hour.

A portrait of Lafayette, hero of the American Revolution, hung behind the main podium, looking down on proceedings with as much solemnity as Elizabeth herself. Both portrait and political campaigner listened as her bill was read once again.

It turned out that many senators had only clocked the bill's title previously and had not grasped the radical nature of what she'd proposed:

a jury trial of *all* inmates currently in the asylum who wanted one, plus penalties if the jury trial law was broken (which itself required administration). The discussions that followed were like a "tug of war."

Elizabeth looked down upon the chaos, aghast. She could see the politicians wobbling, despite the assurances they'd previously given. She feared a repeat of what had happened in Connecticut, when promises to pass her anti-coverture law had proved as empty as a barren woman's womb.

Numerous questions were asked and answered. Elizabeth peered over the gallery's balcony, eyeballing all those she could see, trying silently to remind them of their noble pledge. She felt "in a state of almost breathless suspense."

At length, the vote came around…

Every single senator voted for it. It passed unanimously.

Up in the gallery, a gentleman turned to her. "Mrs. Packard," he said, "your bill is safe!"

Elizabeth's bill is read before the state senate

390

Elizabeth let out the breath she'd been holding. Her bill had passed. She had done it. A jury trial for every single woman on Seventh Ward and beyond. No woman, married or otherwise, could be committed without trial. Never again would a woman suffer what she had. Never again would her friends have to suffer. They would be free, and she would be free too. Free from fear of what Theophilus might do, yet free, too, from the guilt that she'd somehow escaped when others hadn't. She had used her freedom to save them, and with this senate vote, that safety was assured.

"I felt such a relief," she wrote, the words not strong enough to capture her feelings, "accompanied with an indescribable emotion of joy and thankfulness." Her emotion surpassed even what she'd felt at the courtroom in Kankakee, when her own sanity had been declared. "In that decision," she explained, "only the interests of one individual were involved, while on this decision, the personal liberty of hundreds was suspended."

She rose from her seat, walked shakily down the curving staircase, and stood at the door of the senate chamber. As each man left, she grasped him firmly by the hand, uttering thanks that seemed so small in relation to the scale of what he'd done.

After all the machinations to prevent the bill from being passed, Elizabeth did not trust to tradition alone to see it through. Instead, she personally walked it from the house speaker to the senate speaker to the governor himself, securing their formal signatures that would actually make it law. Oglesby signed it on March 5, 1867.

He came out of his office and handed it back to her, saying, "Mrs. Packard, your bill is signed!"

Elizabeth held the bill with one hand and took the governor's with her other.

"In the name of the married women of Illinois," she said gravely, "I thank you for this act."

The politicians gave her a certified copy as a memento. She kept it for years afterward, "a record of my first attempt to serve the State of Illinois." History records that she was "the prime motivator in originating it and securing its passage." It was a legacy indeed.

On August 4, 1863, the summer she'd been released from the asylum, Elizabeth had written to her daughter, "There is not a girl in America who has so capable a mother as you have, and the world will know it soon."

Finally, the world was starting to.

CHAPTER 52

From the moment Oglesby's signature was scrawled upon the bill, the clock began ticking. The asylum trustees now had just sixty days to organize jury trials for those patients who'd been admitted without one.

Elizabeth was perhaps most excited for Sarah Minard. She had no doubt that after nine years in the asylum, Sarah would be declared sane in a trial, along with many other women from Seventh Ward.

It seemed the trustees feared the same. Their stated view on the juries who'd be making the judgments were that they were "imperfectly prepared to perceive the nice distinctions of mental derangement." They protested that many patients were convalescing and therefore "past the stage of their disease where the commonly discoverable evidences of insanity are manifest." Other patients were those who had what McFarland would describe as Elizabeth's type of madness: "dangerous" patients who "possess extreme delusions…perceptible only to skilled observers."

The trustees seemed to fear the consequences if any patients *were* found sane—perhaps expensive court cases claiming damages for improper detainment. In the wake of Elizabeth's trial three years earlier, these had become commonplace, with the AMSAII blasting these "infernal prosecutions." Echoing McFarland's arrogance about the verdict in Elizabeth's trial, the AMSAII criticized the "loose and flawy ways and decisions of judicial officers" because the judgments often went against them. Previously, the doctors had had things almost entirely their own way, but slowly, as Elizabeth put it, "this innovation of recognizing inmates of insane asylums as beings possessing human rights" was beginning to take root.

As such, despite the trustees' antipathic views, the new law *was* the law, and they had to follow it. On May 2, 1867, insanity trials for current patients began, held in the reception room of the hospital and conducted under the direction of two of its trustees, with Judge Whitlock presiding.

Elizabeth was justifiably apprehensive. After all, many of her friends had spent years, if not decades, in the asylum. Could anyone experience such a thing, being sane, and not become insane themselves? She only hoped the salvation of her legal reforms had not come too late to save her sisters.

McFarland was frequently present at proceedings, often called as a witness. Perhaps understandably, his presence did not always inspire positive reactions in his patients. At one man's trial, the patient had been so calm the judge later admitted he'd thought him sane, but as soon as McFarland gave evidence against him, the man became excited, and the judge changed his mind.

Yet he was not the only patient to remain incarcerated.

In trial after trial, verdict after verdict, *every single patient tried was found to be insane.*

Elizabeth couldn't believe it. Not *one* patient sane? That was *not* the reality of the wards she'd lived in. Yet she trusted in the independence of the juries. She could therefore reach only one conclusion: her law *had* come too late. It was devastating. The asylum had driven her friends mad, and there was nothing she could do, now, to rescue them.

The AMSAII, on the other hand, was delighted by the verdicts.

"The conduct of the jury that investigated...was most creditable," the professional body declared. Though they'd previously been aggressively against jury trials, they pronounced the verdicts "confirmatory of the position we have so often assumed, that...our juries may be depended on as safe and humane men, who rarely go grievously wrong."

The newspapers knew exactly who they wanted to blame for this "ridiculous farce."

"The effect of Mrs. Packard's law is to excite the patients and make unnecessary trouble," complained the *Jacksonville Sentinel*. "The reports put in circulation by Mrs. Packard charging gross mismanagement, false imprisonment and oppression on the physicians and attendants at the Hospital, have been proven by strict investigation to be utter groundless—a phantasy of the diseased brain of a former patient... Such disgraceful libel on one of our best State Institutions would seem to demand punishment."

But for Elizabeth, the lack of any sane verdicts was punishment enough.

The only sliver of good news was that Sarah Minard at least had her liberty. She'd been discharged without a trial on May 1, 1867. Though she was freed under the usual asylum processes, Sarah herself still asserted that it was as a result of her friend's personal liberty bill.

Although the trials had not brought the results Elizabeth had anticipated, she tried not to let that—nor the vicious newspaper attacks—derail her. All was not yet lost. She looked now in only one direction: toward the investigating committee.

"The name of General Fuller," crowed *The Bench and Bar of Illinois*, "is a synonym for honor, integrity and fair dealing."

General Allen C. Fuller

As a character reference for the newly appointed chairman of the committee went, it was pretty darn compelling.

General Allen C. Fuller, forty-four, was such a stalwart of Illinois politics that a historian in his own time said, "The history of Illinois could not be written with the name of Allen C. Fuller left out." It was almost quicker to list the jobs he *hadn't* done for the state, but his positions included speaker of the house of representatives, judge, and adjutant general; he'd even deputized for the governor during the Civil War. In every role, he'd proved himself public-spirited, energetic, and methodical, with "every detail...attended to with scrupulous exactness." He wore his balding hair neatly clipped and his fuzzy, pointed beard a good two inches below his chin. He looked out at the world with almost troubled, hooded eyes, as though he'd seen too much of man's dark side. Of his manner, he was known to be "kind, courteous, able and impartial [with] his general...demeanor the perfect model of a gentleman." In all his dealings with his fellow men, he was renowned for treating them with "absolute justice."

Even Andrew McFarland, who was now to be investigated by this titan of Illinois, conceded the committee were "pretty able" men.

Fuller headed up a team of five: two senators, including himself, plus three from the house. All were prominent in the affairs of the state, "of well-known ability and character"; three were "astute lawyers."

As they began their work in May 1867, there was an immediate shock for the hospital's trustees. The resolution that had formed the committee stated that it was to "confer with the Trustees in regard to the speedy correction of any abuses found to exist." The trustees had assumed this meant the two bodies would work hand in glove on the forthcoming investigation: two dance troupes bouncing to the same beat, with not a member out of step.

Yet the committee determined to be completely independent. "The action of the committee at the start," complained the trustees, "evinced a purpose to bestow no recognition on the Board as a co-operative body." Instead, they were kept at arm's length.

But in a way, the trustees were under investigation too. After all, if these reported abuses *were* found to have existed, what exactly had they been doing for the past several years, when they'd found only praise for their friend McFarland and his work?

On May 14, 1867, the committee convened its first meeting at the Dunlap House, a hotel in Jacksonville. Probably as a result of the recent heated newspaper coverage on the issue they were investigating, the committee decided their sessions should be private, with no publication of proceedings until their final report, though all evidence taken would be transcribed. This method aimed to balance transparency with avoidance of a media frenzy.

They also made a series of other calls. First, not to allow McFarland to attend the hearings, a decision perhaps made to avoid the intimidation of witnesses, deliberate or otherwise. He himself was not on trial, after all—it was his *hospital* they were investigating—so they felt he did not need to be present; the trustees were permitted to attend. They also decided to accept the testimony of former patients.

This, McFarland felt, was a ridiculous decision. Patients' accounts, in his view, "should be cast aside as unworthy of notice." Their testimony was merely "perverted representations by those who have been in no condition to form a correct judgment." But the committee concluded, "To reject their testimony, appeared to [us] as calculated to defeat an investigation after the truth, and possibly subvert the ends of public justice."

Elizabeth wholeheartedly agreed. "The representations of the patients are the *truest* representations of the asylums," she avowed. "They are ten times better qualified to report what takes place in the wards, for they are eye-witnesses to it."

The committee also chose to prioritize investigation of the reported cruelty. At that opening session, they took evidence from three witnesses: Elmer Searle, a former patient; Susan Kane, a former attendant, who admitted she herself had been abusive; and Priscilla Graff, the former sewing room directress, who was as prepared to speak out as she'd always been.

Kane gave the most memorable testimony. She recalled how her fellow attendant "would not let [the patients] sit down, and if she found them so sitting, she would take them by the hair of the head and lift them on the seat, and if they resisted she would often shove them back against the wall and choke them, or compel them in some harsh way to comply." That harsh way could include the cold baths Elizabeth had so often heard occurring, where patients were submerged relentlessly under the water, only allowed up, Kane said, to "cast the water from their stomach...the same process continued as long as the patient was thought able to bear it." She added that she "made no complaints to Dr. McFarland of these abuses, because it was understood in the institution that such complaints would receive no attention."

The committee was shocked by what it heard. For the first time since their appointment, they began to have "serious apprehensions that a harsh, if not inhumane and brutal policy had been adopted by the officers and attendants in the treatment of patients."

Therefore, their second meeting was convened quickly, just a few weeks later in early June. To this session, Elizabeth Packard was invited to give evidence. She arrived in Jacksonville on a warm summer's day, accompanied by another witness, Tirzah Shedd, whom she'd recently befriended.

Elizabeth had not been idle in the months since her bill had passed. As she had in 1864, she'd been crisscrossing the state, selling her books and lecturing now, too, on their contents. As she did so, she met more and more women who had their own stories to share of their experiences in the asylum, including Tirzah.

Unlike McFarland, who felt such stories should be silenced, Elizabeth was fascinated by the tales they had to tell. She had never written off patients, whether she thought them mad or not. Elizabeth always saw the people, not the pathology. Even after she'd won her liberty, she'd never forgotten them. She'd never considered these patients as having nothing to say; on the contrary, she wanted to give them agency to say it.

She encouraged the people she met, of course, to give evidence to the committee, but as she listened to their stories, another idea hit her. An idea for a new book: one that collected all these women's voices together and allowed them to be heard. It could be combined with her own asylum journal to allow a whole sisterhood to speak out. She asked Sarah Minard to contribute, Tirzah too, as well as other women she met. She even contacted her old friend Sophia Olsen, now living happily in Wheaton painting maps, and asked if she might turn her own asylum journal into a piece for a new book. Sophia willingly agreed, as did the others. The husband of one woman, Caroline Lake, said candidly, "I hope, Mrs. Packard, you will have all the testimony published, for it ought to be."

That was just what Elizabeth intended—as soon as the committee had completed its work.

In the meantime, she'd been summoned to help with it. On June 6, 1867, she and Tirzah arrived at the Dunlap House with a sense of apprehension, not knowing what giving evidence might be like.

The Dunlap was Jacksonville's premier hotel: a highly attractive brick building set over three stories, with ornate metal balconies on the bottom two floors. It was topped by a handsome observatory from which guests could take in the sights of Jacksonville.

That morning, however, Elizabeth had eyes only for the committee.

They asked Tirzah to give evidence first. She'd been committed in 1865—after what she called a "mock jury trial"—for her spiritualism. Thirty-five, with three children, she'd been committed shortly after her baby Alma had been born; she'd been dragged away from her by six strong men, her hands cuffed to stop her from fighting. She stayed fourteen weeks at the asylum, witnessing water torture and experiencing the same censorship as Elizabeth. After her release, she'd written to McFarland to urge him to resign because of the abuse she'd seen.

He'd sent the letter back to her husband with a single sentence scrawled upon it: "Is Mrs. Shedd becoming more insane?"

In her evidence, she also described McFarland's rather hands-on application of moral treatment—the same kind Elizabeth had experienced.

"He came in and took hold of both my hands," Tirzah testified, "crossed them before me, and pulled me right up close to him. When he drew me up to him…he said, 'If you were my wife, I should want you at home.'"

A ripple of consternation coursed through the committee. They hadn't been expecting evidence like *this*.

On another occasion, Tirzah said, when she donned a new, becoming white dress, the doctor had remarked, "I don't see how a man could put a lady like you away from her home." Tirzah testified that she felt these moments of intimacy were McFarland taking "improper liberties."

Fuller and his fellow men exchanged looks of concern. These allegations reflected on McFarland personally, not just professionally. They felt he should be present. They therefore passed a new resolution at noon that day—"That he (the Superintendent) be invited to examine the testimony, and, if he desires, to cross-examine the witness"—and sent an invitation to the doctor to join their afternoon session at 1:00 p.m.

It meant that when Elizabeth took the stand that afternoon, she would be under the doctor's eyes again and subject to his questions: the first committee witness to be so closely examined. Yet in turn, she would finally have a chance to take the doctor to task in public.

The stage was set for a showdown. It really would be as one headline put it: "Dr. McFarland vs. Mrs. Packard."

CHAPTER 53

Elizabeth came with no lawyer, even though she was speaking under oath—or, perhaps, because of it. "I needed none," she later said, "because truth is its own vindicator."

McFarland, however, was represented, though he, too, seemed intent on telling truths. Upon his arrival, when the committee asked him about Tirzah's allegations, the doctor replied breezily that he thought her testimony "essentially true; as he was aware of remarks of similar purport, in many instances." His whole approach with female patients was to provide a hand to hold and a shoulder to cry on, to take on the role of quasi husband, so that these disobedient women would once again learn to submit to masculine authority. He saw nothing wrong with it; he did it with them all.

Given the short notice, McFarland used one of the trustees, Isaac Morrison, as his attorney. Due to a recently broken leg, Morrison had to be carried into the hotel parlor where the hearings were held, clasped in the arms of four stout men.

Yet broken leg or no, his mind was as sharp as ever. At forty-one, Morrison was renowned as "one of the ablest and most highly reputed lawyers at the Illinois bar." A stout man himself, he had a mustache as bushy as his eyebrows and a thatch of dark hair that he wore in a side parting. He favored bow ties—and excoriating witnesses.

As Elizabeth swore her oath and sat to give her evidence, both McFarland and Morrison watched her closely. McFarland had no real fear of her testimony; he thought her a "crazy woman, whose influence, compared with [mine is] nothing." As the doctor surveyed the gathered politicians, trustees, reporters, and clerks who'd crowded into the room, he had no doubt he would come out on top.

Even when Elizabeth started speaking, he was not perturbed. She read a prepared address to begin with; it was concerned "not so much with the hospital as with the laws of the State, that [had] placed her in the power of her husband." When she eventually got to McFarland, it was really just more of the same. "It is not that Dr. McFarland is so much worse than many other men that we hear such tales of horror from this region of despotism," she testified, "but it is that Illinois has given him power such as no human being can long hold without becoming despotic."

But as the afternoon wore on, the hours passing by one after the other, Elizabeth made the most of the opportunity to describe her asylum experience. It was what she'd longed for ever since she'd started her journal. All those years, she had been subjected and silenced, the doctor so convinced of his absolute power that her every attempt to rebuke him had been taken almost as a joke. How he had sneered when she'd told him he was destined to see her "rising and applauded as the world's reformer." Well, the joke was over now, and no one was laughing. As she spoke in all seriousness, the whole room listened.

She described her initial committal for her religious beliefs, the way she'd been sent to the asylum simply because they no longer tallied with those of her husband, and how McFarland had accepted her as a patient nonetheless. She insisted that "during her entire stay in the hospital she was entirely sane." Though she acknowledged that during her first four months, she'd been treated with respect, she revealed this abruptly changed as soon as she'd reproved the doctor, after which she'd been sent to a far worse ward.

She described the violence she'd suffered at the hands of those dangerous patients—the blows, hair pulling, the dodging of flying forks and knives—and how she'd feared for her life. She related how she'd begged McFarland to move her, but he'd always callously refused. She described the water torture she'd witnessed, the choking of patients, and the gouging of a girl's throat; she perhaps even presented the cloth she'd saved, stained with that same woman's blood. She testified about the unfairness and heartache of the censorship of letters and a myriad other things besides.

And as the hours passed by, both Morrison and McFarland grew rather more agitated. McFarland had long been aware of Elizabeth's eloquence, but Elizabeth Packard under oath proved a far more formidable foe that even he'd anticipated.

To their frustration, however, although Morrison subjected her to "a most searching cross-examination, and re-examination," testing not just "the accuracy of her memory, but the soundness of her mind," she proved unshakable.

"It is but the truth to say," reported General Fuller, "that she sustained herself with great ability in all respects."

Four hours on the stand slipped into five, then six. The summer's day outside the hotel windows began a slow dawdle toward sunset. Still, Morrison kept questioning her. Elizabeth began to get tired, the experience a "long and severe strain upon my nerves and mentality."

"[He] left no point unchallenged," she said wearily, "where Dr. McFarland could gain any advantage over me by way of inconsistencies, absurd opinions in religious belief, or conflicting statements, or by trying to puzzle my mind, so [that he could] impeach the value of my statements as a reliable witness."

She tried to keep her wits about her. She answered every question without hesitation and with as much intelligence as she could. "The prompt and plausible manner in which her views were defended or explained, while on the stand," Fuller later said, "tended to increase the probability of her sanity."

Correctly assessing the reaction in the room, Elizabeth grew more confident. She could see that the doctor's lawyer had "failed to elicit anything to their advantage." When Morrison broke off from questioning her momentarily to have a brief consultation with his client, a gentleman took the chance to whisper in her ear, "Mrs. Packard, I believe you to be a perfectly sane person, and moreover, I believe you always have been."

She could not help but smile.

The smile was perhaps still on her lips as a new line of attack began. Whatever it was to be about, the preface to its introduction had been tense, with McFarland arguing with his lawyer about the course Morrison had urged him to pursue.

With Morrison's leg disabling him, it was McFarland who now rose to quiz Elizabeth, holding a slightly yellowed piece of paper in his hand. He briefly passed it before her eyes.

"[Do you] recognize the handwriting?" he asked.

Elizabeth glanced at it. "It is my own handwriting," she replied promptly, "yet I do not know what the document is."

It was a letter, he told her.

"I have written a good many letters to Dr. McFarland," Elizabeth informed the committee.

McFarland passed the letter to General Fuller. It was formally marked "Exhibit A" and entered into evidence.

Fuller began to read it aloud: "Jacksonville, January 19, 1863."

As soon as she heard that fateful date, she knew exactly what it was.

"Dr. McFarland—My True Friend... I have never seen a man, before I saw you, to whom my whole womanly nature could instinctively pay homage, as my head, as the husband should be to the wife. To such a one, alone, can I entrust the key with which to unlock the fountain of conjugal love within me, whose depths no mortal has ever yet sounded."

She had asked him to consign it to flames. She had assumed he had respected her wishes. But the doctor had kept her promissory note for well over four years—even after she had left the asylum, even after she'd been found sane. Though McFarland had professed to want nothing more to do with her, he'd kept her letter close, and whether as memento or as ammunition did not much matter now.

Hearing her seemingly amorous words read aloud, the whole room "silent and attentive," Elizabeth felt her feelings "writhe." She knew exactly how society would react to her letter. No one would think it a spiritual offering, as she herself saw it, nor acknowledge the fact that it was really a promise for the afterlife as yet unlived. No one would understand the desperate situation she'd been in: denied release by the trustees, believing her book to be the only way out and McFarland the only man to help her. "The most abusive weapon which Dr. McFarland has used against me," she realized bleakly, "is one which I myself put into his own hands."

When she could bring herself to look up, shock and scandalized disapproval were written all over the faces of everyone in the room. Where before there had been admiring glances, impressed by her lucid arguments and unsurpassed intellect, now people would not meet her eye.

Yet there was nothing she could do about it. McFarland had fired his weapon, and her own bullets were striking at her body, a body people now saw in an entirely different light.

"It must be a sacred, profound secret between us, trusted entirely to your honor," Fuller was saying. "Yours in the best of bonds, Elizabeth."

A heavy silence met the final pant of her name, itself already seeming far more sensual. With disquiet, Fuller laid the letter in the file of evidence. He seemed not to know what to say. On first reading, the letter appeared to the committee to be "a brazen offer of marriage by a married lady to a married man." Fuller could choose to take it two ways, neither of which was especially appealing: it was either "the production of a diseased and disordered intellect, or a degrading invitation...of illicit intercourse."

He had not known Elizabeth Packard to be such a woman.

Then again, he had not thought her mad.

But with this letter, surely, she must be one or the other?

Thoughts were flying fast through Elizabeth's mind, none of which she could articulate. She could not say that McFarland producing this letter, which undermined *her* credibility, was no substitute for the doctor defending *himself* on the serious charges he was facing. Where really he should have been on the back foot, providing excuses for his *own* behavior, he had instead gone on the attack, pointing the finger at her when all she'd done was point out his own failings. As a friend of hers later put it, "[It] proves the doctor to be very severely straitened for self-defence, or he would not have resorted to such a straw to save himself from drowning."

But Elizabeth felt as if she was the one who was drowning now. McFarland knew, he *knew*, that her character was stainless, yet he'd still launched this "most cruel and wanton attack...upon my moral character." But without her character, where was she? *Who* was she? It had been hard enough to claw back a place in society with the stigma of insanity haunting her, but her efforts now would be that much harder—if not altogether impossible. Because this letter, to the wider world, meant that she was either mad or bad.

Either way, not a woman society should listen to.

Either way, not a woman who should be given the care of her own children.

Her every dream, every hope, every reason for living hung in the balance.

And it was the doctor who had hung her out to dry.

He'd acted "in defiance of every principle of manly honor, decency, and integrity," she raged silently in her head. Despite everything she'd already been through at his hands, she still felt betrayed. "I have done all I knew how to do to raise this man, from the low level of selfish policy to the higher platform of Christian principle, but all in vain," she later wrote. "I am [now] forced into the unwelcome conviction that he is a most unprincipled man, and on this ground is unworthy of confidence as a man. And much less as a public servant... I [therefore] leave him with his own worst enemy—I leave him with himself."

But these were fighting words she found long after the event. In the fading light of that summer's day, she felt in the twilight of her whole existence. Sunset was coming soon, and with it, the end of everything.

"Mrs. Packard," Fuller said at last, his words breaking through her reverie, "do you recognize that as your own letter?"

Elizabeth straightened up. She was still under oath. "I do," she said assertively and without shame.

"Then you acknowledge it as yours?" the general asked, as though he rather wished she might disown it.

"I do," she said again. She took a deep breath, her tired brain trying to think of an impromptu explanation, when Fuller interrupted.

"Mrs. Packard," he said kindly, seeing her distress, which she was desperately trying to keep private, "you need not speak a word on this subject, on this occasion." He perhaps consulted briefly with his fellow committee members. He fixed his dark, hooded eyes on her. "You may give us your explanation, in writing, tomorrow morning at 10 o'clock in this room."

Elizabeth let out a sigh, trying not to cry at his clemency. "Thank you, General Fuller," she managed. "I esteem it a great privilege you have granted me."

So at close to 8:00 p.m., nearly seven hours after she first took the stand, she was at last allowed to step down. At once, Tirzah came to her side and the women left together, a buzz of scandalized gossip rising behind them like angry bees.

Elizabeth kept it together. She kept it together in the room and in the corridor. Though words and phrases from the past and future were already haunting her, she stuck one foot in front of the other and walked out proudly with her friend. Already she could imagine the kind of comment that would follow her: "The letter is such as no sane virtuous woman could have written…" Those comments felt like cages, trapping her all over again—and this time not with physical locks, which might eventually be opened, but with even more unbreakable bolts: the unforgiving opinions of others.

She made it to the steps of the Dunlap House. But as she and Tirzah walked down them, she felt she was literally descending to her doom. She could keep it together no longer.

"I am ruined!" she cried out despairingly to her friend. "I am ruined!"

She burst into tears, hot and salty. They would have stung, had her wounds been as simple as sores. But Elizabeth was injured in an altogether different way: struck down by the bullets of her very own words, the blood pouring out reputation.

CHAPTER 54

She woke the next morning at 4:00 a.m. It was still dark, but a new day would soon dawn. The hard reality roused her; in six short hours, her defense must be ready. She crept quietly out of bed—being careful not to wake Tirzah, with whom she was sharing a room—and sat before an open window, dressed in a loose wrapper. "In the quietude and stillness of the early hour," she picked up her pen and wrote words to save herself.

Six hours later, she was back on the stand, the stenographer poised to capture every syllable. General Fuller seemed nervous, perhaps for her. Rather than taking his usual seat, he paced the room, every now and again making fruitless attempts to light his fat cigar.

Elizabeth waited for him to sit, but when it became clear he was not going to, she simply had to press on.

"Gentlemen of the Committee," she began. "Truth is my only apology for writing that letter... Since my father...and my husband...had both cast me entirely and solely upon [McFarland] as my only protector of soul and body both, I felt myself driven to seek in him the *protection* I wanted."

She paused. Fuller was still pacing the room, barely listening. She found his rapid walking both a distraction and annoyance but put him out of her mind. She reminded the committee of why they were really all there.

"I tested [McFarland]; I found him wanting," she said. She explained how she'd confronted him about his cruel treatment of patients, "but by so doing I lost all the comforts I had left, and secured only abuse and persecution." When, in 1862, she'd felt he was finally showing some signs of repentance, she "applied myself most assiduously to carry out the instincts of a true woman—which is to forgive man on the ground of repentance... I concentrated all my womanly powers [and] he became my manly protector... [This] instinctively developed in my womanly nature, first the feeling of gratitude, then of reverence, then of love."

She took a deep breath and continued with her story.

> Dr. McFarland had promised to publish my book, and on this hung all and every hope of my personal liberty. This bright hope seemed about to be extinguished in utter darkness by his refusal to publish it as he had promised; leaving naught for me to expect but blasted reputation and a lifelong imprisonment. As my dying hope sought in vain for anything to trust in now almost in a state of desperation I ventured to make one more final appeal...which you find contained in this letter.
>
> [But McFarland had] only assumed the mask of manliness for the malign purpose of betraying my innocence...and the use he is now making of this letter demonstrated that I did not then misjudge him... And the man who is false to a true, pure, virtuous woman... will be sure to be false to others.

She fixed the committee with a hard gaze, her message clear: "Such a man is fit only to disgrace any office or any trust committed to him."

She stared across the room at the doctor. McFarland looked much the same as he had when they'd first met: perhaps a little more salt than pepper in his sideburns, perhaps a bald pate that was now a little larger in scale, but he was still the same handsome man who'd long led her on this not-so-merry dance, a dance she was still wearily performing.

But finally, she was done.

"I hate evil," she announced. "I can no more love evil than I can hate good. In this sense, I now hate Dr. McFarland—that is, I hate his evil, unmanly, brutal acts, while at the same time I pity the poor sinner.

"God knows there is not in my heart one feeling of malice towards Dr. McFarland, even now; [but] I can no [longer] extend fellowship to him."

She brought her defense, such as it was, to a close. It contained not a hint of regret. The truth was she did not regret writing the letter, even though "no act of my life has caused me so keen suffering as this has." But her relationship with McFarland, broken as it was, had still left "a halo of light and joy in [its] rear": the light of her writing life, because he'd been the one to open the door that led her to it. She could not separate one from the other, so she embraced the pain as well as the pleasure. The only thing she truly regretted was "that circumstances do exist that drive defenceless woman to use such means of self-defense."

As soon as she'd finished reading, the chairman of the committee marched up to her, almost before she could draw breath. It was as though Fuller had come to the hearing with his own plan that morning…and had not listened to a word she'd said.

"Do you now, with your present views, regard the offer of marriage with Dr. McFarland, contained in the letter, justifiable?" he pressed her.

She replied honestly: "Under the circumstances, I do." At Fuller's horrified look—he had clearly expected her to say she didn't—she continued, "For the reasons set forth in the written explanation, with others."

"Did you," he tried again, "at the time of writing the letter, know that Dr. McFarland was a married man?"

"Of course I did," she responded.

Fuller looked exasperated. He was trying to help her, in his view, but Elizabeth was under oath and would not lie. "Do you consider the letter," he tried for a third time, "or intend the letter, an offer of marriage to Dr. McFarland?"

"I did," she confirmed, "with those qualifications or conditions named in the letter."

His questions were like a "rack of torture." As the stenographer noted her answers, Elizabeth felt increasing dismay, knowing that all of this would eventually be publicly reported. She knew these answers would make things look worse for her, but as always, she would not lie even to save herself.

After she'd stepped down from the stand, she privately confronted Fuller.

"How could you…ask me such questions?" she demanded. Hadn't he known they would make things worse? It had been obvious from her letter that she'd known McFarland was married, and the defense she'd read that morning had set out all her feelings, for which she'd expressed absolutely no regret. She'd given only explanation.

The general hissed back at her. "I intended to make you back down!" he replied. "That was my object!"

"'Back down!'" she echoed. "General! Do you gain your victories on the battle-field by 'backing down!' or, do you face the enemy with the boldness and assurance which the truth and justice of your cause inspire? I *never* 'back down' on the truth, Mr. Fuller, and if you count on that kind of a conquest, I can insure you defeat, so far as one of your witnesses is concerned!"

"Well, I—!" the general stuttered, stunned. He had expected her to respond differently to his questions in order to save her virtue. He looked her up and down. "You have more boldness than any four women that I ever before saw, combined!"

Elizabeth pulled herself up to her full height. "I claim, Mr. Fuller," she retorted, "that I need a quadruple share of courage to cope with such men as I have had to deal with."

For better or worse, Elizabeth's testimony to the committee was complete. Whether they'd accepted her defense, she did not know. Whether they thought her mad or bad or something else entirely, she had no idea. As to what the public might make of the matter, she at least did not have to find that out until the final report was made public— whenever that might be.

In the meantime, the investigation continued.

———

The committee, in the end, spoke to twenty-two former patients, plus former employees. They heard from erstwhile senator and congressman John Henry, who'd once acted as the asylum's steward. He testified that he'd seen three attendants abuse a patient by "pouring water in his face and nose from a pail." He'd reported it to McFarland, but the doctor "appeared indifferent" and took no action.

"[He] is destitute of common sympathy to the patients," Henry testified, "and [does] not listen to their complaints with kindness; nor give that personal attention to the conduct of the attendants which [is] necessary to a personal knowledge of their treatment."

Most of the complaints relating to McFarland were identical to Henry's account, citing his consistent lack of investigation of allegations of abuse. Mrs. Graff, however, testified that she believed the doctor had once directed a patient to be given a water punishment, while another attendant said that both a patient and Lizzie Bonner had told her McFarland had kicked the patient in the face. The attendant could testify that "one eye was black, and one side of her face was very much bruised and blackened for several days," but she herself had not seen the doctor actually strike the woman. In total, eighteen attendants who'd been cruel were identified.

On November 12, 1867, the committee gathered for what was to be their final session—or so they thought. In fact, due to a cholera epidemic at the asylum in which eight died, McFarland could not be present. Fuller took the opportunity to tell the trustees he would not be taking McFarland's own testimony, which the doctor had asked to give. The trustees were outraged: "The Superintendent was to be tried, judged and degraded without being permitted to open his mouth."

It was, in fact, the same fate married women had endured before Elizabeth's personal liberty law had passed, but this irony was seemingly lost on them.

Given McFarland's absence, another session was added to the diary on November 29. On this date, the committee heard "the balance of the testimony offered by Dr. McFarland," which probably meant the testimony of those witnesses summoned by the doctor to speak in his defense.

Almost a week later, on December 4, the trustees met for their quarterly meeting. They spent the day as usual: enjoying a first-rate lunch and a tour of the hospital wards that were open to them. In the evening, they gathered around a table in a meeting room to conclude their business.

An unexpected knock came upon their door.

When it opened, a man with hooded eyes stood there, his beard hanging fuzzily two inches below his chin. In his hands, he held a stack of papers, more than a hundred pages high. He looked as reluctant to be there as they were to see him.

It was General Fuller—and he had come to read the trustees his final report.

CHAPTER 55

Fuller was invited in, the trustees welcoming him with as much enthusiasm as they might a vampire. He was there at the governor's insistence; Oglesby had said the trustees should hear the report at once. Fuller had followed his boss's instructions. As the six trustees stared at him with unconcealed animosity, he picked up page one and began to read aloud.

As he did, the faces of his audience darkened further. One of the first sections touched on the insanity trials that had taken place earlier that year, at which every patient had been found insane. Elizabeth Packard, whose law had facilitated them, had been pilloried in the press for this time- and money-wasting "ridiculous farce," while she herself had suffered personally in the knowledge that her reforms had come too late to save her sisters.

But Fuller had been studying the asylum's discharge statistics closely. "There were 127 patients discharged between February 28th, the day the committee was appointed, and July 24th, the day of the commencement of inspection of patients [by the committee at the hospital]," Fuller read aloud.

He highlighted that in that short but very relevant period, McFarland had in fact *doubled* the number of patients he'd released as cured.

"This increase in the rate of recovery is a little noticeable," Fuller said pointedly, "but in the absence of proof to the contrary, the committee are bound to suppose the fact incidental, and not the result of a policy to make rapid discharges to avoid examination."

Yet the statistics, in this case, did not lie. It seemed apparent that rather than risk a jury finding his patients sane, McFarland had let them go. That was why Sarah Minard, confined for nine years, had suddenly been released on May 1, 1867: *the day before the trials began.*

Nor was it solely the fear of jury trials that had an impact; the committee's almost year-long focus on the hospital did too. Ten percent more patients were discharged in 1867–68 than in the previous two years. It was, in fact, the highest recorded discharge rate in the hospital's entire history. That same year, McFarland even released the asylum's first-ever patient, the woman who'd been committed for "extreme jealousy," whose insanity had seemingly warranted a sixteen-year seclusion from society. Suddenly, she was free to go.

Elizabeth's law had not come too late after all. She *had* helped her sisters; it was just that they'd been snuck out the back door.

But thanks to McFarland's manipulation of the situation, she didn't even know it.

Fuller moved on to the issue of "unjust commitments." Regarding the question of whether any patients had been unjustly placed in the asylum, the committee concluded, "The answer must be in the affirmative." Of the 205 patients in the Jacksonville asylum who'd been admitted since the passage of the 1865 law, only 57 had "regular and complete" paperwork. A massive 148 had been admitted "without the proper *legal evidence* of their insanity."

"That there should appear so large a proportion of the admissions in violation of law," intoned Fuller in a somber tone, "shows a carelessness on this subject without excuse, and deserving of censure."

The censure continued. On the classification of patients—raised by Elizabeth as an issue when she'd complained of having been moved to Eighth Ward as punishment—Fuller deemed McFarland's policy "fundamentally wrong" and the doctor guilty of "most culpable and cruel conduct."

It had certainly felt cruel to Elizabeth at the time.

Then there were pages and pages of evidence relating to the barbaric treatment of patients, such as choking, beating, and baths that were used not to clean but to control patients. Those were perhaps the most difficult passages for Fuller to read aloud.

Having laid out all the evidence, he reached the committee's conclusions. He focused on their findings regarding McFarland.

> Familiarity with suffering and sorrow has apparently, to some extent, deadened his sensibilities and sympathies; and, long accustomed to govern, he has become about the hospital...a kind of supreme law, and the rule of force has too often usurped the law of love... He assumes that insane patients are never to be believed, and therefore does not listen with favor to their complaints. He substantially denies the right of petition and investigation... He does not require or encourage attendants to report to him each other's delinquencies... His government of patients is believed too severe, and his discipline of attendants too mild...
>
> After...carefully reviewing and considering the evidence, the Committee unanimously resolved that it seemed their imperative duty to recommend: *An immediate change in the office of Superintendent.*

They thought McFarland should be fired for what he'd done.

By the time Fuller finished reading, the trustees were almost apoplectic with rage. They felt as the AMSAII did, that McFarland should be "presumptively entitled to favorable regard, by reason of [his] standing" and to "charitable constructions of [his] acts." But above all they resented the committee's dramatic conclusion, which they felt was more a direct order than a gentle recommendation to a fellow body of men. Fuller was overstepping the mark and by a long way; only the trustees had the legal power to hire or fire the superintendent. They felt he was infringing on their territory.

They also thought the "evidence" he'd collected was literally not worth the paper it was written on. Because who had given all this so-called evidence against their institution? Former patients. People "whose recovery, in all instances, is more than doubtful." Such an unreliable source of information was not "worthy of serious public attention," and they therefore attached "but small importance" to it. As for the attendants turned whistleblowers, the trustees thought them disgruntled former employees: lower-class "servants" who'd found the opportunity to speak out against their "former master...too tempting." They were unreliable too.

But without the witness evidence, there *was* no evidence of patient abuse.

And if the trustees chose to ignore it, McFarland was in the clear.

Having presented his report, Fuller left them to debate their decision, hoping they'd adopt his recommendation. Instead, the trustees unanimously agreed to write at once to the governor to prevent publication. They dashed off a missive on McFarland's letterhead notepaper to request the governor suppress the report, temporarily at least, while they conducted their own inquiry.

They found him amenable. As far as Oglesby was concerned, they could take as long as they liked with their investigation; he was not planning to do anything with the committee's report. Because he'd carefully perused the formal resolutions that had established the committee and concluded "no action on my part" was required. All he had to do, officially, was to *take receipt* of the finished study. After that, nothing. It was his duty only "to retain the custody of [it] until the meeting of the next General Assembly."

Which was in 1869: more than a year away.

In the meantime, he was going to sit on it. Life would continue just as before at the asylum, with McFarland at the helm—no matter what the committee had recommended.

What possible reason might Oglesby have had for sitting on the report for a year? It should not be forgotten that he and McFarland were close friends. So close, in fact, that Oglesby was known to write to the doctor, on behalf of other men, to ask him to retain women a little longer at the hospital. Both were on terms close enough to call in favors. Earlier that year, McFarland had written to Oglesby to do just that, seemingly asking him to intervene in the inquiry. But Oglesby had responded that the general assembly's resolutions "clearly [say] that the whole subject shall be under the control of the investigating committee...I can have nothing to do with their action."

Yet the governor added, "It will be my duty to receive any [report?] they may choose to make...[and] in so far as I shall be able to act upon the matter, you may rest assured that every opportunity will extend to you to vindicate yourself."

Delaying publication for over a year would certainly give McFarland that chance. In the meantime, as far as the public was concerned, the investigated doctor would be left to continue in his role. Almost by default, he would seem faultless.

Elizabeth Packard had waited years for the asylum to be investigated. She'd waited years for the secrets behind the barred windows to be revealed. But it seemed, thanks to the governor's intervention, she would be waiting a little while longer yet.

As for General Fuller, he was reported to toe the official line. Though journalists from at least five different newspapers waylaid him at his hotel in Springfield on December 5, begging him to release the report, he emphatically refused. He gave no reason as to why, being "exceedingly mysterious on the subject." But perhaps he felt uncomfortable revealing that the powers that be were opposed to publication.

At last, he escaped the clamoring reporters and retired to his room. He was staying at the Leland, a fabulous five-story hotel on the northwest corner of Sixth and Capitol. It had opened only that January with a ball deemed "the social sensation of the season" and had already become a favorite watering hole of the prominent men of the city.

Yet Fuller struggled to take pleasure in his surroundings, luxurious as they were.

"She would take them by the hair of the head and lift them on the seat..."

"She would often shove them back against the wall and choke them..."

"One eye was black, and one side of her face was very much bruised..."

"A straight jacket was placed upon them [and] their heads plunged under the water as long as it was safe to leave them..."

Testimony about the abuse the patients had suffered. Testimony he had heard himself. Testimony that perhaps haunted him that December night—voices calling out to him, even though the governor had called for silence.

Could he really leave the patients to this terrible fate for another year?

Could he really countenance what could be conceived as a cover-up?

Could he really let the doctor get away with it?

Fuller had close connections with the *Chicago Tribune*...

Perhaps it was time to call in a favor of his own.

"There is something not merely mysterious but inexplicable in Gen. Fuller's conduct in forthwith rushing up to the *Chicago Tribune* office," the *Illinois Daily State Journal* later wrote. "After his precautions to have [the report] kept secret, we can scarcely reconcile his conduct with what would be expected from a sane man."

But perhaps a sane man, dedicated to justice and humanity, whose name was a synonym for "honor, integrity and fair dealing," might just have decided that the maddest course of action was not to publish the report. Perhaps this sane man now decided to speak out. Whatever his reasons, whether selfish as some said or public-spirited as his reputation suggests, Fuller acted against the wishes of both his boss and the trustees.

He leaked the full report to the *Chicago Tribune*.

"This document," wrote the paper as it splashed its exclusive on December 7, "will produce a profound sensation in the public mind."

They were absolutely right.

For as Illinois's citizens opened up their papers that morning, there was shock after shock after shock. The abuse itself. The callous attitude of the doctor. The fact that patients had been released before they could be tried. The fact that patients had been committed even without evidence of insanity. The recommendation that the doctor be dismissed. It was a horror story of gothic proportions and immediately captured the popular imagination. The story even jumped the Atlantic, with articles published in London and Paris. Like the shocked citizens of Illinois, the Europeans clutched their pearls with dumbfounded dismay.

Perhaps the only person in the whole wide world who was not shocked was Elizabeth Packard.

"Truth...may for a time be crushed to the earth," she said emphatically, "[but] it shall rise again with renovated strength."

With every word she read, Elizabeth felt emotion rising. Because the report set out what she'd always known and always wanted: recognition that McFarland was not fit for his post. Recognition that the abuse she'd witnessed and endured *had* been real and was not some figment of the patients' imaginations, as McFarland had always claimed.

To read about the hosts of patients released before the jury trials was confirmation that the women she'd known and loved *were* sane and did not belong there. Her law *had* saved them, even if that credit had been denied.

As for the fact that McFarland had been admitting patients without evidence of insanity—well, that hardly came as a surprise. He'd been doing that for years when it came to married women. The only difference now was that it was finally against the law.

"The result of this investigation," she wrote with feeling, "confirmed the truth of all my charges against the superintendent."

For years, he had dismissed and belittled her. He'd underestimated her too. McFarland had once held all the power.

But look at him now.

Elizabeth had once written to the doctor, "If you attempt to sustain your character, by defaming mine...you will work out your own destruction."

Finally, that day had come.

Yet Elizabeth had meant what she'd said on the stand in June: she did not hate McFarland. She felt no malice toward him. So it was not revenge that tasted so sweet on that Saturday morning.

It was simple vindication.

CHAPTER 56

April 1869
Boston, Massachusetts

Never had she wanted a train to move faster. Elizabeth Packard, on her way to Boston, stared blindly out the window at the passing landscape of her country. Once, she'd written that she was "the mother of her country," but she'd never forgotten those six children who had a prior and far more powerful claim upon her heart.

Finally, she was on her way to see them again. At least…so she hoped.

She rode not only the train but a wave of public interest in her work. In the wake of the leaking of Fuller's report, Elizabeth Packard had become a household name, albeit not always in the way she might have wished.

McFarland had not gone quietly after Fuller's recommendation that he be dismissed. Instead, he and his allies had unleashed a vicious media strategy, with Elizabeth's personal downfall at its heart. Newspapers supportive to the doctor had swiftly dubbed the official investigation the "Packard-Fuller committee," using her name to undermine it. The more closely they could associate Elizabeth with the inquiry, the easier they hoped it would be for people to ignore. Their motivation was partly financial; the hospital brought prosperity to many, "stimulating business in every direction." Powerful people had pecuniary interests in its continuing to operate as it always had.

Soon references to the "notorious and crack-brained Mrs. Packard" had emerged, with McFarland's supporters reporting that it was only Elizabeth's "insane imaginings" that had prompted the investigation in the first place.

And when this initial attack on Elizabeth's sanity failed, her letter of January 19, 1863, had been predictably leaked to the press. "We submit, in all candor, that the writer of that letter was either insane, or a bad woman," the *Jacksonville Journal* had savagely sneered. "[It] exposes her to the public gaze as a strumpet."

Thus the scandal had unfolded exactly as Elizabeth had feared. She'd become trapped as she'd thought she would be: between bars of public opinion that made her either mad or bad. McFarland's allies had deliberately thrown her under the bus: mere collateral damage deemed necessary to protect an important man. Though the committee, speaking in her defense, said rather naively that "her character as a virtuous lady was not involved" with the allegations McFarland had been called to answer, as any woman who has ever taken the stand in any courtroom knows, her character as a virtuous lady is *always* involved...

Every bleak and horrid word they wrote had cut Elizabeth deeply, red ribbons oozing out. Each one was intended to tie her tongue, to stop her from speaking, to bind her from stepping outside her sphere. It seemed to matter not that, as the committee said, "the charges [against the asylum]...might stand or fall...without reference to [Mrs. Packard's] testimony." McFarland's supporters blithely dismissed that wealth of witness evidence, which ran to over eight hundred pages. Even Fuller himself, the man who'd once deputized for the governor, was derisively dubbed the "renowned follower of Grandmother Packard," who'd become "afflicted with the malady [of madness] himself."

But Elizabeth—and those attacking her—had reckoned without something rather special: public opinion. "The verdict of public sentiment everywhere condemned [McFarland's] conduct as mean, in trying to shield himself under such an ugly mask," Elizabeth wrote, almost in wonder. Readers had flocked to buy her next book, *Mrs. Packard's Prison Life*, which had proved her most successful yet. Her tribute to her asylum sisterhood, containing six women's stories of what had happened to them, was snapped up by a hungry public, to Elizabeth's relief and delight.

McFarland had been shocked. He'd had little fear of Fuller's report at first, deducing correctly that "the trustees and the Governor do not seem to be much disturbed." But with the public's devouring of the report, everything had changed.

"The humiliating feature in the whole business is this," he wrote to a friend. "Here comes in a crazy woman, whose influence, compared with yours, you, at first sight, think as nothing; but when the balance comes to be struck between your reputation and her industrious efforts...you find yourself so much at a discount that your pride, your conceptions of public reputation, and your self love are all scattered at a blow. A whole legislative body is at the feet of a crazy woman, and you are nowhere!"

There was certainly nowhere for McFarland to hide when that legislative body finally reviewed Fuller's report. Though Oglesby kept his promise to McFarland, sitting on it until January 1869—the same month the governor stepped down from his post—by February 20, McFarland's time was up. On that date, the relevant joint committee announced, "From an examination of [the] evidence, we are satisfied that the [committee's] investigation was thorough and impartial [and we] adopt the conclusions."

In short: they supported the firing of McFarland.

As the doctor put it, "I have drunk at the very deepest wells of humiliation and am humiliated."

With McFarland at last held to account, Elizabeth had turned her attention to the matter closest to her heart. She wrote that it was her "grand purpose" to regain custody of her children, the one true "desire of her heart." If she could win her children back, she intended "most cheerfully" to lay aside her public duties, "except the sale of books." And that was why she was en route to Boston, hoping justice might finally be on her side.

Her eldest sons certainly were. "It is my opinion," Isaac swore in a public statement that she carried with her at that very moment, "[my siblings] would be better brought up under her care than under the care of anyone else." Toffy added, "It is my earnest and sincere desire that she may obtain [custody]."

Recently, Elizabeth had even added a third name to her list of supporters: that of her third-born son, Samuel Packard. Why or how he came to reconcile with his mother, when he'd always supported his father before, is not exactly known. Since he'd moved to Chicago in the wake of her trial, the twenty-one-year-old had become a top-notch lawyer. Perhaps he changed his mind about her because so many of his esteemed colleagues, such as James Bradwell, were on his mother's side. Maybe the committee's endorsement of her had given him pause for thought. However it had come about, they'd recently reunited, with Samuel even utilizing his professional skills to draft her latest bill. Mother and son had won a victory when the Illinois legislature passed a watered-down version in March 1869, giving married women the right to their own earnings. It was one more step on Elizabeth's long journey toward freedom from her husband's power.

Samuel clearly enjoyed the process. Later, he wrote to his mother that he wanted to dedicate himself "to carrying on some great & noble reformation—as you do." Far from her being a bad influence as his father had always feared, Elizabeth had in fact become a shining inspiration.

With these three sons now standing behind her, Elizabeth hoped the custody case in Boston might be a shoo-in. After all, in the five years since her husband had left her penniless, she had singlehandedly transformed her situation. As she rode the train to Boston, she was the proud owner of no less than two houses in Illinois, with some $10,000 ($189,685) in savings in the bank.

In contrast, her husband had fallen on hard times. Partly due to the public's outrage at his treatment of his wife, Theophilus hadn't held a permanent pastorship since 1865; by this point, he was rather too comfortably reliant on the charity of friends. Elizabeth knew he must be near destitute, for when she sent him board money for the children, it was not returned, whereas in earlier years, he'd rejected her offers of financial support "with indignant scorn."

In fact, Theophilus's financial situation was better than it once had been. In 1867, despite not having a job, he'd suddenly paid off the $4,000 debt that had plagued him for a decade. Was it mere coincidence that Elizabeth had generously signed away her rights to their shared property that year? She did not need the wealth herself and hoped her children might benefit. In his diary, Theophilus did not credit his wife for his windfall. Instead, he praised "the great mercy of God."

He himself had shown no mercy to Elizabeth in the years since he'd cut her off from her family. He'd not only stopped her from seeing the children; he'd kept her good clothes from her for eighteen months after his desertion. He returned them only when Elizabeth's father—with whom she had at last been reunited—insisted he give them back.

Samuel Ware had realized his daughter was sane as soon as he saw her in person. "It is now my opinion that Mr. Packard has had no cause for treating my daughter Elizabeth as an insane person," he testified. Yet the fact that Elizabeth's male relatives now backed her, having seen through her husband's "tissue of lies," did not mean Theophilus was ready to relinquish his version of the truth.

Even when news of the committee's report had reached him, rather than be horrified at the abuse his wife had suffered, he'd come out fighting for his own reputation. A letter had been quickly dispatched to the *Chicago Tribune* to dispute Elizabeth's supposedly "false statements."

His continued lack of repentance meant Elizabeth expected him to fight her custody suit with every meager resource he had remaining. In truth, he'd never stopped fighting her—and not only privately, in refusing her access to the children, but also in public. Seeing his wife rise to political prominence had been an outrage to Theophilus; he'd embarked on an aggressive media campaign to discredit her. He made frequent "bullying demand[s]" on newspapers to publish his side of the story until even they had had enough. "The persistence of this man in thrusting himself before the public!" one paper exclaimed disapprovingly, declining to publish his submitted articles as they were "such as no respectable paper would publish."

But when he did successfully place pieces—which happened more often than not—he claimed people were being duped by Elizabeth. Like McFarland before him, he cited her new career as evidence. "No other proof of her monomania is necessary than that she is...*roving* from town to town...peddling this pamphlet."

Therefore, when Elizabeth finally arrived in Boston, she immediately hired her old friend Samuel Sewall to represent her in what she expected would be a bitter battle. Back in 1864, McFarland had written, "I have no hesitation in saying that any person of good intelligence, who has had sufficient opportunity of judging, will, sooner or later, share this opinion [that she is insane]." But five years on, this brilliant lawyer remained steadfastly by Elizabeth's side.

It was Sewall who'd told her about the new law that was then passing through the Massachusetts Senate. It would allow a married woman to become the legal guardian of her children. The news had unleashed a chain reaction for Elizabeth, leading her to where she was now: on the cusp of reclaiming her family.

Or so she desperately hoped.

"The case was formally presented," she later remembered, "and met with all the favor from the court we could desire."

But Theophilus's lawyer begged an extension; the case was deferred until July.

Before then, however, Elizabeth received an unexpected letter. On May 24, 1869, Libby, George, and Arthur wrote to her to say, "We will gladly accept of your offer to go out and live with you in Chicago."

In the end, on the frank advice of his lawyer—who saw which way the land lay—Theophilus had simply given the children up.

As she read those precious words, Elizabeth could barely believe it. She replied to them at once: "My fond heart is filled with joy." And in this way, as she put it, "The mother's battle was fought, and the victory won."

———

The water on Lake Michigan had never looked so blue. In the July sunshine, steamers sailed, taking day-trippers out on a wonderful adventure.

Back on shore, people feasted on "pies, cake, strawberries and lemonade," while a band played and children thrilled in games of "velocipede, running, jumping and sack races." It was Saturday, July 3, 1869, and Chicago was already beginning to celebrate Independence Day.

Running parallel to the shoreline was the renowned Prairie Avenue, Chicago's "finest residential area." At number 1497, a mother called out to her children that it was time to leave for church. There was a chorus of voices and a thunder of feet, and as each child exited through the door, that mother counted out her train of stars.

Here came Arthur, a boy of ten, who, in contrast to his siblings, showed no especial flair for his studies. Then dark-haired George, now an impossible fifteen, closer to man than boy. And then there was Libby, a slim, sweet, and very kind woman of nineteen.

The reunited family: Mrs. Packard and all her children

Yet as Elizabeth counted out her not-so-young children, her train of stars did not end there. Three men came carousing through the door too, joining their siblings in the summer sun. Because when Elizabeth had returned to Chicago with her three youngest children triumphantly in tow, her three eldest boys had moved into her home too. They now all lived together as a family of seven. As Samuel, Isaac, and Toffy came out of their shared home, Elizabeth craned her neck back to see them: these strapping sons who were sun and moon and stars as well as so much more.

Together, the family walked as one to the nearby Methodist church.

And someone else walked with them: Theophilus Packard. He'd moved to Chicago when his children had, wanting to be sure his offspring were "safe." Perhaps to his disappointment, he confided in his diary that they "got along living with their mother...comfortably well." Ordinarily, he kept himself to himself at his boardinghouse a mile away, but on this night, perhaps because of the national celebrations, he'd chosen to join his family.

Relations between husband and wife were now cordial. "When he restored the children to my guardianship," Elizabeth said, "although it was a mere act of compulsion on his part...I told him: 'I am happy I can regard this act in the light of an act of restitution on your part so far as to allow me to treat you henceforth as a gentleman.'" When he visited the children—something Elizabeth freely allowed, though he'd never granted her the same gift—she would nod her head or exchange pleasantries but never anything more. He was just a "stranger gentleman" now, as far as she was concerned.

That summer evening, she acknowledged him politely, and the family began their slow stroll to church. To see her children walking around her, to hear their voices, to see their smiles...every moment still seemed impossible. Yet God had "kindly gratified the great desire of my maternal heart."

Against all the odds, she'd gotten her children back.

After church, as they walked home, the flashes of Fourth of July fireworks began exploding over their heads. Those vibrant colors and sounds of celebration joyously honored freedom and independence; they could not have been more apt. Because Elizabeth had won her freedom. She'd won her independence. And she'd done it all through her own endeavors: by standing up for herself and refusing to back down, by speaking her mind, no matter the consequences. And as well as gaining her own freedom through her fight, she'd secured the freedoms of others.

That was certainly something to celebrate.

Just a few weeks after Independence Day, Elizabeth gathered her family together once more. It was just before four on a sunny August afternoon, and the city was strangely busy. The seven of them stepped outside their house. Together with their neighbors, they stared up at the sky.

All across Illinois, other communities were doing the same. Even within the asylum in Jacksonville, the patients crowded to the windows, jostling for position, wanting their own postage-stamp square of sky to see.

It was a perfectly clear day. But even as they watched, that cerulean sky changed to purple, then descended into black. The temperature plummeted; spectators shivered. Yet this was no coming storm darkening their day—something to fear or run from.

Instead, the patients gasped. Some cheered. Some were struck dumb. By the total eclipse of the sun.

The moon, shining silver orb, special and solitary, moved in front of that burning ball of fire. The wind settled as she did. She blocked out all that usually dominated and made the world stop and stare. It was rarer than a once-in-a-lifetime event. It was a spectacle, eyewitnesses said, of "indescribable beauty, and one for which the mind was by no means prepared."

It all sounded rather like a woman named Elizabeth Packard.

And a woman like that could not be put back in her box—not now that she'd taken those giant strides outside it. Though Elizabeth had planned, upon regaining her children, to return forever to her domestic life—to a routine ruled by the whistle of the copper kettle and not by the schedules of the senate—that was not her destiny. She'd anticipated that her work outside the home would become "secondary…to those [duties] of maternity," but she could not have been more wrong.

For we cannot help but be changed by our experiences, and she'd long ago broken the mold of what motherhood meant. Even if she'd wanted to step back into her small, safe sphere and for that sweet song of the kettle to score her days, it would have been impossible. That wasn't who she was anymore. It would never have satisfied her.

She had unfinished business—out in the wide world.

So instead of maternity, she ultimately chose modernity. She would, she declared, dedicate her "undivided energies to the great work [of reformation], [which] I seem peculiarly capacitated by my experiences to perform."

She didn't care that pursuing such a path left her open to more scandal and more cynical negative press. Knowing full well that public duels lay ahead, she didn't hesitate. Society—and superintendents—could sneer all they wanted. Elizabeth Packard cared not a jot.

There was a world out there that needed reforming.

And she was determined to do it.

EPILOGUE

Elizabeth wrote in her asylum diary, "God grant, that the time may never wear away in me this spirit of resistance."

God granted her wish. Over the next three decades, she continued to campaign tirelessly, resisting any and all attempts to silence her. By her own reckoning, she secured the passage of thirty-four bills in forty-four legislatures across twenty-four states. She campaigned for women's equal rights and for the rights of the mentally ill—the former, tellingly, usually a much harder sell than the latter. And she achieved widespread, long-lasting change, including, for example, the establishment of independent bodies that inspected asylums with the power to go above boards of trustees. Remarkably, in certain states, she was even successful in insisting that a female inspector be included.

Perhaps her most lasting achievement, inspired by her own suffering under McFarland's censorship, was securing the postal rights of patients so they were guaranteed uncensored access to their mail. Her legal reforms were copied across numerous states, with the relevant bills often bearing her name; headlines marked the regular passing of "Packard's Law."

Although superintendents complained that her reforms created a dangerous "feeling of independence" in patients, Elizabeth's personal passion made her so persuasive that legislators couldn't say no. "We passed the bill because we could not do otherwise, for Mrs. Packard was so very persistent, we could not bluff her off," admitted one Massachusetts politician. Challenged on her tenacity, Elizabeth said simply, "Sir, I am pleading for those who have…no one to plead for them!"

As the century progressed, however, she found she was no longer alone in fighting for her fellow patients. From the mid-1870s onward, the powerful hold that asylum superintendents had previously maintained on the realm of mental health began to slip. They found themselves under attack from other professionals, criticized for their scientific ignorance and "arrogant guardianship."

"You have far too long maintained the fiction that there is mysterious therapeutic influence to be found behind your walls and locked doors," charged one physician. "We hold the reverse opinion and think your hospitals are never to be used save as a last resort."

In 1880, the National Association for the Protection of the Insane and the Prevention of Insanity was established to encourage patient-friendly legislation and meaningful oversight of asylums. Historians attribute its founding to agitations caused by campaigners, including Elizabeth, who got society so riled up that formal action became essential. The arguments Elizabeth had been making for years now began to be printed in respected medical journals, though of course she was never the mouthpiece.

On the contrary. Although her views were now supported by many in the medical field, Elizabeth still found herself under constant attack, regularly dismissed as a "female paranoiac" and "half-cured lunatic." She felt she had to fight her way "through fire and blood to carry out [her] benevolent purposes to humanity."

"At every inch of progress," she complained, "[I am] compelled to face the barbed arrow of insanity, hurled at [me] by the intolerant and bigoted of [my] age."

And no sooner did she successfully pass a law to protect patients than the asylum superintendents would begin battling to overturn it, grumbling that "just one woman should be able to defeat all the doctors." But defeat them she did. Year after year, she returned to Springfield, Illinois, to defend her landmark personal liberty bill. Lawyer Myra Bradwell supported it too, reminding people that before the law was passed, "A great many people were sent to the insane asylums who were as sane as the person that sent them."

Yet more hurtful to Elizabeth than the allegation she was insane was the way her so-called love letter to McFarland regularly resurfaced to besmirch her virtue. She called it "the greatest obstacle" to her campaigning work, McFarland "my most terrible antagonist."

The doctor was clever in his campaigning against her though. He wrote no articles; he made no grand declarations. Instead, a private letter here, a well-timed visit there, and his opinion of Elizabeth would be conveyed with far more devastating power than a more public attack.

And despite what had happened in Illinois, with the legislature confirming he should be fired, McFarland *did* still have power and influence. Incredibly, he still had his reputation. In the wake of the legislature accepting the committee's recommendations, *all* the hospital's trustees had resigned. They'd long been on McFarland's side, having published a "whitewashing report" in his defense in 1868. It explained away his breaking of the 1865 law as a mere "technical appearance of non-compliance" and described the staff's cruel acts as "accidental collisions" that were simply "styled...abuse." (They even dared congratulate the doctor that "only" 1 in every 125 patients had been abused, though a supporter of McFarland later quoted 1 in 63. "Who would not regard that a success?" the trustees had cheered without irony.) Because by law, the trustees were the only people with the power to fire McFarland, their mass resignation meant the doctor escaped that fate.

In the end, it wasn't until June 8, 1870, that McFarland finally stepped down—of his own volition—two and a half years after Fuller first published his report. Curiously, just as had occurred when the investigating committee had first been appointed, there was a sudden exodus of patients just before the new superintendent started.

Double the usual number of patients were discharged before McFarland left for good.

The *Illinois Daily State Journal* marked his departure by declaring that he was retiring "with the satisfaction of knowing that his pre-eminent fitness for the position he has so long filled...is everywhere recognized."

That was evidently incorrect, but the article demonstrated a convenient rewriting of history that soon settled into supposed fact. Even in 1869, pro-McFarland papers were pushing the narrative that he had been "entirely exhonorated [*sic*]" in an investigation "not composed of... interested officials," by which they meant the trustees' biased report. By 1891, the received wisdom was that Elizabeth's allegations "were not substantiated by the public inquiry."

So the doctor's career remained more than intact; it blossomed. Having departed the asylum an incredibly wealthy man—he had a property and personal wealth portfolio worth $50,000 ($984,622)—McFarland opened a private asylum in Jacksonville called Oak Lawn.

For more than a decade, it took only male patients.

Nevertheless, it was hugely successful, becoming one of the best known institutions in the country. With the white man colonizing new territory in the West, McFarland accommodated all the insane patients from these areas, including Wyoming, Montana, and Oklahoma (whose mental patients, curiously enough, were chiefly Native American).

McFarland, the "distinguished founder" of this respected institution, was so well regarded nationally that he also contributed to two of the most significant insanity cases of the century, being consulted in the trial of President Garfield's assassin and in the case of Lincoln's widow. In the latter, for $100 ($2,345), McFarland gave his professional opinion that Mary Todd Lincoln had a "helpless and irresponsible state of mind" and should be committed indefinitely. Her son, Robert, ultimately ignored his recommendation; soon afterward, Mary was legally declared "restored to reason." No thanks to McFarland, she lived the rest of her life a free woman.

Yet Elizabeth was never free from McFarland's powerful influence. The two were locked in a lifelong dance—wherever Elizabeth campaigned, he was always there, ready to take her in hold again to lead her in steps she did not want to follow. On the cusp of achieving her most ambitious reform—a federal law to protect patients' postal rights, for which she'd personally lobbied President Grant at the White House—McFarland reportedly made a special trip to Washington to inform the committee members of her insanity.

The bill did not pass.

Elizabeth put up with his personal attacks for years, but in 1878, she made a concerted effort to publish her side of the story. *The Mystic Key* was intended to be "an efficient aid in my legislative work, by removing the greatest obstacle I have hitherto encountered in the passing of my reform bills, viz, the false interpretation of my 'love-letter!'"

It was not the only book she published that year. Though she sold it separately, *The Mystic Key* had originally been conceived and published as an appendix. An appendix to what she'd always considered her greatest work: *The Great Drama*.

By 1878, she had finally sold enough books, pamphlets, and copies of her political speeches to raise the capital required to publish the magnum opus she'd written in the asylum. To her credit, she seemingly did not edit or redact it in any way. Her boldness is even more notable because she freely admitted that it was not only want of capital but "want of courage" that had made her reluctant to publish it to date. She'd feared that readers might think her too radical, that she ran risk of another commitment. But, she said, "I now fear God's chastening rod [for not publishing it] more than I do the public criticisms." In the end, she took her own advice: "We must be palsied by no fear to offend, no desire to please, no dependence upon the judgment of others."

It was, perhaps, the crowning moment of her writing career. She dedicated the book to "My beloved sisters, the married women of America."

And those women recognized her in return. One of Elizabeth's most prized possessions was an engraved gold pocket watch she was given in 1880 "by the married women of Oregon for securing their emancipation"; Elizabeth had successfully passed a bill there that equalized the rights of husbands and wives. It became an "inestimable treasure," not least because her campaigning made for a lonely lifestyle. She did not really have a home; she traveled all over the country instead, battling a male- and doctor-dominated world that did not want her in it. After all she'd been through, the watch was a precious gift. She planned to leave it to her children, "as a significant token of their mother's life work."

As for those children, they scattered across the United States. Most married, some had children, and they pursued various careers, with Samuel undoubtedly the most successful, following in his mother's footsteps as he'd hoped to. The lawyer was "ever an advocate of reform and progressive measures" and learned from Elizabeth to create "so strong a sentiment in favor of [his arguments] that it was found impossible" to resist them. Arthur, over whose upbringing Elizabeth had the least influence, was said by the family to be the "least successful" sibling: a "mild, unimpressive sort of man."

By far the saddest story, however, was what happened to Libby. When Elizabeth was in the asylum, knowing her ten-year-old child had been burdened by a weight of responsibility a full-grown woman could be crushed by, she'd written to her daughter encouragingly, saying, "Joys bright and fragrant lie beyond this dark vale thou art now called to tread... The tide will turn."

But that was not what fate had in store for her child.

Libby was "taken deranged," in her father's words. Intriguingly, the first episode of what would prove a lifelong struggle with her mental health apparently struck on April 30, 1870, almost a year after Elizabeth had reclaimed custody. It is conjecture, but perhaps with her mother finally back in her rightful place within the family, Libby could let go of the tension she'd been holding in for the past ten years. Later generations of her family wholly attributed her mental breakdown to the pressure she'd been placed under as a child, and modern medical science supports that. Studies show that a mother's presence can directly influence a child's brain by insulating it from the damaging effects of stress or fear. But children torn from their mothers, like Libby was, and especially for prolonged periods, can suffer such acute stress that the development of their brain is affected, "disrupting a child's ability to regulate their emotions and cope with future stress."

Libby certainly didn't cope. She seesawed between living with her mother and living with her father as a young adult, developing what might have been anorexia ("it seemed as though she would soon waste away and die," wrote her father of his "greatly emaciated" child). Eventually, she became so sick that Elizabeth entirely stopped her reform work for three years to care for Libby full time. She seemingly recovered, later joining Elizabeth on the road as a partner in her book business, and in 1880, she married an Irishman named Henry Gordon. By the 1890s, however, she'd relapsed; her husband committed her to an asylum in California, and they divorced.

As soon as Elizabeth discovered what had happened, she rushed to California and rescued Libby from the hospital. The two women moved in with Toffy's family on the West Coast, with Elizabeth determined to do all she could to nurse her daughter.

But Libby was by no means an unafflicted woman like her mother had been. She was genuinely ill. Yet Elizabeth felt that was all the more reason to keep her at home and to love and care for her personally. After all the horrors she'd seen in the asylum, she would never let her daughter suffer that fate. So what if Libby was noisy and woke Elizabeth in the night? So what if she was quiet and would go days without speaking? Elizabeth was by her side through it all. And when Libby's actions needed at least some kind of control, her mother still made that as humane as she could. She and Libby lived downstairs in the front room of Toffy's house, and Toffy stretched some webbed wire from wall to wall to divide the space so that when she needed to be, Libby could be locked in. But Elizabeth would still sleep in the same room, next to that wall of wire, so she could be there if Libby called to her. Toffy's daughter was often embarrassed because her grandma was always taking Libby outside on frequent walks; the neighbors soon became aware Libby was mad. But Elizabeth seemingly felt no shame at all, proudly walking by her daughter's side as they took the air.

But no matter how much mothers might wish it, they can never live forever, even for their children. Ultimately, despite all Elizabeth's efforts, Libby ended her days in an asylum, passing away at the age of fifty-one.

Theophilus, predictably, blamed Elizabeth for their daughter's breakdown, attributing it to Elizabeth's "wrong treatment" in Chicago. Of his own role, he said nothing, except for one curious line in his diary toward the end of his life: "I acknowledge the Justice of God in this great calamity [his wife's "insanity" and all its consequences] & hope that he in mercy is overruling it for my spiritual welfare."

Did he mean his own actions needed "overruling"? *Was* there something he'd done that God should forgive?

But most likely he simply feared his wife's "irreligious influence" might be held against him on the Day of Judgment. It perhaps suggested another motive for why he'd always pursued her so relentlessly: not for his children but because he'd wanted to save his *own* soul.

Elizabeth certainly felt he never showed an ounce of guilt or regret. She described him to her readers in her later books thus: "His health is poor, and his declining years are mostly spent in the solitude of his lonely room, with but little of the solace of love and human sympathy to cheer his approach to his more lonely tomb."

Ironically, in contrast to Elizabeth's broad world, which now stretched from coast to coast, Theophilus's horizons in his later years reduced down to the four walls of the room he occupied in his sister Sybil's house, in an echo of how he had once reduced Elizabeth's world to the four walls of her asylum cell. But in that small room, far from society's intrusions, Theophilus read his books and prayed his prayers and led a quiet life. One could argue that perhaps that was what *he* had always wanted. He'd never had his wife's curiosity or passion. Maybe in the end, they both became happy in their separate spheres.

As the year 1870 drew to a close, Theophilus wrote in his diary, "The infirmities of old age are now pressing more heavily upon me... [Death] is not far off."

It was a gloomy prediction, typical of the gloomy man. In fact, he lived another fifteen years. But in December 1885, he passed away at Sybil's house aged eighty-three.

Six years later, in a private asylum on the outskirts of Jacksonville, a determined doctor paced the corridors of his own creation. Yet McFarland's strides were no longer as smooth and straight as they had once been; he now walked with difficulty, a symptom of a brain inflammation that was only getting worse. Nevertheless, on that morning of November 22, 1891, he was said to be "quite cheerful."

He had reason to be. Though life had thrown the odd curveball at him, he'd always bounced back—and then some. Back in 1887, the original Oak Lawn had burned down, but he had rebuilt and, only that September, had handed over its management to his doctor son, George, so the McFarland legacy could continue. In 1886, Elizabeth had finally lost her patience and sued him for libel, claiming damages of $25,000 ($686,093) for his constant claims that she was insane. Available records do not indicate a verdict, but McFarland would have won if the case did come to trial. Elizabeth had specifically sued about a letter published in the New Jersey press, but McFarland denied "having written any article," and he was right. It was his *private* correspondence to a fellow superintendent that had been published, and he had no control over whether his letters *happened* to be leaked...

In his own private life, meanwhile, though his first wife died, he remarried only the following year to a woman, Abby Knox, seven years his junior. And though it proved an unhappy marriage—less than nine months after the wedding, Abby had fled the asylum, alleging physical and emotional abuse at her husband's hands—it did not affect McFarland, financially at least. Abby filed for divorce on the grounds of cruelty, requesting maintenance and an equal share of property, but Isaac Morrison, McFarland's longtime lawyer, immediately submitted a cross-bill alleging desertion on her part. Seemingly under pressure, Abby withdrew her bill, so the judge ruled in favor of the doctor.

On that November day in 1891, just as the sun was setting, McFarland paused outside a vacant room. He was in a quiet corridor; only one patient resided in that particular part of the hospital. Working methodically, he removed his hat from his sore head and slipped off his shoes. Then he loosened his necktie and collar before taking them off too. Only once he was shorn of these accoutrements did he step inside that empty room and close the door behind him.

Once inside, he slipped off his jacket, his waistcoat too. Putting his back into it, as his arms no longer worked as they once had, he dragged the washstand closer to the door. He forced his limbs to follow his orders and managed to climb up onto it.

One wonders what thoughts were flitting through his mind. Did he think of the head injury he'd sustained in the Oak Lawn fire, the one he'd recently been told would prove fatal? Did he think of the depression he'd suffered the past few months, ever since he'd received that diagnosis? Or did he think of the requiem he'd already written: "I'm weary; let me rest"?

Did he even think of Elizabeth?

Probably not.

Whatever was going through the doctor's mind, he had made it up. That afternoon, he stepped off the washstand...and into an eternal silence. His inquest declared it was "Death by strangulation...while laboring under temporary mental aberration."

The doctor hung himself.

In almost every one of his obituaries, the journalists namechecked Elizabeth and the "famous Packard investigation." Even in death, they danced their strange duet. The two of them were bound together in history now—and they always would be.

As for Elizabeth, she outlived both the men who'd tried to silence her; she truly had the last word. She continued in good health until the start of her eighth decade, living with Toffy, the son who'd always been such a support, while she cared for Libby in California. In July 1897, she traveled with her daughter to Chicago, perhaps to visit Samuel and his family or to return to her own home on Prairie Avenue. Despite Libby's condition, they made it, but less than a week later, Elizabeth was rushed to the hospital. It was there that she died, aged eighty, from a strangulated hernia. It was July 25, 1897.

Her death was reported all across the country, the news mourned "with sincere sorrow by the thousands of men and women throughout the United States who had aided and sympathized in Mrs. Packard's philanthropic efforts."

"She was remarkably successful," avowed the *Boston Transcript*, "and to her efforts are due the enactment of many measures for ameliorating the condition of such unfortunates. It has been claimed that no woman of her day, except possibly Harriet Beecher Stowe, exerted a wider influence in the interest of humanity."

The *Chicago Tribune* put it more simply: "Wise Friend of the Insane Is Dead."

The papers declared she had left "an enviable record behind." She'd also left her vast raft of bestselling books. Yet despite Elizabeth having lived such an incredibly public life, the final act in her own great drama was pronounced "strictly private." Only family and close friends attended her funeral as she was laid to rest in Rosehill Cemetery.

She did not lie alone. Beside her was her son George, the boy who used to serve her strawberries. He'd died in 1889, aged thirty-five, from tuberculosis. In death, at last, they were together again.

George had no gravestone, but Elizabeth was given one. There were so many epitaphs her family could have chosen, but in the end, they opted for just one word.

Mother.

POSTSCRIPT

"Pray for her," he urged. "She is a very sick person!"

The woman in question stood before him, the only woman in a room of men.

She pointed a finger. She spoke back: a woman who refused to be silenced.

He suspected there was "something wrong with her 'upstairs.'" How else to explain this "unhinged meltdown" in which she dared defy him?

It could have been Elizabeth confronting McFarland in the fall of 1860.

It was Nancy Pelosi versus Donald Trump in October 2019.

History favors reruns.

Because that pernicious accusation of insanity, deliberately intended to undermine, haunts the annals of history like a spirit photograph, unsettling and at times unseen.

It is there in politics, acting as a dead weight to drag back the forces of change. The suffragettes in the 1900s: deemed to be "suffering from hysteria." The civil rights activists in the 1960s: masses diagnosed with schizophrenia—once the diagnostic goalposts had been deliberately moved to accommodate their perceived threat. Martha Beall Mitchell, the Watergate whistleblower: forcibly tranquilized by a psychiatrist when she exposed "dirty politics" in 1972. (Her name is now synonymous with misdiagnoses when facts are dismissed as delusions.)

And it is there, too, in private homes. Women sent to asylums for bearing illegitimate children, for being lesbian, for being themselves. "You have to hide your feelings," said one twentieth-century patient, in a direct echo of the Seventh Ward women, "pretend everything is wonderful, if you want to get out."

It is a tale as old as time. In 1687, Daniel Defoe railed against the "vile practice now so much in vogue...[men] sending their Wives to Mad-Houses at every Whim or Dislike."

And it's still here now, shadowing our society.

There's a reason why. As Elizabeth put it 160 years ago, "What is an insane person's testimony worth?

"*Nothing.*"

And so Janice Dickinson, when confronting Bill Cosby the day after he allegedly raped her, was told dismissively, "You're crazy!"

And Rose McGowan, having demonstrated her determination to expose Harvey Weinstein's crimes, found herself the target of a plot to make her seem "increasingly unglued."

Devalue the words of women and half the battle is won.

And so with Elizabeth Packard. After all, what was her testimony worth in the end in the decades after her death? As the twentieth century unfurled, her legacy slowly tarnished until, if she was remembered at all, it was only ever as a madwoman who'd tried to ruin McFarland. Psychiatrists reviewing her case confidently said she had suffered from a "menopausal...psychosis." Not knowing that Elizabeth in fact campaigned politically almost until her death, the doctors smugly said that at the expiration of her periods, she "settled down to a quiet life...and the subsidence of the mental symptoms." Centenary flashbacks in the local Jacksonville papers commemorated her as "a minor league nut" who "couldn't keep her mouth shut."

McFarland, on the other hand, was honored with a mental health center named after him in Springfield, Illinois. To this day, his oil painting hangs in the lobby, along with his gold-topped cane: a gift from the people of Jacksonville in August 1867—at the height of Fuller's investigation—as a sign of their trust and regard. A memorial plaque celebrates him as a doctor with a national reputation, an unquestioned authority in his chosen field.

To the victors of history, the spoils.

But Elizabeth Packard wrote, "I am determined...to write my own history." *And she did.* Her husband, her doctor, and her very time all tried to silence her, but Elizabeth left her own record behind, and her words now blaze through history, to light the way to the truth. She wrote, "We should set our light blazing as an example to others, and not set it under a bushel." Thanks to her brilliance, her light still burns, inspiring others to follow.

And her legacy, finally, is starting to be reassessed. In *The History and Influence of the American Psychiatric Association* (1987), she was described as an "effective crusader," and her supposed mental illness was not assumed to be a fact but viewed as a possible plot between the men who'd had charge of her life. More recently, historians have credited the origin of organized campaigns for the mentally ill to Elizabeth: the matriarch of all that was to follow, including the important work being done today, when we know at least one in five of us will struggle with our mental health. Meanwhile, feminists keep tapping away at the injustices women still face in law and life, standing on the shoulders of campaigners like Elizabeth, who laid the foundations for the ongoing fight.

At last, we are acknowledging the debt we owe her but have never paid. Ahead of her time, she challenged a patriarchal system and a doctor-dominated world, compelling both to be better and fairer. She did it all alone, bolstered only by her belief that she was right, in a world that continually told her she was wrong. She fought every day of her life to make things better, dedicating her life to others, wanting justice for all.

She was torn down for it, her reputation ravaged. Yet she squared her shoulders and dusted herself off after every single setback. She went back out there to meet that hostile world, with her hoop skirts swishing and her brown eyes gleaming, ready to fight another day.

And yes, they called her crazy.

But if that's crazy, we should stand back and admire.

For just look at what "crazy" can do.

Elizabeth Parsons Ware Packard (1816-1897)

READING GROUP GUIDE

1. Elizabeth is locked up in the asylum because her husband does not agree with her religious views. Do you think modern-day America is more or less tolerant of diverse religions (and controversial viewpoints) than in Packard's time? How free are followers of minority faiths to practice in the U.S. today?

2. Elizabeth employs a variety of tactics—physical resistance, negotiating with hospital staff, writing—to protest her treatment throughout the book. Which techniques were most effective for her? What strategies would you turn to in her place?

3. Novel reading, masturbation, and irregular menstrual cycles are a few of the many reasons that women were admitted to asylums in Elizabeth's time. Which, if any, of these justifications stood out to you? How has our understanding of these "causes of insanity" changed?

4. Dr. Duncanson, the doctor who supports Elizabeth in her insanity trial, testifies that: "I did not agree with…her on many things, but I do not call people insane because they differ with me." How relevant is this statement in America today when political opinions are so divided, and what does it do to public discourse when the idea of insanity is brought into politics? Do you think we might ever

return to a time when people are locked up for holding an opposing viewpoint to those in power?

5. Elizabeth and McFarland have a complicated relationship, to say the least. What did you think of her continuous attempts to redeem him? Did she truly think he would change, or was she just trying to improve her own circumstances? What were the long-lasting effects of the relationship on each of them?

6. When Elizabeth is first released from the asylum, how does her homecoming compare to her daydreams and expectations? Have you ever had a similar experience? How did you handle the difference between your expectations and reality?

7. Elizabeth's landmark case for her sanity was originally a trial regarding habeas corpus. What did you think of the judge's decision to shift focus? Is a jury qualified to confirm or deny someone's sanity?

8. What did you think of the spate of releases that occurred right before the asylum came under scrutiny?

9. Right or wrong, McFarland was completely trusted by the Jacksonville Asylum's Board of Trustees. What impact did this have on his patients? How did the Board respond to Fuller's investigation and recommendations? Can you think of a way to avoid such conflicts of interest?

10. Governor Oglesby was not required to act on the findings of the investigative committee and planned to keep them under wraps until the next meeting of the Illinois General Assembly. What motivated him to keep the report under wraps? Do you think modern politicians play the same games with important information?

11. The book explores the power of rumor and reputation. Even though Elizabeth is declared sane, rumors persist about her sanity for the rest of her life and are used to discredit her. Can you think of

any modern-day examples where, even though someone has been cleared of something, their opponents continue to use that something against them? Do you think this is "fair game," or is it morally wrong?

12. How did Elizabeth's status as a woman, mother, and asylum patient both help and hinder her lobbying efforts? How did she use men's expectations of her to bolster her causes?

13. Which of Elizabeth's many accomplishments do you think she was most proud of? Is there anything else you see as her greatest achievement?

14. Elizabeth writes: "To be lost to reason is a greater misfortune than to be lost to virtue, and the...scorn which the world attaches to it [is] greater." Do you think this is still true today? The American Psychological Association recently stated that only 25 percent of adults with symptoms of mental illness believe that people will be caring and sympathetic toward them. How can we improve sympathy for those who struggle with their mental health? And which do you think carries more societal shame: having a mental health problem or being "lost to virtue"? Is the answer dependent on gender?

A CONVERSATION
WITH THE AUTHOR

How did you first encounter Elizabeth's story? When did you decide that you wanted to write about her?

Before I even knew her name, I actively went looking for Elizabeth's story. The background to that quest: In the fall of 2017, the world was set ablaze by the #MeToo movement, and I wanted to write about some of the issues being raised. Namely, why hadn't women been listened to—and believed—before? Too often, it seemed to me, women had been silenced and discredited with the claim that we were crazy. Was there any woman in history, I wondered, who had been declared insane by a patriarchal society for speaking her mind, but who had somehow, against the odds, proved her sanity and prevailed? (Because I wanted a happy ending for my book!) I went in search of this mystery woman, only hoping she existed. And on January 15, 2018, after having fallen down a rabbit hole of internet searches about women and madness and insane asylums, I first read about Elizabeth Packard in a University of Wisconsin essay that I randomly found online.

That first reference was just a single paragraph in length, but a few Google clicks later, having learned a little more about her life, I was hopeful I had found the central protagonist of my next book. (I noted in my diary she looked "promising.") Yet it wasn't until I had completed my due diligence—reading the other books about her that existed at that time so as to be sure that my vision for her story, a work of narrative nonfiction, hadn't already been published—that I knew for definite she was "The One."

Elizabeth's story relies heavily on her personal tenacity. How do you think she cultivated that strength? What resources do you draw on when you feel like giving up?

I think Elizabeth's strength is absolutely remarkable. Ultimately, I think the bedrock to it was that she *knew* she was in the right, but even more remarkably, she maintained the confidence to *insist* on that truth, something with which some of us struggle. Her faith clearly helped too.

What resources do I draw on? Hope, knowledge that things will always get better (because nothing lasts forever), and sometimes (e.g. when writing a book!) the knowledge that you have to put the hard work in to enjoy the outcome. Nothing worthwhile is easy.

Elizabeth is a great role model for standing up for yourself and always following the truth. Who are your role models, historical or modern?

My role models are the radium girls, who I wrote about in another book. These incredible women are, to me, inspirational beacons of courage and strength. Whenever I'm anxious, I always think of how they might have responded to a situation or simply of what they went through, and they give me the strength to carry on.

You aptly note the ways that our public discourse *hasn't* changed when it comes to denouncing opponents by calling them "insane." Why does that technique have such staying power? How do you think we can combat it?

I think it has staying power because it's *so* dismissive. The accuser isn't even trying to engage with or debate their opponent, probably because they fear they may be bested. I think part of combating it is actually already happening: demystifying those who are genuinely mentally ill and treating them with love and understanding, and with an appreciation that either we or someone we know is likely to suffer with mental health issues. With that changed approach, the former "slur" of being called crazy has less power. And the accusation itself is revealed to be fearful and hollow in nature.

When writing nonfiction, you can't always expect events to be "story-shaped." What kind of work do you do to make a cohesive narrative out of complicated true events? What's the hardest part of that process? The most fun part?

The key thing for me is to complete my research before I write a word of the book. Doing so not only enables me to see the big picture, from which I'll craft the narrative, but it also often throws up intriguing twists that enhance the book's plot. I first plot all my research into a chronological timeline, and only after that do I plot the book itself, which is different, because for dramatic purposes you may want to include "reveals," etc. Even as I'm researching, though, I've got an antenna quivering for possible end-of-chapter slam-dunk quotations and potentially dramatic scenes.

The hardest part of the process? Two answers. One, because I'm writing nonfiction, at times the historic sources simply don't exist to tell you exactly what happened. That can be really frustrating. Two, almost the opposite problem, the act of sifting through the sources and the data that you *do* have and deciding what—or perhaps more importantly, what *not*—to include. It's essential to know the story *you* want to tell from those sources and to stick to it, but that's often easier said than done. I find the editing process is usually essential to help truly distill the narrative you're crafting.

The most fun part? Hands down, actually writing a scene after you've done your research and know all the intimate details that will bring it to life. For example, what the weather was like that day, what clothes the person might have been wearing, the nature of their surroundings and what they looked like, etc. All those details may have come from many different sources, and to combine them as the scene flows out from your pen is a wonderful feeling—you can see this historic scene so clearly in your own mind, brought to life by the collected facts.

Both _The Woman They Could Not Silence_ and your previous book, _The Radium Girls_, required extensive research. How do you work with archives and other sources for primary texts and historical data? What recommendations do you have for other researchers and writers?

I have to give a shout-out to librarians and archivists across the country here. They're always so knowledgeable and helpful. The _how_ of how I work probably boils down to knowing the story I want to tell and how I want to tell it, so I'll mine a source for descriptive details, for example. Staying focused helps you to sort through what is always a mass of data. That said, it's critical to remain open-minded, too, because until the research is finished, you don't necessarily know what is important!

As for tips, I would say be inspired by those who have come before you down a research path. When you're taking your own first steps, it can be useful to consult bibliographies of other books in order to find out what archives even exist. Some of them may prove useful to you too. Secondly, relish pursuing the various serendipitous trails that pop up along the way, whether that's "following the money" to discover corruption and influence or simply saying yes to opportunities for further research that, for example, those wonderful librarians may suggest!

Speaking of research, were there any surprising facts that didn't make it into the final book? What was the most interesting thing you discovered but weren't able to include?

There was so much that didn't make it in! I had to cut an entire part as the first draft was too long. (It was the original part one, which I'd written as a *Crucible*-esque witch hunt, as Elizabeth's religious community tightened the noose of alleged insanity about her neck until she was committed to the asylum.) Similarly, at the other end of the book, I did a heap of research into twentieth-century facts around the book's themes. Here, a surprising fact to me was that it wasn't until 1974, with the passing of the Equal Credit Opportunity Act, that independent women could get credit cards themselves. Until then, a single, divorced, or widowed woman had to get a man to cosign any credit application before it would be granted.

I also regretted deeply that I wasn't able to write more about how Black people face increased prejudice when it comes to alleged insanity. Statistics show that Black women are institutionalized far more frequently than white women with exactly the same symptoms, and they're also disproportionately affected by extreme "treatments," such as, in former times, involuntary sterilizations. Black women made up 85 percent of those legally sterilized in North Carolina in the 1960s; in other operations, Black children as young as five were lobotomized. These things occurred after Elizabeth's time, however, and I wasn't able, in the end, to find a place for them in the postscript (they had featured in my first draft).

What does your writing space look like? How do you keep all your research and drafts organized?

I have written books all over my house, so I don't have a dedicated writing space as such. I wrote *The Radium Girls* at my kitchen table. For *The Woman They Could Not Silence*, I wrote in our tiny, very newly decorated study. It was all very minimalist, as our furniture was still in storage from the renovation. I literally just had a desk, a chair, and a side table with a CD player on it so I could listen to music while I wrote (for this book, generally Ludovico Einaudi's *Eden Roc* or the soundtrack to *The Mission*, composed by Ennio Morricone). The study walls are painted a cream color—for the interest of readers of *The Radium Girls*, it is a shade named Ottawa—and I wrote with four pictures of Elizabeth stuck onto them so that she was always with me.

It's a very tidy space. I just have one A4 printout beside me—my book plan—which I check off and annotate as I go along. My research and various drafts are all stored on my laptop, so there are no piles of paper. On that laptop, the research is organized to the nth degree. Every source has a unique reference number I've given it, which is plotted into my chronological timeline. All that time-consuming, painstaking preparation means I can locate a specific quotation from a source in seconds. This also enables me to write fluidly and fast.

What are you reading these days?

I haven't had much time for reading lately. Rightly or wrongly, when I'm deep in the writing and editing process, I tend not to read so I only have the one story in my head. But the best nonfiction I most recently read was Karen Abbott's *The Ghosts of Eden Park*. And I have Margaret Atwood's *The Testaments* waiting for me on my bookshelf once this book is done.

SELECTED BIBLIOGRAPHY

Books

Abbott, Karen. *Liar, Temptress, Soldier, Spy: Four Women Undercover in the Civil War*. New York: Harper Perennial, 2015.

Baker Brown, Isaac. *On the Curability of Certain Forms of Insanity, Epilepsy, Catalepsy, and Hysteria in Females*. London: Robert Hardwicke, 1866.

Bardwell, Leila Stone. *Vanished Pioneer Homes and Families of Shelburne, Massachusetts*. Northampton, MA: Shelburne Historical Society, 1974.

Callaway, Enoch. *Asylum: A Mid-Century Madhouse and Its Lessons about Our Mentally Ill Today*. Westport, CT: Praeger, 2007.

Carlisle, Linda V. *Elizabeth Packard: A Noble Fight*. Urbana: University of Illinois Press, 2010.

Casson, Herbert N. *Cyrus Hall McCormick: His Life and Work*. 1909. Reprint, Freeport, NY: Books for Libraries Press, 1971.

Chesler, Phyllis. *Women and Madness*. New York: Doubleday, 1972.

Doyle, Don Harrison. *The Social Order of a Frontier Community: Jacksonville, Illinois, 1825–70*. Urbana: University of Illinois Press, 1978.

Duis, Perry R. *Challenging Chicago: Coping with Everyday Life, 1837–1920*. Urbana: University of Illinois Press, 1998.

Geller, Jeffrey L., and Maxine Harris. *Women of the Asylum: Voices from Behind the Walls, 1840–1945*. New York: Doubleday, 1994.

Grob, Gerald N. *The Mad Among Us: A History of the Care of America's Mentally Ill*. New York: Free Press, 1994.

———. *Mental Institutions in America: Social Policy to 1875*. New York: Free Press, 1973.

———. *The State and the Mentally Ill: A History of Worcester State Hospital in Massachusetts, 1830–1920*. Durham: University of North Carolina Press, 1966.

Hutchinson, William T. *Cyrus Hall McCormick: Harvest 1856–1884*. New York and London: D. Appleton-Century, 1935.

James, Edward T., Janet Wilson James, and Paul S. Boyer, eds. *Notable American Women 1607–1950: A Biographical Dictionary Vol. II*. Cambridge, MA: The Belknap Press of Harvard University Press, 1971.

Karamanski, Theodore J., and Eileen M. McMahon, eds. *Civil War Chicago: Eyewitness to History*. Athens: Ohio University Press, 2014.

Kenaga, William F., and George R. Letourneau. *History of Kankakee County*. Vol. 2. Chicago: Middle-West, 1906.

Lusk, D. W. *Eighty Years of Illinois: Politics and Politicians, Anecdotes and Incidents, a Succinct History of the State, 1809–1889*. Springfield, IL: H. W. Rokker, 1889.

McFarland, Andrew. *The Escape, or Loiterings Amid the Scenes of Story and Song*. Boston: B. B. Mussey, 1851.

Mehr, Joseph J. *Illinois Public Mental Health Services, 1847 to 2000: An Illustrated History*. Victoria, BC: Trafford, 2002.

Merwin, Madelyn (Madge) Bourell, ed. *Area History of Manteno, Illinois*. Dallas, TX: Curtis Media Corporation, 1993.

Morrissey, Joseph P., Howard H. Goldman, Lorraine V. Klerman, and Associates. *The Enduring Asylum: Cycles of Institutional Reform at Worcester State Hospital*. New York: Grune & Stratton, 1980.

Neely, Mark E., Jr., and R. Gerald McMurtry. *The Insanity File: The Case of Mary Todd Lincoln*. Carbondale and Edwardsville: Southern Illinois University Press, 1986.

O'Connor, Thomas H. *Civil War Boston: Home Front and Battlefield*. Boston: Northeastern University Press, 1997.

Packard, Elizabeth Parsons Ware. *The Exposure on Board the Atlantic & Pacific Car of Emancipation for the Slaves of Old Columbia, Engineered by the Lightning Express, or Christianity & Calvinism Compared. With an Appeal to the Government to Emancipate the Slaves of the Marriage Union*. Chicago, 1864.

———. *The Great Drama: or, The Millennial Harbinger*. 4 vols. Hartford, CT, 1878.

———. *Marital Power Exemplified in Mrs. Packard's Trial, and Self-Defence from the Charge of Insanity; or Three Years' Imprisonment for Religious Belief, by the Arbitrary Will of a Husband, with an Appeal to the Government to so Change the Laws as to Afford Legal Protection to Married Women*. Chicago: Clarke, 1870.

———. *Modern Persecution, or Insane Asylums Unveiled, as Demonstrated by the Report of the Investigating Committee of the Legislature of Illinois*. Vol. 1. New York, 1873.

———. *Modern Persecution, or Married Woman's Liabilities, as Demonstrated by the Action of the Illinois Legislature.* Vol. 2. Hartford, CT, 1874.

———. *Mrs. Packard's Reproof to Dr. McFarland for His Abuse of His Patients, and for Which He Called Her Hopelessly Insane.* Chicago, 1864.

———. *The Mystic Key, or The Asylum Secret Unlocked.* Hartford, CT, 1886.

———. *The Prisoners' Hidden Life, or Insane Asylums Unveiled: As Demonstrated by the Report of the Investigating Committee of the Legislature of Illinois together with Mrs. Packard's Coadjutors' Testimony.* Chicago, 1868.

Palmer, John M., ed. *The Bench and Bar of Illinois: Historical and Reminiscent.* 2 vols. Chicago: Lewis, 1899.

Pease, Rev. Charles Stanley, ed. *History of Conway (Massachusetts), 1767–1917.* Springfield, MA: Springfield Printing and Binding, 1917.

Portrait and Biographical Record of Kankakee County, Illinois. Chicago: Lake City, 1893.

Reiss, Benjamin. *Theaters of Madness: Insane Asylums and Nineteenth-Century American Culture.* Chicago and London: University of Chicago Press, 2008.

Reminiscences of Chicago During the Civil War. Chicago: Lakeside, 1914.

Sapinsley, Barbara. *The Private War of Mrs. Packard.* New York: Paragon House, 1991.

Short, William F., ed. *Historical Encyclopedia of Illinois & History of Morgan County.* Chicago: Munsell, 1906.

Showalter, Elaine. *The Female Malady: Women, Madness and English Culture, 1830–1980.* London: Virago, 1987.

Stanton, Elizabeth Cady, Susan B. Anthony, and Matilda Joslyn Gage, eds. *History of Woman Suffrage*, Vol. 1, *1848–1861.* 2nd ed. Rochester, NY: Susan B. Anthony, 1889. https://www.gutenberg.org/files/28020/28020-h/28020-h.htm.

———. *History of Woman Suffrage*, Vol. 3, *1876–1885.* Rochester, NY: Susan B. Anthony, 1887.

Stevens, Norman S., and the Kankakee County Historical Society. *Images of America: Kankakee, 1853–1910.* Charleston, SC: Arcadia Publishing, 2004.

Tiffany, Nina Moore. *Samuel E. Sewall: A Memoir.* Boston and New York: Houghton Mifflin, 1898.

Miscellaneous Articles and Publications

American Journal of Insanity, various editions from the 1850s and 1860s.

Baur, Nicole, and Joseph Melling. "Dressing and Addressing the Mental Patient: The Uses of Clothing in the Admission, Care and Employment of Residents in English

Provincial Mental Hospitals, c. 1860–1960." *Textile History* 45, no. 2 (2014): 145–170. https://doi.org/10.1179/0040496914Z.00000000045.

Bazar, Jennifer L., and Jeremy T. Burman. "Asylum Tourism." *American Psychological Association* 45, no. 2 (February 2014): 68. https://www.apa.org/monitor/2014/02/asylum-tourism.

Biennial Reports of the Illinois State Hospital for the Insane, various editions, from 1864 onward.

Blakemore, Erin. "Did Victorians Really Get Brain Fever?" JSTOR Daily, March 30, 2017. https://daily.jstor.org/did-victorians-really-get-brain-fever/.

Burnham, Mrs. Walter E., et al., eds. *History and Tradition of Shelburne, Massachusetts*. Shelburne, MA: History and Tradition of Shelburne Committee, 1958.

Cartwright, Dr. Samuel A. "Diseases and Peculiarities of the Negro Race." *De Bow's Review: Southern and Western States* 11 (1851).

City directories for Jacksonville and Chicago, IL, 1860s.

Clark, Emily. "Mad Literature: Insane Asylums in Nineteenth-Century America." *Arizona Journal of Interdisciplinary Studies* 4 (Spring 2015): 42–64.

Cruea, Susan M. "Changing Ideals of Womanhood During the Nineteenth-Century Woman Movement." *General Studies Writing Faculty Publications* 1 (2005): 187–204.

Digby, Anne. "Victorian Values and Women in Public and Private." *Proceedings of the British Academy* 78 (1992): 195–215. https://www.thebritishacademy.ac.uk/sites/default/files/78p195.pdf.

Dunton, W. R., Jr. "Mrs. Packard and Her Influence Upon Laws for the Commitment of the Insane." *Johns Hopkins Hospital Bulletin* 18 (October 1907): 419–424.

Eighth Annual Report of the Trustees of the State Lunatic Hospital, at Northampton, October, 1863, 1864. Northampton State Hospital Annual Reports (RB 035). Special Collections and University Archives, University of Massachusetts Amherst Libraries. http://credo.library.umass.edu/view/full/murb035-y1863-i001.

Falret, Dr. Jules. "On Moral Insanity." *American Journal of Insanity* 23, nos. 3–4 (April 1867): 409–424, 516–535.

First Congregational Church, Shelburne, MA. 200th Anniversary commemorative publication.

Fortson, S. Donald, III. "Old New Calvinism: The New School Presbyterian Spirit." *Reformed Faith & Practice: The Journal of Reformed Theological Seminary* 1, no. 3 (December 2016). https://journal.rts.edu/article/old-new-calvinism-the-new-school-presbyterian-spirit/.

Grob, Gerald N. "Abuse in American Mental Hospitals in Historical Perspective: Myth and Reality." In *Sickness and Health in America: Readings in the History of Medicine and Public Health*, edited by Judith Walzer Leavitt and Ronald L. Numbers, 298–309. Madison: University of Wisconsin Press, 1985.

———. "Class, Ethnicity, and Race in American Mental Hospitals, 1830–75." In *Theory and Practice in American Medicine*, edited by Gert H. Brieger, 227–249. New York: Science History Publications, 1976.

Groneman, Carol. "Nymphomania: The Historical Construction of Female Sexuality." *Signs: Journal of Women in Culture and Society* 19, no. 2 (Winter 1994): 337–367. http://www.brown.uk.com/brownlibrary/GRONE.htm.

Guimond, Virgil. *A History of Manteno Township, 1740–1990*. Manteno, IL: Manteno News, 1991.

Haahr, Kristina. "Restored to Reason: A Case Study of Women's Use of Legislative Reform for the Purpose of Legal Equality." Master's thesis, Wichita State University, 2015. https://soar.wichita.edu/bitstream/handle/10057/11628/t15010_Haahr.pdf?sequence=1&isAllowed=y.

Harper, Leslie Ann. "'They Had No Key That Would Fit My Mouth': Women's Struggles with Cultural Constructions of Madness in Victorian and Modern England and America." PhD diss., University of Louisville, 2014. https://doi.org/10.18297/etd/576.

Hartog, Hendrik. "Mrs. Packard on Dependency." *Yale Journal of Law & the Humanities* 1, no. 1 (1989): 79–103. https://digitalcommons.law.yale.edu/yjlh/vol1/iss1/6/.

Himelhoch, Myra Samuels, with Arthur H. Shaffer. "Elizabeth Packard: Nineteenth-Century Crusader for the Rights of Mental Patients." *Journal of American Studies* 13, no. 3 (December 1979): 343–375. https://doi.org/10.1017/S0021875800007404.

Hughes, John S. "Labeling and Treating Black Mental Illness in Alabama, 1861–1910." *Journal of Southern History* 58, no. 3 (August 1992): 435–460. https://doi.org/10.2307/2210163.

"The Hysterical Female." Restoring Perspective: Life and Treatment at the London Asylum. 1920. Thesis, www.lib.uwo.ca/archives/virtualexhibits/londonasylum/hysteria.html.

Johnson, Lacey. "Evolution of Fashion: Clothing of Upper Class American Women from 1865 to 1920." Thesis, Ouachita Baptist University, 2014. https://scholarlycommons.obu.edu/honors_theses/220.

Joinson, Carla. "How to Commit." Canton Asylum for Insane Indians. January 17, 2016. http://cantonasylumforinsaneindians.com/history_blog/how-to-commit/.

Journals of the House and Senate, various editions from the legislatures in Illinois and Massachusetts, 1860s.

Kaelber, Lutz, ed. "Eugenics: Compulsory Sterilization in 50 American States—Illinois." March 2009. www.uvm.edu/~lkaelber/eugenics/IL/IL.html.

Kim, Jonathan, ed. "Habeas Corpus." Legal Information Institute, June 2017. https://www.law.cornell.edu/wex/habeas_corpus.

Kraychik, Robert. "Hysterical and Angry Clinton Shrieks at Town Hall When Asked About Goldman Sachs Speeches." *Daily Wire*, February 19, 2016. https://www.dailywire.com/news/hysterical-and-angry-clinton-shrieks-town-hall-robert-kraychik.

LoBue, Vanessa. "The Effects of Separating Children from Their Parents." *Psychology Today*, July 5, 2018. https://www.psychologytoday.com/gb/blog/the-baby-scientist/201807/the-effects-separating-children-their-parents.

Lombardo, Paul A. "Mrs. Packard's Revenge." *BioLaw* 2, nos. 59/60 (March/April 1992): 791–797. https://www.researchgate.net/publication/261949275_Mrs_Packard's_Revenge.

Marsh, Jan. "Gender Ideology & Separate Spheres in the 19th Century." Victoria and Albert Museum. http://www.vam.ac.uk/content/articles/g/gender-ideology-and-separate-spheres-19th-century/.

McCauley, Elizabeth. "Martha Mitchell: The Woman Nobody Believed About Watergate." All That's Interesting, September 17, 2018. https://allthatsinteresting.com/martha-mitchell.

McFarland, Andrew. "Association Reminiscences and Reflections." *American Journal of Insanity* 34 (January 1878): 342–59.

———. "Attendants in Institutions for the Insane." *American Journal of Insanity* 17 (July 1860): 53–60.

———. "The Better Way, or Considerations Upon the Natural System of Providing for the Treatment of the Insane." Standalone pamphlet publication, originally extracted from the *St. Louis Medical and Surgical Journal* (1872).

———. "Insanity and Intemperance." *American Journal of Insanity* 19 (April 1863): 448–70.

———. "Minor Mental Maladies." *American Journal of Insanity* 20 (July 1863): 10–26.

National Register of Historic Places Registration Form for Kankakee County Courthouse. United States Department of the Interior, National Park Service, January 18, 2007. http://gis.hpa.state.il.us/pdfs/223437.pdf.

Ne'eman, Ari. "Another Tragedy, Another Scapegoat." *American Prospect*, February 27, 2018. https://prospect.org/justice/another-tragedy-another-scapegoat/.

Paz, Franco A. "The Uprisings of Nat Turner and John Brown: Response and Treatment from the Abolitionist Movement and the Press." *Inquiries Journal* 8. no. 5 (2016). http://www.inquiriesjournal.com/a?id=1409.

Pouba, Katherine, and Ashley Tianen. "Lunacy in the 19th Century: Women's Admission to Asylums in United States of America." *Oshkosh Scholar* 1 (April 2006): 95–103.

"Rape victims say military labels them 'crazy.'" CNN, April 14, 2012. http://edition.cnn .com/2012/04/14/health/military-sexual-assaults-personality-disorder/index.html.

Ray, Dr. Isaac. "Doubtful Recoveries." *American Journal of Insanity* 20 (July 1863): 26–44.

Reports and Other Documents Relating to the State Lunatic Hospital at Worcester, Massachusetts. Boston: Dutton and Wentworth, 1837.

Reports of the Illinois State Hospital for the Insane 1847–1862. Chicago: F. Fulton, 1863.

Reports of the New Hampshire Asylum for the Insane, various editions, from 1845 onward.

Rothschild, Mike. "The Craziest Medical Practices Doctors Thought Made Sense." *Ranker,* September 11, 2019. https://www.ranker.com/list/weird-medical-practices /mike-rothschild?ref=collections&l=2462717&collectionId=2101.

Sheehan, Elizabeth A. "Victorian Clitoridectomy: Isaac Baker Brown and His Harmless Operative Procedure." In *The Gender/Sexuality Reader: Culture, History, Political Economy,* edited by Micaela di Leonardo and Roger N. Lancaster, 325–334. New York: Routledge, 1997.

Shelton, Jacob. "12 Twisted Before & After Stories of Lobotomy Victims." *Ranker,* January 17, 2020. https://www.ranker.com/list/lobotomies-before-and-after/jacob-shelton.

Sigurðardóttir, Elísabet Rakel. "Women and Madness in the 19th Century: The effects of oppression on women's mental health." Bachelor's thesis, September 2013. https:// skemman.is/bitstream/1946/16449/1/BA-ElisabetRakelSigurdar.pdf.

Smith, Matthew. "The Healing Waters: The Long History of Using Water to Cure Madness." *Psychology Today,* October 9, 2015. https://www.psychologytoday.com/us /blog/short-history-mental-health/201510/the-healing-waters.

Special Report of the Trustees of the Illinois State Hospital for the Insane. Springfield, IL, 1868.

Tasca, Cecilia, Mariangela Rapetti, Mauro Giovanni Carta, and Bianca Fadda. "Women and Hysteria in the History of Mental Health." *Clinical Practice & Epidemiology in Mental Health* 8 (2012): 110–119. https://doi.org/10.2174/1745017901208010110.

Testa, Megan, and Sara G. West. "Civil Commitment in the United States." *Psychiatry (Edgmont)* 7, no. 10 (2010): 30–40. https://www.ncbi.nlm.nih.gov/pmc/articles /PMC3392176/.

Tolman, Gilbert Alden. "Reminiscences of Randolph" and "Randolph Reminiscences." *Randolph Register and News,* 1897–1902.

Topp, Leslie. "Single Rooms, Seclusion and the Non-Restraint Movement in British Asylums, 1838–1844." *Social History of Medicine* 31, no. 4 (November 2018): 754–73. https://doi.org/10.1093/shm/hky015.

Umeh, Uchenna. "Mental Illness in Black Community, 1700–2019: A Short History." *Black Past*, March 11, 2019. https://www.blackpast.org/african-american-history /mental-illness-in-black-community-1700–2019-a-short-history/.

Vital Records of Shelburne, Massachusetts. Salem, MA: Essex Institute, 1931.

Walter, Madaline Reeder. "Insanity, Rhetoric, and Women: Nineteenth-Century Women's Asylum Narratives." PhD diss., University of Missouri-Kansas City, 2011. https:// mospace.umsystem.edu/xmlui/bitstream/handle/10355/11577/WalterInsRheWom .pdf?sequence=1&isAllowed=y.

Wazer, Caroline. "Victorian Doctors Thought Reading Novels Made Women 'Incurably Insane.'" *History Buff*, March 22, 2016. https://greenviewasylum.word press.com/2016/04/12/victorian-doctors-thought-reading-novels-made-women -incurably-insane/.

Williams, Florence et al. "The Wonderful Land: A History and Geography of Kankakee." Kankakee, IL: Thomas Edison School, 1965.

Woodward, Samuel B. "Medical Ethics." *New England Journal of Medicine* 202, no. 18 (May 1930): 843–853.

Newspapers

Boston Daily Advertiser

Boston Journal

Boston Post

Boston Transcript

Chicago Post

Chicago Tribune

Evening Standard (London, UK)

Gazette & Mercury (Greenfield, MA)

Gazette and Courier (Greenfield, MA)

Greenfield Courier

Guardian (UK)

Hampshire Express

Hartford Courant

Illinois Daily State Journal

Illinois State Register

Illinois State Sentinel

Inter Ocean, Chicago

Jacksonville Journal

Jacksonville Sentinel

Kankakee Gazette

Monmouth Democrat (Freehold, NJ)

New York Herald

New York Post

New York Times

Northampton Free Press

San Francisco Chronicle

Seattle Times

St. Louis Post-Dispatch

Special Collections

American Antiquarian Society, Worcester, MA.

Archives of the First Presbyterian Church of Manteno. Community Presbyterian Church, Manteno, IL.

Barbara Sapinsley Papers. Oskar Diethelm Library, DeWitt Wallace Institute of Psychiatry, Weill Cornell Medical College, NY.

Chicago History Museum, Chicago, IL.

Concord Public Library, Concord, NH.

Dorothea Lynde Dix Papers. MS Am 1838 (123). Houghton Library, Harvard University, Boston, MA.

Edward Jarvis Papers. Rare Books & Special Collections, Francis Countway Library, Harvard Medical School, Boston, MA.

Harold Washington Library, Chicago, IL.

Illinois State Archives, Springfield, IL.

Jacksonville Public Library, Jacksonville, IL.

Jones Library, Amherst, MA.

Kankakee County Records. Kankakee County Court House, Kankakee, IL.

Kankakee Public Library, Kankakee, IL.

Lincoln Library, Springfield, IL.

Manteno Public Library, Manteno, IL.

Memorial Libraries, Deerfield, MA.

Morgan County Records. Morgan County Circuit Court. Jacksonville, IL.

Records of the New Hampshire Asylum for the Insane. New Hampshire Historical Society, Concord, NH.

Shelburne Public Library, Shelburne, MA.

Shelburne Free Public Library Fidelia Fiske Collection, Mount Holyoke College Archives and Special Collections, South Hadley, MA.

State Library of Massachusetts, Boston, MA.

Wellcome Collection, London, UK.

Websites

Ancestry.com

BBC.co.uk

Britannica.com

FindAGrave.com

HathiTrust.org

History.com

In2013Dollars.com

Newspapers.com

NPS.gov

OldandInteresting.com

ScienceMuseum.org.uk

TheAtlantic.com

TheExploressPodcast.com

Timeline.com

PICTURE
ACKNOWLEDGMENTS

page 8   Used courtesy of the Packard family and Judy Domhoff Stenovich.
Sourced from *The Private War of Mrs. Packard* by Barbara Sapinsley
(New York: Paragon House, 1991).

page 19   Used courtesy of the Packard family and Judy Domhoff Stenovich.
Sourced from *The Private War*.

page 30   *Marital Power Exemplified in Mrs. Packard's Trial, and Self-Defence
from the Charge of Insanity; or Three Years' Imprisonment for Religious
Belief, by the Arbitrary Will of a Husband, with an Appeal to the
Government to so Change the Laws as to Afford Legal Protection to
Married Women* by E. P. W. Packard (Chicago, 1870), inside cover.

page 33   *Modern Persecution, or Insane Asylums Unveiled, as Demonstrated by the
Report of the Investigating Committee of the Legislature of Illinois*, vol. 1,
by E. P. W. Packard (New York, 1873), 64 (hereafter cited as *MP1*).

page 36   *Tenth Biennial Report of the Trustees, Superintendent and Treasurer of the
Illinois State Hospital for the Insane at Jacksonville* (Springfield: Baker,
Bailhache & Co., 1866), inside cover. Courtesy of Oskar Diethelm
Library, DeWitt Wallace Institute of Psychiatry: History, Policy, & the
Arts, Weill Cornell Medical College.

page 39   Table IV from *Tenth Biennial Report*, 20. Courtesy of Oskar Diethelm
Library, DeWitt Wallace Institute of Psychiatry: History, Policy, & the
Arts, Weill Cornell Medical College.

page 45   Jacksonville State Hospital Souvenir Booklet (undated). Sourced from
"Jacksonville State Hospital" research file, courtesy of the Jacksonville
Public Library, Jacksonville, Illinois.

page 48   *Photographs of Pioneers and Early Settlers of Morgan County: Vol. 1*
           (Morgan County Historical Society), 7. Courtesy of the Jacksonville
           Public Library, Jacksonville, Illinois.

page 55   *MP1*, 256.

page 149   Jacksonville Mental Health and Developmental Center, "Institutional
           Photographic Files," Record Series 252.021, Illinois State Archives.

page 152   Elizabeth Packard's letter to Fidelia Fiske, March 3, 1846. Letter
           sourced from and used courtesy of Shelburne Free Public Library
           Fidelia Fiske Collection, Mount Holyoke College Archives and
           Special Collections, South Hadley, MA.

page 183   *MP1*, 288.

page 305   *Portrait and Biographical Record of Kankakee County, Illinois* (Chicago,
           1893), 209.

page 352   *Mrs. Packard's Reproof to Dr. McFarland for His Abuse of His Patients,
           and for Which He Called Her Hopelessly Insane* (Chicago, 1864), front
           cover. Courtesy of Oskar Diethelm Library, DeWitt Wallace Institute
           of Psychiatry: History, Policy, & the Arts, Weill Cornell Medical
           College.

page 363   *Three Years' Imprisonment for Religious Belief: A Narrative of Facts* by
           Mrs. E. P. W. Packard, front matter. Courtesy of Oskar Diethelm
           Library, DeWitt Wallace Institute of Psychiatry: History, Policy, & the
           Arts, Weill Cornell Medical College.

page 372   Courtesy of the Abraham Lincoln Presidential Library & Museum.

page 390   *Modern Persecution, or Married Woman's Liabilities, as Demonstrated by
           the Action of the Illinois Legislature*, vol. 2 (Hartford, CT, 1874), 204
           (hereafter cited as *MP2*).

page 396   Courtesy of the Abraham Lincoln Presidential Library & Museum.

page 432   *MP2*, 379.

page 455   From the collection of Elizabeth Hattie Leach Desjardins; used cour-
           tesy of her grandson, Michael G. Draper.

ABBREVIATIONS

AM	Dr. Andrew McFarland
EP	Elizabeth Packard
SO	Sophia Olsen
TP	Theophilus Packard

AJOI	*American Journal of Insanity*
AMSAII	Association of Medical Superintendents of American Institutions for the Insane
GD	*The Great Drama: or, The Millennial Harbinger* by E. P. W. Packard
GT	"The Great Trial of Mrs. Elizabeth P. W. Packard" by Stephen R. Moore, published in *MPE* (see below)
MK	*The Mystic Key, or The Asylum Secret Unlocked* by E. P. W. Packard
MO	"Mrs. Olsen's Narrative of Her One Year's Imprisonment, at Jacksonville Insane Asylum" by Sophia Olsen, published in *PHL* (see below)
MP1	*Modern Persecution, or Insane Asylums Unveiled, as Demonstrated by the Report of the Investigating Committee of the Legislature of Illinois*, Vol. 1, by E. P. W. Packard
MP2	*Modern Persecution, or Married Woman's Liabilities, as Demonstrated by the Action of the Illinois Legislature*, Vol. 2, by E. P. W. Packard

MPE   *Marital Power Exemplified in Mrs. Packard's Trial, and Self-Defence from the Charge of Insanity; or Three Years' Imprisonment for Religious Belief, by the Arbitrary Will of a Husband, with an Appeal to the Government to so Change the Laws as to Afford Legal Protection to Married Women* by E. P. W. Packard

PHL   *The Prisoners' Hidden Life, or Insane Asylums Unveiled: As Demonstrated by the Report of the Investigating Committee of the Legislature of Illinois together with Mrs. Packard's Coadjutors' Testimony* by E. P. W. Packard

TE   *The Exposure on Board the Atlantic & Pacific Car of Emancipation for the Slaves of Old Columbia, Engineered by the Lightning Express, or Christianity & Calvinism Compared. With an Appeal to the Government to Emancipate the Slaves of the Marriage Union* by E. P. W. Packard

TPD   Theophilus Packard's diary

NOTES

BOOK EPIGRAPHS

"There's no more": Holly Bourne, "Jokes about 'Snowflakes' Ignore the Crisis in Young Mental Health," *Guardian*, September 20, 2018, https://www.theguardian.com/books/2018/sep/20/jokes-about-snowflakes-ignore-the -crisis-in-young-mental-health.

"Confusion has seized": Maria Weston Chapman, "The Times That Try Men's Souls" (1840), in *History of Woman Suffrage*, ed. Elizabeth Cady Stanton, Susan B. Anthony, and Matilda Joslyn Gage, vol. 1, 1848–1861, 2nd ed. (Rochester, New York: Charles Mann, 1889), 82, https://www.gutenberg.org/files/28020/28020-h/28020-h.htm.

PROLOGUE

"Is there no": Rebecca Blessing, quoted in E. P. W. Packard (EP), *The Prisoners' Hidden Life, or Insane Asylums Unveiled: As Demonstrated by the Report of the Investigating Committee of the Legislature of Illinois together with Mrs. Packard's Coadjutors' Testimony* (Chicago, 1868), 47 (hereafter cited as *PHL*).

"silent and almost": EP, *Marital Power Exemplified in Mrs. Packard's Trial, and Self-Defence from the Charge of Insanity; or Three Years' Imprisonment for Religious Belief, by the Arbitrary Will of a Husband, with an Appeal to the Government to so Change the Laws as to Afford Legal Protection to Married Women* (Chicago: Clarke, 1870), 4 (hereafter cited as *MPE*).

PART ONE: BRAVE NEW WORLD

EPIGRAPHS

"A wife once": *Chicago Jokes and Anecdotes for Railroad Travelers and Fun Lovers* (Chicago: John R. Walsh, 1866), 116.

"Unruly women are": Roxane Gay, "Unruly Women Are Always Witches: Outlander S1 E10," The Butter, *The Toast* (blog), April 18, 2015, https://the-toast.net/2015/04/18/unruly-women-are-always-witches-outlander -s1-e-10/.

CHAPTER 1

"mother-boy": EP, *The Great Drama: or, The Millennial Harbinger*, 4 vols. (Hartford, CT, 1878), 1:335 (hereafter cited as *GD*).

"an all-absorbing": EP, *The Mystic Key; or, The Asylum Secret Unlocked* (Hartford, CT: Case, Lockwood & Brainard Co., 1886), 50 (hereafter cited as *MK*).

"the sun, moon": EP, *The Exposure on Board the Atlantic & Pacific Car of Emancipation for the Slaves of Old Columbia, Engineered by the Lightning Express, or Christianity & Calvinism Compared. With an Appeal to the Government to Emancipate the Slaves of the Marriage Union* (Chicago, 1864), 5 (hereafter cited as *TE*).

"jewels": Ibid.

"*train of stars*": EP, *GD*, 2:95.

"*happy faces*": Ibid., 1:219.

"*always rejoicing*": Ibid., 2:336.

"*anxious foreboding*": EP, *PHL*, 36.

"*noiselessly searching*": Ibid., 42.

"*When I was*": EP, *GD*, 1:135.

"*woman's chief office*": Ibid., 2:86.

"*natural for the*": Ibid., 2:82.

"*green*": Ibid., 1:347.

"*dusty*": Ibid., 2:17.

"*did not seem*": Ibid., 2:190.

"*to please*": Ibid., 4:68.

"*with all the*": EP, *PHL*, 60.

"*to be a*": EP, ibid., 63.

"*To make him*": EP, *GD*, 2:28.

"*That's all I*": Ibid., 1:352.

"*dull*": Theophilus Packard (TP), Theophilus Packard's diary, 51, November 26, 1829, Barbara Sapinsley Papers, Oskar Diethelm Library, DeWitt Wallace Institute of Psychiatry, Weill Cornell Medical College, New York (hereafter cited as TPD).

"*This Sabbath is*": Ibid., 47 (March 1, 1829).

"*cheerless*": EP, *GD*, 2:85.

"*The polar regions*": Ibid., 2:66.

"*totally indifferent*": Ibid., 2:23.

"*not know how*": EP, *PHL*, 63.

"*blighting, love strangling*": Ibid., 64–65.

"*Wives are not*": EP, *GD*, 1:320.

"*a woman has*" and following quotation: EP, *MPE*, 78.

"*a most rare*": Dr. Andrew McFarland (AM), letter to TP, August 11, 1860, in "The Question of Mrs. Packard's Sanity," *Northampton Free Press*, April 13, 1866.

"*jealousy*": EP, *MPE*, 80.

"*stung to the*": EP, *GD*, 2:328.

"*My wife was*": TP, TPD, 77 (1856).

"*I, though a*": EP, *TE*, 112.

"*I have got*": EP, *GD*, 1:135.

"*wives, obey your*": Eph. 5:22 (Worldwide English New Testament). EP describes TP quoting this verse repeatedly to her in *GD*, 4:119.

"*with equal justice*": EP, *TE*, 113.

"*sad reason to*": EP quoting TP's letters to her relatives, *MPE*, 78.

"*Action is the*": EP, *GD*, 2:248.

"*woman's mind*": Ibid., 2:59.

"*No man shall*": Ibid., 2:41.

"*used to tell*" and following quotation: Ibid., 4:133–34.

"*wrong by nature*": TP, TPD, 72 (1844).

"*Be your own*": EP, *GD*, 1:278.

"*irreligious influence*": TP, TPD, 41 ("Wife's Insanity—1860").

"*unspeakable grief*": Ibid.

"*good talking times*": EP, *PHL*, 119.

"*Laughing!*": TP, quoted in *GD*, 1:220.

"*assumed a tangible*" and following quotation: EP, *PHL*, 42.

KATE MOORE

"[I] felt so": EP, *GD*, 2:179.

"I ask you": EP, "Rights of Private Judgment," in *PHL*, 22.

"an irresistible magnetism": Sophia Olsen (SO), "Mrs. Olsen's Narrative of Her One Year's Imprisonment, at Jacksonville Insane Asylum" (hereafter cited as MO), 72, in *PHL*, page 426 in PDF.

"unusual timidity": TPD, 6, August 1818.

"I am willing" and following quotations: *PHL*, 17.

"I had rather": EP, *MPE*, 74.

"to act the": Ibid., 5.

"I do not": EP, *TE*, 113.

"I shall put": TP, quoted in EP, *GD*, 1:134.

"fugitive lunatics": *New York Herald*, 1850, quoted in Leslie Ann Harper, "'They Had No Key That Would Fit My Mouth': Women's Struggles with Cultural Constructions of Madness in Victorian and Modern England and America" (PhD diss., University of Louisville, 2014), 70, https://doi.org/10.18297/etd/576.

"Can [a woman]": EP, *MPE*, 63.

"the result of": TP, in EP, *PHL*, 22.

"attack of derangement" and following quotations: TP, "An Account of the Insanity Case of Mrs. E. P. W. Packard of Manteno, Illinois," *Gazette and Courier*, April 4, 1864.

"Why do you": EP, *TE*, 109.

"To…be false": EP, *MPE*, 74.

"withdrawn from conversation": Advice of Dr. Christopher Knott of what EP needed at this time, from Knott's evidence at the trial, quoted in Stephen R. Moore, "The Great Trial of Mrs. Elizabeth P. W. Packard" (hereafter cited as GT) in *MPE*, 18.

"kept from observers": EP, *GD*, 1:331.

CHAPTER 2

"every motion": SO, MO, 13, in *PHL*, page 367 in PDF.

"As soon as": AM, "The Better Way, or Considerations Upon the Natural System of Providing for the Treatment of the Insane," standalone pamphlet publication, originally extracted from the *St. Louis Medical and Surgical Journal* 1872: 29.

"There still lingers": AM, in *Ninth Biennial Report of the Trustees, Superintendent and Treasurer of the Illinois State Hospital for the Insane at Jacksonville* (Springfield, IL, 1864), 13.

"crushing scrutiny": SO, MO, 13, in *PHL*, page 367 in PDF.

"Whatever I say": EP, *MPE*, 75.

"an instinctive aversion": EP, *PHL*, 66.

"angry…and showed": Sarah Rumsey, court testimony, GT, in *MPE*, 29.

"dislike to her": Mrs. F. E. Dickson, affidavit, August 21, 1862, in "The Question of Mrs. Packard's Sanity," *Northampton Free Press*, May 8, 1866.

"derangement of mind": Ibid.

"to feel indifferent": Nineteenth-century book, quoted in Rachelle Bergstein, "The Beauty Routine of a Victorian Woman Was Anything But Glamorous," *New York Post*, October 23, 2016, https://nypost.com/2016/10/23/the-beauty-routine-of-a-victorian-woman-was-anything-but-glamorous/.

"ungovernable": Dr. John Conolly, *A Remonstrance with the Lord Chief Baron Touching the Case Nottidge versus Ripley*, 3rd ed. (London: John Churchill, 1849), 9.

"more than usual": F. C. Skey, *Hysteria: Remote Causes of Disease in General. Treatment of Diseases by Tonic Agency. Local Or Surgical Forms of Hysteria, Etc.* (London: Longmans, Green, Reader, & Dyer, 1867), 55.

"of strong resolution": Ibid.

"to have her": Parishioners' petition, May 22, 1860, in "The Question of Mrs. Packard's Sanity," *Northampton Free Press*, May 1, 1866.

"Just think": EP, *GD*, 1:230–31.

"Such a pack": Ibid., 2:18.

"suffocating and choking": EP, *PHL*, 178.

"earnest conversation": Ibid., 39.

"[I will] talk": EP's declaration, as recounted by Sybil Dole, court testimony, in Moore, GT, in *MPE*, 26.

"They will have": EP's children, quoted by EP, *PHL*, 39.

"tender-hearted and devoted": Ibid., 40.

"a mild": EP, letter to Fidelia Fiske, March 3, 1846, Shelburne Free Public Library Fidelia Fiske Collection, Mount Holyoke College Archives and Special Collections, South Hadley, MA.

"wholly unfounded": Isaac Packard, letter of endorsement for EP, April 12, 1869, in EP, *Modern Persecution, or Married Woman's Liabilities, as Demonstrated by the Action of the Illinois Legislature*, vol. 2 (Hartford, CT, 1874), 376 (hereafter cited as *MP2*).

"She went from": Deacon Charles A. Spring, affidavit, in "The Question of Mrs. Packard's Sanity," *Northampton Free Press*, May 1, 1866.

"aroused a rabid": TP, TPD, 40 ("Wife's Insanity—1860").

"That woman endured": Isaac Blessing, quoted by EP, *TE*, 101.

"quack": TP, TPD, 40 ("Wife's Insanity—1860").

"I must first": Isaac Packard, quoted by EP, *PHL*, 42.

"too noble": EP, *GD*, 2:160.

"gentle respectful attentions": Ibid., 2:145.

"could look up": Ibid., 2:178.

"right of disposal": Isaac Ray, "American Legislation on Insanity," *AJOI* 21 (July 1864): 49–50.

"The insane were": Myra Samuels Himelhoch and Arthur H. Shaffer, "Elizabeth Packard: Nineteenth-Century Crusader for the Rights of Mental Patients," *Journal of American Studies* 13, no. 3 (December 1979): 345, https://doi.org/10.1017/S0021875800007404.

"only available means": EP, *PHL*, 99.

"into written form": EP, *MPE*, 33.

"a thorough": EP, "Mrs. Packard's Address to the Illinois Legislature," 2, in *MPE*, page 146 in PDF.

"I have picked": George Packard, quoted by EP, *PHL*, 42.

"Come, George,": TP, quoted by EP, ibid., 42–43.

"winter of perpetual": *Kankakee Gazette*, article reproduced in "The Case of Mrs. Packard," *Chicago Tribune*, January 28, 1864.

"gleam": Witness for the defense in EP's 1886 libel suit against AM, Elizabeth P. W. Packard v. Andrew McFarland et al., suit filed May 10, 1886, Kankakee Circuit Court, Kankakee, Illinois, quoted in Linda V. Carlisle, *Elizabeth Packard: A Noble Fight* (Urbana: University of Illinois Press, 2010), 191.

"stranger gentleman": EP, *MPE*, 3.

CHAPTER 3

"The 'forms of'": TP, quoted by EP, *PHL*, 43.

"I am doing": TP, quoted by EP, *Modern Persecution, or Insane Asylums Unveiled, as Demonstrated by the Report of the Investigating Committee of the Legislature of Illinois*, vol. 1 (New York, 1873), 53 (hereafter cited as *MP1*).

"so far deranged": Parishioners' petition, May 22, 1860, in "The Question of Mrs. Packard's Sanity," *Northampton Free Press*, May 1, 1866.

"by the request": Clause 6, "An act to amend an act entitled 'An act to establish the Illinois State Hospital for the Insane,' in force March 1, 1847," approved February 12, 1853, quoted in *Reports of the Illinois State Hospital for the Insane, 1847–1862*, Chicago: F. Fulton & Co., 1863, 390.

"civilly dead": Declaration of Sentiments, 1848, quoted in *History of Woman Suffrage*, 1:70.

"The husband and": Blackstone's Commentaries on the Laws of England, quoted in ibid., 1:738.

"to deprive her": Declaration of Sentiments, 1848, quoted in ibid., 1:70.

"without the evidence": Clause 10, "An act to amend the act establishing the Illinois State Hospital for the Insane," approved February 15, 1851, in *Reports of the Illinois*, 386.

"if the Medical": Clause 6, *Reports of the Illinois*, 390.

"I...have married": EP, *GD*, 2:196.

"If it had": Ibid., 2:321.

"[The] man to": EP, *MPE*, 51.

CHAPTER 4

Conversation between TP and EP: quoted by EP, *MP1*, 53–56.

"deep emotion": EP, *PHL*, 45.

"most bland": EP, *MP1*, 57.

"Mr. Packard": Ibid.

"more and more": EP, *GD*, 2:255.

"business that God": Ibid., 1:278.

"to be...": EP, in a self-written prayer said aloud to her family on June 14, 1860, as reported in the certificate of Sarah Rumsey, in "The Question of Mrs. Packard's Sanity," *Northampton Free Press*, April 20, 1866.

"holding on to": EP, *GD*, 4:67.

"A peace based": Ibid., 2:72.

"saddle-seat": EP, *PHL*, 47.

"stranger gentleman": EP, *MPE*, 3.

"imploringly and silently": EP, *PHL*, 47.

"silent and almost": EP, *MPE*, 4.

"like dead faith": EP, *GD*, 2:133.

"All the oppressor": Ibid., 2:141–42.

"The hungry wolf": Ibid., 2:217–18.

"You will not": Isaac Simington, quoted by EP in "Mrs. Packard's Address," 3, in *MPE*, page 147 in PDF.

"in a few": EP, *PHL*, 75.

"speedy liberation": EP, printed appeal to members of the General Assembly, in "Wife Behind the Bars of a Madhouse," *Chicago Tribune*, March 1, 1891.

"I did not": Isaac Blessing, court testimony, in Moore, *GT*, in *MPE*, 35.

"double-minded" and following quotation: EP, *GD*, 2:150.

"Is there no": Rebecca Blessing, quoted in EP, *PHL*, 47.

"to guard against": Ibid., 48.

"O!": Ibid.

"deep gush": Ibid.

"almost unceasingly": Ibid., 50.

CHAPTER 5

"awe both deep": AM, "The Better Way," 18.

"chilling sense": Ibid.

"only the best": Gilbert Alden Tolman, "Randolph Reminiscences," *Randolph Register and News*, February 15, 1902.

"mental labor": EP's "supposed cause" of insanity, "Fourth Report of the Superintendent of the State Lunatic Hospital, Worcester, Massachusetts, from December 1st, 1835, to November 30th, 1836, inclusive," in *Reports and Other Documents Relating to the State Lunatic Hospital at Worcester, Massachusetts* (Boston: Dutton and Wentworth, 1837), 145.

"training your girls": Sir Charles Fox, quoted by Isaac Ray, "Proceedings of the Thirteenth Annual Meeting of the AMSAII," *AJOI* 15 (July 1858): 131.

"derangements of": Edward H. Clarke, *Sex in Education; or, A Fair Chance for Girls* (Boston: James R. Osgood, 1875), 18.

"minds of limited": AM, in *Reports of the Board of Visitors and Trustees and of the Superintendent of the New Hampshire Asylum for the Insane: June Session, 1847* (Concord, NH, 1847), 21.

"medicalization of female": Carol Groneman, "Nymphomania: The Historical Construction of Female Sexuality," *Signs: Journal of Women in Culture and Society* 19, no. 2 (Winter 1994): 337–67, http://www.brown.uk.com /brownlibrary/GRONE.htm.

"novel reading": Table IV, "Supposed Exciting Causes of Insanity in Cases Admitted since December 1, 1864," *Tenth Biennial Report of the Trustees, Superintendent, and Treasurer of the Illinois State Hospital for the Insane at Jacksonville* (Springfield, IL, 1866), 20.

"pernicious habit": Dr. John Harvey Kellogg, quoted in Caroline Wazer, "Victorian Doctors Thought Reading Novels Made Women 'Incurably Insane,'" *History Buff*, March 22, 2016, found in article of same name on Greenview Asylum website, April 12, 2016, https://greenviewasylum.wordpress.com/2016/04/12 /victorian-doctors-thought-reading-novels-made-women-incurably-insane/.

"a dreamy kind": AM, in *Reports of the Trustees and Superintendent of the New Hampshire Asylum for the Insane: June Session, 1846* (Concord, NH, 1846), 19.

"improper literature": Reverend Theophilus Packard Sr. to Deacon Pratt, early 1850s, quoted in *History and Tradition of Shelburne, Massachusetts*, ed. Mrs. Walter E. Burnham et al. of the History and Tradition of Shelburne Committee (1958), 88.

"very needlessly": EP, *TE*, 38.

"a tender brother": EP, *PHL*, 129.

"horrid and sickening": Lyman E. De Wolf, "Public Institutions," *Daily Illinois State Register*, February 21, 1867.

"the peculiar taint": AM, in *Reports of the Board of Visitors and Trustees and of the Superintendent of the New Hampshire Asylum for the Insane: June Session, 1849* (Concord, NH, 1849), 34.

"notion and custard-pies": EP, *GD*, 2:157.

"all the viands": "Excursion to Jacksonville," *Illinois Journal*, January 11, 1867.

"unearthly sounds": EP, *MPE*, 95.

"dear fragments": EP, *PHL*, 60.

CHAPTER 6

"submission is": EP, *GD*, 2:10.

"to secure her": EP, *PHL*, 125.

"That class of": Ibid.

"almost uninhabitable": AM, "Sixth Biennial Report of the Trustees, Superintendent, and Treasurer of the Illinois State Hospital for the Insane at Jacksonville: December 1858," *Reports of the Illinois*, 272.

"the most pleasant": SO, *MO*, 15, in *PHL*, page 369 in PDF.

"lady-like civility": EP, *PHL*, 62.

"ought not to": Superintendent of the Worcester State Lunatic Hospital, *Annual Report*, 1854, quoted in Gerald N. Grob, "Class, Ethnicity, and Race in American Mental Hospitals, 1830–75," in *Theory and Practice in American Medicine: Historical Studies from the Journal of the History of Medicine & Allied Sciences*, ed. Gert H. Brieger (New York: Science History Publications, 1976), 240.

"may retard": Ibid.

"noisy, destructive": AM, in "Proceedings of the Twelfth Annual Meeting of the AMSAII," *AJOI* 14 (July 1857): 79.

"vulgar and obscene": Case note from Worcester State Hospital (Case No. 4710, Case Book No. 28, p. 240, Record Storage Section, Worcester State Hospital, Worcester, MA), 1854, quoted in Grob, "Class, Ethnicity, and Race," 241.

"low grade": AM, in "Proceedings of the Twelfth," 103.

"highly civilized": Elaine Showalter, *The Female Malady: Women, Madness and English Culture, 1830–1980* (London: Virago, 1987), 24.

"We seldom meet": Dr. Andrew Halliday, *A General View of the Present State of Lunatics and Lunatic Asylums in Great Britain and Ireland* (London: Underwood, 1828), 79–80.

"freedom": The "exciting" cause of the madness of John Patterson (a pseudonym), patient #295, Admissions Book, Staff Library (Bryce Hospital, Tuscaloosa, AL), 1867, quoted in John S. Hughes, "Labeling and Treating Black Mental Illness in Alabama, 1861–1910," *The Journal of Southern History* 58, no. 3 (August 1992): 435, https://doi.org/10.2307/2210163.

"drapetomania": Dr. Samuel A. Cartwright, "Diseases and Peculiarities of the Negro Race," *De Bow's Review: Southern and Western States* 11 (1851).

"whipping the devil": Ibid.

"very plain and": EP, *PHL*, 62.

"hurry up!": SO, MO, 69, in *PHL*, page 423 in PDF.

"the use of": EP, printed appeal, in "Wife Behind the Bars."

"for THINKING": EP, *TE*, title page.

"a fine-looking gentleman": EP, *PHL*, 66.

"true man": EP, *MK*, 57.

"you can feel": EP, *GD*, 2:81.

"of the classic": Frank P. Norbury, "Historical Remarks Pertaining to State Hospitals, the Jacksonville State Hospital and of Dr. Andrew McFarland and Dr. Henry F. Carriel," read before the Morgan County Medical Society, in "Jacksonville State Hospital in Earlier Years," *Jacksonville Daily Journal*, May 31, 1925.

"an unfailing fund": AM, *The Escape, or Loiterings Amid the Scenes of Story and Song* (Boston: B. B. Mussey, 1851), 27.

"bearing marks": Review of AM's poem "The Vision," *Jacksonville Sentinel*, March 21, 1867.

"hardly be eclipsed": EP, *GD*, 2:140.

"enthusiast": AM, letter to Dr. Edward Jarvis, August 12, 1868, Edward Jarvis Papers, Rare Books & Special Collections, Francis Countway Library, Harvard Medical School.

"the best men": AM, "The Better Way," 12.

"executive ability": *Special Report of the Trustees of the Illinois State Hospital for the Insane: In Review of a Report of a Legislative Committee Appointed by the Twenty-Fifth General Assembly* (Springfield, IL: Baker, Bailhache & Co., 1868), 98.

"There is no": "An Infamous Lie," *Illinois State Daily Journal*, July 5, 1869.

"kindly, dignified": Norbury, "Historical Remarks."

"to be restored": EP, *PHL*, 66.

"harmony" and following quotation: AM, in "Sixth Biennial Report," 254.

CHAPTER 7

"the progressive ideas": EP, *PHL*, 66.

"dying by inches": EP, *GD*, 1:122.

"a feast of": EP, *PHL*, 67.

"particularly avoided": Ibid., 66.

"womanly instincts": Ibid., 67.

"good looks": AM, letter to Superintendent Smith of the Bureau of Associated Charities at Newark, New Jersey, in "A Curious Case," *Monmouth Democrat*, December 31, 1885.

"extraordinary powers": AM, in "Annual Meeting of the AMSAII," 91.

"the sad risk": TP, TPD, 69 (1839).

"a model wife": AM, letter to the *Chicago Tribune*, January 29, 1864, in "The Packard Insanity Case," *Chicago Tribune*, February 4, 1864.

"appeared to human": TP, TPD, 69 (1839).

"plea of defence": EP, *PHL*, 66.

"I do believe": Ibid., 68–69.

"the Athens of": Charles M. Eames, *Historic Morgan and Classic Jacksonville* (Jacksonville, IL, 1885), 223.

"the beasts": Quoted in Jennifer L. Bazar and Jeremy T. Burman, "Asylum Tourism," *American Psychological Association* 45, no. 2 (February 2014): 68, https://www.apa.org/monitor/2014/02/asylum-tourism.

"the pure air": EP, *PHL*, 68.

"a cloud": AM, in *Ninth Biennial Report*, 46.

"ample expanse": SO, MO, 17, in *PHL*, page 371 in PDF.

"shade as well": "First Biennial Report of the Trustees of the Illinois State Hospital for the Insane" (1847–48), *Reports of the Illinois*, 55.

"all but Paradisiacal": SO, MO, 17, in *PHL*, page 371 in PDF.

"Is there no": EP, *PHL*, 68.

"very pleasant": Ibid., 69.

Conversation between TP and EP: Quoted by EP, ibid., 70–71.

"a little ray": Ibid., 69.

"derangement of mind": Certificate of Dr. C. W. Knott, June 5, 1860, in "The Question of Mrs. Packard's Sanity," *Northampton Free Press*, April 13, 1866.

"religious matters": Dr. Knott, court testimony, in Moore, GT, in *MPE*, 17.

"incessant talking": Dr. A. B. Newkirk, affidavit, in "The Question of Mrs. Packard's Sanity," *Northampton Free Press*, May 1, 1866.

"designed to convey": Dr. Knott, court testimony, in Moore, GT, in *MPE*, 17.

"deficiency of science": "Dr. Dunglison's Statistics of Insanity in the United States," *AJOI* 17 (July 1860): 111.

"for the purpose": Dr. Knott, court testimony, in Moore, GT, in *MPE*, 18.

"unusual zealousness": Ibid.

"strong will": Ibid.

"slightly insane": Elizabeth Packard's admittance record at the Illinois State Hospital, Jacksonville Record 1:232, June 19, 1860, Barbara Sapinsley Papers. Access to these admittance records is now restricted by law.

"present attack": Ibid.

"excessive application": Ibid.

"placed there by": EP, *TE*, title page.

"one look of": EP, *PHL*, 72.

"Never had I": Ibid.

"kisses from": Ibid.

"happy adieu": Ibid.

"dying hope": Ibid., 69.

CHAPTER 8

"from sister spirits": EP, *GD*, 1:91.

"no bruises": EP, *PHL*, xi.

"in agony": Ibid.

"drunkard husband": EP, *MP1*, 171.

"half of": Ibid.

"Of course": EP, *PHL*, 121.

"The manifestations": Dr. Jules Falret, "On Moral Insanity," *AJOI* 23, nos. 3–4 (April 1867): 534.

"preserve the appearance": Ibid.

"It isn't fair": EP, *GD*, 1:287.

"premature marks": SO, MO, 24, in *PHL*, page 378 in PDF.

"the only religious": *History of Woman Suffrage*, ed. Elizabeth Cady Stanton, Susan B. Anthony, and Matilda Joslyn Gage, vol. 3, *1876–1885* (Rochester, NY: Susan B. Anthony, 1887), 530.

"It is not": Sarah Minard, "Testimony of Mrs. Sarah Minard, of St. Charles, Ill.," in "Mrs. Packard's Coadjutor's Testimony," 129, in *PHL*, page 483 in PDF.

"busy fingers": SO, MO, 23, in *PHL*, page 377 in PDF.

"universal respect": Ibid.

"In many instances": EP, Bill No. 2, presented to the Committee on the Commitment of the Insane in Boston State House on March 29, 1865, quoted in *MPE*, 56 [italics added].

"It was a": EP, *PHL*, 80.

"the greatest annoyances": Dr. DeWolf recalling an application to his asylum, in "Proceedings of the Nineteenth Annual Meeting of the AMSAII," *AJOI* 22, nos. 1–2 (July 1865): 54.

"all domestic control": Conolly, *A Remonstrance*, 10.

"storage unit": http://social.rollins.edu/wpsites/thirdsight/2013/09/23/women-in-insane-asylums/ (site inaccessible as of publication time).

"put here": EP, *MPE*, 96.

"massive Thor": *Chicago Daily Press*, 1858, quoted in *Encyclopaedia Britannica*, s.v. "Cyrus McCormick," last modified June 10, 2020, https://www.britannica.com/biography/Cyrus-McCormick.

"men of lesser": Herbert N. Casson, *Cyrus Hall McCormick: His Life and Work* (1909; repr., Freeport, NY: Books for Libraries Press, 1971), 154.

"smaller men could": Ibid.

"no authority": Declaration of the General Assembly of the Old School Presbyterian Church, 1845, quoted in William T. Hutchinson, *Cyrus Hall McCormick: Harvest 1856–1884* (New York and London: D. Appleton-Century, 1935), 6n5.

"subsidizing the preaching": Hutchinson, *Cyrus Hall McCormick*, 14.

"The oppressed ought": EP, *GD*, 1:134.

"I think he": Ibid.

"Self-interest": TP, TPD, 65 (December 28, 1832).

"may not be": TP, quoted by EP, *TE*, 109.

"so entirely disregarded": Letter from TP's parishioners and deacons to EP, May 24, 1860, in "The Question of Mrs. Packard's Sanity," *Northampton Free Press*, April 13, 1866.

"We all have": Sybil Dole, quoted by EP, *GD*, 2:254.

"my deluded": Ibid., 2:72.

"She would not": Abijah Dole, court testimony, in Moore, GT, in *MPE*, 24.

"a covert": EP, *TE*, 101.

"how many hopes": AM, "The Better Way," 20.

"characters, feelings, connections": Luther V. Bell, quoted in Gerald N. Grob, *The Mad Among Us: A History of the Care of America's Mentally Ill* (New York: Free Press, 1994), 83.

"fountains of sympathy": AM, *The Escape*, vii.

"a heart of": L. M. Glover, letter to the Ministers of the Gospel in Illinois, "Hospital for the Insane," *Jacksonville Journal*, December 19, 1867.

"extraordinary mental capacity": AM, in "Annual Meeting of the AMSAII," 91.

"a labor": AM, "The Better Way," 12.

"feast": EP, *PHL*, 67.

"after-claps": EP, *GD*, 1:133.

"the perfection": AM, letter to Mrs. Alma E. Eaton, March 21, 1866, in "Packard Controversy," *Hampshire Express*, April 19, 1866.

"minutest movements": AM, in *Reports of the Board of Visitors, Trustees, Building Committee, and of the Superintendent of the New Hampshire Asylum for the Insane: June Session, 1850* (Concord, NH, 1850), 25.

"I felt that": EP, *PHL*, 78.

"were anticipated": EP, *MK*, 56.

"never could sing": AM, *The Escape*, 29.

"a man of": EP, *MK*, 56.

"affectionate": EP, *PHL*, 78.

"longer continued": Ibid.

"I was then": Ibid.

"I do not": AM, quoted by EP, letter to her children and husband, July 14, 1860, in *MPE*, 94.

CHAPTER 9

"Asylum favorite": EP, *PHL*, 87.

"almost queen-like": EP, *MK*, 56.

"had liberty": Dr. Henry F. Carriel, letter to Dorothea Dix, July 22, 1875, Dorothea Lynde Dix Papers MS Am 1838 (123). Houghton Library, Harvard University.

"her consummate tact": AM, "Packard Insanity Case."

"997 pillowcases" and other sewing statistics: "Seventh Biennial Report," *Reports of the Illinois*, 321.

"my best friend": EP, *TE*, 69.

"in a few": EP, *PHL*, 75.

"She is the": Dr. Shirley, quoted by EP, *PHL*, 75.

"did not begin": EP, *TE*, 101.

"Indeed I do": Ibid., 102.

"But I must": Ibid.

"public indignation meeting": EP, *PHL*, 75.

"the liberation": Chief Justice Marshall (the first Chief Justice of the U.S. Supreme Court), 1830, quoted in "Habeas Corpus," Legal Information Institute, June 2017, https://www.law.cornell.edu/wex/habeas_corpus.

"universal application": "Illinois Legislation Regarding Hospitals for the Insane," *AJOI* 26 (October 1869): 223.

"the gentlemanly Superintendent": EP, *PHL*, 80.

"a monstrous-sized": Ibid., 73.

"Is Mr. Packard": EP's fellow patients, quoted in ibid.

"One ray of": EP, ibid.

"in a state": Ibid.

"next to finding": Ibid., 74.

"We are glad": Letter from Elizabeth "Libby" Packard, quoted in ibid.

"most troublesome": EP, *GD*, 4:120.

"naught to do": EP, *PHL*, 72.

"coming under": Ibid., 74.

"Being sane": EP, *GD*, 2:364.

"with the most": EP, *MK*, 56.

CHAPTER 10

"subsidiary use": AM, in *Reports of the Board of Visitors, Trustees, Building Committee, and of the Superintendent of the N.H. Asylum for the Insane: June Session, 1851* (Concord, NH, 1851), 31–32.

"more frequently": Dr. Cutter, in "Proceedings of the Twelfth," 87.

"very common": Ibid.

"A lunatic asylum": New York City Lunatic Asylum, Blackwell's Island, *Annual Report* 1861, 18, quoted in Grob, "Class, Ethnicity, and Race," 242.

"eccentricity of conduct": James Cowles Prichard, 1835, quoted in Anne Digby, "Victorian Values and Women in Public and Private," *Proceedings of the British Academy* 78 (1992): 197, https://www.thebritishacademy.ac.uk /sites/default/files/78p195.pdf.

"perversion of the": Eric T. Carlson and Norman Dain, "The Meaning of Moral Insanity," *Bulletin of the History of Medicine* 36, no. 2 (March-April 1962): 131, https://www.jstor.org/stable/44449786.

"arise in the": Dr. Gray, in "Annual Meeting of the AMSAII," 72.

"misfortune for science": Professor Griesinger in his "treatise on mental diseases," 355, quoted in Falret, "On Moral Insanity," 412.

"faster than institutions": AM, in *Ninth Biennial Report*, 31.

"to keep me": EP, *MPE*, 94.

"fully determined": EP, *GD*, 2:258.

"I will be": Dr. Tenny, quoted by SO, MO, 31, in *PHL*, page 385 in PDF.

"the law of": Dr. Samuel Woodward, quoted in "An Appeal in Behalf of the Insane," *American Psychological Journal* 1, no. 5 (September 1853): 137.

"my counselor": EP, *TE*, 118.

"a most noble": Ibid., 101.

"proper values": "Mental Hospital Reform," 1, Barbara Sapinsley Papers.

"therapeutic intervention": Michel Foucault, *Mental Illness and Psychology*, trans. Alan Sheridan (Berkeley: University of California Press, 1987), 71.

"quiet, decorous": Dr. John Conolly, *Treatment of the Insane Without Mechanical Restraints* (1856; repr. London: Dawsons, 1973), 127–28.

"Self-defense forbids": EP, *TE*, 74.

"I have done": EP, *GD*, 2:351.

"Old Packard will": Ibid., 1:151.

"I think it": EP, *PHL*, 65.

"model wife": AM, in "Packard Insanity Case."

"impregnable, invincible fortress": EP, *PHL*, 285.

"mere emotional impulses": AM, in "Annual Meeting of the AMSAII," 88.

"hardly deserve": Ibid.

"intellectual impairment": Ibid., 91.

"fine mind": AM, letter to TP, August 11, 1860, in "The Question of Mrs. Packard's Sanity," *Northampton Free Press*, April 13, 1866.

"interesting study": Ibid.

"made comfortable": Dr. J. Sanbourne Bockoven, *Moral Treatment in American Psychiatry* (New York: Springer, 1963), 12.

"feelings of tranquillity": EP, *MK*, 58.

"permeated into": Ibid.

"my kind friend": EP, *TE*, 112.

"your faithful Eva": EP, "My Reproof to Dr. McFarland for his Abuse of his Patients," *MP1*, 136.

"extraordinary tact": "Andrew McFarland," *Biographical and Portrait Album of Morgan and Scott Counties* (Chicago: Chapman Brothers, 1889), 303.

"intimate and effective": AM, "Attendants in Institutions for the Insane," *AJOI* 17 (July 1860): 54.

"a self-control": L. M. Glover, in "Hospital for the Insane," *Jacksonville Journal*, December 19, 1867.

"one of his": EP, *GD*, 1:189.

"took possession": EP, *MK*, 57.

"dare[d] not come": EP, *TE*, 97.

"manly protector": Repeated references throughout EP's books, including EP, *MK*, 95.

"[I] do so": EP, *GD*, 4:76.

"buds of hope": EP, *MK*, 57.

"kindred spirit[s]": EP, *GD*, 1:189.

"O, how I": EP, *MPE*, 96.

"base charges": EP, *MK*, 60.

"order and system": Ibid., 59.

"Go with": EP, "My Reproof," *MP1*, 128.

"It is of": Ibid., 129.

"hallucinations": EP, *MK*, 60.

"silent eye": EP, *TE*, 117.

CHAPTER 11

"ignorant of all": EP, *TE*, 117.

"system of compulsory": SO, MO, 95, in *PHL*, page 449 in PDF.

"Their rules": Phebe B. Davis, *Two Years and Three Months in the New York Lunatic Asylum at Utica* (1855), in Jeffrey L. Geller and Maxine Harris, *Women of the Asylum: Voices from Behind the Walls, 1840–1945* (New York: Doubleday, 1994), 57.

"You mustn't cry": Attendants quoted by EP, *GD*, 2:214.

"It is always": Dr. Isaac Ray, "Doubtful Recoveries," *AJOI* 20 (July 1863): 37.

"lingering spark": Ibid., 39.

"as hard to": EP, *GD*, 4:26.

"grieving and talking": Ibid., 1:302.

"We must seem": Caroline E. Lake, "Testimony of Mrs. Caroline E. Lake, of Aurora, Ill.," in "Mrs. Packard's Coadjutor's Testimony," 141, in *PHL*, page 495 in PDF.

"being violent": Testimony of Dr. W. Ward to the Select Committee, Commissioners in Lunacy on Bethlem Hospital, July 7, 1851, in Great Britain, *Parliamentary Papers*, 6:271, quoted in Showalter, *Female Malady*, 81.

"silently and meekly": EP, "My Reproof," *MP1*, 121.

"confidant": EP, *MPE*, 96.

"did not listen": Testimony of John Henry, former steward of the Illinois State Hospital, Report of the Investigating Committee (1867), 42.

"indifferent when complaints": Ibid.

"We are free": EP, *GD*, 2:55.

"These two dear": EP, *MK*, 42.

"with all the": EP, *MPE*, 127.

"tower of strength": EP, *MK*, 44.

"Mother": Toffy Packard, quoted by EP, *MPE*, 128 [italics added].

"When all the": EP, *TE*, 5.

"Scarcely anyone seems": EP, *GD*, 2:74.

"passed beyond": Ibid., 1:5.

"Sometimes": EP, *PHL*, 197.

"wail of horror": EP, "My Reproof," *MP1*, 129.

"a lady of": Ibid., 133.

"sisters in bonds": SO, MO, 26, in *PHL*, page 380 in PDF.

"If you ever": Mrs. Hosmer, quoted by EP, *GD*, 1:303.

"So long as": Ibid.

"I know more": Ibid.

CHAPTER 12

"Mrs. Packard…": EP says of the patients of the lower wards, "Several times…I was saluted by name, from these windows," *MK*, 60.

"never could see": EP, *GD*, 2:94.

"No one was": SO, MO, 72, in *PHL*, page 426 in PDF.

"false imprisonment": J. C. and Celia Coe, in notices "sent to several New England and Western papers a short time since," quoted in "An Appeal in Behalf of the Insane" (June 18, 1862), reproduced in *Mrs. Packard's Reproof to Dr. McFarland for His Abuse of His Patients, and for Which He Called Her Hopelessly Insane*, (Chicago, 1864), 26.

"She is not": Ibid. EP also quotes Farmer Jones saying the same thing in *TE*, 88–89.

"All…we get": EP, *GD*, 4:56.

"so much more": Ibid., 180. For those interested in the specific wages of asylum attendants, the most recent source for these in relation to Elizabeth's time comes from the Third Biennial Report of the Illinois State Hospital,

covering the years 1851–52. Most female attendants took home $10 a month (about $336 today). In contrast, male attendants were paid $20 a month (about $672 today). See *Reports of the Illinois*, 130.

"intelligent, educated" and following quotation: AM, "Appendix: Superintendent's Letter," February 28, 1868, in *Special Report of the Trustees*, 102.

"colored races": AM, "Attendants in Institutions," 57–60.

"The unworthy": AM, "Appendix: Superintendent's Letter," 102.

"what they needed": EP, *GD*, 2:231.

"I never saw": Ibid., 1:152.

"a little ale": EP, *PHL*, 78.

"laying on": Ibid.

"almost universally": Ibid.

"I can tell": EP, *GD*, 1:152.

"always acted upon": AM, in "Proceedings of the Twelfth," 96.

"The insane hospital": Ibid.

"[A] curb must": AM, "The Better Way," 29.

"notable only for": Gerald N. Grob, "Institutional Origins and Early Transformation," in Joseph P. Morrissey, Howard H. Goldman, and Lorraine V. Klerman, *The Enduring Asylum: Cycles of Institutional Reform at Worcester State Hospital* (New York: Grune & Stratton, 1980), 31.

"impropriety": Dr. Brown, referring to the views of Dr. Churchill of Dublin, in "Proceedings of the AMSAII," *AJOI* 26 (October 1869): 169.

"mischievous": Ibid., 170.

"almost always": Ibid.

"harmless": Quoted in Elizabeth A. Sheehan, "Victorian Clitoridectomy: Isaac Baker Brown and His Harmless Operative Procedure," in *The Gender/Sexuality Reader: Culture, History, Political Economy*, ed. Roger N. Lancaster and Micaela di Leonardo (New York: Routledge, 1997), 333.

"foiled in dealing": Isaac Baker Brown, *On the Curability of Certain Forms of Insanity, Epilepsy, Catalepsy, and Hysteria in Females* (London: Robert Hardwicke, 1866), vi.

"without being able": Ibid.

"peripheral excitement": Ibid.

"down to the": Ibid., 43.

"by scissors": Ibid., 17.

"The rapid improvement": Ibid., 18.

"distaste for marital": Ibid., 22.

"distaste for the": Ibid., 26.

"sterility or": Ibid., 16.

"in serious reading": Ibid., 37.

"restless and excited": Ibid., 14–15.

"became in every": Ibid., 30.

"unsexed": Ibid., 79.

"nothing of the": Ibid.

"most wretched": Ibid.

"Daily experience convinces": Ibid., vi.

"Would anyone strip": T. Spencer Wells, Alfred Hegar, and Robert Battey, "Castration in Nervous Diseases: A Symposium," *American Journal of Medical Science* 92, no. 10 (1886): 466.

"mutilation of helpless": Criticism of Dr. R. Maurice Bucke of the London Asylum, Ontario, Canada, quoted in "The Hysterical Female," Restoring Perspective: Life and Treatment at the London Asylum, https://www.lib.uwo.ca/archives/virtualexhibits/londonasylum/hysteria.html.

"emotional disorder": Sheehan, "Victorian Clitoridectomy," 333.

"tincture of veratria": Dr. McIlhenny, in "Proceedings of the Twelfth," 98.

"for the purpose": Dr. Earle, ibid., 99.

"singular sensation": Ibid.

"boisterous": Dr. Bemis, in "Proceedings of the Thirteenth," 94.

"not only temporarily": Dr. Athon, in "Proceedings of the Fourteenth Annual Meeting of the AMSAII," *AJOI* 16 (July 1859): 50.

"I use it": Dr. Hills, in "Proceedings of the Thirteenth," 93.

"to prevent its": "Eighth Biennial Report of the Trustees, Superintendent, and Treasurer of the Illinois State Hospital for the Insane at Jacksonville: December 1862," *Reports of the Illinois*, 334.

"deaf adder": EP repeatedly uses this as a metaphor for AM, including *PHL*, 112 and 262.

"It is too": EP, "My Reproof," *MP1*, 129.

"His word could": EP, *PHL*, 77.

CHAPTER 13

"Mrs. Packard, who": AM, quoted by EP, *MPE*, 89.

"Every means possible": EP, *PHL*, 197.

"injurious": AM, in "Eighth Biennial Report," 359.

"let [them] alone": Ibid., 358.

"sterling commandment": Ibid.

"immediately destroyed": S. A. Kain (Susan Kane), letter to the governor, January 1866, reproduced in both the *State Register* and *MP2*, 223.

"the sense of": EP, *GD*, 4:164.

"It [is] hard": Ibid., 4:193.

"the dominant and": AM, "Attendants in Institutions," 53.

"with feelings of": System of Regulations for the State Lunatic Hospital, Worcester, Mass. (Worcester, MA, 1839), 7, quoted in Gerald N. Grob, *The State and the Mentally Ill: A History of Worcester State Hospital in Massachusetts, 1830–1920* (Durham: University of North Carolina Press, 1966), 66.

"his judgment is": EP quoting AM's words, *PHL*, 143.

"shape [their] manner": AM, "Attendants in Institutions," 53.

"The superior": Ibid.

"modify his thoughts": Review of *Moral Medicine in the Treatment of Nervous Diseases* by Atde. Padioleau, *AJOI* 21 (July 1864): 160.

"benignant Prospero": AM, "Attendants in Institutions," 53.

"elevated by his": Ibid.

"laying on of": EP, *PHL*, 78.

"large numbers of": AM, in "Seventh Biennial Report of the Trustees, Superintendent, and Treasurer of the Illinois State Hospital for the Insane at Jacksonville: December 1860," *Reports of the Illinois*, 318.

"Is such ease": EP, *GD*, 4:28.

"that I should": Ibid., 4:29.

"dark corner": Ibid., 4:42.

"all by ourselves": Ibid.

"I will see": AM, quoted by EP, *PHL*, 79–80.

"Dr. McFarland didn't force": EP, *GD*, 4:66.

"a mere impulsive": EP, *PHL*, 80.

"Dr. McFarland": Ibid.

"stepping-stone to": EP, *MK*, 66.

"imperative necessity": Ibid., 61.

"The Doctor orders": Attendants, quoted by EP, ibid., 59.

"If the doctor": EP, *GD*, 4:37.

"all reasonable time": EP, "A Defense," *TE*, 93.

"intelligently and knowingly": Ibid.

"I will not": EP, "My Reproof," *MP1*, 131 [italics added].

"championship of": EP, *MK*, 65.

"[You have] no": EP, *PHL*, 89.

"Mrs. Packard": Ibid.

"manly protector": Repeated references throughout EP's books, including EP, *MK*, 95.

"I therefore shall": EP, "A Defense," *TE*, 117.

"on simple hearsay": EP, *PHL*, 80–81.

"The Approaching Revolution": *New York Herald*, October 26, 1860, reproduced in *Jacksonville Sentinel*, November 9, 1860.

CHAPTER 14

"I, your sane": EP, "A Defense," *TE*, 93–95.

"I am a": Ibid., 109.

"Have you not": Ibid., 95.

"a class of": Ibid.

"Excitements among them": AM, in "Seventh Biennial Report," 318.

"understanding": EP, "A Defense," *TE*, 96.

"act honorably": Ibid., 117.

"O, my friend": Ibid., 116.

"I am fully": Ibid., 93.

"He has forced": Ibid., 111.

"to fill any": Ibid., 118.

"support myself": Ibid.

"Am I under": Ibid., 102.

"the privilege of": Ibid., 118.

"[Make] me an": Ibid., 103.

"as a Moses": Ibid.

"I know these": Ibid., 99.

"no fancy sketch": Ibid.

"the pictures": Ibid.

"I hate him": EP, *GD*, 2:48.

"He has by": EP, *PHL*, 191.

"the most inhuman": EP, *GD*, 2:350.

"loathing and disgust": Ibid., 2:124.

"a perverted and": EP, "A Defense," *TE*, 107.

"David's prayer": Ibid., 116.

"He remembered not": "David's prayer," quoted by EP, ibid.

"Her hatred of": AM, in "Annual Meeting of the AMSAII," 91.

"refused to honor": Cecilia Tasca, Mariangela Rapetti, Mauro Giovanni Carta, and Bianca Fadda, "Women and Hysteria in the History of Mental Health," *Clinical Practice & Epidemiology in Mental Health* 8 (2012): 110–19, https://doi.org/10.2174/1745017901208010110.

"to join": Ibid.

"recovered": Ibid.

"their love is": Falret, "On Moral Insanity," 530.

"They excite": Ibid., 531.

"I fear nothing": EP, "A Defense," *TE*, 110–11 and 94.

"Dr. McFarland, I beg": Ibid., 111, 114, 118.

"Your sane patient": Ibid., 119.

"He can see": EP, MPE, 101.

"I have no": Mrs. Tirzah F. Shedd, "Testimony of Mrs. Tirzah F. Shedd, of Aurora, Ill.," in "Mrs. Packard's Coadjutor's Testimony," 133, in PHL, page 487 in PDF.

"who always finds": SO, MO, 119, in PHL, page 473 in PDF.

"Motives higher than": EP, PHL, 87.

"surprise": Ibid., 86.

"I will back": Seventh Ward patient, quoted by EP, "My Reproof," MP1, 137.

"I will stand": Ibid.

"I tell my": EP, "My Reproof," MP1, 131.

"I love my": EP, GD, 1:244.

"fixed to neat": AM, in "Fifth Biennial Report of the Trustees, Superintendent, and Treasurer of the Illinois State Hospital for the Insane at Jacksonville: December 1856," Reports of the Illinois, 231.

CHAPTER 15

"the most expressive": EP, PHL, 87.

"I do not approve": EP, "My Reproof," MP1, 120.

"a kind act": Ibid., 131.

"others are better": Ibid., 122.

"give up their": Ibid.

"Dr. McFarland": Ibid., 120–21.

"I came here": Ibid., 132.

"I shall make": Ibid.

"iron pen": Ibid.

"I feel called": Ibid., 123.

"no right to": Ibid., 125.

"The patients are": Asylum employee, quoted by EP, ibid., 132.

"Dr. McFarland keeps": Ibid.

"If it were": Ibid., 133.

"This is but": EP, ibid.

"Perhaps it was": Ibid., 126, 131.

"You can": Ibid., 124–25.

"I defy all": Ibid., 125.

"rising and applauded": Ibid.

"You need not": Ibid., 130.

"Of one thing": Ibid.

"fear her artillery": Ibid., 126.

"class of oppressed": EP, "A Defense," TE, 95.

"communicable to others": AM, "Appendix," in Special Report of the Trustees, 100.

"spread, like": Ibid.

"the minds of": Ibid.

"most trying": AM, in Ninth Biennial Report, 34.

"I do want": EP, "My Reproof," MP1, 127.

"when you thought": Ibid., 136.

"his feelings burst": EP, MK, 62.

"He seemed determined": Ibid.

"Remember, Dr. McFarland": EP, "My Reproof," MP1, 137.

"presentiment of coming": EP, PHL, 89.

"put every article": Ibid.

"so cold that": EP, "My Reproof," MP1, 128.

"the almost monastic": AM, in "Sixth Biennial Report," 256.

"neat and well-arranged": AM, in "Fourth Biennial Report of the Trustees, Superintendent, and Treasurer of the Illinois State Hospital for the Insane at Jacksonville: December 1854," *Reports of the Illinois*, 176.

"pleasing anticipation": Ibid., 177.

"soul-cheering doctrine": EP, *GD*, 1:256.

"most fetid scent": EP, *PHL*, 90.

"screaming, fighting": Ibid.

"rough, tangled": Ibid., 95.

"unfragrant puddles": Ibid., 91.

"to wade": Ibid.

"You may occupy": AM, quoted by EP, *PHL*, 88.

PART TWO: DARK BEFORE THE DAWN

EPIGRAPHS

"Much Madness is": Emily Dickinson, "Much Madness is divinest Sense—(620)," *The Poems of Emily Dickinson: Variorum Edition*, ed. Ralph W. Franklin (Cambridge, MA: Belknap Press of Harvard University Press, 1998).

"She did not": Obituary of Lucy Strong Parsons Ware, "Died," *Gazette and Courier*, November 28, 1843.

CHAPTER 16

"The maniac's ward": SO, MO, 33, in *PHL*, page 387 in PDF.

Conversation between EP and Miss Tenney: Quoted by EP, *PHL*, 88.

"except when the": SO, MO, 37, in *PHL*, page 391 in PDF.

"like wild beasts": De Wolf, "Public Institutions."

"there was scarcely": EP, *PHL*, 90.

"mild and peaceful": SO, MO, 36–37, in *PHL*, pages 390–91 in PDF.

"fluttering bird": EP, *GD*, 4:65.

"She saw I": Ibid.

"Pray aloud!": Bridget, quoted by EP, *PHL*, 111.

"quiet, inoffensive": EP, *PHL*, 110.

"exclaiming with great": Ibid., 111.

"Let Dr. McFarland": Bridget, quoted by EP, ibid.

"human passions": EP, ibid., 189.

"O, my dear": Jenny Haslett, quoted by EP, *PHL*, 128.

"sobbing and": SO, MO, 39, in *PHL*, page 393 in PDF.

"swearing, cursing": SO, MO, 38, in *PHL*, page 392 in PDF.

"silent musings": EP, *MK*, 65.

"Comfort, attention": EP, *PHL*, 87.

"blackest night": EP, *MK*, 63.

CHAPTER 17

"Duties are ours": EP, *GD*, 12.

"pretend to be": Ibid., 360.

"in consequence": EP, *PHL*, 93.

"mere empty bubbles": EP, "My Reproof," *MP1*, 136.

"The only way": EP, *GD*, 12.

"I determined": EP, *PHL*, 94.

"filthy insane": Phrase cited in Grob, *The Mad Among Us*, 85.

"their beds": New York State official, quoted in ibid.

"an exceedingly": EP, *PHL*, 94.

"their personal cleanliness": Ibid.

"with a scream": AM, "The Better Way," 28.

"I cannot forget": EP, *PHL*, 95.

"Good morning": AM, quoted by EP, ibid.

"Doctor, I find": EP, ibid.

"Yes": AM, quoted by EP, ibid.

"It is no": EP, ibid., 96.

"I do not": Ibid., 173.

"I find, from": EP, *GD*, 1:184.

"brute beasts": EP, *PHL*, 186.

"as black as": Ibid., 96.

"Mrs. Packard": Minerva Tenney, quoted by EP, ibid., 92.

"To [Minnie's] kindness": EP, ibid.

"like a sister": Ibid.

"stripped of every": EP, *MK*, 64.

"feelings of delicacy": EP, *PHL*, 91.

"disappointed affection": Ibid., 128.

"human wreck": Ibid.

"a handsome, delicate": Ibid.

"most desperately upon": EP, *GD*, 1:229.

"Dear mamma!": Arthur Packard, quoted by EP, *PHL*, 41.

"loving caresses": EP, *GD*, 1:330.

"sweet spirit": Ibid., 2:302.

"pleasure almost unalloyed": Ibid., 1:229.

"I must love": Ibid., 4:164.

"more like the": EP, *PHL*, 128.

"I am going": Jenny Haslett, quoted by EP, ibid.

CHAPTER 18

"sudden frenzies": EP, *PHL*, 128.

"O, Mrs. Packard": Minerva Tenney, quoted by EP, ibid.

"It is no": AM, quoted by EP, ibid., 129.

"the most dangerous": EP, ibid.

"Old Mother Triplet": EP, *GD*, 2:395.

"rare and extraordinary": SO, MO, 67, in *PHL*, page 421 in PDF.

"ordinary": Ibid.

"I will kill": Mrs. Triplet, quoted by EP, *MK*, 70.

"tones the most": EP, ibid.

"I considered myself": EP, *PHL*, 130.

"seize the tumblers": Ibid.

"hurled in promiscuous": EP, "Mrs. Packard's Address," 4, in *MPE*, page 148 in PDF.

"constantly exposed": EP, printed appeal, in "Wife Behind the Bars."

"almost daily": EP, *PHL*, 127.

"begged and besought": EP, "Mrs. Packard's Address," 4, in *MPE*, page 148 in PDF.

"Even before I": EP, *PHL*, 130.

"a very cruel": Ibid., 132.

"he laid his": Ibid., 78.

"Dr. McFarland did": EP, *MPE*, 103.

"While I have": EP, *GD*, 4:184.

"Human endurance is": Davis, *Two Years and Three Months*, in Geller and Harris, *Women of the Asylum*, 49.

"Most of [the]": Ibid., 48.

"INSANE ASYLUM": Adeline T. P. Lunt, excerpts from *Behind Bars* (1871), in Geller and Harris, *Women of the Asylum*, 123.

"I fully believe": EP, *PHL*, 88.

CHAPTER 19

"Her case is": AM, letter to TP, August 11, 1860, in "The Question of Mrs. Packard's Sanity," *Northampton Free Press*, April 13, 1866.

"no outward form": AM, "Insanity and Intemperance," *AJOI* 19 (April 1863): 464.

"When I have": AM, in "Annual Meeting of the AMSAII," 98.

"a natural growth": EP, *TE*, 38.

"absence of": AM, "Minor Mental Maladies," *AJOI* 20 (July 1863): 19.

"Apparently motiveless conduct": Dr. Thomas Mayo, "Summary," *AJOI* 18 (July 1861): 83.

"no positive trace": Ray, "Doubtful Recoveries," 29.

"work, talk and": Dr. Edward Jarvis, in "Annual Meeting of the AMSAII," 112.

"insanity has its": Dr. Bell, unpublished paper, quoted in Dr. John E. Tyler, "Tests of Insanity," *AJOI* 22, nos. 1–2 (October 1865): 146.

"It was some": Dr. Gray, in "Annual Meeting of the AMSAII," 73.

"although he had": Dr. Chipley, in "Proceedings of the Nineteenth," 54.

"sooner or later": AM, in *Reports of the New Hampshire Asylum, 1846*, 17.

"well marked insanity": Ibid.

"No human being": EP, "My Reproof," *MP1*, 120.

"less able than": AM, *Reports of the New Hampshire Asylum, 1846*, 17.

"less suitable subjects": Ibid.

"Being capable of": Ibid., 16–17.

"an artfulness in": AM, letter to TP, August 11, 1860, in "The Question of Mrs. Packard's Sanity," *Northampton Free Press*, April 13, 1866.

"discontent and disaffection": Trustees of the Illinois State Hospital, *Special Report of the Trustees*, 31.

"I believed that": AM, in "Annual Meeting of the AMSAII," 93.

CHAPTER 20

"bad taste": EP, *PHL*, 177.

"I must soon": Ibid., 90.

"I smelled and": EP, *GD*, 4:51.

"poor, shriveled wheat": EP, *MPE*, 95.

"God says I": EP, *GD*, 1:241 [italics added].

"miracle": EP, "Mrs. Packard's Address," 12, in *MPE*, page 156 in PDF.

"God's grace": Ibid.

"some foreign country": Dr. Richard Dewey, c. 1871, quoted in Joseph J. Mehr, *Illinois Public Mental Health Services, 1847 to 2000: An Illustrated History* (Victoria, BC: Trafford, 2002), 77.

"emaciated almost": SO, MO, 76, in *PHL*, page 430 in PDF.

"from the ends": EP, *PHL*, 242.

"act of self-defense": Ibid.

"spells' of excessive": Ibid., 148.

"divested herself of": Ibid.

"gross indulgence": Dr. Workman, in "Proceedings of the Thirteenth," 118.

"the eating of": Ibid.

"imparting genuine sympathy": EP, *PHL*, 244.

"She is diseased": Ibid., 242.

"I have wept": EP, *GD*, 4:86.

"In alleviating their": EP, *MK*, 68.

"hug me still": EP, *GD*, 4:65.

"When we suffered": SO, MO, 72, in *PHL*, page 426 in PDF.

"I always stand": EP, *GD*, 1:157.

"Mine was the": EP, *GD*, 4:13.

"even the sight": EP, *PHL*, 145.

"I must not": Ibid., 288.

"O, Dr. McFarland": Ibid., 158.

"I can live": Ibid., 90.

"aimless purpose": EP, *GD*, 2:29.

"an absolute essential": AM, in *Tenth Biennial Report*, 26.

"restraints and neglect": Dr. John Conolly, quoted in Grob, "Institutional Origins," 36.

"so simple and": AM, in "Seventh Biennial Report," 311.

"fully alive to" and following quotations: AM, in "Proceedings of the Fourteenth," 64–65.

"rarely found necessary": Dr. Choate, in "Proceedings of the Twelfth," 74–75.

"from five to": Ibid.

"abused patients was": EP, *MP2*, 225.

"The working of": EP, *PHL*, 125.

"the journal of": Ibid.

"a secret journal": EP, *MPE*, 99.

"It shall be": EP, *PHL*, 125.

CHAPTER 21

"I put a": EP, *PHL*, 120.

"buy the privilege": Ibid., 160.

"the medium of": EP, *TE*, 69.

"I have had": Mrs. P. L. Hosmer, "Mrs. P. L. Hosmer's Letter to the Trustees," September 1863, reproduced in *Mrs. Packard's Reproof*, 29.

"The pain I": Mrs. Hosmer, letter to AM, Jan 1852 (?), New Hampshire Asylum for the Insane, call no. 1979.008, series 4, box 1, folder 14, "Patient Corres. & Bills, 1852–54," New Hampshire Historical Society, Concord, NH.

"a man who": Mrs. Hosmer, "Mrs. P. L. Hosmer's Letter," in *Mrs. Packard's Reproof*, 29.

"uninterrupted power": Ibid.

"The Doctor is": Mrs. Hosmer, quoted by EP, *PHL*, 132.

"tell facts of": Ibid.

"flesh creep": Ibid.

"I encircled this": EP, ibid., 99.

"the air in": AM, in *Tenth Biennial Report*, 35.

"the bad construction": Ibid.

"Holidays!": *Jacksonville Sentinel*, December 21, 1860.

"the mothers don't": EP, *GD*, 1:267.

"The evils of": EP, *PHL*, 125.

"trusted my deliverance": EP, *TE*, 71.

"by my own": Ibid.

"Mrs. Packard": Mrs. Hosmer, quoted by EP, ibid.

"This period of": EP, *PHL*, 125.

"*I must defend*": EP, *GD*, 1:128 [italics added].

"*The worst that*": EP, *MPE*, 69–70.

"*I can stand*": EP, *GD*, 1:252 [italics added].

"*I feel that*": EP, *MPE*, 70.

"*This Insane Asylum*": Ibid., 97.

"*For woman's sake*": EP, *PHL*, 124–25.

"*My will and*": EP, *GD*, 2:122.

"*I am not*": Ibid., 1:355.

"*The fact is*": Ibid., 1:183.

"*Woman is too*": EP, *GD*, 2:279 [italics added].

PART THREE: MY PEN SHALL RAGE

EPIGRAPHS

"*A word after*": Margaret Atwood, "Spelling," *True Stories* (New York: Simon & Schuster, 1981), 64. Reproduced with permission of Curtis Brown Group Ltd, London, on behalf of Margaret Atwood. Copyright © Margaret Atwood, 1982.

"*When I was*": Phebe B. Davis, *Two Years and Three Months*, in Geller and Harris, *Women of the Asylum*, 49.

CHAPTER 22

"*In the matter*": AM, letter to TP, April 3, 1862, in "The Question of Mrs. Packard's Sanity," *Northampton Free Press*, April 13, 1866.

"*By my experiences*": EP, *PHL*, 14.

"*smelted by*": EP, *TE*, 44.

"*thinking machine*": EP, *GD*, 2:20.

"*I never needed*": Ibid., 2:75.

"*hurricane-blast*": Ibid., 2:98.

"*humanity-crushing institution*": Ibid., 2:211.

"*a feeling of*": EP, *PHL*, 273.

"*extreme jealousy*": Diagnosis of the first patient admitted to the Illinois State Hospital, hospital admissions book, November 3, 1851, quoted in several sources, including Heather Harlan Bacus, "Old Buildings and Impaired Minds," undated newspaper article but likely c. 1972; in Jacksonville State Hospital folder, Sangamon Valley Collection, Lincoln Library, Springfield, IL.

"*If the prisoner*": Shedd, "Testimony of Mrs. Tirzah F. Shedd," in "Mrs. Packard's Coadjutor's Testimony," 137, in *PHL*, page 491 in PDF.

"*subduing treatment*": EP, printed appeal, in "Wife Behind the Bars."

"*the patient who*": AM, in *Reports of the New Hampshire Asylum, 1846*, 23.

"*I have in*": AM, letter to TP, February 2, 1861, in "The Question of Mrs. Packard's Sanity," *Northampton Free Press*, April 13, 1866.

"*the possibility of*": AM, in "Packard Insanity Case."

"*He is trying*": EP, *PHL*, 116.

"*all the work*": TP, letter to EP, c. spring 1861, quoted in *PHL*, 115.

"*My daughter did*": TP, *TPD*, 80 (1861).

"*very important age*": EP, *MK*, 49.

"*How can a*": EP, *PHL*, 115.

"*Is there not*": EP, *TE*, 111.

"*When I visited*": TP, *TPD*, 79 (1861).

"*I have done*": EP, *GD*, 2:351.

"*He is answerable*": EP, *TE*, 48.

"a being whom": Ibid., 34.

"I can protect": EP, *GD*, 1:128–29.

"Yes, husband": EP, *TE*, 34.

"Everything in her": AM, letter to TP, April 3, 1862, in "The Question of Mrs. Packard's Sanity," *Northampton Free Press*, April 13, 1866.

"Mrs. Packard, do": AM, quoted by EP, *MP2*, 156.

"would be an": EP, *PHL*, 192.

"I never saw": TP, speech as reported by patient Mrs. Page, quoted by EP, ibid., 53.

"new effort for": Samuel Ware, letter to TP, July 17, 1861, in "The Question of Mrs. Packard's Sanity," *Northampton Free Press*, May 1, 1866.

"Mrs. Packard": AM, letter to EP's friends, including Mr. David Field, as quoted by EP, *PHL*, 285.

"slight": Elizabeth Packard's admittance record at the Illinois State Hospital, June 19, 1860, Barbara Sapinsley Papers.

"has become": AM, letter to EP's friends, including Mr. David Field, as quoted by EP, *PHL*, 285.

"I do not": AM, letter to David Field, ibid.

"forms of law": TP, quoted by EP, ibid., 43.

"no hope of": EP, ibid., 76.

"think this place": EP, *GD*, 4:58.

"I shall never": EP, *TE*, 31.

"You, Dr. McFarland": EP, *PHL*, 213.

"I never regretted": Ibid., 214.

"slow constitutional deterioration": AM, in "Sixth Biennial Report," 275.

"The cheek": Ibid.

"sedative influence": "Autobiography of the Insane," *Journal of Psychological Medicine and Mental Pathology* 8 (1855): 353.

"power and": Ibid.

"What is very": EP, *GD*, 1:154.

"Underground Express": Mentioned throughout EP's books, including ibid., 2:323.

"assist in any": Appendix, "Extracts from Rules and Regulations Referred to in this Report," Chapter X: Attendants and Assistants, General Rules, Section 15, *Special Report of the Trustees*, 108.

"Where woman is": EP, *PHL*, 154.

"aroused the just": Ibid., 183.

"possessed more than": EP, *GD*, 4:57.

"apples in abundance": EP, *PHL*, 287.

"You know I": Ibid., 252 [italics added].

"a mission upon": AM, in *Ninth Biennial Report*, 34.

"With resolution": EP, *PHL*, 252–53.

"To be God's": Ibid., 253.

"a disposition wantonly": AM, "Minor Mental Maladies," 18.

"more than lawyer-like": AM, in "Packard Insanity Case."

"She gives us": AM, letter to TP, April 3, 1862, in "The Question of Mrs. Packard's Sanity," *Northampton Free Press*, April 13, 1866.

CHAPTER 23

"a quiet class": EP, *GD*, 4:47.

"Quiet maniacs!": Ibid.

"until my soul": Mrs. Hosmer, "Mrs. Hosmer's Letter to Miss Dix," reproduced in *Mrs. Packard's Reproof*, 30.

Conversation between EP and attendant: EP, *PHL*, 109.

"I am becoming": Ibid., 216.

"Mrs. Packard, stop": Ibid., 108.

"locked in her": Ibid., 107.

"accompanied with": Ibid.

"calculated to convert": Ibid.

"red with the": Ibid., 108.

"so convulsed her" and following quotations: Ibid., 228.

"their hands and feet" and following quotations: Testimony of Miss Kane, former attendant at the Illinois State Hospital for the Insane, Report of the Investigating Committee (1867), 38.

"silly behaviour": Quoted in Matthew Smith, "The Healing Waters: The Long History of Using Water to Cure Madness," *Psychology Today*, October 9, 2015, https://www.psychologytoday.com/us/blog/short-history-mental-health/201510/the-healing-waters.

"convenience" and following quotations: AM, "The Better Way," 17.

"but to confess": AM, "Appendix," in *Special Report of the Trustees*, 103.

"The best attendants": Dr. John E. Tyler, "On the Care of the Violent Insane," read as part of "Proceedings of the Twelfth," 73.

"No humane regulations": AM, "The Better Way," 28.

"never to be": Report of the Investigating Committee (1867), quoted in *MP2*, 263.

"the right of": Ibid.

"The remark is": AM, in "Eighth Biennial Report," 360.

"in proportion as": Testimony of Dr. Richard J. Patterson before the investigating committee, in *Special Report of the Trustees*, 77.

"on the best": Appendix, "Extracts from Rules and Regulations Referred to in this Report," Chapter XI: Supervisors and Their Especial Duties, in ibid., 108.

"Giving vent to": EP, *GD*, 4:103.

"where [their] word": Lake, "Testimony of Mrs. Caroline E. Lake," in "Mrs. Packard's Coadjutor's Testimony," 140, in *PHL*, page 494 in PDF.

"mere phantoms": EP, *PHL*, 210–11.

"It is of": Lake, "Testimony of Mrs. Caroline E. Lake," in "Mrs. Packard's Coadjutor's Testimony," 141, in *PHL*, page 495 in PDF.

"What is an": EP, *PHL*, 122.

"The record of": Ibid., 175.

"You cannot imagine": Ibid., 201.

"this field of": Ibid., 136.

CHAPTER 24

"An appeal in": "Appeal" (June 18, 1862), reproduced in *Mrs. Packard's Reproof*, 22.

"at the request": *Mrs. Packard's Reproof*, 22.

"burden": J. C. and Celia Coe, "Appeal," reproduced in *Mrs. Packard's Reproof*, 27.

"large, coarse": EP, *PHL*, 206.

"an expression of": SO, *MO*, 46, in *PHL*, page 400 in PDF.

"I have many": Ibid., 52, in *PHL*, page 406 in PDF.

"[I] found Miss": J. C. and Celia Coe, "Appeal," reproduced in *Mrs. Packard's Reproof*, 23–24.

"until their faces": Ibid., 25.

"It is the": Ibid.

"May this mute": Ibid., 27.

"in readiness": Ibid.

"How would you": EP, "My Reproof," *MP1*, 133.

"If Dr. McFarland": Mrs. Grere, quoted by EP, *PHL*, 263.

CHAPTER 25

"Madness was upon": Elizabeth Van Lew, "Occasional Journal," Van Lew Papers, New York Public Library, quoted in Karen Abbott, *Liar, Temptress, Soldier, Spy: Four Women Undercover in the Civil War* (New York: Harper Perennial, 2015), 41.

"entombed alive": EP, *PHL*, 222.

"of what is": Ibid.

"You may join": EP, *GD*, 1:335.

"dared to espouse" and following quotation: Ibid., 4:39.

"giant evil": EP, *GD*, 2:171.

"The North may": Ibid., 2:121.

"For as is": EP, *TE*, 156.

"mischievous purposes": AM, during his cross-examination of Dr. Richard J. Patterson before the investigating committee, quoted in *Special Report of the Trustees*, 79.

"evil influences": AM, "Appendix," in *Special Report of the Trustees*, 101.

"my treasures": EP, *PHL*, 330.

"insulting and abusive": SO, MO, 44, in *PHL*, page 398 in PDF.

"lift up my": EP, *TE*, 117.

"get out of": EP, *GD*, 4:77.

"temporal destiny entirely": EP, *PHL*, 270.

"My reason and": Ibid., 259.

"Still, there is": Ibid.

"If something is": President Abraham Lincoln, in Harry Hansen, *The Civil War: A History* (New York: Penguin, 1991), 174.

"I do hope": EP, *GD*, 1:214.

"that in every": EP, *PHL*, 313.

"Could I not": Ibid.

"fan this embryo": EP, *MK*, 94.

"I intend to": EP, *PHL*, 188.

"modify [their] thoughts": Review of *Moral Medicine*, 160.

"exceedingly sorrowful": EP, *PHL*, 259.

"beloved sisters": SO, MO, 26, in *PHL*, page 380 in PDF.

"dare to do": EP, "A Defense," *TE*, 95.

"protector, instead": Ibid.

"I find it": Natascha Kampusch, 2010 interview with the *Guardian*, quoted in Kathryn Westcott, "What Is Stockholm Syndrome?" BBC News, August 22, 2013, https://www.bbc.co.uk/news/magazine-22447726 [italics added].

CHAPTER 26

"a reasonable and": EP, *PHL*, 266.

"new spirit seemed": Ibid., 152–53.

"free and full": Ibid., 305–6.

"It is a rule": Ray, "Doubtful Recoveries," 31.

"it was thought": EP on what Dr. Tenny reportedly said, *Mrs. Packard's Reproof*, 20.

"every [strait]jacket": Mrs. S. A. Kain, "Letter from an Attendant in the Jacksonville Insane Asylum," January 1866, in "Insanity a Crime!" *Daily Illinois State Register*, February 22, 1867.

"no more than": *Special Report of the Trustees*, 27.

"liars by nature": Isaac Ray, "The Popular Feeling Toward the Hospitals for the Insane," *AJOI* 9 (1852): 36–65, in Geller and Harris, *Women of the Asylum*, 28.

"tendency to have": Ibid.

"but small importance": *Special Report of the Trustees*, 85.

"unreliability of": Ibid.

"had great influence": "Third Annual Report of the Trustees of State Lunatic Hospital, December, 1835," in *Reports and Other Documents*, 95.

"intimate friends": Dr. J. Parigot, "Legislation on Lunacy," *AJOI* 21 (October 1864): 215.

"but relatives by": Ibid.

"imprisoned…simply": EP, "Mrs. Packard's Address," 2, in *MPE*, page 146 in PDF.

"tasteful head-dress": EP, *PHL*, 306.

"queenlike feeling": Ibid.

"I have been": Ibid., 287.

"the sanctimonious gravity": Ibid., 308.

"Mrs. Packard": Mr. Brown, quoted by EP, *MPE*, 6.

"in a quiet": EP, ibid.

"could almost hear": EP, *PHL*, 307.

"a spiritual woman": EP, "Statement Before the Trustees," *TE*, 23.

"I now ask": Ibid., 24.

"so still": EP, *MPE*, 7.

"You say": EP, "Statement Before the Trustees," *TE*, 24–25.

"They did not": EP, *MPE*, 7.

"the darkest parts": Ibid.

"exposed their wicked": Ibid.

"So long as": EP, *TE*, 28.

"manifested a kindly": Ibid., 39.

"benevolent intentions": EP, *GD*, 1:208.

"not as [she]": EP, *TE*, 37.

"a natural growth": Ibid., 38.

"My husband placing": Ibid.

"roar of laughter": Ibid.

"accompanied by": Ibid.

"hear roars and": Ibid., 29.

"protested against": AM, in "Annual Meeting of the AMSAII," 91.

"In relation to": Trustees' Records, September 4, 1862, quoted in *Special Report of the Trustees*, 31.

"I regard them": EP, *TE*, 39.

"I am satisfied": Ibid., 31.

"The tide has": Ibid.

"I proposed to": AM, in "Annual Meeting of the AMSAII," 91.

CHAPTER 27

Conversation between AM and EP: Recounted by EP in *PHL*, 310.

"Write what you": AM, quoted by EP, *MPE*, 111.

"Well done": EP, *PHL*, 311.

"to liberty": "A Friend of Justice," *Chicago Tribune*, December 26, 1867, in *MK*, 101.

"It seems to": EP, *MPE*, 82.

"hitherto prison-bound": Ibid., 112.

"The subject so": EP, *TE*, 18.

"Reason taught me": EP, *GD*, 4:137.

"so that my": Ibid.

"the most delightful": EP, *MPE*, 112.

"Write it out": AM, quoted by EP, *PHL*, 311.

"their names will": EP, *GD*, 2:166.

"only a 'glance'": Ibid., 1:10.

"an ordinary book": EP, *MPE*, 111.

"I leave the": EP, *GD*, 1:10.

"Now we are": Ibid., 2:55.

"I intend to": Ibid., 2:115.

"When I get": Ibid., 1:296.

"Home! Sweet home!": Ibid., 2:308.

"Mrs. Packard often": Ibid., 1:360–61.

"see my baby": Ibid., 1:165.

"upon keeping the": EP, *TE*, 16.

"great battery": EP, *MPE*, 100.

"My book is": EP, *GD*, 2:167.

"pet": EP, *TE*, 62.

"pride": Ibid.

"a transcript of": Ibid., 7.

"They seemed to": EP, *GD*, 1:87.

"one breath": Ibid., 1:88.

"I tell you": Ibid., 2:18.

CHAPTER 28

"shall be then": Abraham Lincoln, Emancipation Proclamation, January 1, 1863, https://www.archives.gov/exhibits/featured-documents/emancipation-proclamation/transcript.html.

"If you continue": EP, *GD*, 2:56–57.

"The [insane] patient": Ibid., 2:212.

"be allowed to": Ibid., 2:31.

"I intend to": Ibid., 2:210.

"Does our government": Ibid., 1:269 and 1:287.

"mean, and ungenerous": Ibid., 2:359.

"We don't want": Ibid., 2:47.

"half affair": Ibid., 1:269.

"Put woman into": Ibid., 2:359.

"Never let a": Ibid., 2:220–21.

"Dare to do": Ibid., 2:223.

"He trusts me": Ibid., 2:19.

"great want": EP, *PHL*, 318.

"No man on": Mrs. Packard's *Reproof*, 3.

"noble protector": EP, *GD*, 1:224.

"bound with joy": EP, *PHL*, 316.

"the inauguration": Ibid.

"such a tranquilizing": EP, *MK*, 76–77.

"This I do": Ibid., 77.

"magnetisms mingled": Ibid.

"not one word": Ibid.

"He is the first": Ibid.

"As he had": EP, *PHL*, 318.

"I don't see": Isaac Packard, quoted by EP, *GD*, 4:181–82.

"that he feared": TP's letter to Toffy Packard, as quoted by Toffy, in EP, *TE*, 57.

CHAPTER 29

"a very common": EP, *MPE*, 112–13.

"universal sensation": Attendant, quoted by EP, *PHL*, 335.

"I will die": EP, *GD*, 1:170.

"to sit under": EP, *TE*, 84–85.

"extraordinary power": AM, letter to TP, March 14, 1863, in "The Question of Mrs. Packard's Sanity," *Northampton Free Press*, April 13, 1866.

"a mental level": AM, in "Eighth Biennial Report," 367.

"The wonderful power": SO, MO, 72, in *PHL*, page 426 in PDF.

"read in our": Feedback from a male reader, as quoted by EP, *MPE*, 115.

"She'll be in": Quoted by EP, ibid., 113.

"If this prophetess": Ibid.

"When she came": SO, MO, 72, in *PHL*, page 426 in PDF.

"Such an ardent": Ibid.

"The boldness with": Ibid.

"the brightest oasis": EP, *MP1*, 288.

"beautifully wrought white": SO, MO, 53, in PHL, page 406 in PDF.

"pledge of her": SO, MO, 53, in *PHL*, page 407 in PDF.

"This inestimable woman": Ibid., 35, in *PHL*, page 389 in PDF.

"You needn't speak": Mary Bailey (attendant), quoted by SO, ibid., 44, in *PHL*, page 398 in PDF.

"If Mrs. Olsen": Mrs. McFarland, ibid., 43, in *PHL*, page 397 in PDF.

"unmanageable, mischief-making": Mary Bailey's report of SO to AM, quoted by SO, ibid., 45, in *PHL*, page 399 in PDF.

"She don't like": EP, *GD*, 2:25.

"She calls me": Ibid.

"I wonder": Ibid.

"frighten away": EP, *TE*, 9.

"weep with joy": SO, MO, 71, in *PHL*, page 425 in PDF.

"conversed in very": Ibid., 73, in *PHL*, page 427 in PDF.

"there wasn't quite": Testimony of Dr. H. A. Johnson before the investigating committee, in *Special Report of the Trustees*, 80.

"charnel house": SO, MO, 46, in *PHL*, page 400 in PDF.

"very filthy women": Ibid., 47, in *PHL*, page 401 in PDF.

"indecently torn": Ibid.

"unfragrant water": Ibid., 47–48, in *PHL*, pages 401–2 in PDF.

"did not see": Ibid., 71, in *PHL*, page 425 in PDF.

"Sometimes it appeared": Ibid., 52–53, in *PHL*, pages 406–7 in PDF.

"Dr. McFarland knows": Lizzie Bonner, quoted in ibid., 53, in *PHL*, page 407 in PDF.

"Repentance or exposure": EP, "My Reproof," *MP1*, 137.

"All intercourse between": "Proclamation," quoted by SO, MO, 75, in *PHL*, page 429 in PDF.

"universal sensation": Attendant, quoted by EP, *PHL*, 335.

"silent hisses": SO, MO, 75, in *PHL*, page 429 in PDF.

"bitter tears": Ibid.

"We all felt": Ibid., 74, in *PHL*, page 428 in PDF.

"reign of terror": Ibid., 76, in *PHL*, page 430 in PDF.

"We were seldom": Ibid., 75, in *PHL*, page 429 in PDF.

"and all who": Ibid., 76, in *PHL*, page 430 in PDF.

"Don't kill me": Ibid.

"its most valuable": Trustees of the Illinois State Hospital, *Special Report of the Trustees*, 59.

"even an unworthy": Testimony of Patterson, in *Special Report of the Trustees*, 73.

"I feel that": EP, *GD*, 4:279.

"no use, and": Ibid.

"mild and gentle": SO, MO, 77, in *PHL*, page 431 in PDF.

"unmistakeable portents": Ibid., 76, in *PHL*, page 430 in PDF.

CHAPTER 30

"good talking times": EP, *PHL*, 119.

"reign of terror": SO, MO, 76, in *PHL*, page 430 in PDF.

"the capacity": "Eighth Biennial Report," 332.

"full to overflowing": AM, in ibid., 372.

"extreme limit": Ibid., 351.

"been in so": "Eighth Biennial Report," 331.

"great professional skill": Ibid., 332.

"indefinitely postponed": Trustees' Records, December 3, 1862, quoted in *Special Report of the Trustees*, 31.

"I never felt": EP, *TE*, 83.

"shut their ears": Ibid., 82.

"There is no": Ibid.

"sickened": Ibid., 81.

"If grief can": Ibid., 83.

"broken and": Ibid.

"It is proper": Trustees of the Illinois State Hospital, *Special Report of the Trustees*, 31.

"In the…retaining": "Eighth Biennial Report," 337.

"very much grieved": EP, *TE*, 83.

Conversation between EP and AM: Recounted by EP, ibid., 81–82.

"It shall be": EP, *GD*, 2:71–72.

"Perhaps I am": EP, *TE*, 83.

"dead cart": Shedd, "Testimony of Mrs. Tirzah F. Shedd," in "Mrs. Packard's Coadjutor's Testimony," 136, in *PHL*, page 490 in PDF.

"hasty spade": SO, MO, 40, in *PHL*, page 394 in PDF.

"a beast": EP, *MP2*, 271.

"in the dead": Ibid., 270.

"the saddest month": SO, MO, 78, in *PHL*, page 432 in PDF.

"sense of utter": Ibid.

"daughters of affliction": Ibid.

"dim, shadowy": Ibid.

"undermining of every": Ibid.

"grass before the": Francis Augustin O'Reilly, *The Fredericksburg Campaign* (Baton Rouge: Louisiana State University Press, 2003), 318.

"Doubt—suspense—uncertainty": EP, *TE*, 84.

"The faces of all": SO, MO, 78, in *PHL*, page 432 in PDF.

"Darkness, cold and": Ibid.

"the bell heavily": Ibid.

PART FOUR: DEAL WITH THE DEVIL?

EPIGRAPHS

"We must have": Marie Curie, as quoted in *Madame Curie: A Biography* (Hachette Books, 1937) by Eve Curie, 158.

"She stood in": Elizabeth Edwards, as quoted in Sarah Netter, "Elizabeth Edwards: In Her Own Words," ABC News, December 7, 2010, https://abcnews.go.com/US/elizabeth-edwards-words/story?id=12337723.

CHAPTER 31

"On this book": EP, *MK*, 83.

"single anchor": Ibid.

"sinking ship": Ibid.

"He has given": EP, *GD*, 2:404.

"argued and discussed": EP, *MK*, 83.

"Vain my logic": Ibid.

"Nothing but a": Ibid., 82.

"reign of terror": SO, MO, 76, in *PHL*, page 430 in PDF.

"only a protraction": Ibid., 79, in *PHL*, page 433 in PDF.

"all felt ourselves": Ibid., 81, in *PHL*, page 435 in PDF.

"At every opportunity": Ibid.

"military activity": Ibid., 85, in *PHL*, page 439 in PDF.

"tangled up in": Ibid., 84, in *PHL*, page 438 in PDF.

"Looking glasses": Ibid., 85, in *PHL*, page 439 in PDF.

"little uneasiness": Ibid., 86, in *PHL*, page 440 in PDF.

"The wind was": Ibid., 83, in *PHL*, page 437 in PDF.

"so scattered": Ibid.

"Orders were suddenly": Ibid., 87, in *PHL*, page 441 in PDF.

"blasted reputation": EP, *MK*, 95.

"in a state": Ibid.

"This book is": Ibid.

"It is my": Ibid., 83.

"as an act": Ibid., 82.

"my heart had": Ibid., 86.

"willingly offered": EP, *PHL*, 327.

"Dr. McFarland": EP, letter to AM, January 19, 1863, reproduced in *MK*, 83–85.

"our future existence": EP, *MK*, 86.

"I did then": EP, *MP1*, 382.

"This note must": EP, letter to AM, January 19, 1863, reproduced in *MK*, 85.

"without uttering one": EP, *MK*, 87.

"low, respectful bow": Ibid.

"with a slight": Ibid.

"the highest expectations": Ibid.

"I considered this": Ibid.

CHAPTER 32

"If you fail": EP, letter to AM, quoted in *PHL*, 320.

"almost hear my": EP, *PHL*, 320.

Conversation between EP and AM: Recounted by EP, ibid.

"Good sleep": Ibid., 321.

"as good an": Ibid.

"Duties are ours": EP, *GD*, 2:12 [italics added].

Conversation between EP and AM: Recounted by EP, *PHL*, 322.

"God's purpose would": EP, *GD*, 2:415.

"knowing the dog": Ibid.

"He will return": EP, *MK*, 88.

"There seemed": Ibid.

"this secret": Ibid.

"This…was": Ibid.

"unasked, with an": EP, *PHL*, 326.

"delightful work": Ibid.

"I never": Ibid.

"entire trust": Ibid.

"should trust him": EP, *TE*, 28.

"I had no": EP, *PHL*, 326.

"dearest friend": EP, *GD*, 2:351.

"browbeat her": EP, *MPE*, 81.

"foul play": Ibid.

"open to all": Eighth Annual Report of the Trustees of the State Lunatic Hospital, at Northampton, October, 1863 (Boston: Wright & Potter, 1864), 9, Northampton State Hospital Annual Reports (RB 035), Special Collections and University Archives, University of Massachusetts Amherst Libraries, http://credo.library.umass.edu/view /full/murb035-y1863-i001.

"none have ever": Ibid., 10.

"Elizabeth P. W.": Trustees' Records, March 4, 1863, quoted in *Special Report of the Trustees*, 31.

CHAPTER 33

"a theme of": SO, MO, 103, in *PHL*, page 457 in PDF.

"I felt that": EP, *GD*, 4:219.

"to secure for": Ibid., 4:218.

"I felt": Ibid., 4:220.

"I had full": Ibid., 4:219–20.

"I considered myself": Ibid., 4:222.

"sufficient ability": "Eighth Biennial Report," 338.

"a hodgepodge": Don Harrison Doyle, *The Social Order of a Frontier Community: Jacksonville, Illinois, 1825–70* (Urbana: University of Illinois Press, 1978), 199.

"simply a boarder": EP, *GD*, 4:222.

"I really felt": EP, *PHL*, 329.

CHAPTER 34

"dazzles and bewilders": "The Metropolitan Hotel," *New York Herald*, September 2, 1852.

"palaces of": Ibid.

"rich and inviting": Ibid.

"got tired": AM, in "Annual Meeting of the AMSAII," 91.

"infinite trouble": Ibid.

"I proposed to": Ibid.

"at any time": Daily Illinois State Register, November 29, 1883.

"free and full": EP, *PHL*, 305–6.

"I do not": AM, in "Annual Meeting of the AMSAII," 91.

"a spiritual woman": EP, "Statement Before the Trustees," *TE*, 23.

"Write what you": AM, quoted by EP, *MPE*, 111.

"dexterously": AM, in *Ninth Biennial Report*, 33.

"may utter almost": Ibid.

"As there always": AM, letter to TP, March 14, 1863, in "The Question of Mrs. Packard's Sanity," *Northampton Free Press*, April 13, 1866.

"convince the most": Ibid.

"most effectually": Ibid.

"absurd and childish": Ibid.

"Are not women": EP, *GD*, 1:269.

"Put woman into": Ibid., 2:359 [italics added].

"unconcerned about what": Ibid., 2:19.

"The delusion was": AM, in "Annual Meeting of the AMSAII," 92.

"Her insanity consists": AM, official certificate regarding EP's sanity, May 5, 1863, in "The Question of Mrs. Packard's Sanity," *Northampton Free Press*, May 8, 1866.

"Is not a": EP, *GD*, 2:228 [italics added].

"He can't be": Ibid., 2:395.

"stirring up the": TP reporting what AM told him by letter about EP, TPD, 80 (1862).

"most welcome": AM, in *Ninth Biennial Report*, 35.

"The extraordinary amount": AM, letter to TP, March 14, 1863, in "The Question of Mrs. Packard's Sanity," *Northampton Free Press*, April 13, 1866.

"I hereby certify": AM, official certificate regarding EP's sanity, May 5, 1863, in "The Question of Mrs. Packard's Sanity," *Northampton Free Press*, May 8, 1866.

"I care nothing": AM, letter to Mrs. Alma E. Eaton, in "Packard Controversy."

CHAPTER 35

"Mrs. Packard must": Attendant, quoted by EP, *PHL*, 331.

"He then shook": EP, *GD*, 4:226.

"As to accompanying": EP, *PHL*, 331.

"tremor of excitement": EP, *GD*, 4:91.

"No flash of": SO, MO, 105, in *PHL*, page 459 in PDF.

"Mrs. Packard": Dr. Tenny, quoted by EP, *PHL*, 332.

"like water spilt": EP, *GD*, 4:231.

"Dr. Tenny": EP, *PHL*, 332 [italics added].

"Take Mrs. Packard": Ibid.

"I held myself": Ibid.

"None came": EP, *GD*, 4:227.

"Mr. Packard's wishes": Ibid.

"No, sir": Ibid.

"I knew not": EP, *PHL*, 333–34.

"throbbing heart": SO, MO, 105, in *PHL*, page 459 in PDF.

"fast gathering": Ibid.

"She has gone": Ibid.

"Some lectured on": Ibid., 106, in *PHL*, page 460 in PDF.

"I maintain": EP, *TE*, 92.

"June 18/63": Elizabeth Packard's discharge record at the Illinois State Hospital, Jacksonville Record 1:232, June 18, 1863, Barbara Sapinsley Papers.

"The one": EP, *GD*, 4:228.

"I had found": Ibid., 4:243.

"We shall miss": Attendant, quoted by EP, *PHL*, 335.

"in any suspicious": EP, *GD*, 4:241.

"as if I": Ibid., 4:241–42.

"I had no": Ibid., 4:238.

PART FIVE: TURNING POINTS

EPIGRAPHS

"I am not": Audre Lorde, "The Uses of Anger: Women Responding to Racism," keynote speech, National Women's Studies Association Conference, June 1981, Storrs, CT, transcript, https://www.blackpast.org /african-american-history/speeches-african-american-history/1981-audre-lorde-uses-anger-women -responding-racism/.

"Woman has her": Elizabeth Blackwell (the first woman to receive a medical degree in the United States), letter to Emily Collins, August 12, 1848, quoted in *History of Woman Suffrage*, 1:90.

CHAPTER 36

"my truest and": EP, *GD*, 4:238.

"as welcome": Ibid., 4:239.

"little, weak-minded": Ibid., 4:265.

"If she ever": TP, quoted by EP, *MP2*, 9.

"as a kind": EP, *PHL*, 274.

"I cried so hard": EP, *GD*, 4:246.

"first and chief": Ibid., 4:245.

"field of letters": Ibid.

"tiresome negotiations": SO, MO, 111, in *PHL*, page 465 in PDF.

"in no respect": EP in De Wolf, "Public Institutions."

"entertained none": Ibid.

"There is not": EP, letter to Libby Packard, August 4, 1863, in "The Question of Mrs. Packard's Sanity," *Northampton Free Press*, May 8, 1866.

"I found the": EP, *MK*, 9.

"I find it": EP, *GD*, 4:251.

"my treacherous friend": EP, letter to AM, August 10, 1863, in ibid., 4:250.

"Mr. Packard is": EP, ibid., 4:261.

"an act of treachery": Ibid., 4:276.

"thought the book": Ibid.

"one spring of": EP, *MK*, 57.

"He is no less": EP, *GD*, 4:276.

"rattlesnakes": Ibid., 4:261.

"and then drag": Ibid.

"The very word": Ibid., 1:96.

"abandon the project": EP, *MK*, 9.

"for the present": Ibid.

"The stone of truth": EP, letter to AM, August 10, 1863, in *GD*, 4:252.

"even in defiance": EP, *MK*, 10.

"should self-defense": EP, *TE*, 121.

"It shall be": EP, *PHL*, 125.

"done what she": Ibid.

"The pain is": EP, *GD*, 2:309.

"alienated from me": EP, letter to TP, July 3, 1863, in "The Question of Mrs. Packard's Sanity," *Northampton Free Press*, April 13, 1866.

CHAPTER 37

"wet and sloppy": EP, *MP2*, 10.

Conversation between EP and boy: Ibid., 11.

"good talking": EP, *PHL*, 119.

Conversation between EP and George Packard: Recounted by EP, *MP2*, 11–12.

"only one side": EP, *MPE*, 89.

"The other side": Ibid.

"The result": Ibid.

"injurious interference": TP, "An Account of the Insanity Case of Mrs. E. P. W. Packard of Manteno, Illinois," *Gazette and Courier*, April 4, 1864.

"Their speeches came": Ibid.

"great trouble to": TP, *TPD*, 80 (1861).

"he preached until": EP on what she was told about TP, *MPE*, 77.

"in order to": EP, *MK*, 35.

"We lived without": TP, *TPD*, 80 (1863).

"desolate-looking": EP, *MP2*, 13.

"extra amount of": Ibid.

"to do my": Ibid.

"the marriage contract": EP, letter to TP, July 1, 1863, in "The Question of Mrs. Packard's Sanity," *Northampton Free Press*, May 8, 1866.

"the most efficient": EP, *MPE*, 10.

CHAPTER 38

"[You are] going": EP, *MP2*, 13.

"perfect image": Dr. Chandler, quoted by EP, *GD*, 2:301.

"as good and": EP, ibid., 2:302.

"little daughter" and following quotation: Lizzie Packard (the name TP used for Libby Packard), certificate, July 6, 1864, in "The Question of Mrs. Packard's Sanity," *Northampton Free Press*, May 1, 1866.

"My daughter": EP, *MP2*, 13.

"No": TP, quoted in ibid.

"You shall hear": Ibid., 14.

"they needed cleaning": Mrs. Blessing, court testimony, in Moore, GT, in *MPE*, 36.

"It looked as": Mrs. Haslett, court testimony, in ibid.

"bathing, toilet duties": EP, *MP2*, 16.

"required them to": Ibid.

"It don't need": TP, quoted in ibid., 14.

"Let me show": EP, ibid.

"his hand upraised": Ibid.

"loud and most": Ibid.

"I forbid your": TP, quoted in ibid.

"I exchanged no": EP, ibid., 13.

"three years was": EP, *MP1*, 65.

"not to respect": *Kankakee Gazette*, reproduced in "The Case of Mrs. Packard," *Chicago Tribune*, January 28, 1864.

"I have seen": Joseph E. Labrie, court testimony, in Moore, GT, in *MPE*, 32.

"until they had": EP, *MK*, 17.

"mischievous intermeddlers": TP, "Account of the Insanity Case."

"meeting her secretly": Ibid.

"A Manteno mob": TP, *TPD*, 81 (1863).

"a couple of": Ibid.

"the chief instigators": TP, "Account of the Insanity Case."

"O what scenes": TP, TPD, 81 (1863).

"to regulate": Ibid.

"I cannot": Ibid.

"good treatment": TP, citing the certificates of Hervey Severance, Mrs. Sybil T. Dole, Samuel Packard, and Elizabeth W. Packard (Libby) about their observations of this meeting, in "Account of the Insanity Case."

"had a great": Ibid.

"did not wish": Ibid.

"left the room": Ibid.

CHAPTER 39

"great comfort": TP, TPD, 37.

"prejudicing and influencing": Thomas P. Bonfield, certificate supplied to TP, February 19, 1864, in "Reply to Mr. Sewall's Rejoinder," *Boston Daily Advertiser*, May 3, 1865.

"took an inventory": EP, MP2, 15.

"The entire house": Ibid.

"every stone": Ibid.

"I...refused a woman": Samuel Packard, certificate supplied to TP, June 1, 1864, in "Reply to Mr. Sewall's Rejoinder."

"This nation, under": Abraham Lincoln, "The Gettysburg Address," November 19, 1863, https://www.history.com/topics/american-civil-war/gettysburg-address.

"would not let": Mrs. Blessing, court testimony, in Moore, GT, in *MPE*, 36.

"striking": Bill of complaint for divorce, Kankakee County Circuit Court, February 8, 1864.

"dragging [her] by": Ibid.

"His sympathy": EP, GD, 2:112.

"false and slanderous": Abijah H. Dole, Hervey Severance, Sibyl T. Dole, and Laura E. Dole, certificate supplied to TP, November 24, 1863, in "The Question of Mrs. Packard's Sanity," *Northampton Free Press*, May 8, 1866.

"Mrs. Packard, the": Ibid.

"To deprive the": Ray, "American Legislation on Insanity," 25.

"The door to": Joseph E. Labrie, court testimony, in Moore, GT, in *MPE*, 33.

"released from her": Mrs. Haslett, court testimony, in ibid., 36.

"protection from": Ibid.

"I advised her": Ibid.

"Would it not": EP, MPE, 63.

"favored her": AM, letter to TP, December 18, 1863, quoted by EP, ibid., 9.

CHAPTER 40

"Mr. Packard had": Dr. J. D. Mann, court testimony, in Moore, GT, in *MPE*, 32.

"I was there": Ibid.

"She said she": Joseph H. Way, court testimony, in ibid., 21.

Following quotations: Ibid.

"some calamity would": J. W. Brown, court testimony, in ibid., 21.

"It [is] my": TP, TPD, 81 (1864).

"She gave it": Ibid.

"almost totally": "The Weather," *Chicago Tribune*, January 13, 1864.

"Four intermeddlers": TP, TPD, 41 ("Wife's Insanity—1860").

"Thus was my": EP, MP2, 15–16.

KATE MOORE

CHAPTER 41

"We command you": State of Illinois, Kankakee County, "The People of the State of Illinois, to Theophilus Packard," January 11, 1864, as reproduced in Moore, GT, in *MPE*, 15–16.

"a rise of": "The Cold Term," *Chicago Tribune*, January 14, 1864.

"to avail myself": EP, *MP2*, 17.

"as a case": Dr. Prince, Superintendent of the State Lunatic Hospital at Northampton, Massachusetts, letter to TP, quoted by EP, ibid.

"O, when one": EP, *PHL*, 273.

"Three long years": EP, "My Plea for Married Women's Emancipation made before Connecticut Legislature in New Haven State House, June 1866," in *MP2*, 405.

"I should run": EP, *GD*, 1:171–72.

"In a few days": EP, *MPE*, 10.

"Stranger, please": EP, *MP2*, 20.

"If I should": EP, *MPE*, 10.

"responsible citizens": *Kankakee Gazette*, article reproduced in "The Case of Mrs. Packard," *Chicago Tribune*, January 28, 1864.

"ill-arranged seats": "The Court House," *Kankakee Gazette*, January 23, 1868.

"very difficult": Ibid.

"enraged": TP, "The Charge Against Rev. Mr. Packard," *Boston Daily Advertiser*, April 4, 1865.

"seething": Ibid.

"I have neglected": EP, *PHL*, 194.

"Devoid of all": *Portrait and Biographical Record of Kankakee County, Illinois* (Chicago: Lake City, 1893), 242.

"Steve": John M. Palmer, ed., *The Bench and Bar of Illinois: Historical and Reminiscent*, vol. 2 (Chicago: Lewis, 1899), 980.

"the life and soul": Ibid.

"hosts of friends": Ibid.

"one of the": Ibid., 979.

"benevolent and charitable": Ibid., 980.

"He gives his": Ibid.

"without any expectation": Stephen R. Moore, letter to the editors, *Boston Daily Advertiser*, May 16, 1865, reproduced in *MPE*, 123.

"distinguished by the": *Portrait and Biographical Record*, 213.

"very short time": Thomas P. Bonfield, certificate supplied to TP, February 19, 1864, in "Reply to Mr. Sewall's Rejoinder."

"I…denied the": TP, "Account of the Insanity Case."

"as one who": *Kankakee Gazette*, article reproduced in "The Case of Mrs. Packard," *Chicago Tribune*, January 28, 1864.

"genuine imaginative powers": "Literary," *Kankakee Gazette*, January 23, 1868.

"Prove it!": Judge Starr, quoted by EP, *MPE*, 11.

CHAPTER 42

"without the": Clause 10, "An act to amend the act establishing the Illinois State Hospital for the Insane," approved February 15, 1851, in *Reports of the Illinois*, 386.

"It was illegal": TP, "The Question of Mrs. Packard's Sanity," *Northampton Free Press*, April 20, 1866.

"impudent, violent": Ibid.

"The direct votes": TP, "Account of the Insanity Case."

"of a different": Ibid.

"excited by": Ibid.

"a jury could": Thomas P. Bonfield, certificate supplied to TP, February 19, 1864, in "Reply to Mr. Sewall's Rejoinder."

"the reverse of": Portrait and Biographical Record, 464.

"The case was": TP, TPD, 34 ("School Lawsuit 1832").

"I am a practicing" and following quotations: Dr. Knott, court testimony, in Moore, GT, in MPE, 17–18.

"Hisses even": TP, "Charge Against Rev. Mr. Packard."

"Her insanity was" and following quotations: Dr. Knott, court testimony, in Moore, GT, in MPE, 18.

"almost unparalleled": Brown's advertisement for his services, Kankakee Gazette, December 19, 1856.

"the high-flown": EP, PHL, 107.

"extended conference" and following quotations: J. W. Brown, court testimony, in Moore, GT, in MPE, 18–19.

"clear and lucid": Palmer, Bench and Bar of Illinois, 980.

"Dr., what particular" and following quotations: Court testimony, in Moore, GT, in MPE, 19–21.

"Now I beseech": 1 Cor. 1:10 (King James Version).

CHAPTER 43

"much attention": "Excitement in Kankakee," Chicago Tribune, January 21, 1864.

"one of the": Ibid.

"Mrs. Packard": EP quoting "multitudes of his [TP's] people who attended my trial, whom I know defended him at the time he kidnapped me," MPE, 77.

"hypnotic and compelling": Emma Packard (daughter-in-law of Samuel Packard), letter to Barbara Sapinsley, January 5, 1965, Barbara Sapinsley Papers.

"One morning early" and following quotations: Abijah Dole, court testimony, in Moore, GT, in MPE, 22–24.

"clinging to her": Moore, ibid., 25.

"to keep her": Isaac Packard describing his sister's reaction to Elizabeth's long-term commitment, quoted by EP, GD, 1:178.

"snatched the child": Moore, GT, in MPE, 25.

"Come away": Sybil Dole, quoted by Moore, ibid.

"Not a mother's": Moore, ibid.

"I was elected": Josephus B. Smith, court testimony, ibid.

"Her natural disposition" and following quotations: Sybil Dole, court testimony, ibid., 25–26.

"Mrs. Packard was": Sarah Rumsey, court testimony, ibid., 27.

"The least mistake": EP, PHL, 247.

"I approved taking": Sarah Rumsey, court testimony, in Moore, GT, in MPE, 29.

"bore evidence": Ibid., 28.

"I cannot": Ibid.

"in a decisive": Portrait and Biographical Record, 242.

"very important": TP's lawyers, quoted by Moore, GT, in MPE, 30.

CHAPTER 44

"unheard-of": Moore, GT, in MPE, 30.

"to enable": Ibid.

"submit the case": Ibid., 31.

"Incompetent testimony": Ibid.

"debarred the defense": Ibid.

"acknowledged leader": Portrait and Biographical Record, 241.

"convincing personality": William F. Kenaga and George R. Letourneau, History of Kankakee County, vol. 2 (Chicago: Middle-West, 1906), 827.

"more than ordinary": Portrait and Biographical Record, 241–42.

"Of the existence": AM, official certificate regarding EP's sanity, May 5, 1863, in "The Question of Mrs. Packard's Sanity," Northampton Free Press, May 8, 1866.

"The officers of": AM, letter to TP, December 1863, quoted by Moore, GT, in MPE, 31.

"The defence had": Moore, letter to the editors, *Boston Daily Advertiser*, May 16, 1865, reproduced in *MPE*, 125.

"I always said" and following quotations: Joseph E. Labrie, court testimony, in Moore, GT, in *MPE*, 32–33.

"Her insanity": AM, official certificate regarding EP's sanity, May 5, 1863, in "The Question of Mrs. Packard's Sanity," *Northampton Free Press*, May 8, 1866.

"[We would like]" and following quotations: Moore, GT, in *MPE*, 33.

"unnatural": Pastoral Letter, 1837, quoted in *History of Woman Suffrage*, 1:81.

"fall in shame": Ibid.

"a lady of": Moore, GT, in *MPE*, 13.

"masculine thinker": Ibid.

"She drew all": SO, MO, 72 in *PHL*, page 426 in PDF.

"under the spell": AM, letter to Mrs. Alma E. Eaton, in "Packard Controversy."

"I think we" and following quotations: EP, "How Godliness is Profitable," in Moore, GT, in *MPE*, 34.

"a murmur of": Moore, ibid., 35.

"I never thought": Mr. Blessing, court testimony, ibid.

"The popular verdict": EP, *MPE*, 75.

"the disorderly demonstrations": Sybil T. Dole, Sarah Rumsey, J. B. Smith, and A. H. Dole, certificate supplied to TP, February 18, 1865, in "The Question of Mrs. Packard's Sanity," *Northampton Free Press*, April 20, 1866.

"vulgar hisses issued": TP, "Account of the Insanity Case."

"surrounded by": Account of the trial from "a highly respected gentleman," quoted by TP in "The Question of Mrs. Packard's Sanity," *Northampton Free Press*, April 20, 1866.

"feeble attempt": TP, "Account of the Insanity Case."

"I never saw" and following quotations: Mrs. Haslett, court testimony, in Moore, GT, in *MPE*, 36.

"rabid, ferocious": TP, "Account of the Insanity Case."

"It was unmistakably": Ibid.

"the bitter spirit": Ibid.

"lawless violence": Ibid.

"ready to sacrifice": Ibid.

CHAPTER 45

"I live here" and following quotations: Dr. Duncanson, court testimony, in Moore, GT, in *MPE*, 37.

"It has always": EP, *TE*, 7.

"So with Mrs.": Dr. Duncanson, court testimony, in Moore, GT, in *MPE*, 37–38.

"I pronounce her": Ibid., 38.

"ably and at": Moore, ibid.

"a painful case": TP, letter to editors, February 5, 1864, in "A Sad Case," *Gazette and Courier*, February 8, 1864 [italics added].

"venturesome driver": EP, *GD*, 4:62.

"likes to see": Ibid.

"We, the undersigned": State of Illinois, Kankakee County, jury verdict, January 18, 1864, as reproduced in Moore, GT, in *MPE*, 38.

"cheers rose": Moore, ibid.

"to have the": Quoted in EP, *MK*, 22.

"grateful joy": EP, *MP2*, 204.

"It is hereby": State of Illinois, Kankakee County, official court order signed by Charles R. Starr, Judge of the 20th Judicial Circuit of the State of Illinois, January 18, 1864, as reproduced in Moore, GT, in *MPE*, 39.

"His troubles": AM, letter to Mrs. Alma E. Eaton, in "Packard Controversy."

"death agonies": EP, *TE*, 6.

"soul and body": Ibid.

"living death of": EP, *MP2*, 93.

"I want to": EP, *MPE*, 62.

"I am thrown": Ibid., 130.

CHAPTER 46

"with the promise": EP, *MPE*, 42.

"grope about in": EP, *GD*, 4:5.

EP's conversation with her lawyers: Recounted by EP in *MPE*, 46.

"annihilates all": EP, *PHL*, 309.

"I am not": Ibid., 114.

"I…appealed to": EP, *MP2*, 67.

EP's conversation with her lawyers: Recounted by EP, ibid., 265.

"[I have] no": EP, *PHL*, 126.

"And can one": EP, *MPE*, 47.

"On the principle": EP's lawyers quoted by EP, *MP2*, 68.

"You can have": Ibid., 365.

"The idea of": Hendrik Hartog, "Mrs. Packard on Dependency," *Yale Journal of Law & the Humanities* 1, no. 1 (1989): 91, https://digitalcommons.law.yale.edu/yjlh/vol1/iss1/6/.

"conscientiously get": EP, *MP2*, 67.

"When Will the": "When Will the War End?" *Chicago Tribune*, January 21, 1864.

"Depravity of a": "Depravity of a Clergyman," *Chicago Tribune*, January 28, 1864.

"a willing tool": Ibid.

"I may here": AM, "Packard Insanity Case."

"respectfully request": TP, "Sad Case."

"sham": TP, "Charge Against Rev. Mr. Packard."

"illegal and oppressive": TP, "Account of the Insanity Case."

"the impudent": TP, "The Question of Mrs. Packard's Sanity," *Northampton Free Press*, April 20, 1866.

"the reliable": TP, letter to the editor, *Chicago Tribune*, February 1, 1864, in "The Packard Case," *Chicago Tribune*, February 6, 1864.

"I see not": Reverend Robert Crawford, letter to William Bross, editor of the *Chicago Tribune*, February 23, 1864, in "The Packard Case," *Chicago Tribune*, March 12, 1864.

"two talented men": EP, *MK*, 13.

"repeated and": Bill of complaint for divorce, Kankakee County Circuit Court, February 8, 1864.

"using violence": Ibid.

"unhallowed influence": TP, "Account of the Insanity Case."

"I do say": EP, *GD*, 1:141.

"Woman cannot be": Ibid., 2:241.

"doubt, despondency": EP, *MP2*, 366.

"supplanted by plenty": Ibid.

"become my own": Ibid., 72.

"17.5 cents a shirt": Statistic from Thomas H. O'Connor, *Civil War Boston: Home Front and Battlefield* (Boston: Northeastern University Press, 1997), 166.

"$1.54 (about $25)": Ibid.

"$7 (about $115)" and following salary statistic: *Chicago Times*, February 3, 1864, in Theodore J. Karamanski and Eileen M. McMahon, eds., *Civil War Chicago: Eyewitness to History* (Athens: Ohio University Press, 2014), 187.

"sugar, a unit": Cost of living statistics from *Chicago Tribune*, July 20, 1864, in ibid., 188.

"No talent can": EP, letter to Fidelia Fiske, March 3, 1846, Shelburne Free Public Library Fidelia Fiske Collection.

"the many thousands": *Mrs. Packard's Reproof*, 3.

"Knowing as I do": Ibid.

"enlighten the public": Ibid., 31.

"caus[e] their": Ibid.

"immense mass": "The Packard Case," *Chicago Tribune*, March 12, 1864.

Following quotations: Ibid.

CHAPTER 47

"dazzling entrance": EP, *GD*, 2:141.

"the unmistakable signs": *Chicago Tribune*, October 8, 1863, in *Reminiscences of Chicago During the Civil War* (Chicago: Lakeside, 1914), xi–xii.

"a combination of": Franc Wilkie, 1860, quoted in Perry R. Duis, *Challenging Chicago: Coping with Everyday Life, 1837–1920* (Urbana: University of Illinois Press, 1998), 11.

"more ostentation": TP, TPD, 67 (April 1834).

"The facts of": EP, *MPE*, 117.

"My skirts are": *Mrs. Packard's Reproof*, 31.

"fit for [his]": Ibid., 17.

"I shan't trouble": EP, *GD*, 1:279.

"health, education": EP, *MP2*, 380.

"invincible determination": Ibid., 86.

"sham": TP, "Charge Against Rev. Mr. Packard."

"much study": EP, *MP2*, 85.

"I must first": Ibid.

"The Bearer is": EP's "tickets," as reproduced in ibid.

"The subscriber wishes": "Notice: The Great Drama," *Chicago Tribune*, March 23, 1864.

"risked ruining": Susan M. Cruea, "Changing Ideals of Womanhood During the Nineteenth-Century Woman Movement," *General Studies Writing Faculty Publications* 1 (2005): 194.

"I write in": T. Packard Jr. (Toffy Packard), letter to Samuel Ware, March 29, 1864, in "The Question of Mrs. Packard's Sanity," *Northampton Free Press*, May 15, 1866.

"The more freedom": EP, *GD*, 4:12 [italics added].

"Mrs. Packard": Mayor Sherman, as quoted by EP, *MPE*, 51.

"I must say": Ibid.

"The only way": EP, *MK*, 15 [italics added].

"I chose the": Ibid.

"I don't want": EP, *TE*, 16.

"Being in the": EP, *MK*, 41.

"My case is": EP, "Appeal to the Government for Protection," in *TE*, 154–58.

"I am resolved": EP, *PHL*, 253.

"her page became": Madaline Reeder Walter, "Insanity, Rhetoric, and Women: Nineteenth-Century Women's Asylum Narratives," (PhD diss., University of Missouri-Kansas City, 2011), 82, https://mospace.umsystem.edu/xmlui/bitstream/handle/10355/11577/WalterInsRheWom.pdf?sequence=1&isAllowed=y.

"To my beloved": EP, *TE*, 5.

"The mother has": Ibid., 6.

"Women are made": EP, *GD*, 1:275.

PART SIX: SHE WILL RISE

EPIGRAPHS

"Every woman who": Rebecca Solnit, *Men Explain Things To Me* (Chicago: Haymarket Books, 2014).

"Prostitute. Whore": Janet Fitch, *White Oleander* (New York: Little, Brown, 1999).

CHAPTER 48

"house…upon": "Levee at the Governor's," *Illinois Journal*, January 23, 1867.

"I intend to": EP, *GD*, 2:115.

"I am now": EP, letter to the *Gazette and Courier*, in "Mrs. Packard's Book," *Gazette and Courier*, June 13, 1864.

"Reforms succeed": EP, *MK*, 54.

"My experience": EP, *MPE*, 61.

"platform of": Ibid., 107.

"many persons": "Levee at the Governor's."

"the complicated machinery": EP, *MP2*, 209.

"ignorantly…upon": Ibid.

"Where do you": EP, *TE*, 75.

"In woman!": Ibid.

"another kidnapping": EP, *MK*, 33.

"Our society": Samuel E. Sewall, letter to Samuel J. May, 1868, in Nina Moore Tiffany, *Samuel E. Sewall: A Memoir* (Boston and New York: Houghton Mifflin, 1898), 141.

"in a most": EP, *MPE*, 108.

"I say I have": EP, *GD*, 2:49.

"secret frameups": "Evolution of Mental Health Laws in Nineteenth Century United States," Encyclopaedia Britannica Library Research Service, 5, Barbara Sapinsley Papers. Original source is possibly Albert Deutsch, *The Mentally Ill in America* (New York: Columbia University Press, 1962), 420–28.

"a dozen": *Boston Daily Advertiser*, quoted in Thomas H. O'Connor, *Civil War Boston: Home Front and Battlefield* (Boston: Northeastern University Press, 1997), 228.

"any woman entering": EP's proposed bill, as submitted to the Connecticut General Assembly of 1866, quoted in *MP2*, 406.

"inexpedient to make": Mr. Wait, chairman of the Judiciary Committee, as quoted by EP, ibid., 294.

"No such thing": EP, *MK*, 54.

"My work ain't": EP, *GD*, 2:76.

"one uniform testimony": EP in De Wolf, "Public Institutions."

"lest their own": Ibid.

"These letters came": AM, quoted by EP, ibid.

"Ah!": EP, ibid. [italics added].

"the verdict of": EP, *MPE*, 85.

"severe comment": *Kankakee Gazette*, article reproduced in "The Case of Mrs. Packard," *Chicago Tribune*, January 28, 1864.

"a substantial dinner" and following quotations: "A Day Among the State Institutions," *Jacksonville Sentinel*, January 31, 1867.

"perfectly in raptures": "Excursion to Jacksonville," *Illinois Journal*, January 11, 1867.

"well conducted": "Day Among the State Institutions."

"able and accomplished": "Insane Hospital Report," *Jacksonville Sentinel*, February 2, 1867.

"sham trial": AM, letter to Mrs. Alma E. Eaton, in "Packard Controversy."

"very high degree": Ibid.

"I wonder that": Ibid.

"I intend to": EP, *MPE*, 99.

CHAPTER 49

"Nothing venture": EP, *MK*, 127.

"What is the object" and following quotations: Conversation between Governor Richard Oglesby and EP, recounted by EP in *MP2*, 191.

"prudent management": Richard J. Oglesby, "Message from Governor Oglesby to the Twenty-Fifth General Assembly," January 7, 1867, 11, Special Collections, Harold Washington Library, Chicago, IL.

"a dead letter": EP, *MP2*, 219.

"to relieve all": EP in De Wolf, "Public Institutions."

"some of the": EP, *MP2*, 190.

"a studious and": Palmer, *Bench and Bar of Illinois*, 1151.

"tone and manner": EP, *MP2*, 192.

"wise, just": Palmer, *Bench and Bar of Illinois*, 1153–54.

"a very respectable": EP, *MP2*, 193.

"Gentlemen, it does" and following quotations: EP's dialogue with the Judiciary Committee, as quoted by EP, ibid.

"sensational novel": *Illinois Journal*, January 15, 1867, reprised in "January 15, 1867," *Illinois State Journal*, January 15, 1934.

"ought to be": De Wolf, "Public Institutions."

"[It] is injurious": AM, letter to Ralph Parsons (a New York asylum superintendent), undated but c. 1876–1881, in D. Hack Tuke, "Psychological Retrospect," *Journal of Mental Science* 31 (1885–86): 99, quoted in Himelhoch, "Elizabeth Packard," 373.

"the haphazard opinions": "Summary," *AJOI* 27 (October 1870): 261, https://doi.org/10.1176/ajp.27.2.260.

"In nearly three": AM, in *Tenth Biennial Report*, 39.

"Has the Doctor": Letter attributed to "A Lover of Justice," January 21, 1867, in "Dr. McFarland's Report Opposed to Jury Trials," *Illinois Journal*, January 26, 1867. EP also republished the letter in *MP2*, 214–16.

"Mrs. Packard's case": Ibid.

"offensive class": Quoted by EP, *MP2*, 313.

"You are reasonable": Ibid.

"constantly growing": EP, ibid., 197.

"Horrible revelations": "Horrible Revelations," *Jacksonville Journal*, April 29, 1867.

"much gratification": Article from January 29, 1867, as recorded by Barbara Sapinsley in her research notes, Barbara Sapinsley Papers.

CHAPTER 50

"after the first": EP, *MK*, 113.

"Gentlemen of Illinois" and following quotations: "Mrs. Packard's Address," in *MPE*, pages 145–60 in PDF [italics added on "I am not the only one…"].

"with the most": EP, *MK*, 12.

"spell-bound": *Boise Republican*, January 1, 1881, quoted in Carlisle, *Elizabeth Packard*, 186.

"sensation": *Chicago Tribune*, September 23, 1869.

CHAPTER 51

"The success of": *Jacksonville Journal*, March 31, 1864, quoted in Doyle, *Social Order of a Frontier Community*, 218.

"excessive quantity of": "Legislative Visit to Jacksonville," *Illinois Journal*, February 14, 1867.

"How long have" and following quotations: Conversation between unnamed gentleman and Mrs. Minard quoted in De Wolf, "Public Institutions."

"irresistible conviction" and following quotations: De Wolf, "Public Institutions."

"liable to any": "Illinois Legislation Regarding Hospitals," 214.

"no father": Ibid.

"fruitless annoyance": Dr. Isaac Ray, quoted in "Report of Commission on Insanity," *AJOI* 21 (October 1864): 267.

"Such a commission": Ibid., 266.

"not only wholly": Resolution of the AMSAII, "Proceedings of the Association," *AJOI* 21 (July 1864): 152.

"so pointed were": "The Insane Asylum," *Kankakee Gazette*, December 19, 1867.

"examined into these": Mr. Ward, chairman of the Finance Committee, in "The Insane Asylum," *Illinois Journal*, February 25, 1867.

"thorough investigation": Ibid.

"had been": Ibid.

"His statement seemed": Ibid.

"We have every": "State Institutions at Jacksonville," *Jacksonville Journal*, February 8, 1867.

"[I have] waited": T. B. Wakeman, in *Illinois Journal*, February 26, 1867.

"The appointment": "The Report of the Committee of Investigation of the State Institutions at Jacksonville," *Daily Illinois State Register*, December 6, 1867.

"If Dr. McFarland": Mrs. Grere, quoted by EP, *PHL*, 263.

"to ascertain whether": Joint resolution adopted by the Twenty-Fifth General Assembly in 1867, quoted in "Governor Oglesby's Message," January 4, 1869, 12, Special Collections, Harold Washington Library, Chicago, IL.

"O, yes": EP, *PHL*, 263 [italics added].

"Mrs. Packard's Personal": "Mrs. Packard's Personal Liberty Law," *Jacksonville Sentinel*, May 9, 1867.

"tug of war": EP, *MP2*, 203.

"in a state": Ibid., 204.

"Mrs. Packard": Gentleman quoted by EP, ibid.

"I felt such": EP, ibid.

"In that decision": Ibid.

"Mrs. Packard, your": Oglesby, quoted by EP, ibid., 208.

"In the name": EP, ibid., 208–9.

"a record of": Ibid., 209.

"the prime motivator": Richard Dewey, "The Jury Law for the Commitment of the Insane in Illinois, 1867–1893 and Mrs. E. P. W. Packard, its author. Also, Later Developments in Lunacy Legislation in Illinois," read before the American Medical Psychological Association, May 29, 1912, *Chicago Medical Recorder* 35, no. 1: 72, Barbara Sapinsley Papers.

"There is not": EP, letter to Libby Packard, August 4, 1863, in "The Question of Mrs. Packard's Sanity," *Northampton Free Press*, May 8, 1866.

CHAPTER 52

"imperfectly prepared": "Illinois Legislation Regarding Hospitals," 220.

"past the stage": *Eleventh Biennial Report of the Trustees, Superintendent and Treasurer of the Illinois State Hospital for the Insane at Jacksonville* (Springfield, IL, 1868), 9.

"dangerous": Ibid.

"possess extreme": Ibid., 9–10.

"infernal prosecutions": A. H. Van Nostrand, "Proceedings of the Twentieth Annual Meeting of the AMSAII," *AJOI* 23 (July 1866): 115.

"loose and flawy": "Habeas Corpus and Lunacy," *AJOI* 26 (January 1870): 336.

"this innovation": EP, *MP2*, 323.

"The conduct of": "Illinois Legislation Regarding Hospitals," 221.

"confirmatory": Ibid.

"ridiculous farce": *Jacksonville Sentinel*, May 30, 1867.

"The effect of": "Mrs. Packard's Personal Liberty Law."

"The reports put": "Mrs. Packard's Personal Liberty Law Again," *Jacksonville Sentinel*, May 16, 1867.

"The name of": Palmer, *Bench and Bar of Illinois*, 790.

"The history of": A "learned historian of this state," quoted in ibid.

"every detail": Palmer, ibid.

"kind, courteous": Resolution of the Illinois House of Representatives, quoted in ibid., 789.

"absolute justice": Palmer, ibid., 790.

"pretty able": AM, letter to Dr. Edward Jarvis, January 2, 1868, Edward Jarvis Papers.

"of well-known": "The Insane Asylum," *Kankakee Gazette*, December 19, 1867.

"astute lawyers": Trustees of the Illinois State Hospital, *Special Report of the Trustees*, 43.

"confer with the": Resolution of the Illinois House of Representatives, quoted in ibid., 3.

"The action of": Trustees of the Illinois State Hospital, ibid., 5.

"should be cast": AM, "The Better Way," 11.

"perverted representations": Ibid.

"To reject their": EP summarizing the committee's opinion, *PHL*, vi.

"The representations": EP, *GD*, 2:210 [italics added].

"would not let": Testimony of Miss Kane before the investigating committee, in Report of the Investigating Committee, 38.

"cast the water": Ibid.

"made no complaints": Ibid., 39.

"serious apprehensions": Report of the Investigating Committee, 8.

"I hope": EP quoting the husband of Mrs. Caroline E. Lake, in "Mrs. Packard's Coadjutor's Testimony," 143, in *PHL*, page 497 in PDF.

"mock jury trial": Shedd, "Testimony of Mrs. Tirzah F. Shedd," in ibid., 132, in *PHL*, page 486 in PDF.

"Is Mrs. Shedd": AM's letter, quoted in ibid., 134, in *PHL*, page 488 in PDF.

"He came in": Testimony of Mrs. Shedd before the investigating committee, in *Special Report of the Trustees*, 29.

"I don't see": AM, quoted in "Testimony of Mrs. Tirzah F. Shedd," in "Mrs. Packard's Coadjutor's Testimony," 134, in *PHL*, page 488 in PDF.

"improper liberties": Testimony of Mrs. Shedd before the investigating committee, in *Special Report of the Trustees*, 29.

"That he": Resolution of the Investigating Committee, in ibid., 30.

"Dr. McFarland vs.": "The Insane Asylum: Dr. McFarland vs. Mrs. Packard," *Chicago Tribune*, December 26, 1867.

CHAPTER 53

"I needed none": EP, *MK*, 91–92.

"essentially true": AM's response quoted by the trustees in *Special Report of the Trustees*, 30.

"one of the": William F. Short, ed., *Historical Encyclopedia of Illinois & History of Morgan County* (Chicago: Munsell, 1906).

"crazy woman": AM, letter to Dr. Edward Jarvis, August 12, 1868, Edward Jarvis Papers.

"not so much": "The Insane Hospital Investigation," *Illinois Journal*, June 10, 1867.

"It is not that": Testimony of EP before the investigating committee, in *Special Report of the Trustees*, 32.

"rising and applauded": EP, "My Reproof," *MP1*, 125.

"during her entire": Testimony of EP before the investigating committee, in Report of the Investigating Committee, 48.

"a most searching": Report of the Investigating Committee, 51.

"the accuracy of": Ibid.

"It is but": Ibid.

"long and severe": EP, *MK*, 91.

"[He] left no": Ibid.

"The prompt and": Report of the Investigating Committee, 55.

"failed to elicit": EP, *MK*, 91.

"Mrs. Packard, I": Quoted by EP, *PHL*, 337.

"[Do you] recognize": AM, quoted by EP, *MK*, 90.

"It is my": EP, ibid.

"I have written": Testimony of EP before the investigating committee, in *Special Report of the Trustees*, 34.

"Jacksonville, January": EP's letter to AM, January 19, 1863, quoted in account of EP's testimony before the investigating committee, ibid.

"Dr. McFarland": Ibid.

"silent and attentive": EP, *MK*, 90.

"writhe": Ibid., 88.

"The most abusive": Ibid., 8.

"It must be": EP's letter to AM, January 19, 1863, quoted in account of EP's testimony before the investigating committee, *Special Report of the Trustees*, 35.

"a brazen offer": Report of the Investigating Committee, 52.

"the production of": Ibid.

"[It] proves the": Letter from "A Friend of Justice" (likely SO) to the editor, *Chicago Tribune*, December 26, 1867, in "Mrs. Packard's Letter to Superintendent McFarland," *Chicago Tribune*, December 28, 1867.

"most cruel and": EP, *PHL*, 337.

"in defiance of": EP, *MK*, 86.

"I have done": EP, *PHL*, 337.

"Mrs. Packard" and following quotations: Dialogue between Fuller and EP quoted by EP, *MK*, 90–91.

"The letter is": *Jacksonville Sentinel*, December 26, 1867.

"I am ruined!": EP, *MK*, 92.

CHAPTER 54

"In the quietude": EP, *MK*, 93.

"Gentlemen of the" and following quotations: EP's defense of the love letter, as presented to the investigating committee, in *Special Report of the Trustees*, 35–37.

"no act of": EP, *MK*, 88.

"a halo of": Ibid., 80.

"that circumstances": Ibid., 88–89.

"Do you now" and following quotations: Transcript of dialogue between EP and Fuller before the investigating committee, *Special Report of the Trustees*, 37.

"rack of torture": EP, *MK*, 97.

"How could you" and following quotations: Dialogue between EP and Fuller recounted by EP, ibid., 97–98.

"pouring water in": Testimony of John Henry, former steward of the Illinois State Hospital, Report of the Investigating Committee, 41.

"appeared indifferent": Ibid., 42.

"[He] is destitute": Ibid.

"one eye was": Testimony of Mary Cassell, former assistant matron of the Illinois State Hospital, Report of the Investigating Committee, 47.

"The Superintendent was": *Special Report of the Trustees*, 45.

"the balance of": Report of the Investigating Committee, 9.

CHAPTER 55

"ridiculous farce": *Jacksonville Sentinel*, May 30, 1867.

"There were 127": Report of the Investigating Committee, 31.

"This increase in": Ibid.

"extreme jealousy": Diagnosis of the first patient admitted to the Illinois State Hospital, hospital admissions book, November 3, 1851, quoted in several sources, including Bacus, "Old Buildings and Impaired Minds."

"unjust commitments" and following quotations: Report of the Investigating Committee, 31–2.

"fundamentally wrong": Ibid., 66.

"most culpable": Ibid., 67.

"Familiarity with suffering": Report of the Investigating Committee, quoted by EP, *MP2*, 262–63.

"presumptively entitled to": "Illinois Legislation Regarding Hospitals," 211.

"charitable constructions": Ibid., 212.

"whose recovery": *Special Report of the Trustees*, 18.

"worthy of serious": Ibid., 17.

"but small importance": Ibid., 85.

"servants": Ibid., 19.

"former master": Ibid.

"no action on": "Governor Oglesby's Message," 13.

"to retain": Ibid.

"clearly [say] that": Oglesby, letter to AM, September 18, 1867, Barbara Sapinsley Papers.

"It will be": Ibid.

"exceedingly mysterious": "A Question of Courtesy," *Illinois Journal*, December 10, 1867.

"the social sensation": *Illinois State Journal*, January 1867, in "Leland Hotel," SangamonLink, July 8, 2016, https://sangamoncountyhistory.org/wp/?p=8661.

"She would take": Testimony of Miss Kane before the investigating committee, in *Report of the Investigating Committee*, 38.

"She would often": Ibid.

"One eye was": Testimony of Mary Cassell, ibid., 47.

"A straight jacket": Testimony of Miss Kane, ibid., 38.

"There is something": "A Premature Deliverance," *Illinois Daily State Journal*, December 13, 1867.

"honor, integrity": Palmer, *Bench and Bar of Illinois*, 790.

"This document": "Startling Report—Illinois Insane Asylum," *Chicago Tribune*, December 7, 1867.

"Truth…may": EP, *MPE*, 106.

"The result of": EP, *MK*, 12.

"If you attempt": EP, letter to AM, April 28, 1862, in *PHL*, 258.

CHAPTER 56

"the mother of": EP, *TE*, 6.

"Packard-Fuller committee": *Jacksonville Sentinel*, February 13, 1868.

"stimulating business": John C. W. Bailey, "Sketch of Jacksonville," *Jacksonville City Directory* (1866), 323.

"notorious and crack-brained": *Jacksonville Journal*, c. November 1867, back page, quoted in Barbara Sapinsley, *The Private War of Mrs. Packard* (New York: Paragon House, 1991), 154.

"insane imaginings": *Special Report of the Trustees*, 92.

"We submit": "Mrs. Packard's Love Letter to Dr. McFarland," *Jacksonville Journal*, December 21, 1867.

"her character as": Report of the Investigating Committee, 52.

"the charges": Ibid., 48.

"renowned follower": *Jacksonville Journal*, December 31, 1867.

"afflicted with": "The Insane Hospital Committee's Report," *Jacksonville Sentinel*, January 2, 1868.

"The verdict of": EP, *MK*, 99.

"the trustees and": AM, letter to Dr. Edward Jarvis, January 2, 1868, Edward Jarvis Papers.

"The humiliating": AM, letter to Dr. Edward Jarvis, August 12, 1868, Edward Jarvis Papers.

"From an examination": *Journal of the House of Representatives of the Twenty-Sixth General Assembly of the State of Illinois* (Springfield, IL, 1869), 128.

"I have drunk": AM, letter to Dr. Edward Jarvis, August 12, 1868, Edward Jarvis Papers.

"grand purpose": EP, *MK*, 50.

"desire of her": Testimonial of Isaac Packard, April 12, 1869, in *MP2*, 377.

"most cheerfully": EP, ibid., 381.

"except the sale": Ibid.

"It is my opinion": Testimonial of Isaac Packard, April 12, 1869, in ibid., 377.

"It is my earnest": Testimonial of Theophilus Packard Jr. (Toffy), April 10, 1869, in ibid., 376.

"to carrying on": Samuel Packard, letter to EP, 1874, Barbara Sapinsley Papers.

"with indignant scorn": EP, *MK*, 38.

"the great mercy": TP, TPD, 82 (1867).

"It is now": Rev. Samuel Ware's Certificate to the Public, August 21, 1866, in *MPE*, 138.

"tissue of lies": EP, ibid., 87.

"false statements": TP, letter to the editor, *Chicago Tribune*, January 20, 1868, in "The Insane Hospital Investigation—Letter from Mr. Packard," *Chicago Tribune*, January 25, 1868.

"bullying demand[s]" and following quotations: "Rev. T. Packard—Again," *Hampshire Express*, June 28, 1866.

"No other proof": TP, "Charge Against Rev. Mr. Packard."

"I have no": AM, "Packard Insanity Case."

"The case was": EP, *MP2*, 379.

"We will gladly": Elizabeth W. Packard (Libby), George H. Packard, and Arthur D. Packard, letter to EP, May 24, 1869, in "The End of the Packard Matter," *Illinois Journal*, June 4, 1869.

"My fond heart": EP, letter to Elizabeth (Libby), George, and Arthur Packard, May 25, 1869, in ibid.

"The mother's battle": EP, *MP2*, 379.

"pies, cake": "The Fourth," *Chicago Tribune*, July 4, 1869.

"velocipede": Ibid.

"finest residential area": Chicago School of Architecture Foundation and the Prairie Avenue Historic District Committee, "Prairie Avenue Historic District" (self-pub., July 1975), Foreword, 1.

"safe": TP, TPD, 41 ("Wife's Insanity—1860").

"got along": Ibid., 84 (1869).

"When he restored": EP, *MP2*, 383.

"stranger gentleman": Ibid.

"kindly gratified": Ibid., 384.

"indescribable beauty": James. M. Pierce, Harvard scientist, Congressional report, quoted in Joe McFarland, "When Was the Last Total Solar Eclipse in Illinois? It's Been a Long Time," *Daily Herald*, August 18, 2017, https://www.dailyherald.com/news/20170817/when-was-the-last-total-solar-eclipse-in-illinois-its-been-a-long-time.

"secondary": EP, *MP2*, 381.

"undivided energies": Ibid., 384.

EPILOGUE

"God grant": EP, *PHL*, 162–63.

"Packard's Law": Quoted in Carlisle, *Elizabeth Packard*, 165.

"feeling of independence": Dr. Ranney, Iowa Superintendent, quoted in Himelhoch, "Elizabeth Packard," 368.

"We passed the": A member of the Massachusetts Legislative Committee, quoted by EP, *MK*, 137.

"Sir, I am": EP, ibid.

"arrogant guardianship": National Association for the Protection of the Insane and the Prevention of Insanity, quoted in Carlisle, *Elizabeth Packard*, 188.

"You have far": S. Weir Mitchell, "Address before the Fiftieth Annual Meeting of the American Medico-Psychological Association," *Journal of Nervous and Mental Disease* 21, no. 2 (1894): 427.

"female paranoiac": Dr. James G. Kiernan, comment made at the joint meeting of the Chicago Medical Society and the Chicago Medico-Legal Society, February 16, 1891, quoted in Himelhoch, "Elizabeth Packard," 373.

"half-cured lunatic": Clement Walker, "Proceedings of the Annual Meeting of the AMSAII," *AJOI* 32 (January 1876): 352, in Carlisle, *Elizabeth Packard*, 176.

"through fire and": EP, *PHL*, 172.

"At every inch": Ibid.

"just one": Dr. D. R. Brower, *Transactions of the 43rd Annual Meeting of the Illinois State Medical Society* (Chicago, 1893): 485, in Himelhoch, "Elizabeth Packard," 374.

"A great many": Myra Bradwell, *Chicago Legal News*, March 3, 1879, 267:3–4, in Carlisle, *Elizabeth Packard*, 179.

"the greatest obstacle": EP, *MK*, 7.

"my most terrible": Ibid., 99.

"whitewashing report": *Daily Illinois State Register*, June 29, 1869.

"technical appearance": "Illinois Legislation Regarding Hospitals," 220.

"accidental collisions": *Special Report of the Trustees*, 46.

"styled…abuse": Ibid., 85.

"Who would not": Ibid., 59.

"with the satisfaction": "New Superintendent of the Illinois Hospital for the Insane," *Illinois State Journal*, June 10, 1870.

"entirely exhonorated": "An Infamous Lie," *Illinois State Journal*, July 5, 1869.

"not composed": Ibid.

"were not substantiated": "The Late Dr. M'Farland," *St. Louis Post-Dispatch*, November 24, 1891.

"distinguished founder": Ibid.

"helpless and irresponsible": AM to Robert Todd Lincoln, September 8, 1875, in Mark E. Neely Jr. and R. Gerald McMurtry, *The Insanity File: The Case of Mary Todd Lincoln* (Carbondale and Edwardsville: Southern Illinois University Press, 1986), 72.

"restored to reason": Jury's verdict in the trial of Mary Todd Lincoln, June 15, 1876, in ibid., 104.

"an efficient aid": EP, *MK*, 7.

"want of courage": EP, *GD*, 1:11.

"I now fear": Ibid., 1:12.

"We must be": EP, *PHL*, 13.

"My beloved sisters": EP, *GD*, 1:3.

"by the married": Message engraved on watch, quoted by EP, letter to the editor, in "The Emancipation Watch," *Daily Inter Ocean*, September 15, 1889.

"inestimable treasure": Ibid.

"as a significant": Ibid.

"ever an advocate": Palmer, *Bench and Bar of Illinois*, 1026.

"so strong a": Ibid.

"least successful": Emma L. Packard, letter to Barbara Sapinsley, October 6, 1965. Barbara Sapinsley Papers.

"mild, unimpressive": Ibid.

"Joys bright and": EP, *GD*, 2:230.

"taken deranged": TP, TPD, 42 ("Wife's Insanity—1860").

"disrupting a child's": Vanessa LoBue, "The Effects of Separating Children from Their Parents," *Psychology Today*, July 5, 2018, https://www.psychologytoday.com/gb/blog/the-baby-scientist/201807/the-effects-separating -children-their-parents.

"it seemed as": TP, TPD, 42 ("Wife's Insanity—1860").

"greatly emaciated": Ibid.

"wrong treatment": Ibid., 85 (October 16, 1871).

"I acknowledge": Ibid., 41.

"irreligious influence": Ibid.

"His health is": EP, *MK*, 51.

"The infirmities": TP, TPD, 42 ("Wife's Insanity—1860").

"quite cheerful": Joseph H. Smart, attendant at Oak Lawn, evidence to coroner's inquest, "Dr. Andrew McFarland," *Illinois Daily Courier*, November 23, 1891.

"having written any": "The Other Side of the Story," *Chicago Tribune*, May 14, 1886.

"I'm weary": AM, "Requiem," reproduced in "The Last Sad Rites," *Illinois Weekly Courier*, November 25, 1891.

"Death by strangulation": Official verdict of the jury at AM's inquest, in "Dr. Andrew McFarland."

"Famous Packard investigation": "Sensational Suicide," *Daily Illinois State Register*, November 24, 1891.

"with sincere sorrow": "Mrs. S. M. P. Packard" [sic], *Daily Inter Ocean* (Chicago), July 27, 1897.

"She was remarkably": "A Noted Woman," *Boston Transcript*, July 28, 1897.

"Wise Friend": "Wise Friend of the Insane Is Dead," *Chicago Tribune*, July 27, 1897.

"an enviable record": "Mrs. E. T. W. Packard Leaves an Enviable Record Behind" [*sic*], *Tennessean*, July 27, 1897.

"strictly private": "Mrs. S. M. P. Packard" [*sic*].

POSTSCRIPT

"Pray for her" and following quotations: Donald J. Trump (@realDonaldTrump), "Nancy Pelosi needs help fast!" Twitter, October 17, 2019, 1:00 a.m., https://twitter.com/realdonaldtrump/status/1184620202480193537 ?lang=en. This Twitter account has since been suspended.

"unhinged meltdown": Donald J. Trump (@realDonaldTrump), "Nervous Nancy's unhinged meltdown!" Twitter, October 16, 2019, 10:29 a.m., https://twitter.com/realDonaldTrump/status/1184597281808498688.

"suffering from hysteria": *The Times* (UK), December 11, 1908, quoted in Digby, "Victorian Values," 212.

"dirty politics": Quoted in Elizabeth McCauley, "Martha Mitchell: The Woman Nobody Believed About Watergate," All That's Interesting, September 17, 2018, https://allthatsinteresting.com/martha-mitchell.

"You have to": Laura, quoted in Phyllis Chesler, *Women and Madness* (New York: Doubleday, 1972), 169.

"vile practice": Daniel Defoe, 1687, quoted in ibid., 163.

"What is an": EP, *PHL*, 122.

"You're crazy": Janice Dickinson's court evidence, quoted in "US model 'wanted to punch' Bill Cosby after alleged rape," BBC News, April 12, 2018, https://www.bbc.co.uk/news/world-us-canada-43747223.

"increasingly unglued": Memo of Lisa Bloom, 2016, quoted in Jodi Kantor and Megan Twohey, *She Said: Breaking the Sexual Harassment Story That Helped Ignite A Movement* (New York: Penguin, 2019), 101.

"menopausal…psychosis": W. R. Dunton Jr., "Mrs. Packard and Her Influence Upon Laws for the Commitment of the Insane," *Johns Hopkins Hospital Bulletin* 18, no. 199 (October 1907): 422.

"settled down to": Ibid.

"a minor league": "A Sane Lady Such As I: Part II," *Jacksonville Journal Courier*, June 18, 1967.

"couldn't keep her": "A Sane Lady Such As I," *Jacksonville Journal Courier*, June 11, 1967.

"I am determined": EP, *PHL*, 145.

"We should set": EP, *GD*, 4:10.

"effective crusader": Walter E. Barton, *The History and Influence of the American Psychiatric Association* (Washington: American Psychiatric Press, 1987), 64.

INDEX

A

abolition, 13, 62–63, 327, 365. *See also*
    slavery
abuse, domestic, 59
abuse at Illinois State Hospital, 175–180,
    182–184. *See also* attendants; reproof
    of McFarland; violence
    after *The Great Drama*, 222–223
    on Eighth Ward, 210
    Elizabeth's recording of, 188
    exposé about, 274 (See also *Exposure, The*)
    on Fifth Ward, 219–220
    in *The Great Drama*, 220–221
    investigating committee and, 418–419, 422
        (*See also* investigating committee)
    McFarland's awareness of, 100
    patients' protest against, 234–236
    in press, 378
    reports of, 185
    Sophia's accounts of, 225
agency, 10, 347. *See also* independence
"Appeal in behalf of the insane"
    (Packard), 274, 349
"Appeal to the Government for
    Protection" (Packard), 358

assertiveness, as threat, 242
assessments, 56–57
Association of Medical Superintendents
    of American Institutions for the
    Insane (AMSAII), 49–50, 90, 111,
    140, 251, 386, 393–395, 420
asylum tourism, 53
asylum(s). *See also* Illinois State Hospital
    Elizabeth threatened with, 13
    Elizabeth's first stay in, 38–41, 78
    Northampton asylum, 245–246, 256, 262,
        301–302, 305
    overcrowding in, 76, 89
    petition to have Elizabeth placed in, 17, 315
    as tool of social control, 74
attendants, 87–88. *See also* abuse at
    Illinois State Hospital
    on abuse, 378
    Bonner, 182–184, 219, 220, 222, 223, 234,
        415
    on Eighth Ward, 121, 182–184, 188, 192,
        210
    female, 88
    unkindness of, 82

B

Bailey, Mary, 188

Baldwin, Elmer, 374

bathtubs, 174, 177–179

Beedy, Daniel, 303, 328

Bible class, 12, 22, 57, 138

Bible class essays, 21–22, 289, 292–293, 321, 325–328

Blessing (family), 19–20, 69, 84, 94, 168, 278–280, 281, 287

Blessing, Isaac, 33, 69, 328

Blessing, Rebecca, 34, 69, 278, 291, 297, 328–329

Bonfield, Thomas, 304, 307, 308, 309, 314, 321, 322, 323, 329

Bonner, Lizzie, 182–184, 219, 220, 222, 223, 234, 415

books. *See* reading

books, Elizabeth's. See also *Great Drama, The*; writings, Elizabeth's

    The Exposure, 220–221, 244, 353–358, 363–364

    Mrs. Packard's Prison Life, 427

    The Mystic Key, 441

Bradwell, James, 373

Bradwell, Myra, 373, 439

brain, exercise of, 39, 40. *See also* independence; reading; thinking; writings, Elizabeth's

Bridgman, Emeline, 147

Brown, Isaac Baker, 90–92

Brown, J. W., 310–314

Brown, William, 195. *See also* trustees

C

certificates of insanity, 56–57, 365

    Knott's, 304, 309

    Mann's refusal to issue, 295, 324

    McFarland's, 256, 271, 295, 301, 323–324

    Way's, 295–296, 314

chapel, asylum, 116

Chapman, Maria, 60–61, 384–385

Chicago, 351–352

children, as property of husband, 343–344

children, Packard, 6, 43, 71, 158. *See also* Packard, George; Packard, Isaac; Packard, Libby; Packard, Theophilus III (Toffy)

    after Elizabeth's return, 285–286

    attachment to Elizabeth, 168

    convinced of Elizabeth's insanity, 286, 290–293

    custody of, 428

    Elizabeth prohibited from seeing, 269–270, 273, 367

    Elizabeth's concern for, 55

    Elizabeth's desire to see, 194–195

    Elizabeth's reunions with, 283–284, 431–434

    at Elizabeth's trial, 318–319

    Elizabeth's trip to see, 274–278

    The Exposure dedicated to, 359

    in *The Great Drama*, 206

    influence of Theophilus on, 72–73

    letters from, 72

    letters to, 271

    loyalty to Elizabeth, 18–19, 20

    reaction to Elizabeth's commitment, 34–35

    religion and, 196

    support for Elizabeth, 428

    Theophilus's concern for, 11

    Theophilus's taking of, 338–341

    used to tempt Elizabeth into submission, 165–166

church, Theophilus's. *See also* Bible class; religion

change in creed, 12, 61

Elizabeth's departure from, 14–15, 63–64, 317

parishioners' petition for Elizabeth's commitment, 17, 315

position on slavery, 62

split of, 280

Civil War, 102, 155, 186–187, 207, 229, 274, 347–348, 367

Clarke, Betsy, 146

clitoridectomies, 90–92

clothing, Elizabeth's, 70–71, 116, 287

Coe, Celia, 99, 171, 182–185, 187, 274

Coe, James, 182–185, 187, 274

commitment laws, 21. *See also* certificates of insanity; insanity trials; laws; legal reform

married women and, 25, 307 (*See also* insanity trials)

in Massachusetts, 365

relatives' "right of disposal", 21

Comstock, Mr., 19, 20–21, 25

control, drugs and, 92–93

coverture, 342, 356, 367–368. *See also* legal reform; women, married

crowdfunding, 353, 366

D

dancing, 98–99

defense of sanity, Elizabeth's, 100–102, 103–108, 247. *See also* insanity trial, Elizabeth's

depression, 147

desertion, 341

divorce, 293, 329–330, 343–344, 346–347, 357

Dix, Dorothea, 185, 349

doctors, 56–57

Dole, Abijah, 23, 32, 34, 64, 292, 317–318, 329

Dole, Sybil, 18, 288, 292, 318, 319, 320, 329

dream, Elizabeth's, 155–157

drugs, 92–93, 150

Duncanson, Alexander A., 332–335

E

education, Elizabeth's, 21

Eighth Ward, 419

abuse on, 210

conditions on, 122–125, 127

Elizabeth moved to, 117–118

Elizabeth's cleaning of, 127–130

Elizabeth's refusal to leave, 169–170

patients on, 146–148

removal of violent patients from, 175

restraints used on, 149–151

violence on, 131–137, 144–145

Emancipation Proclamation, 208, 233

emotions, 75, 82–83

employment opportunities for women, 347–348

epilepsy, 146

exercise, 181

Exposure, The (Packard), 220–221, 244, 353–358, 363–364

F

female genital mutilation, 90–92

feminism, 114. *See also* women's rights

Field, Angeline, 168, 245, 265, 269–270, 353

Field, David, 169, 269–270

Fifth Ward, 135, 219–220

"filthy insane," 127. *See also* Eighth Ward

finances, Elizabeth's, 347, 354

fitness, Elizabeth's, 181

freedom. *See* independence; release, Elizabeth's

friends, Elizabeth's. *See also* support for Elizabeth; *specific friends*

    efforts to secure release, 168–169

    on Eighth Ward, 146–148

    Elizabeth's campaign for, 368–371

    in Manteno, 19–20

    Olsen, 216–220, 222, 234–236, 259, 399

    prayer circle and, 80

    separation from, 187–188, 217–218, 221–222, 329

    on Seventh Ward, 86

    support for Elizabeth, 270, 272

    trials for, 393–395

Fuller, Allen C., 395–396, 404, 405, 410, 413, 415, 422–424. *See also* investigating committee

G

Gettysburg Address, 291

Goldsby, Emily, 146

Graff, Priscilla (Priscilla Hosmer), 86, 93, 94, 100, 104, 153–154, 157, 175, 185, 187, 349, 378, 415

Granville, Illinois, 273, 281. *See also* Field, Angeline; friends, Elizabeth's

Great Drama, The (Packard), 377

    abuse after, 222–223

    abuse in, 220–221

    Annie McFarland's reaction to, 218

    completion of, 213

    confiscation of, 244

    letter to McFarland and, 237–239, 406–414, 426

    McFarland and, 209, 218, 228, 233–234

    patients' reaction to, 214–224

    politics in, 208–209

    as proof of Elizabeth's insanity, 272

    publication of, 441–442

    publishers' rejection of, 271

    as self-defense, 247

    vision for, 203–207

    women's rights in, 209

Grere, Mrs., 185

Grimké sisters, 327

H

habeas corpus, 69–70, 169, 279, 298–299, 300–303. *See also* insanity trial, Elizabeth's

Hanford, Abigail "Nabby," 291, 297

Hanford, Zalmon, 302

Haslett (family), 19–20, 168, 287

Haslett, Caroline Ann (Sarah), 278, 281, 293, 302, 329

Haslett, Jenny, 131–134

Haslett, William, 302

Henry, John, 414–415

Holy Ghost, 253, 254–255, 312, 313, 333. *See also* religion

Hosmer, Priscilla (Priscilla Graff), 86, 93, 94, 100, 104, 153–154, 157, 175, 185, 187, 349, 378, 415

house, Packards', 52

    cleaning of, 284

    Elizabeth imprisoned in, 290–291, 298–299, 305, 329

    Elizabeth's return to, 282

hygiene, in Illinois State Hospital, 45–46, 127–130, 174

hysteria, 40

I

Illinois State Hospital. *See also* asylum(s);
attendants; Eighth Ward; Fifth
Ward; investigating committee;
McFarland, Andrew; Seventh Ward;
trustees
classification of patients at, 174–175, 419
conditions in, 42–43, 45–46, 80–81, 127–
130, 174
description of, 37
Elizabeth's first night in, 41–43
Elizabeth's formal admission to, 56
financial position of, 116, 249
grounds of, 53
lower ward patients, 80–81, 87, 93–94
overcrowding in, 45, 226
politicians' visit to, 384–385 (*See also* investigating committee)
segregation in, 46
staff (*See* attendants; Hosmer, Priscilla
(Priscilla Graff); McFarland, Andrew)
superintendent (*See* McFarland, Andrew)
Theophilus's desire to return Elizabeth to,
291, 293–294
independence, 9–15, 105. *See also* freedom; women's rights
considered insanity, 17
Elizabeth's, 157–159, 354, 364
Elizabeth's insistence on, 166–167
of women, 209
individuality, as cause for admittance, 61
industrial therapy, 68. *See also* sewing
insanity
recovery from, 193
slavery and, 47
talking as evidence of, 56
insanity, Elizabeth's
allegations of, 14, 16

behavior as proof of, 320–321
McFarland's belief in, 138–143, 172, 379
McFarland's proof of, 370–371
Theophilus's account of, 52
writings as proof of, 253–255, 272
insanity, female
acceptance of men's word about, 59–60
causes of, 38–40
symptoms of, 56–57
views of men and, 107
insanity, invisible, 139
insanity, moral, 75–76, 78, 139, 172
insanity trial, Elizabeth's, 17, 307. *See also*
Bonfield, Thomas; Moore, Stephen;
Starr, Charles
Abijah Dole in, 317–318
Bible class essays in, 325–328
Elizabeth's witnesses, 324–330, 332–335
friends' efforts for, 279
legality of, 307
McFarland's documentation in, 321–324
McFarland's rejection of verdict, 345
mock, 17, 20
Moore's account of, 358
religion and, 308, 309, 311–314, 317, 321,
330, 333–334
support for Elizabeth during, 316, 329, 330
Sybil Dole in, 320
Theophilus's case, 308–309
verdict in, 337–338
insanity trials. *See also* certificates of
insanity
married women and, 25, 307, 373, 391,
393–395
McFarland's objections to, 376
of patients, 417–418
required, 21
inspections, independent, 386

intellectual impairment, 139

intellectual insanity, 140

intelligence, Elizabeth's, 142

investigating committee, 387–388, 395–422

    Elizabeth's letter to McFarland and, 406–414

    leak of report, 422–424

    patients' testimony before, 397–401

    report of, 417–422, 427–428

J

journal, Elizabeth's, 151, 171, 188, 358, 403. *See also* writings, Elizabeth's

K

Kankakee, 302, 303. *See also* insanity trial, Elizabeth's

kidnapper, identifying with, 191

kidnapping, Elizabeth's, 23–25, 27–35, 365

kindness, 129

Knott, Christopher, 57, 303–304, 309, 315, 335

L

labor, unpaid, 68, 153, 215

Labrie, Joseph, 287, 293, 324

Lake, Caroline, 400

Lake, Chauncey A., 318

law of love, 76. *See also* moral treatment

laws. *See also* commitment laws; habeas corpus; insanity trials

    Elizabeth's campaign to change, 357 (*See also* legal reform)

    Elizabeth's confinement and, 279

    lack of legal protections for patients, 21

    married women and, 25–26, 307, 342–344, 356, 367–368 (*See also* insanity trials)

lawyers, Elizabeth's, 304, 322. *See also* Moore, Stephen

lawyers, Theophilus's, 303, 305, 318. *See also* Bonfield, Thomas

laying on of hands. *See* moral treatment

legal reform, 357. *See also* coverture; investigating committee

    Elizabeth's campaigns for, 365

    Elizabeth's strategy in, 377

    in Illinois, 368–371, 380–383

    insanity trials and, 373

    Marital Power Exemplified and, 364

    in Massachusetts, 366

    personal liberty bill, 380–383, 388–392, 439

    politicians' visit to asylum, 384–385

    postal rights of patients, 437–438, 441

    support for, 373–375, 387

letters

    confiscated by McFarland, 94, 96, 168–169, 278

    lack of, 155

    to newspapers, 182–185, 274, 349

    postal rights of patients, 437–438, 441

liberty. *See* freedom; release, Elizabeth's

library, public, 39

Lincoln, Abraham, 110, 187, 189, 208, 233, 291, 367

Lincoln, Mary Todd, 441

loneliness, Elizabeth's, 79

Loomis, Mason, 303

Loring, Harrison, 304, 335

Low, Sallie, 146

M

madness. *See* insanity

mail. *See* letters

management, focus on, 89–90

Mann, James, 295, 324, 335

Manteno, Illinois. *See also* friends,
    Elizabeth's; house, Packards'
  Elizabeth's return to, 275–282
  reaction to Elizabeth's seizure in, 32–34
Marital Power Exemplified (Packard),
    364
marriage, Packards', 7–8, 10, 21–22, 26–27
Massachusetts. *See also* Northampton
    asylum
  commitment law in, 365
  Elizabeth's campaigning in, 365
  legal reform in, 366
  married women in, 431
  Theophilus's move to, 338–341
masturbation, 91, 146
McCormick, Cyrus H., 61, 63
McFarland, Andrew, 65, 369–371
  abuse of patients, 179–180
  after reproof, 134–137
  at AMSAII meeting, 251
  arrogance of, 97, 242, 393
  attacks on Elizabeth, 439
  betrayal of Elizabeth, 108, 272, 411–412
  death of, 447
  defense of reputation, 345
  described, 48–50
  Elizabeth's challenges of, 172
  Elizabeth's faith in, 248, 250, 258
  Elizabeth's first meeting with, 51–52
  Elizabeth's forgiveness of, 210
  Elizabeth's letter to, 237–239, 406–414, 426
  Elizabeth's loss of trust in, 94–96
  Elizabeth's opinion of, 412, 424
  Elizabeth's plan to change into ally, 189–191
  Elizabeth's trial and, 321–324
  Hosmer's view of, 154
  investigating committee and, 402, 419,
    427–428

  methods of, 89–90, 111
  Oak Lawn asylum, 440–441, 446
  objections to proposed reform, 375–376,
    386–387
  power of, 124, 403, 439
  prognosis for Elizabeth, 165
  relationship with Elizabeth, 64–65, 76–77,
    79, 97–100, 210, 237–239
  relationship with patients, 400–401
  reputation of, 441
  retirement of, 440
  sessions with Elizabeth, 78–79
  support for, 372, 378, 440
  updates on Elizabeth, 163–165
McFarland, Annie, 171, 174, 218
medical history, Elizabeth's, 52
medicalization of female behavior, 38–39
medicines, 92–93, 150
men
  admission of women to asylums and, 59–60
  superiority of, 7
menstrual cycles, 39–40, 82
mental health. *See* insanity; sanity
Merrick, Dr., 23
Milk, Lemuel, 308
Minard, Sarah, 60, 85, 368–369, 384–
    385, 393, 395
Moore, Stephen, 304, 308, 311–312, 314,
    319, 322, 323, 324, 327, 331, 333,
    358
moral insanity, 75–76, 78, 139, 172
moral treatment, 76, 78, 89, 97, 98, 400–
    401, 402
Morrison, Isaac, 402, 404, 405
Mrs. Packard's Prison Life (Packard),
    427
Mystic Key, The (Packard), 441

N

National Association for the Protection of the Insane and the Prevention of Insanity, 438

Newkirk, Dr., 23, 25, 56

newspapers. *See also* press
    Civil War in, 186–187
    Elizabeth's access to, 186–187
    letters to, 182–185, 274, 349

Northampton asylum, 245–246, 256, 262, 301–302, 305

O

Oak Lawn asylum, 440–441, 446

obedience, 82. *See also* submission

Oglesby, Richard J., 372–373, 387, 391, 420–422

Olsen, Sophia, 216–220, 222, 234–236, 259, 399

opinions, expression of, 57

Orr, James, 304, 335

P

Packard, Arthur, 442. *See also* children, Packard

Packard, Elizabeth
    children of (*See* children, Packard; *individual children*)
    death of, 448
    father of (*See* Ware, Samuel)

Packard, George, 22–23, 277–278, 448. *See also* children, Packard

Packard, Isaac, 19, 20, 23, 186, 212–213, 319, 428. *See also* children, Packard

Packard, Libby, 20, 166, 271, 281, 284, 288, 289, 317. *See also* children, Packard

mental health of, 443–445
    at trial, 318–319

Packard, Samuel, 288, 290–291, 293, 316, 345–346, 428, 442

Packard, Theophilus, 5
    after Elizabeth's release, 263–264
    betrayal of Elizabeth, 27
    campaign against Elizabeth, 18
    in Chicago, 433
    control of Elizabeth, 7, 10
    disappearance of, 336
    Elizabeth's hatred of, 140, 166–167, 252–253, 263, 309–310, 320
    Elizabeth's refusal to return to, 105
    financial situation, 63, 249, 429
    lack of repentance, 430
    later years, 445–446
    loss of job, 280
    motivations of, 61
    move to Massachusetts, 338–341
    personality of, 8
    presentation to trustees, 195
    in press, 346, 350
    resignation of, 213
    surveillance of Elizabeth, 288

Packard, Theophilus III (Toffy), 19, 84, 94, 212–213, 247, 249, 355, 428. *See also* children, Packard

patients. *See also* friends, Elizabeth's; Illinois State Hospital
    classification of, 174–175, 419
    Elizabeth's campaign for, 368–371
    interaction between, 104
    lack of legal protections for, 21
    postal rights of, 437–438, 441
    testimony of, 397–401
    trials for, 393–395, 417–418

pauper patient, Elizabeth as, 249

personal liberty bill, 380–383, 388–392,
439. *See also* legal reform; women,
married
Pinel, Philippe, 75
possessions, Elizabeth's, 130. *See also*
wardrobe, Elizabeth's
postal rights of patients, 437–438, 441
prayer circle, 80, 84, 86, 93, 104, 174
prayers, 130, 147
press. *See also* newspapers
abuse in, 378
attacks on Elizabeth, 425–426
defense of Theophilus in, 346, 350
Elizabeth's letters to, 182–185, 274, 349
report leaked to, 422–424
support for Elizabeth in, 345
support for legal reform in, 375
trial in, 316
Prichard, James Cowles, 75
property, women as, 25–26
protest, patients', 234–236
psychiatrists, 75, 88. *See also* AMSAII;
McFarland, Andrew
public indignation meeting, 69
public opinion, 157, 427
public speaking, 327, 379
punishments, 82

R

reading, as cause of insanity, 39
real estate, 292–293, 324, 325, 429
rebellion, patient, 234–236
recovery, recognition of insanity and, 193
release, Elizabeth's. *See also* freedom;
trustees
book and, 206
day of departure, 258–262
denied by trustees, 226–230

discharge date, 246
Elizabeth's demand for, 105
Elizabeth's plans for, 47
expectations of, 213, 225
friends' efforts for, 69–70, 168–169, 245, 279
McFarland's prediction of, 66–67
McFarland's recommendation for, 201,
251–257
submission as condition of, 73
religion. *See also* Bible class; church,
Theophilus's
abolition and, 62
certificate of insanity and, 296
commitment and, 403
Elizabeth's trial and, 303, 308, 309, 311–314,
317, 321, 330, 333–334
Holy Ghost, 253, 254–255, 312, 313, 333
Packards' disagreement over, 11–13
in presentation to trustees, 195–196
spiritualism, 60, 215, 400
Theophilus's beliefs, 37
reproof of McFarland, 100–101, 109–
115, 141, 142, 185, 349, 352
reputation, Elizabeth's, 272
restraints, 86, 149–151, 242. *See also*
abuse at Illinois State Hospital;
straitjackets
rules, 82–83. *See also* abuse at Illinois
State Hospital; attendants
Rumsey, Sarah, 18, 27

S

sabotage, 234–236
sanity, Elizabeth's, 287. *See also* insanity,
Elizabeth's; insanity trial, Elizabeth's
defense of, 100–102, 103–108, 247
scold's bridle, 150
screen room, 242

self-defense, Elizabeth's, 272–273

self-reliance. *See* independence

Seventh Ward, 60, 80. *See also* friends, Elizabeth's

Severance, Hervey, 288

Sewall, Samuel, 365–366, 431

sewing, 67–68, 153

sewing-machine salesman, 296, 310

Shedd, Tirzah, 399, 400, 409

Simington, Isaac, 287, 324

slavery, 187

    abolished, 367

    abolition, 13, 62–63, 327, 365

    Emancipation Proclamation, 208, 233

    mental health and, 47

smells, in Illinois State Hospital, 45–46

Smith, Deacon, 318, 319

Smith, Miss, 188, 192, 210

social control, 74. *See also* moral insanity; submission

solitary confinement, 176, 242

spiritualism, 60, 215, 400

Spring, Deacon, 17, 19, 62, 63

Stanton, Elizabeth Cady, 60

Starr, Charles, 304–305, 307, 322, 328, 337

State Lunatic Hospital (Worcester, Massachusetts), 38–41, 78

straitjackets, 86, 149–151, 176. *See also* restraints; violence

submission, 44, 73. *See also* obedience

suicides, 223–224, 447

superintendent. *See* McFarland, Andrew

support for Elizabeth, 270, 272. *See also* friends, Elizabeth's

    in Granville, 273–274

    in Kankakee, 303

    in press, 345

    religion and, 308

    during trial, 316, 329, 330

survival, 191

Swedenborgianism, 61, 333, 334

T

talking

    as evidence of insanity, 56

    scold's bridle and, 150

    Theophilus's reactions to, 65

teaching career, Elizabeth's, 21, 38

Tenney sisters, 121, 127, 128, 129, 175

Tenny, Dr., 41, 261, 262

testimony, insane person's, 179–180

thinking

    at Illinois State Hospital, 84

    as symptom of insanity, 57

threats. *See* reproof of McFarland

treatments

    drugs, 92–93, 150

    focus on women's sexual organs, 90–92

    industrial therapy, 68

    lack of, 89

    McFarland's approach to, 89

    moral treatment, 76, 78, 89, 97, 98, 400–401, 402

trials, insanity. *See* insanity trial, Elizabeth's; insanity trials

Triplet, Sarah, 135

trunk, Elizabeth's, 70–71

trustees, 225, 402

    deferment of decision, 199–200

    Elizabeth's attempts to contact, 193

    Elizabeth's presentation to, 192, 194–199, 202–203

    inspections by, 193

    investigating committee and, 415–416, 417, 420

jury trials and, 393–394

objections to proposed reform, 386

release and, 193

resignation of, 439–440

Tryon, Adelaide, 192

V

violence, 86, 131–137, 144–145, 404. *See also* abuse at Illinois State Hospital

visitors, 84–85, 165, 186, 212–213

W

wages, women's, 347–348, 428–429

Wakeman, T. B., 387

Ward, Joseph, 374

wardrobe, Elizabeth's, 70–71, 116, 287

Ware, Samuel, 353, 355, 430

Way, Joseph, 295–296, 314–315

Weaver, Miss, 122, 147

will, Elizabeth's, 163

women

    employment opportunities for, 347–348

    lack of power, 34, 191

    laws and, 25–26 (*See also* legal reform)

    need for protection, 79–80, 377

    oppression of, 187

    public speaking by, 327

women, married, 442

    commitment laws and, 25, 307

    earnings of, 347–348, 428–429

    guardianship of children and, 431

    insanity trials required for, 307, 373, 391, 393–395

    lack of legal protection for, 25, 307, 342–344, 356, 367–368 (*See also* legal reform)

    personal liberty bill, 380–383, 388–392, 439

women of color, 46–47

women's rights, 115, 208, 228. *See also*

legal reform

    divorce and, 293

    Elizabeth's introduction to, 8–9

    in *The Great Drama*, 209

    Sewall and, 365–366

    vision for books and, 203–207

Worcester, asylum in, 38–41

writing privileges, Elizabeth's, 137–138, 148

writings, Elizabeth's. *See also* defense of sanity, Elizabeth's; *Great Drama, The*; reproof of McFarland

    after move to Eighth Ward, 152–154

    Bible class essays, 21–22, 289, 292–293, 321, 325–328

    entrusted to Haslett, 281

    The Exposure, 220–221, 244, 353–358, 363–364

    journal, 151, 171, 188, 358, 403

    letter to McFarland, 237–239, 406–414, 426

    letters to newspapers, 182–185

    letters to press, 349

    Marital Power Exemplified, 364

    McFarland's confiscation of, 243–244

    Mrs. Packard's Prison Life, 427

    The Mystic Key, 441

    as proof of insanity, 253–255

Y

Younglove, Joseph, 302

ACKNOWLEDGMENTS

I want to start by thanking the radium girls, the subjects of my first American history book and my absolute heroines. Without them, I never would have had the opportunity to tell Elizabeth's story. Ladies, you contributed so much to the world. In a way, this book, too, is another of your legacies. Thank you. All of you. *Always.*

I am also indebted to my publisher, Sourcebooks, which consistently demonstrates such incredible faith in me as a writer. My dream team of editors: Grace Menary-Winefield, the book's first champion; Shana Drehs, the midwife who helped me find its shape as it came into the world; Bridget Connolly, who read so many versions; and last but by no means least Anna Michels, who helped to hone the book with clarity and wisdom. Thank you all for your enthusiasm, patience, and expertise. Thank you to Sabrina Baskey, Brenda Horrigan, and Heather Hall for their work on the text. And thank you to Jillian Rahn for her work on the pages.

To the entire team at Sourcebooks—including but not limited to Liz Kelsch, Valerie Pierce, Margaret Coffee, Lizzie Lewandowski, Dominique Raccah, Caitlin Lawler, and everyone else!—thank you for so generously lending your remarkable individual talents to getting this book into readers' hands, and for your passion for both my work and yours. I'll be forever grateful.

As I will be to my readers. You are the best. Thank you for your hearts and heads and for reading these stories with such appetite. I hope you will all enjoy this latest book.

I want to thank two University of Wisconsin students, Katherine Pouba and Ashley Tianen. It was in their essay, found online, that I first read about a woman named Elizabeth Packard. I also want to thank the other writers who have previously shone a spotlight on her. Thank you to Myra Himelhoch for her insight, Phyllis Chesler for her ground-breaking revelations, and Linda Carlisle for her thorough bibliography, which provided many helpful starting points for my own journey with this remarkable woman.

Very special thanks are also due to author Barbara Sapinsley. Barbara, your academic generosity in donating your decades of research on Elizabeth to the Oskar Diethelm Library has provided a treasure trove for all those who now come after you. Thank you for your diligence and for persevering when all doors were slammed in your face. The world benefits greatly from the valuable legacy you've left us.

A book of this nature is nothing without its research. I'd like to thank three authors whose books were especially insightful—Elaine Showalter, Jeffery L. Geller, and Maxine Harris—but above all I am indebted to those expert librarians who assisted me in uncovering the bones of Elizabeth's experiences through the historical records. Particular thanks are due to Elizabeth Antaya of the Shelburne Free Public Library, Ellen Keith of the Chicago History Museum Research Center, and Hillary Peppers, Chris Ashmore, and Sarah Snyder of the Jacksonville Public Library in Illinois, all of whom generously went the extra mile—and more—to assist me in my research.

Grateful thanks also to: Marisa Shaari and Nicole Topich at the Oskar Diethelm Library in New York; John Rathe at the New York

Public Library; Paul Friday at the New Hampshire Historical Society; Robbin Bailey and Ashley at the Concord Public Library; Jessica Murphy and Heather Mumford at the Francis Countway Library; Karen Trop at the Houghton Library; Beth Carroll-Horrocks at the State Library in MA; Sharon Parrington Wright at the Turner Free Library, Randolph, MA; Ashley Cataldo, Dan Boudreau, Beth, and the team at the American Antiquarian Society in Worcester, MA; Wendy Essery at the Worcester Historical Museum; Laurie Nivison at the Deerfield Memorial Libraries; Leslie Fields at Mount Holyoke College Archives and Special Collections; Cynthia Harbeson and Katherine Whitcomb at the Jones Library, Amherst; Blake Spitz at UMass Amherst Libraries; Courtney Posing at the Manteno Public Library in Illinois; Curtis Mann at the Lincoln Library in Springfield, Illinois; Catheryne Popovitch at the Illinois State Archives; Jennifer Bonjean at the Morgan County Circuit Court; Johanna Russ, Glenn Humphreys, Michelle, and Roslyn at the Harold Washington Library in Chicago; Sally J, archivist at the Wisconsin Historical Society; Emily A. Schroeder, archivist at the Kennebec Historical Society; Sherry DeVito of the Illinois State Medical Society; the team at the Kankakee County Museum, including Jorie Walters and Jack Klasey; and to the Illinois Historical Society too.

But research does not stop at a library door. I'm also grateful to those individuals who kindly helped with various elements of my dogged digging, including Mike Draper, Levi Bridges, Pastor Chrystal Abbott, Judy Kulp, Greg Olson, Al Shaw, Penny Vagg, Beth Gribble, Liz Mossop, Anna Beeton, the unwitting real estate agent who showed me around Theophilus's childhood home, and Julian Moldovan and Christine Rutledge at Rosehill Cemetery. Enormous thanks, too, to Elizabeth's relatives who assisted me, including Lynn Barker and most especially

Judy Domhoff Stenovich, whose enthusiasm and support for this project are priceless. Thank you so much, Judy. I hope I did her justice.

I'd also like to thank author Karen Abbott and creative supremo Lin-Manuel Miranda. Their own historical works inspired me endlessly during this project, showing me how it's done.

This was a hard book to write, and I'd have struggled without a dream team behind me. I'd like to thank my literary agent, Simon Lipskar of Writers House, and his assistant, Celia J. Taylor Mobley, for their thoughtful guidance as we embarked together on this new journey. Thanks also to my dramatic rights agent, Joel Gotler, for his wonderful passion and support.

Closer to home, I am the luckiest to have a loving, supportive family always cheerleading me. Thank you Mum, Dad, Penny, Sarah, and the whole gang. A special thank-you to Mackenzie for his patience and for being so chill. And thank you to my friends for always seeming interested in the story so far!

There is one man without whom I would be lost, however. One man who keeps the show on the road, who is always willing to read one more version, who gives superb creative feedback with wisdom, insight, and understanding. One man who is able to reach me when my head is under the duvet and I'm despairing of finding a way forward, who is also by my side to see the smiles when it goes right.

Thank you, Duncan. I love you.

Finally, thank you to Elizabeth Packard. *What* a woman. I hope I've done enough to make you proud—of everything that *you* achieved.

Kate Moore
London, 2020